W9-DCV-604

Tyranny of Kindness

Tyranny of Kindness

Dismantling the Welfare System
to End Poverty in America

Theresa Funiciello

THE ATLANTIC MONTHLY PRESS
NEW YORK

Copyright © 1993 by Theresa Funiciello

Published simultaneously in Canada
Printed in the United States of America

Library of Congress Cataloging-in-Publication Data

Funiciello, Theresa.
Tyranny of kindness: dismantling the welfare system to end
poverty in America / Theresa Funiciello.
1. Public welfare—United States.   2. Poverty—United States.
3. Welfare recipients—United States.   4. United States—Social
policy. I. Title.
HV95.F86   1993   361.973—dc20   93-14649

ISBN 0-87113-578-7(pbk.)

DESIGN BY LAURA HOUGH

The Atlantic Monthly Press
841 Broadway
New York, NY 10003

2   4   6   8   10   9   7   5   3   1

Especially for Nanine,

whose love, wit, patience,

and smile never fail.

ACKNOWLEDGMENTS

"Together we can move mountains, alone we can't move at all." That song became the unofficial anthem of the Downtown Welfare Advocate Center. Written by Bev Grant and performed by the Human Condition, it symbolized our vision of DWAC. But it also was reality. Alone, few of us would have survived our personal fight, much less had the courage and strength to take on the political one.

When I first began talking to people about writing the story of DWAC and describing the vision that came out of it, my thoughts turned to the thousands of women on welfare I have known, the endless meetings, the stories of children growing, and the pain that, for all our efforts, we could not prevent or stop. As the research and reflection evolved, it became clear that the organization made a lot of noise over a troubling issue as it pursued its objectives, and the noise had purpose. The other life of DWAC, however, is found in the quiet moments when mothers' love for their children caused them to question our contemporary notions of a civilized society. While motherhood is sometimes touted, mothers are accorded little common respect and no claim to the public purse absent the requisite and sometimes brutal indignities of charitable, judicial, or administrative scrutiny. That was all quite private, quite silent—which is why DWAC was not. It took the courage of many women and some men to make it work.

To some, our claims seemed radical. But we were not attempting to shatter the settled world of public values. Our needs, as we defined them, were quite modest. When I look at the children of the many welfare mothers I have known, I see the wisdom of a thousand small decisions gone right; I see grace amidst adversity; I see the hopes (we are said not to have) materialized; I see the common sense that kept us pushing as if to hold back the tidal wave of nearly universal disapproval.

I have tried in writing this book to remain faithful to the views, experiences, and aspirations of the welfare mothers I worked with. While there are differing views among welfare recipients, as there are within any group, the experiences we shared are remarkably similar. I could not have offered this portrait of welfare mothers and the welfare system without the constant strength, reinforcement, and thinking of those who participated in the Downtown Welfare Advocate Center and the Redistribute America Movement, as well as the many other poor women's grass-roots organizations in this country. It is impossible to acknowledge fully the participation and friendship of a number of individuals with whom I have worked. You know who you are. Thank you very much.

Some of the many sisters (and brothers) with whom I was fortunate to stand side by side (literally and figuratively) in the struggle for the dignity of welfare recipients are Carmen Agosta, Diana Autin, Dolores Barry, Lily Benjamin, Mary Blackburn, Marlene Blount, Edna Blue, Ebie Brown, Anna Cruz, Mary Devitt, Julia Dinsmore, Angel Falcone, Robin Fenley, Jackie Goeings, Ruby Grace, Ronnie Gray, Margeurita Guttierez, Elsie Harry, Ann Hermann, Sharon Hunt, Josephine Hurrinus, Frankie Jeter, Marion Kramer, Christine Larson, Yvonne Lewis, Cindy Mann, Deborah May, Marcy May, Florence Monroe, Pat Moore, Vicki Moore, Rosa Negron, Barbara Neighbors-Glass, Alice Orr, Avis Parke, Shirley Smith Peoples, Pedra Ponce, Ernestine Royster, Beulah Sanders, Gussie Scott, Eddie Shuler, Elisabeth Solomon, Yolanda Soto, Dottie Stevens, Linda Storm, Elly Spicer, Maureen Sweeny, Frances Taylor, Karren Thomas, Johnnie Tillman, Lucy Toomy, Jim Travers, Diana Voelker, Cynthia Wilcox, and Doreen Zelman.

I have also been blessed by a multitude of professional colleagues and personal friends (many serving both roles) who assisted and encouraged the effort to bring a poor people's voice to the public debate on welfare, sometimes at personal and political risk to themselves. Among them are Bella Abzug, Msgr. John Ahern, Judy Austermiller, Jean Bandler, Steve Banks, Harriet Barlow, John Beam, Carol Bellamy, Dan Bomberry, Richard Boone, Mary Ellen Boyd, Gale Brewer, Rudy Bryant, Tim Casey, Nancy Castleman, Rev. Robert Chapman, Assemblymember Barbara Clarke, Andy Cooper, Anna Lou DeHavenon, Bert

DeLeeuw, Gary Delgado, Barbara Deming, Helen DesFossess, Leslie
Dunbar, Pablo Eisenberg, W. H. and Carol Bernstein Ferry, Joseph
Francois, Henry Freedman, Miriam Friedlander, Leah Fritz, Annette
Fuentes, Bob Gangi, Eli Ginzburg, Owen Goldfarb, Sister Mary Heg-
gerty, Bruce Hanson, Wretha Wiley Hanson, Bob Harris, Joy Hausman,
Elizabeth Hay, Sister Ann Hayes, Robert Hayes, Pat Hewitt, Anita
Hoffman, Leslie Holmes, Steve Horvath, Jonathan House, Hulbert
James, Andrea Kydd, Phil Latimer, Sylvia Law, Alan Levine, Rhoda
Linton, New York State Assemblymember Nettie Mayersohn, Peggy
McManus, New York State Senator Olga Mendez, Mari Mennel, Man-
hattan Borough President Ruth Messinger, John Mohawk, New York
State Senator Velmanette Montgomery, Rev. Howard Moody, John
Moukad, Ralph Murphy, Sam Myers, Frank Negron, Michael O'Con-
nor, Val Orselli, Bob Ostrow, Representative Major Owens, New York
City Councilmember Mary Pinkett, Calvin Pressley, David Ramage,
Helen Reicherter, Maurice Reid, Judy Remet, Ann Roberts, Florence
Roberts, Alida Rockerfeller, Ramon Rodriguez, Dolores Sanzillo, Fran-
cis Sanzillo, Karen Saum, Steve Savner, Sandy Schram, Laura Scudder,
Norman Seigel, Allan Sheahen, Stanley Schear, Ron Shiffman, Gloria
Steinem, I. F. Stone, Dinny Stranahan, Bill Tabb, Bob Theobald, Mir-
iam Thompson, David Tobis, Alair Townsend, Christina Walker, Pau-
lette Walther, Carmen Ward, Marilyn Waring, Phil Weitzman, Judy
Wessler, Jane Wholey, Stephanie Whidden, and Dan Wise.

Finally, while I have written this book and all its failings are my
own, it could not have been produced without considerable support
from a number of special people. Pat Courtney, David Greene, Edite
Kroll, and Joe Lubow read and commented on various drafts. Nancy
Pointek Farley suffered through the entire text at its longest. Tracy
Huling sat through hours of discourse and debate that helped to solidify
the ideas flowing from the experiences. I. F. Stone was among the first
instigators to prompt me to write a book about welfare. Robin Morgan
continued the agitation, and, even when I felt inadequate to the task, she
somehow convinced me otherwise. Gloria Steinem gently nourished me
at a time when I thought I'd never get to the end. Ann Sellew "kept me
together" through the long and frustrating writing process. My agent,
Nancy Rose, took me and this tome that seemed like it would never be
published and, with good cheer, made it happen. A special thanks to my

ACKNOWLEDGMENTS

editor, Anton Mueller, who became familiar with a whole new topic on short notice and improved this book immensely. Most important, I want to thank my husband, Tom Sanzillo, who did all those things and more, and without whose support and devotion, both to me and to the subject matter, this book would never have been written. And he made me laugh.

CONTENTS

CONTENTS

There will be justice in Athens only when the uninjured parties are as indignant as the injured parties.

—*Ancient Greeks*

INTRODUCTION

My first experience with Aid to Families with Dependent Children (AFDC)—welfare—was in upstate New York, three months after the birth of my daughter, on the heels of the departure of her father. It was 1973. I was twenty-six years old, nursing an infant, and alone. Welfare was humiliating on a personal level, and administratively it was nuts. But there wasn't anything I could do about it. At least that's what I thought.

In 1975 I moved to New York City. Like so many others, I was searching for opportunity. When I couldn't find paying work, I had my second encounter with welfare. It was nuts here, too.

Fortunately, in the city there were many thousands of others in the same boat. Looking for sympathetic advice, I stumbled onto a sturdy little volunteer organization of mostly welfare mothers, the Downtown Welfare Advocate Center (DWAC.) The women at DWAC thought something could be done about the welfare, and they set about doing it. They helped people with problems negotiate the chaotic system and they helped change the way welfare mothers felt about themselves in relation to it. They also tried to influence the welfare bureaucracy. They said mothering was work. They said single mothers and children made up 95 percent of the entire AFDC population. They said welfare was a women's issue. I came back for more.

My third, fourth, and hundred-and-fifth encounters with the welfare system took place on behalf of other women as I, too, learned how to sort out the mess and be an "advocate." By late 1976, I was also organizing to change the way people thought about welfare—essential to changing the entire system from bottom to top. Over the next few years,

DWAC sponsored a membership organization, which peeked at about six thousand members in 1981. Almost all were welfare mothers.

It was during this period that DWAC began to interact with the mega-charities on a fairly regular basis. These were agencies with millions of dollars in their coffers and nifty salaries for employees who "helped the poor." Actually, many of the social welfare professionals seemed to do little more than refer people who needed help to us and have luncheons to discuss the problem. It took many more years and many incarnations to find out what they were really about.

I moved on from DWAC to work at a small "change-oriented" (as they liked to call themselves) foundation that purported to give money to projects that poor people worked on. That was maybe ten percent true. So, in 1983, when Mario Cuomo became governor and his newly appointed commissioner of the New York State Department of Social Services (DSS) offered me a job, I was ready to take on the beast from inside the belly. Just maybe things could be changed from the inside.

At DSS, my worst nightmares became fire-breathing realities. Millions of dollars were regularly dispensed in contracts to virtually useless "nonprofit" agencies. DSS was a patronage trough. Poor people were not the beneficiaries. They weren't even in on the deal.

Nevertheless, I'd learned a couple important lessons at DSS. One was that incompetence is a heavy contender with greed as prime motivator of the bureaucracy. Second, any time there's money to be had, every manner of opportunist crawls out for a piece. Combined, these fundamentals form the basis of public policy.

It didn't take too much intelligence to figure out the idiocy of paying thousands of dollars a month to "shelter" a homeless family instead of paying for a real apartment. Various layers of government blamed one another—but .*they* were setting the rules, not Martians. Taxpayers were bilked and poor people were sacrificed as hundreds of millions of dollars were poured into the sinkholes of the social welfare establishment. Shelters. Soup kitchens. Name it. Nationwide, poverty is big business—as long as you are politically connected.

The consequence to poor people of this ever-expanding poverty industry has been that over the past two decades, the purchasing power of welfare benefits has fallen in every state in the country, in spite of the fact that aggregate spending on most other social programs has soared. It was not quite by accident, nor quite by design. Boosted by the unseeing but hardly innocent eye of the media, the poverty industry has become a veritable fifth estate. Acting as stand-ins for actual poor people, they mediate the politics of poverty with government officials. The fifth estate is a large and ever-growing power bloc that routinely and by whatever means necessary trades off the interests of poor people to advance its own parochial agenda. From the charities fleecing the state and the public, to the champagne fund-raisers charged off to Uncle Sam, to the corporations developing ever more ways of getting tax deductions for having their trash hauled away free of charge, the fix is in.

Charities have been powerful since they first popped on the scene during the middle of the nineteenth century. Run exclusively by men, they were originally premised solely on the negative—stopping behaviors they believed to be inbred and causally connected to poverty. They believed the problem would continue unchecked if poor people were able to resist their services and exist outside of charity-run poorhouses. The charities fought long and hard against "outdoor relief" (cash assistance) for poor families. The struggle was temporarily checked with the passage of the Social Security Act, which established AFDC in 1935. Poor mothers could live in their own homes and raise their children. The compromise wrested by the nascent social work profession was that, unlike social security insurance, wherein a check would go directly from the federal government to the recipient, AFDC would be mediated by them. Both the public welfare bureaucracy and its private extension (charities) expanded.

Almost every president since has promised some sort of reform of the welfare system. But it wasn't until the 1960s that the welfare rolls exploded, landing the issue back onto center stage. Launching the Great Society, President Johnson declared "War on Poverty" and spewed social service dollars in every direction (except into the pockets of poor people, that is). In part, the new programs would stimulate the economy, as tens of thousands of jobs were created to "help the poor." Few poor people got any of these jobs, however. Most of the decent ones went to middle-class social welfare professionals, who were perceived to be an important cog in a deteriorating Democratic party machine.[1]

Despite the largess of the Great Society, a chain reaction of inner-city riots spanning several years soon shocked the nation. The rioting was a total enigma to most people—in the wake of all the anti-poverty legislative gifts. But poor people were neither receiving the money directly nor truly influencing how it would be spent. In addition to the generalized anomie caused by poverty, the indignities of welfare and unemployment, and long-repressed racial bitterness, the riots were an expression of grave despair over a government agenda and monies said to be *for them* that for the most part were getting nowhere near actual poor people.

As the agencies that *did* cash in grew and reinvented themselves, it became apparent that they were in an inherent conflict of interest with poor people. Welfare mothers, for instance, wanted an adequate guaranteed income, which would have rendered many of the activities of the social welfare professionals meaningless.[2] The agencies wanted a guaranteed income, too: for themselves. With the money and power to lobby effectively, they got it.

As the misery of poor people increased, so did the cacophony of private interests competing for government contracts, foundation grants, donations by individuals and corporations, and tax advantages for the donations to "correct" their version of the problem. The only people who did not cash in, the only ones absent from the debate in any public way, as ever, were poor. It was not for lack of trying. Many poor women, myself included, attempted to reframe the debate, but the charitable opposition was too comfortable and powerful.

Over a period of nearly two decades, I went from being a homeless welfare mother to being an organizer of welfare mothers, an establishment insider at DSS, an adviser to some members of the New York state legislature, and a consultant for various prominent social welfare agencies. I have seen it from all sides now. I remain appalled.

The view from the bottom is substantially different from that of any other vantage point. Usually, you won't learn about it in books. Certainly it can't be found in classrooms, newsrooms, boardrooms, or bedrooms of the not so poor or the rich and famous. Part I of a *Tyranny of Kindness* is an abridged history of the Downtown Welfare Advocate Center, especially its early years, as I remember it. The constant bombardment of families in crisis was the backdrop against which our political perspective was formed. This section is neither entirely chronological nor by any means exhaustive. There were many more players and events than could be covered here. I have attempted to remain faithful to the core of the discussions of the many welfare mothers and others whose thinking helped frame my own analysis.

Part II of this book examines social deception, exposing such rip-offs as the secondary market of soup kitchens and pantries, spawned in behalf of poor people, that will never feed a fraction of those who need food *when* they need it. Not to worry. It only costs us billions. Countless middle-class people were making money, building careers, becoming powerful, and otherwise benefiting from poverty. It didn't have to *be* and it wasn't help. The poverty industry once again substituted its own interests for that of poor people and got away with it. To me, that's welfare fraud.

During this seemingly endless period of social greed, the issue of justice has all but disappeared. We have drained the resources of the poorest communities and people by passing them on to a more powerful group of middle-class social welfare professionals. It's time to reverse that trend. Part III of this book suggests how.

The national psyche purged itself from the mid-1960s through the mid-1970s in the War on Poverty only to wage war on poor *people*. *Tyranny of Kindness* tells how it happened, why it happened, and what can be done about it. The basic tenets are simple: A) Poor people, especially welfare mothers and their children are increasingly, and more desperately, poor; B) Charities that purport to represent poor people abuse the public trust in an endless quest for larger budgets, career advancement, and political power; C) An entire mythology about welfare and the people on it has been developed and strengthened to reinforce stereotypes that justify the expenditures of billions of tax dollars and preserve the status quo; D) Politicians and policy makers help to prop up the charities by dishing out government contracts and supportive legislation in covert quid pro quo arrangements. Still, at some point they must adapt to the challenge of structural changes in the economy that increase the proportion of people estranged from a dwindling job market, and accept that no amount of social workers can alter those dynamics or distribute essential goods to people who need them; E) The only way to reverse the trend of the increasing povertization, particularly of poor families, is to increase their income security through some form of guaranteed income. F) The money's all there—it's just being spent on an army of social welfare professionals whose interests are protected by the elected officials they help put into office and by the press that naively reports on all of it at face value.

Tyranny of Kindness takes a look at social policy in the United States from the perspective of people who live with the consequences. I do not pretend to be "objective." I don't believe anyone can be. I do try to present some barely known history and facts that are often misinterpreted or kept discreetly, esoterically buried in reams of public and private documents. Judge for yourself, but judge. Perhaps we can work together to address the issue of poverty in ways that are truly meaningful.

PART I

The Welfare: Inside Out

Chapter 1

The Mothers' Shift

The personal is political.   —Robin Morgan

I felt like I had a dreaded, contagious disease. The bacteria from
the disease spread slowly; it took the strength from my muscles
causing me to feel ugly; it took the hope from my heart causing me
to feel discouraged; it took ideas from my mind causing me to feel
useless.   —Martha Maxwell, welfare mother

Firefighters returning from a false alarm in Queens, New York, one
beautiful October day in 1989 were gazing into the sky when they passed
a tall apartment complex. Ten stories up, a body was dangling from the
window. They yelled up front to get the rig turned around. Just as it
arrived, a little girl, naked, hit the ground. Hector Faberlle and his
partner ran to resuscitate her as two other firefighters dashed into the
building.

According to Faberlle, "We tried to stabilize her. Just as she was
breathing on her own, I heard people screaming. I couldn't imagine what
the commotion was, because it looked like she was going to make it. I
looked up and saw another small child spinning down." Witnesses said
the mother had seemed to dangle him for a while before she let go of
him. Rasheed, age three, fell on his seven-year-old sister. "After that we
couldn't get a pulse from her, and blood was spilling from her mouth."

Fatima Ali,[1] a thirty-two-year-old middle-class Muslim housewife, was attempting to send all five of her children back to Allah, through their apartment window. Her daughter Taisha was pronounced dead at the hospital. Rasheed, critically injured, survived. Just as Ms. Ali was about to toss out her one-year-old, firefighters burst into her apartment. As they were overtaking her, she urged the children to go quickly, as if they would go on their own. All were naked. According to one news report, she said, "We came into this world with nothing, and that's how we're going to leave." Three children and their mother, who intended to jump when she completed the task, were rescued.

Ms. Ali was charged with murder, attempted murder, first- and second-degree assault, reckless endangerment, and endangering the welfare of a child. Neighbors said the mother was loving and the children were always polite and clean, as if that somehow rendered the occurrence more mysterious. And then Fatima Ali and her children vanished from our collective memory, almost as swiftly as they had entered.

When I was young, I could not possibly have understood or forgiven the acts of Fatima Ali. Some of that youth I spent as a Muslim—drapes for clothes, virtually nonstop prayers, my two feet of hair cordoned with a bolt of white cloth bound so tightly I could never really forget it was there. I took this religion as seriously as the religions that preceded it in my life, starting with Catholicism (I went to church every day till I was eighteen). My religion was as solid as a rock mountain, vulnerable only to major earthquakes and dripping water by the century. In later years, feminism finally crept up on me.

In Islam everything, from sex to eating, is ritualized. That's how I know what Fatima Ali was doing with apparent calm while she held Rasheed out the window before letting go. She was praying. In form and function, as in other patriarchal religions, women in Islam are buried alive in an avalanche of contradictions. They are equal; no, superior; no, inferior to men, to snakes, to witches. The female self is sublimated under a mass of religious debris. Make no mistake: an Islamic woman without a man, especially a woman with children, isn't remotely like a fish without a bicycle.

This woman had five children, aged one to eight years, and was recently separated from her husband. She had trouble making her last month's rent. She had been trapped in one alienating system and was

4

about to become trapped in another. She surely feared a descent into poverty, alienation, and probably homelessness. After all, once removed from attachment to a man, her labor as a wife and mother was all but worthless. It would not have been difficult for her to imagine a terrifying future. The streets. Welfare. Welfare hotels. Drugs, prostitution, guns, knives, gambling, drunkenness, and all manner of spiritual death. But for a woman with the option of deliverance, it wasn't inevitable.

A homeless mother of five has virtually no chance of being taken in by friends or family for more than a night or two. In fact, were Ms. Ali to become homeless, she would have only a 16 percent chance of keeping her children with her for the duration of their homelessness. The odds are not that much better for mothers of fewer children, who would be more typical. In all cases, relatively young mothers and their children who find themselves suddenly without the income a father (or the unlikely trust fund) might bring in, are in a situation fraught with peril.

If the Ali family had become homeless, exactly what would have happened cannot be said with absolute certainty. Still, there are commonalities shared by women of all races and religions, from coast to coast, experiencing either rural or urban poverty. The merciless anxiety and humiliation of being shuttled back and forth like herded animals, the stress of keeping kids in school are constant. Only the little details vary.

In New York City, if she were able to keep her family together, at some point they would approach an emergency assistance unit (EAU), which is obligated to shelter them in some way. This would mean waiting for hours, sometimes days, on plastic chairs, metal desks, or the bare floor. If the family didn't eat pork, they'd eat nothing, since baloney sandwiches would be about all they'd get for the next several meals. Some nights (often after midnight) they might be placed in a roach-, lice-, and rat-infested welfare hotel for just a few hours till a more "permanent," equally squalid temporary placement was arranged. First thing in the morning, the family would be roused and shuttled back to the EAU to wait again.

If they were extremely lucky, they would finally be placed in a welfare hotel or "transitional" shelter together. The latter often provide less space per family member than is required of jail cells. Because the Ali

5

family is so large, they wouldn't even get apartment referrals from city workers until after they'd been in this hell for many months. (One rural homeless mother told me her family was placed in a motel with bars where windows should have been and without a store or school within walking distance. Every time she needed something, she was at the mercy of a barely functional shuttle system for homeless people.)

At first, many mothers try to continue taking their children to their previous schools. In New York City, this usually means traveling with them (other babies in tow) to another borough in the morning and returning for them in the afternoon. When one of the children is too sick to travel, none will go to school. After a while, mothers might try to place their children in a school closer to the shelter. Legal, yes. Easy, no. If a mother accomplishes this, sooner or later other kids in the new school will realize that her kids are "untouchables." School life will become anathema to her kids. They'll begin to adopt the coping mechanisms of the homeless kids who will associate with them.

Night brings scant respite. Sounds of sirens, gunshots from outside or down the hall. Families fighting. Too many people and too few beds, often with neither sheets nor blankets, much less pillows. The mattresses have long since burst like pastry puffs, and each day finds more of their insides outside. Bedbugs pinch.

Those who are lucky have a little stove in the room. I will never forget the first time I used such a stove in a welfare hotel. I had just added eggs to the frying pan when swarms of roaches scrambled out of the fire in every direction, including right into the frying pan. It was days before I could bring myself to try it again. The things most people take for granted become little horrors, each stacked on top of the one before.

If the Ali family were to emerge from the "temporary" shelter intact and be placed in an apartment, the rest of the world would think their problems solved. But they would still be only beginning. Almost any place the family could expect to live would be its own ghoulish chamber. But now the family would be a welfare family. Overnight, social policy would swerve away from even the pretense of caring. Ms. Ali would change from pitied social victim to society's victimizer. Her living conditions would not improve, nor would her stress diminish; her agony would not subside, but she would be stripped of her poverty rank, joining the much larger class of poor women—the thoroughly despised "abusers of the system"—welfare mothers. To have come this far would have been a heroic feat, but it would be said of her that she's a drain on the national resources, has too many children she shouldn't have had if she couldn't afford to, and doesn't "work."

Like most welfare mothers, Ms. Ali will raise her children without the modern conveniences most mothers take for granted. No washing machines. Often no heat in the winter or utilities in the summer. The baby will be likely to sleep in a cardboard box or dresser drawer because even a secondhand crib is too expensive. Shopping for food will become an exploit. Supermarkets are rarely accessible because they often don't exist where poor women live, and transportation to them can be prohibitively expensive. She will raise her kids in a high-crime neighborhood teeming with drug abuse and other life-defeating modes of survival.

If any woman were absolutely penniless today and went to apply for welfare to feed her children, she would not receive her first welfare check for about a month. This is not because the welfare is prohibited from giving money any sooner but because they are *allowed* to take thirty days to determine the obvious—that she is poor. The thirty-day deadline might come and go with no relief. Or, if she makes it onto welfare, destructive policies combined with bureaucratic bungling might cut her off despite her continued eligibility (this happens to at least one million needy families in the United States every year). This process has been given the name *churning* by the welfare department itself, as people are routinely cut off only to be put back on again months later.

Once on welfare, a family's chances of having enough money to live in a remotely decent neighborhood and pay for all basic human needs are nil, even in New York, where welfare benefits are said to be "high." On the sunny day in 1989 when the Ali family almost came to a total halt, the *maximum* monthly grant in New York City for a mother and five children was $814.20—or less than three fifths of the federal poverty threshold for the same size family. The *average* New York grant for six was approximately $655.00 per month.[2] (The average family on welfare has only three persons, a mother and two children. In New York City, the average grant for a three-person family was about $441.00 per month.)

Assuming the Ali family received the maximum, the rent allotment would have been $349.00. Assuming the absurd—that they could find habitable housing for that price in New York or most any other U.S. city—they would be left with $465.20, or about $2.50 per person per day, for most of their food. (Food stamps would have provided less than two weeks of nutritionally adequate food for the month.) That *same* $2.50 must also cover some medical expenses and *all* utilities, toothpaste, toilet paper, furniture, soap, baby bottles, diapers, laundry, transportation, kitchen utensils, clothing, and so on. If Ms. Ali lived in South Dakota, she'd have had just about $1.88 for all those things. In New York, if she took one ride on the subway in search of the elusive job, she would use up more than 90 percent of her daily ration. If she were menstruating and needed to buy a box of tampons, she would have to dip into her children's share. There is no state in the country where welfare benefits reach the poverty line, though twenty years ago they did in some states, including New York.

Like millions of women, Ms. Ali had only one commodity at her disposal guaranteed to produce sufficient income in the short term to keep her family together: her body. To a devout Muslim, as to many others, even survival does not justify such a damning act. And, from her perspective, to kill *only* herself would have been irresponsible. Had Mr. Ali died instead of leaving, things would have been very different.

First, Ms. Ali would then have been the recipient of universal sympathy and support. As a widow with minor children, she would have become a social security "survivor" or widow instead of a welfare mother. The maximum family benefit for survivor families on social security in 1989—$1,896 per month—could have been enough to continue living modestly where she was. While this sum is hardly lavish, the family would have remained above poverty. And no bureaucrats, social policy experts, politicians, or journalists would have gone nuts because she didn't have a "job." In fact, she would have been thought to be a good mother for taking care of her children full-time, at least while they were young.

If and when she did get a paying job, she could earn thousands of dollars without any reduction in her social security check. When the threshold was reached at which her social security would begin to be taxed, it would be 50 cents on the dollar. On welfare, income from a job would have been taxed at a 100 percent rate. From day one, aside from minimal work-related expenses and a negligible "bonus" for working outside the home, her welfare check would be reduced a dollar for every dollar she was paid.

No one has suggested the mother on social security suffers from "dependency," yet everyone seems concerned about dependency when it comes to welfare. There is no rational public policy basis for treating families in essentially identical circumstances in such radically different ways. It was the very same act—the Social Security Act of 1935—that created both these income maintenance programs. The only real difference between "survivor" and "welfare" families, then and now, is the imprimatur of the father. The message: the needs and rights of women and children are determined not by universal standards but by the nature of their prior relationship to a man. Why punish the mother and children for the negligence or inability of the father to provide?

Over 90 percent of the *adults* on welfare are women with children. *Children are poor because their mothers are poor.* Financially "secure" mothers don't know the gritty details, but they can be certain in some deep place that if the economic rug is pulled out from under them, they and their children may never recover.

Fatima Ali's tragic acts may not have been so mysterious after all. Choosing exposure to untold evils for your children can be like choosing death, if not of the body then of the spirit. The miracle is why more women facing similar crises don't do the same.

My own rude awakening came when, in my midtwenties, I became a welfare mother. I was single and had a baby whose father was better at providing fear than the necessities of life. When my daughter was three months old, I kicked him out. It had finally dawned on me that he (1) might kill me one of these days, (2) might try to hurt her, or (3) might kill us both in one of his blind drunks.

I didn't dwell on the consequences of kicking him out. I didn't even think about having to go on welfare. Even if I had thought about it, the result would have been the same. My father was dead, and my mother lived on social security. My father had been superstitious, so he had no private life insurance. In any event, without parents or other resources to fall back on, I did what I had to do. I soon became slave to what we (welfare mothers in New York) called "the welfare." It is a crude and irrational system of income distribution, usually capricious and often downright cruel. I have spent the better part of my adult life trying to figure it out. During the first four of those years, I was on and off the rolls intermittently.

The first time I applied for welfare was in early December of 1973. I was crushed when I received no welfare check until after Christmas. I experienced a profound sadness for my three-month-old daughter on Christmas Eve; her future seemed to loom so bleak. I wasn't the crying type, but every now and then I felt these tears rolling down my cheeks, almost as if they belonged to someone else.

A year and a half later, I got a summer job miles from where we lived, so I had to move. Since the job was in a resort town, I couldn't afford to live there either. We moved from one county to another, and I worked in still a third. I had a hunch that I might be entitled to some help with child-care expenses, but I didn't have anyone besides the welfare department to ask. I did that in all three counties. I was told that I didn't qualify for "day care" because *day care* meant daytime, and I worked nights. This, as it turned out, was not true, but at the time I didn't know it. What's more, though I was also entitled to other supple- mental welfare benefits[3] (of which I was equally ignorant), I never got them either. Instead, because I took the job, I was cut off welfare entirely, lost my food stamps and my medicaid. The job paid more than minimum wage. Nonetheless, I was worse off than before. First, I worked nights, like many single mothers, so that I could spend most of my daughter's waking hours with her. This meant that she was sleeping while I was awake, and I had to be awake when she was. By Labor Day, I was, to put it mildly, overtired, overweary, overstrained, overdriven, overfatigued, overspent, and worn out.

There were countless problems associated with money. In theory I had more than when we were on welfare. In practice it wasn't quite the case. On welfare, I could wear whatever passed for clothes without giving much thought to it. On my paying job, the expectations were not so lax. I had less energy for cooking items like dried beans half the day, baking bread, or fashioning nutritious soups out of assorted food scraps. I was living in a small city now, so I could not grow any food because I had no garden in which to sow seeds. I quickly discovered that the faster the food, the more it cost. I also had the expense of traveling back and forth to this job five nights a week. Not only did this extract gas dollars but my car had a seemingly endless capacity to languish at the mechanic's when I couldn't figure out how to fix it myself. Getting sick was out of the question. Not only would I go unpaid if I didn't show up at work but I could not afford a doctor for myself under any circumstances and I would have been reluctant to take my daughter to one had she gotten sick.

By far the most traumatic dilemma for both me and the baby, though, was child care. I could afford very little. Capitulating to the social pressure to be off welfare, I left my daughter at age one and a half with people who could not begin to match my parenting skills. And for what? For her? For me? For money? Or so people would stop watching what I bought at the grocery store? (When you pull out your food stamps at a checkout counter, all eyes within fifty feet—with the exception of those like you, who will be soon facing the music—run a quick tabulation and analysis of your purchases.)

When that job ended, I went to a state employment office in Albany, looking for better-paying work. Foolishly, I told the truth on my application. When the employment official found out I was a single mother who had recently been on welfare, he told me he was not allowed to refer me for a job. He explained that the department had to compete with private employment firms and that it was customary not to send single mothers out for job interviews since employers generally didn't want them, no matter what their skills were. At the time, there was a coding system at employment agencies to tell prospective interviewers in advance such things as your marital status (for women only) and the color of your skin (for nonwhites, of course). This ensured that certain undesirable "types" didn't get sent on interviews. Another staff person approached me and asked if I would like to file a lawsuit against them for the practice, saying he could get me a free lawyer. I gave it only brief consideration. My political consciousness at the time was, to say the least, limited. I also figured that if I went along with them I'd be stuck on welfare for years to come while I waited around for this lawsuit.

Instead, just after my daughter's second birthday in September of 1975, I moved to New York City. I was convinced we'd never escape poverty if I couldn't find better-paying work, so I went stalking "opportunity" in the city. As it turned out, I was shortly looking to get back on welfare, finding no job coupled with acceptable child care screaming out for my skills, such as they were. There didn't seem to be much of a market for brains, and I couldn't type. I could only answer one phone line at a time. I had a college degree (acquired on scholarships), but it wasn't worth much in a city teeming with hundreds of thousands of other baby-boom graduates, many of whom had connections and no babies.

I went to the welfare with all my papers and baby in tow. After waiting interminable days for an appointment, I was finally told that I didn't qualify because I didn't have a place to live. I said that I didn't have any place to live because I didn't have any money with which to rent an apartment, and, if they would just help me, I could remedy that. I was sent packing.

In no time, I obtained a letter from a friend saying I lived in her apartment and went back to the welfare, only this time at another center, to avoid being recognized. (New York City had some forty-six welfare centers at the time. One out of every eleven welfare recipients in the country lives there.) I went through the same process, filling out reams of forms and waiting anxiously for my "appointment." There was a sign on the wall in this center stating, NO MATTER WHAT TIME YOUR APPOINTMENT IS, IF YOU ARE NOT HERE BY 8:30 A.M., YOU WILL NOT BE SEEN. After examining my application, the intake worker told me we were not eligible for welfare because we had no furniture. I started to panic but refrained from strangling her. She told me to go back where I had come from. But I couldn't.

When I got enough of a grip on myself to act, I realized that I needed to know what you had to *have*, not simply what you *didn't* have, to get on welfare in New York, because, though I didn't have any of it, I was willing to say I did. Of course, what they were telling me was not true, but, once again, I was not privy to that little piece of information. Even if I had known, I wouldn't have had the slightest idea what to do about it. I converted one of the few dollars I had left into dimes, got hold of a phone book, and proceeded to call organizations listed in the yellow pages. After a series of unproductive calls, it occurred to me to call New York NOW. I had noticed, after all, that most of the people in the centers were women with kids. I'd heard from a friend who was on welfare, but with whom I was unable to get in touch, that there was some

12

kind of welfare mothers' group in New York, and I inquired about it. They actually knew of it and gave me the number for the Downtown Welfare Advocate Center (DWAC, which whites usually pronounced phonetically and blacks pronounced with a flair I preferred: "DEE-wac").

Some weeks later, with the help of a law student, John Morken, who volunteered at the center, I received a welfare check and got a room in an apartment share for my baby and me. John and my friend Ann Phillips kept trying to convince me to come to DWAC some Sunday for meetings of welfare mothers who talked about their problems and about the notion of "welfare rights," whatever that was. Having virtually no political interests, I was disinclined. Sometime later, I finally relented. There were only a handful of women present at the meeting that first day I went. I don't remember what I expected, but it was more or less a consciousness-raising session for welfare mothers. It was 1975, and little did I know that I would be involved with this organization for more than a decade.

One woman there, Diana Voelker, was particularly impressive. She had grown up on the streets of New York, been a gang member. She, too, was a welfare mother, with a beautiful blond child about seven years old. Diana acted tough, but I was later to find out that was all cover. Throughout the meeting she, and to some extent the others, was "organizing" me, although I didn't know it at the time. Diana said things like "They try to make you feel guilty like you've done something wrong. There's nothing wrong with you; it's the system that's all screwed up. You're a mother, and that's a job and it's an important one." There was a poster on the wall that said WOMEN HOLD UP HALF THE SKY.

I came back the next Sunday and the next. I learned the history of this organization. Diana was one of the founders, along with Anita Hoffman, Abbie's wife. When Abbie went underground, Anita and their son, then called Amerika, had to go on welfare. As I understand it, Abbie had made a fair amount of money on his books, but much of it was given away and the rest was spent on his legal defense. Suddenly thrust into this alien world of welfare, Anita felt politically abandoned by most of their former friends. So she started this consciousness-raising group of welfare mothers. Soon the women realized that they needed to know what their legal rights were, as the welfare was so unpredictable in responding to people's needs. Other women heard about the group through the grapevine and called Anita with increasing frequency to ask for advice. Given her prominence in the "progressive" community, she was able to raise a small amount of seed money for office space and a phone. Supplies like paper, pens, scissors, tape, and glue were usually supplied piecemeal, often from other people's offices.

When I started at DWAC, Anita was weary from the nearly overwhelming tasks of keeping the place afloat, and she rarely showed up at the meetings. In fact, I only met her twice before she went underground to join Abbie with Amerika. She struck me as a truly creative thinker. Clearly she had a broader vision of the Downtown Welfare Advocate Center as a political force. Had she remained involved, the organization may have evolved pretty much as it ultimately did. Some years after she resurfaced from the underground, we met again. She told me that welfare was the true radicalizing experience of her life.

Six months after I first walked in the door, I started to talk in the meetings. There are those who would say I haven't shut up since. I also began working there full-time. I didn't get paid for it in the beginning, but I did get free child care. There were two phones in the room, ostensibly for different grass-roots "self-help" organizations, but most of the calls that came in were from welfare mothers (or prospective ones) with problems. If I had to work alone, I'd run from desk to desk answering the nearly nonstop rings in spite of the fact that I knew almost nothing about welfare in New York. I promised to look up answers for people but usually could not call them back, as they were at pay phones, so I would get answers and wait to hear back from them. Virtually every caller was in a state of terror I knew well. Fortunately, between the books and manuals in the office, the other women who sometimes also worked there, and the occasional welfare lawyer or law student willing to advise me, I was usually able to respond effectively. In time, I became the organization's de facto leader.

Women called or came in from every borough of the city, and they came by the droves. Even a woman named Whoopi Goldberg called for help a couple of times. We were getting about 200 calls a week. I began to wonder how they got our number, so we started asking. We compiled a list of over 100 agencies throughout the city that referred people to us. They ran the gamut—from the gigantic, like the Community Service Society (the largest privately endowed social welfare organization in New York) to the local "multiservice centers" scattered about the city's neighborhoods. The police sent women, the welfare workers sent women, the public library sent women, hospitals, firefighters, colleges, even the Red Cross. All of them had substantial budgets—hundreds of thousands, even millions of dollars. To say the least, they were well funded, and why they didn't do more than refer so many people on to us was beyond me at the time. We had almost nothing. No paid staff. No amenities. (In the winter we worked with our coats on; in the summer we sweltered.) I knew nothing about the politics of social welfare and had no preconceived notions about the "helping" organizations or the players in them. This, too, I would learn.

Helping women with the constant welfare hassles (and their by-products) brought me into contact with hundreds and even thousands of lives. They were all types. Some started out poor, and, even if they had previously had a poorly paying job, found themselves in need of welfare; others had medicaid or food stamp problems; some had been "middle class" until hubby split and they landed right where the rest of us did. There were even a few who had been married to very wealthy men, millionaires who refused to support either their former wives or their current children. Welfare was the great equalizer. It was often said at that time that every woman was only one man away from welfare. For the most part, it was true.

As I met more welfare mothers, I was struck by the number who had lost children. One Christmas, the news reported that a baby had died in a heatless apartment in New York. At the office, we jumped to the logical conclusion that the family was poor and probably on welfare. When we spoke to the doctor at the hospital, he told us the only unusual thing about this case was that it was reported in the news media. He maintained that this was a fairly common occurrence in poor communities. The cause of death is never listed as poverty, though. Pneumonia, hypothermia, heart failure, and the like are medical terms obscuring the truth.

A little more digging revealed the unreported facts. The infant had been hospitalized earlier in the week but had been discharged. The mother was a single parent on welfare with two other children. She was also on what is called a two-party rent check. These checks can only be cashed when both the recipient and the landlord endorse them, effectively ensuring payment to the landlord regardless of housing conditions. The mother had no heat (which was the responsibility of the landlord in this case), no hot water, and no electricity. She was also on recoupments, which means that her welfare check was being garnisheed by up to 15 percent to pay back an "advance" or loan that had been provided by welfare to cover a previous emergency.

The night of the incident was particularly cold, even for late December. She put all three of her children in bed with her in the hope of keeping them warm. In the morning, two of her children woke up next to a dead infant.

At the time, had her total welfare budget been sufficient to meet the state's definition of need, the mother and her children would have been at considerable risk. However, her total cash grant was about 50 percent less than the state itself had deemed "necessary" when it set the so-called standard of need in 1970. At most she could have been getting $218 a month for rent for a four-person family—all of which was designated for the landlord. This portion of her grant was completely unavailable to her for self-help measures such as more blankets, because of the two-party check.

The nonrent portion of her grant, often called the basic grant, would normally have been $258 per month, but since she was on recoupments, she was getting less. Her maximum available cash income would have been between $1.51 and $1.70 per person per day. If her infant needed shoes (and babies' feet change sizes every three months or so), she would have had to starve the other kids (each of whom would also soon be needing shoes) for a few days or go without some other essential. Clearly she was going without a lot of essentials. If she needed toilet paper and soap on the same day she had to do the laundry (at the Laundromat, no doubt), the whole family's allotment for the day would be gone. This was in the heyday of Jimmy Carter's presidency, in what was considered a liberal (almost lavish, with respect to its poor) state.

Another survivor I became acquainted with was actually a grandmother who was being "recouped" for spending her rent money on a crib for her grandchild. She came to see me for advice about her recoupment. I did the calculations on her budget and discovered that the Human Resources Administration (HRA, New York City's euphemism for the welfare department) was taking back more than she owed. At first Aretha's story seemed like a fairly ordinary one—we just had to get the welfare to stop the recoupments and pay her back the excess. As I was finishing the details of her case, she began explaining why she had used the rent money.

Her daughter had a baby and didn't have money for a crib. No one they knew had one available to lend them. Aretha had good reason to worry. Only a year earlier, her own son, for whom she had not had a crib, had died of lead poisoning. She was convinced that a crib would have prevented him from getting at the paint chips. It had been impossible to see and stop him every time he put one in his mouth. He was diagnosed with lead poisoning when he was two. He died at nine. He had been an invalid all his short life—never got out of diapers, never walked, barely learned to talk. He never went to school. Aretha was never able to leave him and take a job outside the home, as she had done before he was born. She had repeatedly asked her social worker to allow them to move to a different apartment. Her file at the welfare department was a foot thick with requests and rejections. Two weeks after her son died, they moved her.

I met Aretha about fifteen years ago. What I didn't know then is that I would come to know many like her. Every time I see a welfare baby sleeping in a cardboard box or a dresser drawer, I think about Aretha.

By almost any measure, poverty is the number-one killer of children in the United States. Doctors don't say so, at least not in so many words, because poverty isn't a medical affliction—it's an economic and social one. It kills all the same. Twelve times as many poor children as nonpoor children die in fires. Eight times as many die of disease, according to a study done by the state of Maine, where, by the way, 98 percent of the population is white. Thirty times as many low-birth-weight babies die as normal-weight babies in the United States. In 1987, one in two homeless mothers in New York reported *losing* weight during pregnancy.[4] Even at the bottom, luck plays a distinct role: whose kid is hit by a stray bullet, whose kitchen stove explodes because it was used nonstop as the only source of heat in a frozen apartment, whose infant dies of pneumonia. These figures, and the ghastly, tragic stories that lie behind them are the results of the failure of U.S. social policy. Murder, by malfeasance. It is not a secret to anyone who lives in an "inner city" *or* to the public officials whose policies create the conditions.

However, most people in the United States have never been to an inner city. There are many all across the land. Few are worse than East New York in Brooklyn. The majority of the families there are on fixed incomes—usually welfare. I once brought a UNICEF organizer from Bombay into East New York at his request. He was so stunned there were tears in his eyes. He told me that the conditions there were more life threatening than those of the poorest people in Bombay. Another outsider I took there said it reminded him of the pictures he had seen after the atomic bomb was dropped on Hiroshima.

I can't say these reactions were surprising. I had been there many times before. It was certainly "life threatening." On one occasion, Jackie Goeings, a member of DWAC, asked me to accompany her to see a young white woman with two small children who lived in East New York. Until recently, they had lived in a welfare hotel. Like most of the homeless families who get apartments following a period in the city's shelter system, she had no real choice about where she was sent. Jackie (who was a black grandmother) had met this woman at a welfare center and was concerned—among other reasons—because, although this was not a safe neighborhood for anyone, it could be particularly alienating for a young white family since virtually everyone else in the neighborhood was black or Hispanic.

When we arrived at the building, we saw notices posted from the Department of Housing Preservation and Development (HPD) indicating that the place had been condemned and that no one at all was supposed to be living there. However, the welfare department was clearly not only *not* moving families out but continuing to move people in. The condition of the building spoke volumes. The stone steps leading up to the entrance were jagged and cracked in half. The front door obviously had once been finely crafted of wrought iron and glass, but all the glass had been broken out of it except random shards. There was no lock on the door. Without even turning the handle, we were able to push our way in. At the entryway was a second door. A solid metal door, this one would have served well to keep out unwanted intruders, except that where there should have been a doorknob and lock there was only a hole. Another light push and we were inside. A bare bulb lit our way.

The first apartment on our left had no door at all. The only living residents in it were rats and vermin. It was literally a garbage dump, and obviously had been for some time. Paint was peeling, the plaster crumbling, and the walls were actually buckling everywhere we looked. The stairway in front of us was an obstacle course of broken steps and debris from the ceiling. Fortunately, we didn't need to use it. The woman we had come to visit lived on the first floor to our right. We knocked and were greeted by a black woman and her kids, who seemed to be waiting for us. She told us that Lydia would be back soon. For some odd reason, Lydia had to leave even though she knew we were coming. We were nonetheless welcome to wait.

Had I not seen other residences like it before, I would have been shocked. There were two "rooms" to this apartment, a kitchen and another open space off it. There was a stove in the kitchen with no knobs, so it clearly didn't work. The mother had converted it into a shelf to hold salt and hot sauce, a few dishes and a glass. A nearby sink had cold water on tap. No hot. There was enough space for a table and chairs, but there were neither. There was a refrigerator, but it didn't work. I wondered silently if it was left there by HPD for the kids to play in.

Some milk and a few other food items were lined up on the windowsill, which functioned fairly well as a refrigeration unit because the windowpanes were almost all broken and it was December. Lydia had obviously attempted to do some repair work on her own; dark green garbage bags were taped across the wounded panes. Still, the place was quite cold. The only source of warmth was a once-upon-a-time toaster oven, the innards of which were fully exposed and red with heat. The wire leading out of the oven was frayed every few inches, and where it plugged into the socket the wall was charred black.

The only piece of furniture in the entire apartment was a single cot. Keep in mind, this apartment housed a woman with two children. Over in the far corner was a broken stroller and two little stacks of neatly folded clothes. These were all the worldly possessions of this family. Lydia, too, had been a victim of spouse abuse, becoming homeless with nothing to her name except two small children. Putting her in this apartment without essential furniture and kitchen equipment, much less heat, was, of course, not proper procedure. Forget that the building was condemned.

We had been waiting for some time when the woman across the hall came to ask if we would look in her apartment, too. So we did. Anna, a short, plump Puerto Rican woman, had only one child, who looked about two or three years old. She was a lovely little girl, with her arm in a cast. We were told that she fell, but I felt a wave of nausea as I wondered what she could possibly have fallen off to have broken her arm. I suspected, as did Jackie, that a boyfriend factored into this household. It struck me that, unlike most other welfare mothers I knew, Anna seemed to be singularly unintelligent. How would she survive if pushed into a forced-work program?

Anna had a stove that worked and served the dual functions of cooking and, to a lesser extent, heating. Her apartment had the same mechanism for refrigeration as Lydia's. What she didn't have was tap water—neither hot nor cold. At least not in the kitchen. She took us to the bathroom, which did have water—spraying out of the upper walls. Inside the tub, chunks of plaster from the ceiling floated in a pool of rust-colored water collected from above. Adding humor to the home-spun charm, Anna had rigged an umbrella over the toilet seat to minimize the forced shower that accompanied any attempt to relieve oneself. There was one anomaly in the bathroom that I'll never forget. It was a brand-new little pink sink. Anna said it had been installed about six months previously by HPD, but no one ever returned to finish the job, so it never produced water. She told us it was the only time during the two years she had been there that any work was done on her apartment.

We were interrupted by a commotion from upstairs, prompting us to go out into the hall. Jackie had been informed that a gang of young hoodlums had taken over an upstairs apartment, from which drugs were being sold—and neighbors terrorized. One young thug with menacing eyes came down to tell us to "get the fuck out of the building." He claimed to be quite certain that Lydia would not be back any time soon. Throughout the short time we'd been there, a dozen or more young men had come and gone. Soon five or six of them swelled into the stairway. A door on one of the upper floors creaked open, and an old black man in a tee-shirt peered down at us through the banisters. He was the only other male in the building. Sadly, he knew he was no match for the young men. Neither were we. So we left for the night, making our way through the phalanx of young men then milling around the stoop.

This building and the people in it are not a composite, not a figment of anyone's imagination. I was there. How many people live like this? There is no absolute raw data, but, judging from the waiting list for public housing in the city (which only the fairly desperate want to get into), the number is now in excess of 250,000 families. About half the inner-city families are on welfare, and another 10 percent receive some form of public assistance. Across the country, the total must exceed a million. And a million families translates to about 3 million people. They are not measurably better off than homeless families. But they are out of sight until something like the riots in South Central Los Angeles hits. Then everyone asks Why?

For most on welfare, life is an intense survival struggle, always robbing Peter to pay Paul (except you're always Peter, and somebody else is always Paul), sometimes experiencing a festering desperation, a sense of being swallowed alive. Still, there are times that are happy—poor babies smile and coo like any other babies.

On many occasions, those of us who worked at DWAC pooled our money for someone worse off than ourselves. We knew without any question what she wanted and needed. And we left the decision on spending it to her. A family who had been burned out might need emergency clothing—diapers at the very least. On occasion a family would show up living in a car, desperate for food while waiting for a welfare determination—a process that would take longer if the family applied for "emergency assistance" than if they applied without mentioning the word *emergency*.

When a child died, friends and neighbors went into action, determined to help get the child buried. The first time I participated in this morbid ritual known only to poor communities was when the son of one of our leaders died. At the time, the welfare would give only up to $250 for the burial. Problem was, no undertaker would do the job for $250. This left two options. First, the child could be given over to the city, to be buried in an unmarked pauper's grave, usually far from where the mother lived. Most mothers simply could not bear to have their dead offspring carted away, never to be able to visit their gravesites. The second option was to raise the money necessary for a "proper" burial. Those who could, those who had at least a few close relatives or neighbors in the community, chose this option.

However, once enough money was available to move the undertaker to action, the welfare would refuse, *as a matter of written policy,* to give the $250. They would argue that if a woman could raise the additional cash necessary to bury a child, she must have access to resources she had failed to report in the past! Even upon the death of a child, the Byzantine logic of the welfare always prevailed. And it masked a cruelty of immeasurable proportions visited upon the poorest citizens of one of the wealthiest nations in the world.

The horrors continued to parade through our day-to-day lives at DWAC. Each new crisis intensified our need to understand why and to figure out how to change "the system." The personal was indeed political, and vice versa. In those early years at DWAC, we believed that if we could simply tell people what was happening to very poor people, someone would put a stop to it. We thought all we had to do was make it public; take these invisible private nightmares and expose them for all the world to see. We couldn't have begun to understand how hard this would be to accomplish, how difficult it would be to reveal the simple truth, how much myth was attached to welfare, and what forces would be brought to bear to prevent us from telling our story.

How do you make public what so many people more powerful than you are trying their damnedest to keep secret? Short of owning your own television network or the lion's share of the stock in *The New York Times,* your opportunities for mass communication are pitiful. Freedom of the press, as they say, belongs to those who own one. Bad enough you've got this sob story to tell, but you're trying to tell it about the dirtiest word in the English language: welfare. It's a word that curdles on most people's tongues, whether they are living under its tyranny as recipients or living with the belief that it's picking their pockets. Almost no one has a dispassionate view of welfare. Fortunately, we didn't know all that when we started. We only knew that welfare was an American tragedy that others needed to know about and that work outside the home for a poor single woman with kids was rarely any better and often even worse.

Besides, the system was personal—for me and most of the women who came to work at DWAC. In the beginning, most of us couldn't see our own way out, but we weren't going to let it bury us without a fight. Too much had happened to us individually and vicariously, through the women who continued to come to us for help.

We knew we had to act collectively, or life on welfare would continue to be a constant game of Russian roulette whose participants did not have to be willing but would have to play. It was against this backdrop of a million personal tragedies, hundreds of whom came to us each week, that we sought to insert our voices and theirs into the public debate on poverty and welfare policies and practices. There were just a few little problems: we were poor individually and organizationally, we were political lepers, and we didn't know anything about building a political base. And that was just for starters.

Chapter 2

The Brutality of the Bureaucracy

Poverty is the worst form of violence.   —Mahatma Gandhi

*In our own time, attention to experience may signal that the
greatest threat to due process principles is formal reason severed from
the insights of passion. . . . In the bureaucratic welfare state of the
late twentieth century, it may be that what we need most acutely is
the passion that understands the pulse of life beneath the official
version of events . . . the characteristic complaint of our time seems
to be not that government provides no reasons, but that its reasons
often seem remote from the human beings who must live with their
consequences.*   —Justice William J. Brennan, Jr.

Think of the worst experience you've ever had with a clerk in some
government service job—motor vehicles, hospital, whatever—and add
the life-threatening condition of impending starvation or homelessness
to the waiting line, multiply the anxiety by an exponent of ten, and
have some idea of what it's like in a welfare center. You wait and wait,
shuttling back and forth in various lines like cattle to the slaughter. You
want to wring the workers' necks, but you don't dare talk back. The
slightest remark can set your case back hours, days, weeks, or forever.
Occasionally someone loses it and starts cursing at the top of her lungs.
Then she's carted away by security guards. In the early days, I thought
this meant she was getting served faster for having had the nerve to lay
it all out. It wasn't long before it became evident that these were among
the ones who would be arrested and sometimes beaten up. It's truly
amazing that more welfare workers aren't killed; the torment so many of

them inflict would break the patience of anyone whose life wasn't on the line. But that's always their ace in the hole. No check, no life.

Babies and other small children are squirming all over the place, and always at least one worker shoots verbal bullets if they cry or run around. Half the time they're hungry as well as bored, but the mother has run out of the food she brought, had none to begin with, or can't leave to get some for fear her number will be called while she's out tracking down an apple, candy bar, or quart of milk. If she yells at the kid, a worker yells at her. If she doesn't yell at the kid, a worker yells at her.

You run the same risk taking one of the kids or yourself to the bathroom, so "accidents" are common. In any event, the bathrooms in welfare centers are not to be believed. The stalls have no doors, and there's rarely any toilet paper. If they are ever cleaned, it must be on holidays; they are putrid with the stench of weeks-old rags piled up anywhere because there are usually no bins to put them in. You could yearn for the good life in a prison after walking into a welfare center bathroom.

Not all workers were ghouls, but they all had to contend with their own predicaments, too. What should have happened and didn't was in many ways the consequence of the draw—what worker you got on what day of the week. Most workers know little about the actual law governing eligibility for public assistance, and even those who start out with good intentions often get blown away by the ever-changing legal script. Each month, new regulations by the dozens are distributed. Most of the workers are so overwhelmed with the sheer volume of clients that only the truly stalwart keep up with the changes.

On the one side, the department is constantly trying to figure itself out, so as "to minimize waste and abuse." On the other, slews of lawsuits are constantly changing policies out of compliance with state or federal laws. And, because most lawmakers are oblivious of the Constitution as it pertains to poor people, it is not uncommon for laws that are unconstitutional to be passed, put into operation, challenged, and overturned. A welfare worker in Kingston, New York, once told one of our members, "When you sign up for welfare, that's when you sign all your rights away." Though this attitude is pervasive throughout the system, it is simply not true.

If you have the uncanny luck of getting a worker who knows the law, you also have to get that person on a good day—which makes all the difference between being treated decently and being treated inhumanely. Inhumanity, by the nature of the job, is the more common treatment. God forbid your worker had a fight with a family member that morning. If the worker has previously been on welfare herself, she might be more helpful, but it's more likely that she'll be more bitter about having to "work" at this low-paying, essentially dead-end job while someone else makes off with a welfare check. Still other workers have this attitude that the welfare is coming right out of their pockets— an outlook the hierarchy likes to cultivate. Some welfare centers even had a system of rewards for intake workers who denied the most applications or cut off the most recipients in a given period.

When you walk into a center, you have the right to get and file an application. To do that, you must first be deemed worthy of one by the person whose job it is to hand them out and initiate the herding process. Often people never get past point one, because the worker *who is obligated by law* to give you that application, not to question or determine your eligibility, often refuses to do so. When that happens, people who are rejected at the door, who have no resources to turn to for advice, just fall through the cracks. They are included in no statistics, anywhere. For all practical intents and purposes, from the state's point of view, they do not exist unless they have submitted an application. At DWAC we used to get many people with this problem. There had to be thousands of others, because we were such a small, virtually unknown operation at the time.

Getting the application into the hands of an "intake worker" who will interview you and check that you have proper documentation—like birth certificates, leases, and social security numbers—is the next hurdle. We were convinced that some of the workers were sadists and would find any excuse to humiliate an applicant, like the one who raged that an applicant was using a verboten red pen. The applicant had made a quarter-inch mark on the form, not even completing the first letter of her name. "You can't use red ink," bellowed the application approver nearby. Okay. The applicant switched to black ink and continued. But over an hour later, as the applicant handed the worker the completed form in black ink, she was told that the entire application was no good because of the tiny red mark on it.

This worker, whose job was to look at applications to determine if

26

they were completely filled out, simply refused to pass the form on to the intake worker. She insisted the applicant do the whole thing over again. She could have told her to get a new form the moment she spotted the red mark. She could have simply handed her another. She could have ignored the obviously irrelevant red mark. But this may have been the only part of her life in which she held the reins of power. She obviously liked it.

There is no rational, uniform method for qualifying for welfare. The attitude of the worker prevails on the one end and that of the state on the other, with rules of the federal government (subject to the politics of the moment) having some jurisdiction over all. At a minimum, there are fifty administrative systems for welfare, one in each state. That's then subdivided into whatever local categories the state chooses—like by county. In New York at the time, to qualify for welfare under the best of circumstances, you could have zero dollars in your possession, and if you had outside income (from a job or child support) it had to be less than the maximum you could have gotten on welfare if you had nothing. As a practical matter, if you walked in and said you had fifty dollars to your name, which the worker would know could not possibly last until your case was accepted, you could not qualify for welfare. If you had any asset whatsoever that the worker deemed sellable—like an old wedding ring—it had to be sold. *All* your resources had to be expended before you were eligible. One of the few things that improved for New Yorkers at least, during the Reagan administration, was the establishment of a one-thousand-dollar "resource limit," which meant an applicant could hold on to any asset deemed worth less than a thousand dollars and still qualify as long as all the other income requirements were met.

In states like Mississippi, income of more than $48 a month for a three-person family would, as a practical matter, disqualify them for welfare eligibility. In New York City, the maximum possible benefit for a three-person family at that time was $332. Job or other outside net income would have to be less than that.[1]

When the intake worker gets through with you, the case supervisor normally has the final thumbs up or down. So all the variables that affected your outcome with the intake worker are once again operative with the supervisor. The case supervisor can demand that you see still other workers to approve this or that required document or answer on your seventeen-page application form. You can be sent to a dozen places before a determination is made. Pregnant women virtually ready to give birth must supply a doctor's verification of their pregnancies. Processing the application takes weeks, sometimes even months (in spite of the law, which says a determination must be made within thirty days). Even after you are determined eligible, you can wait days for the money to come through. Whether you are in heartrending, desperate, obvious need with a sick baby on your lap does not matter. People can fake heartrending, desperate, obvious need. That possibility guides the entire department as well as the local, state, and federal policies. For the poor there is no honor system like the one that guides paying taxes. No innocent until proven guilty like in the criminal justice system. No siree, Betsy.

More often than not, it was quite the opposite. There was a woman who had been raped and was being denied welfare for "refusing to comply" by naming the father. Father? Who the hell were they talking about? This young woman was leaving her infant home alone in a makeshift apartment in someone's attic while she worked a few hours a night in an all-night diner. She was taking home $41 a week. She called in tears. She simply couldn't make it on $41 a week.

If the welfare system worked the way it should, it would still not give people enough to live on. But securing and keeping what little it is possible to get would be difficult for an FBI agent. For instance, since the rape victim had only $41 a week for herself and her child, she was eligible for the difference between what she was paid on her job and the amount set for a welfare grant for two people. However, when asked who the father of her child was, she was in an impossible bind. He had told her neither his name nor his address during the rape, and she'd never seen him before in her life. Her inability to supply his name drove the case worker into a paroxysm of doubt. If she had known who the father was and he was not providing for the child, even if they were married she would still have been eligible for welfare.

Once the worker was dissatisfied with the answer to the name-that-father question, whole avenues of questions followed. Among them: had she reported the rape to the police? She hadn't. Now the worker felt justified in rejecting the application or postponing action until the woman went to the police to report a rape that had occurred over a year ago, securing proof of the report in the process. As you might imagine, this intrusion on their day-to-day work does not make the police happy and can and usually does evolve into another hassle.

Though the welfare is required to assist the applicant in obtaining documents that might be difficult for her to obtain on her own, this assistance is rarely given. Reluctantly, she went to the police, who resisted the paperwork. She called me from the police station, frustrated by another bureaucracy. I had to pressure them to give her a statement verifying that she made the report, which they thought was crazy, given the time lapse. Then it was back to the welfare department for the next round. We hoped she had satisfied them, but they wouldn't say. She was told only that she would hear by mail.

This time they rejected her for lack of an address at which to contact a man whose name she did not know. And so on and on. In cases like these, the only way an applicant usually gets through the maze is by getting the aggressive intervention of an advocate or friend who knows the rules and how to enforce them or by going to court, which, given the dearth of lawyers who can or will take such a case, is rare.

Another woman presented herself on DWAC's doorstep, a small child's hand in each of hers. They were homeless and victims of family violence in the days before homelessness and battering were known to exist except by those to whom they happened. She had just run away. It was approaching evening when she arrived, and the welfare centers—all but the all-night emergency assistance unit (EAU) at 241 Broadway—were closed for the day. I sent her over with instructions to call if they didn't help her immediately. Heh.

As it was late when she called, and forcing the unit to act would have taken a great deal of time that night, I called a nun I knew who occasionally took in homeless women for brief periods. It was rare that I could prevail on her to take in one with children, but she acquiesced. The woman and kids went there for the night.

The next morning I sent her to the closest welfare center, again with instructions to call. In the meantime, several of us at DWAC pooled our food stamps and shared them with her so she could feed the kids during the upcoming welfare marathon. Helping women at the welfare centers was DWAC's primary and never-ending function. Over time we developed our tactics into a fine art. Chaos was the one constant with the welfare department. If organizations could be declared crazy, this one would have been carted off to Bellevue. At first some of the problems women came for help with seemed impossibly nuts. After a while, nothing was too hard to imagine. We could safely begin with the assumption that the woman's story was true and work from there. Poised for battle, we went into full gear, calling up and down the "chain of command" until we were able to get this woman placed on an emergency basis in a welfare hotel. Welfare center directors at several locations knew DWAC by name, and some of us individually, so we could usually sooner or later prevail on them to force an intake worker to act in accordance with the law. But generally only after we had exhausted the center's entire bureaucratic chain, several people deep. As a practical matter, if the directors hadn't insisted on this, they'd never have gotten peace from us, because we would have put them at the top of our list instead of near the bottom.

If going through the center director failed, we went to "central office" (the headquarters of New York's welfare department), which was the best way to get action but also normally required exhausting the other routes first. Central office was less personally involved, and they knew that our persistence would cost them, taking up the valuable time of innumerable officials if we were right—which, 99 percent of the time, we were. When you stop to think about it, who in their right minds would put themselves through incredible humiliation and risk jail over the paltry sums to be had by committing welfare fraud? Certainly not people with options.

Not all cases were so complicated. Many could be settled through a simple phone call. Often women just wanted to know what their rights were. With a relatively benign piece of information like "tell them they are required by law to give you an application," they could unglue their own cases. In part, that was why so many women came to us. We took them at their word, we presumed the information they were giving us was accurate, we didn't *have to see* their paperwork as long as they could read it to us over the phone, and we helped them with as little rigmarole as we could. We required no forms and no explanations beyond what was necessary to take care of the problem.

If they called Legal Services, they could get no information without going to the Legal Services office to flag all their papers in front of an attorney or paralegal. To boot, they would generally be unable to make an appointment at a Legal Services office unless they were holding something like a three-day notice of eviction—only the most desperate could find help there because of the sheer volume of people in need and the snail's-pace office procedures. There was a catch-22 at nearly all the "helping" agencies that could intervene in a welfare dispute. Most wouldn't help anyone who wasn't in their "catchment" area. That means an organization from downtown Manhattan wouldn't help a person from uptown (and vice versa) because they weren't paid by their funding sources to do so. That was in part why so many organizations with big budgets were always referring people to us: we would help anybody who needed it, anytime, anywhere.

The constant bombardment of families in crisis had its own kind of allure, strangely enough. When you knew the answer to their questions, when you got them over whatever bureaucratic hurdle they were stuck on, you leveraged a desperate family's total income for months or even years to come. You saved them from starvation, you prevented them from becoming homeless, you delivered them from the streets to a place they could call home, however dilapidated. You accessed such luxuries as clean diapers and toothpaste. It could be exhilarating—probably like being a firefighter or a cop, a female Tarzan for that matter—only you could do it ten or twenty times a day if you were good.

But it could be drudgery, too. No pay didn't excite potential advocates either. Turnover at DWAC was frequent. Advocates came and went, one or two at a time. Some women would drop out when their own cases became tangled. Others got jobs, left the city to go to law school, whatever. Usually, that was the last we'd see of them. Diana Voelker, who had been instrumental in pulling me into DWAC, had been job hunting for some time and finally snagged a decent job as a result of a talk she gave at some conference. I was depressed to see her go but committed myself to staying. Besides, Diana wasn't dropping out, she just wouldn't be around as often. John Morken, who had first helped me at DWAC, was in law school most days, and his regular participation had trickled to a near halt. It fell to me to keep the place going.

Coincidentally, a temporary paying job became available in the room where DWAC was housed. John encouraged me to apply for it, which I did in spite of misgivings. In particular, I was reluctant to give up that one benefit of welfare: even though I worked all the time, I felt my time was one of the few things in my control. Being under the thumb of an employer again would change that. The job was offered to me. With continued trepidation, I took it.

Because the pay was so low, I qualified for much reduced, but nevertheless important, welfare benefits. Unlike during my last job, this time I knew how to get everything coming to me. For instance, I was able to retain my medicaid card. Like most low-paying jobs, this one didn't offer health insurance.

Getting my partial welfare checks became a recurring battle, though. I assumed the problem derived from the fact that I was a regular pain in the ass at the welfare centers, fighting for other people's checks on a daily basis. Just about every time my check was due, I'd have to wait the requisite week (to be certain that I wasn't trying to commit welfare fraud by getting them to issue a duplicate check). In other words, they didn't wait to see if I had actually committed welfare fraud before leaving me without the necessary resources to live on. At least I had a place to live and a small but steady source of additional income.

The waiting rule, however, applied equally to people with no other income. No matter how bare the cupboard, every month thousands of families waited to replace a check that hadn't arrived in the mail. All were guilty until proven innocent. Next to these, my biweekly ritual was insignificant.

No one seemed able to supply any satisfactory explanation for my dilemma. My checks continued to disappear before they got to me, so I was put on what was called R/O (route to office). My checks were sent to the welfare center (instead of to my home address) and handed to me there twice a month. At least this way I would get my check on check day, even if I had to wait hours for it. I wondered what would have happened if I'd had a job from which I couldn't take time off to visit a center. Soon I would know the answer to that question, as many former low-wage employees lost their jobs and came to DWAC for help getting back on a full welfare check. As ever, the system was nothing if not perverse.

After I'd been working at this new job for less than six months, the other shoe dropped. A letter came in the mail from the inspector general at the State Department of Social Services indicating that I was under investigation for committing welfare fraud. I called the number on the letter and was informed that an inspector would meet me at my office the following week to go over my case. If I wasn't already paranoid—with the check mix-ups and all—this would have done the trick. It seemed like a pattern was emerging. Were they hounding me for the work I was doing? Who knows. Fortunately for me, the inspector who came was a reasonable woman. She had to wait a couple times while I dealt with calls from other recipients. When she saw what I was doing, I think she was embarrassed about the whole thing, especially after analyzing my budget. According to her calculations, I was getting even less than I was supposed to get. That's another thing about the welfare—the regulations are so complicated, no two people working there would come to the same conclusions. Who was I to argue? I wiped the sweat off my brow, gratefully accepted an upward adjustment in my grant, and returned to work.

I prayed for new volunteers. We often fantasized about raising money to hire staff for DWAC, but it seemed like a pipe dream to me. I couldn't imagine someone giving us money to make trouble. Still, doing this work without having to maneuver around my paying job had a lot of appeal.

One day a young woman named Christine Larson walked through the door looking to put in some time. She had heard of us somewhere along the line and felt that this would suit her just fine. She was quite striking, with very long, straight, blond hair and a chiseled profile. She was everything you wouldn't expect to find in a welfare advocate center. She'd been to Williams College and displayed all the markings of a wealthy WASP upbringing.

I was to discover differently. Like me, Christine came from a low-income family and had gone to college on a scholarship. She had the will of a bulldozer, and guts to match. She believed that her birth mother had died as a direct consequence of giving birth to her. Her strong feelings about mothers sacrificing for their children were probably part of the reason she came to DWAC. Perhaps most telling in her background, she was raised in a black neighborhood in Chicago and had attended an African-American public school. She was a little girl when Dr. Martin Luther King was shot. The next day, she and her brothers and sister, all white as snow, were attacked in the schoolyard. Luckily, they were saved from what they felt was certain death by a black man who stepped in and pulled them away to safety. When I got to know Christine, I realized that she was still trapped somewhere between being attacked and being saved—both by blacks.

By night she was a waitress at The Bitter End. By day she was a welfare warrior. Petite, delicate Christine. Hard drinking and smoking in both roles. Occasionally scattered, usually responsible. She expressed a desire to become a minister and years later attended Union Theological Seminary. She was a bundle of contradictions, which suited me just fine. She became my right arm for several years, my loyal friend, someone I could rely on under any kind of fire. There was plenty of that. She also took to the evolving politics of DWAC, naturally and with gusto. Something about it was personal for her, too.

In the evenings I would pick up my three-year-old daughter at the day-care center across the hall. She loved day care, my little social butterfly. In that respect she was turning out to be my opposite, comfortable in most any social situation, with children or adults. If we didn't have grocery shopping to do first, we would go home, where I'd cook dinner for the two of us and anyone else who happened to be around. Often Christine would join us, as did other co-workers and supporters of DWAC as time went by.

After my daughter was asleep, we talked. Usually it was about the welfare and the day's events, especially the women whose cases we could not quite seem to get resolved, the ones that could drag on for weeks or even months. These were the ones that made us breathe fire, because some petty bureaucrat was getting off on making a poor wretch even more miserable. Now that there were two of us on a pretty regular basis, one could accompany an applicant or temporarily disconnected recipient down to a center more often. The bodily presence of a witness, particularly one who could be counted on to start bringing the chain of command to bear on a case, often sped things up.

If it wasn't workers at the centers bashing recipients directly, it was the extremist policies and practices emanating from the higher-ups. At

34

one point, the ever-vigilant Human Resources Administration secured a hired gun to track down absent fathers. The organization was named Gulf Coast Services. We called them bounty hunters. They got paid by the head—$75 for the lead, more if they could make it stick. One woman whose husband had died three years earlier (she had a death certificate) came to us when she was cut off after Gulf Coast claimed to have verified that the father was still living at home. The "verification" was done by sending a piece of mail return receipt requested to the father at the family's address. This woman, like many widows, signed for the mail, assuming it was family business that continued to be carried on in his name. We finally got her reinstated. She had been off welfare for sixty days. Sixty days without income for a family with no reserves. They had resorted to begging.

When we weren't talking about cases and the general filth in all senses of the word that pervaded welfare centers, we talked about how to get DWAC off the ground in a more coherent fashion. The files, for instance, were a lesson in collective chaos. Every volunteer who stepped into the center for more than ten minutes had put his or her imprimatur on them. About the only way to find anything was to leaf through every file, drawer by drawer. Files were arbitrarily named, only infrequently in alphabetical order, and the contents of any given file were scrambled.

This had its advantages, believe it or not. We kept what passed for our fiscal records (our checkbook and checks) in a garbage bag stuffed into one of the file drawers. The standard explanation was that no potential thief would ever have looked for it there. The scary part was, someone could also mistake it for garbage and accidentally throw it out in a cleaning frenzy. Fortunately, that never happened.

We also needed to recruit more workers who would throw themselves on our funeral pyre. We had nothing but intensity to offer. And of that there was plenty to go around. With two of us, the phones seemed to ring even more frequently, if only because nobody had to be kept on hold while one skated across the room to answer the other phone. At least not if we were both in the office.

And we talked about politics—what was really going on in the world of welfare. We were ensnared in the ugliest system for responding to people in dire need that could be imagined. It was beyond belief, a bottomless pit of cruelty. Recipients were treated like untouchables in the newspapers, by all the politicians who opened their mouths about us, by every institution we came into contact with.

They might as well have painted a scarlet *W* on recipients' foreheads. Once you got the hang of it, you could spot one of us, white or black, a mile away. We exuded poverty. But we were just people, just mothers for the most part, trying to raise up our children through adversity that would be hard to exaggerate. Given those circumstances, it was finally not difficult to understand why Christine and later others would walk the red-hot coals to our office. At least someone in the world had to care.

Not long after Christine's arrival, Dolores started dropping by more frequently. She had been helped by John over quite a long period, with a case that seemed to stay bollixed up. I guess John pressed her to put in some time. She was also going to social work school and probably figured DWAC would be a good place to get some experience. Couldn't beat that logic.

Dolores was about ten years older than I, but you couldn't tell that by looking at her. She had three kids and had only recently found herself in the welfare lines. Her husband of nineteen years had just told her he was gay and moved out of the house to fulfill his dreams. Problem was, she'd married him when she was still a teenager, and she had been a full-time mother ever since. With no history of employment outside the home, she was in the same sour pickle millions of others have experienced over the years. The whole thing had come as an enormous shock to her. Unlike many welfare mothers, she had lived quite a comfortable middle-class existence most of her life. This lack of abundance was for the birds, not to mention that she'd had no inkling of her husband's other sex life until the day he told her before walking out. Worse was the fact that almost the minute he announced he was leaving home, he let it be known that he wouldn't be paying the rent anymore either. She was bereft of a nearly lifelong partner, suddenly the single mother of three children, and penniless all in one fell swoop.

When Dolores went to the welfare, which was really her only option in the beginning, she received two pertinent suggestions. First, "You're a good-looking chick. Why don't you just go out and peddle your ass?" Second, her intake worker recommended she put the children in foster care till she got on her feet. By that time, she was at her wits' end and actually went home to give that suggestion some consideration. Her rent was late. Before long she might be evicted. She had no money for the ordinary things her children had come to take for granted, like ice-cream cones or a movie. They had no idea what had transpired between their parents, so they blamed her for their radical shift in life-style as well as for their father's sudden absence from the household.

After a couple of weepy days in which she felt paralyzed—only adding to her self-loathing—she got angry. At her husband and at the welfare. I guess that's when she found her way to DWAC for the first time. As a consequence of her fortitude and John's intervention at the welfare center, she surrendered neither her children nor her apartment.

Before I got to know Dolores well, a man named Hulbert James appeared on the DWAC scene. How he got there, I'm not exactly sure. My guess is that he originally had contact, directly or indirectly, with Anita Hoffman. John must have been the person who set things up this time around. All I knew was that James would be attending a meeting at our office.

I made arrangements to be at the meeting myself but could not understand all the anticipation regarding James's impending appearance. Diana was coming; so was Cindy Mann, another law student I had met only a couple of times previously. So, apparently, were some women from the by then essentially defunct National Welfare Rights Organization (NWRO), about which I knew very little. Before coming to DWAC, I'd never even heard of it. I came to understand that NWRO had been a considerable political force as a national membership group of welfare recipients (mainly mothers) from the late 1960s till about 1972.

The room was full that evening. A lot of people I'd seen only a few times before had shown up. Among those I recognized from a prior meeting I had attended since being at DWAC were Marion Kramer and Beulah Sanders. Neither spoke highfalutin English (as my mother would have referred to it), but, could they ever talk! Both were black. Marion was petite and pretty, while Beulah was large and fearsome. Beulah had refined her body language to communicate like a fine instrument, albeit a bass drum. She had been president of the New York Welfare Rights Organization during its brief heyday and vice president of the national organization, where, no doubt, her histrionics had come in quite handy.

There was a distinct sort of patter that peppered meetings like these, no matter what the subject was. Presidents, governors, mayors, and politicians generally were portrayed as true lowlifes. Virtually everybody in the country was on some sort of welfare (farm subsidies, corporate bailouts, college scholarships, social security, and the like), but they all pretended not to be. Social workers were the butt of endless jokes. In this context, welfare recipients were insiders; everyone else was outside. I liked that.

Sitting quietly, I picked up the lingo, the ideas, the politics, and found I could identify with it the same way I had at those early DWAC meetings I'd attended. In fact, I had more in common with poor women, black or white, than I had with anyone else anywhere I had ever been.

Whoever introduced Hulbert James indicated that he had been director of Citywide, the accepted euphemism for the New York City branch of NWRO, which had been further broken down into borough groupings like B-WAC (Brooklyn Welfare Action Coalition) and then local chapters. When he spoke, most eyes and ears were attentive. A hum of approval punctuated his talk. Little did I know that his reappearance in New York would change DWAC forever.

In those days I was more often moved by events than a mover of them. So when Hulbert appeared in my office the next day, I sensed he was going to try to change things, and I didn't want any part of it. The night before there had been talk of a protest march over proposed budget cuts in the state legislature and much fond recollection of the good old days of NWRO. All that protesting stuff made me nervous. It certainly wasn't for me. I was tied to phones that just kept on ringing, and I couldn't imagine waltzing around Wall Street and Federal Plaza for the show of it, much less wasting precious time trying to get other people to do it, no matter what the governor was proposing.

Hulbert wasn't easy to brush off, though. He was working for the United Church of Christ at the time. But for some reason he wanted our office for the headquarters of this march and presumed that we would be delighted to share the space with him. I found at least a dozen reasons why it wasn't a good idea—tying up the phone lines, the cost of the calls, the disruption of all the comings and goings. Worse, he kept talking about *organizing* right there in the office. At the time, I thought organizing was illegal, and although I wasn't by nature opposed to it, I'd seen enough FBI types crawling around DWAC (most likely looking for Abbie) that I was sure all this radical stuff would bring us to a crunching halt.

I asked him to be cool with that talk. He must have thought I was a real dingbat. No doubt he figured he could talk me into it anyway. So he told me what I now recognize as the standard parable of organizing. That's the one about a person walking by a riverbank who suddenly notices another person drowning and jumps in to save him. The next day, the person is out walking by the riverbank again when the same thing happens and again he jumps in to save the drowning person. Day after day the scenario is played out, till one day the person who's been fishing these others out of the river all this time decides to go up to the bridge to stop whoever is throwing everybody over in the first place. Clearly I was on the riverbank, with bodies floating by so fast that under the best of circumstances I could never succeed in fishing more than a fraction of the total out. Years later I'd be telling that story over and over to new staff and members. DWAC became the headquarters for this march.

Christine and I participated in the nuts and bolts of pulling off the march while continuing to juggle the phones. We learned such essentials as how to design leaflets, how to use the Gestetner for burning stencils and the printer to put out copies by the thousands. The competing demands of women in need here and now were a real strain. At the same time, there was something kind of electric about the office. On the day of the march, we had mixed emotions. Sashaying down a street in public shouting chants was really bush league. Once we shook that feeling, though, we enjoyed it in spite of ourselves.

There wasn't much media coverage of the event. Fewer than 200 people turned out, and half of them were from the various do-good agencies happy to have Hulbert James back in New York. Still, it made a certain amount of sense. What little was covered was very different from the profoundly negative feed about welfare recipients that was emanating from the governor's office almost daily in order to pass the welfare cuts. It was during this time that the first mention of bringing back the soup kitchens to decrease welfare expenditures was tossed out for public consumption. The worst of then Governor Hugh Carey's proposals would have cut sixteen- to twenty-one-year-olds off welfare unless they could prove emancipated minor status—like by having a baby. It was really targeted at black boys, at a time when their unemployment rate was soaring.

The governor's bill handily passed in the legislature. Almost as quickly, Legal Services attorneys led by Mike O'Conner (New York's primo welfare law jock) got an injunction to prevent it from being carried out while they prepared a lawsuit to stop it permanently. No matter. The welfare centers were already primed to move these legislative intentions. Suddenly our offices were under siege by teenage boys alone or with their mothers trying to undo the damage. It was astonishing how fast the welfare centers could implement this rule change. It took a great deal more time and effort to reverse their actions, in spite of the injunction and other legal maneuvers that stopped the plan, at least in New York.

In spite of the legal victory, the ideas had been planted. They took root. Other states moved even more cuts aimed at single men and, incidentally, single women on welfare and got away with it. The homeless adult crisis was triggered. (Ronald Reagan's presidency continued this onslaught against welfare recipients, as if there were jobs galore going unfilled for this constituency, which was soon expanded to include poor mothers.) On the surface, the premise was that if these people were denied welfare, they would go out and get jobs. Practically speaking, since the jobs were simply not there, the more likely motivation was to get them to move away (to some state where general assistance still existed) or just disappear. In any case, it was believed that, if they could not get on welfare period, they would cease to be a burden to the states in question. Wrong. The development of an expensive array of soup kitchens and shelters was sure to follow.[2]

During the weeks preceding the march, Hulbert spent a lot of time at our office, flitting in and out several times a day. He also spent time educating us. He said to read the newspapers so we would know what was going on in New York. He said things like "Those who sit at the table write the agenda." We chewed on that mystic pizza for a while. He sat down and rattled off a list of possible funding sources for DWAC, including those that would give what he called "seed money." He didn't seem to fathom how foreign concepts like "board" and "seed money" were to us. He also insisted we introduce DWAC to the key players at social work agencies like the Community Council of Greater New York. I took voluminous notes. Standing by as the springs of social justice were recoiling certainly clarified the need for a more consistent and powerful voice for welfare recipients. Maybe I was just beginning to understand how to go beyond the one-on-one advocacy DWAC did.

Hulbert didn't tell me how many of these people I was about to meet would make my skin crawl. There was that "some of my best friends are welfare recipients" quality about so many of them. Susan Kinoy staffed a do-gooder committee at the council. Shortly after I agreed to be on the committee, she took to slinging her arm around my shoulder and introducing me to everybody as her "favorite welfare mother." In spite of the indignities of these relationships, we hoped to be getting closer to the table where the agenda was written.

Hulbert took off shortly for another city. I was upset when he went, because he seemed to have been talking about building something one day and be gone the next. I had no idea that he probably thought something was started that would go on and he could move on to the next place. As it happened, the loose network that had been established while he was in town continued to meet, however infrequently.

The weeks that followed that first march went like lightning. In the limited circles that followed welfare policy, DWAC's reputation was jumping. That was how Sharon Hunt happened into our lives. When she went looking for what she called "the poop" on current welfare issues, she was referred to us. At that point, she was on unemployment, having been laid off months earlier. She had been on welfare in the past and expected she and her kids would be back there in the not-too-distant future. The troika of Christine, Dolores, and me was soon expanded to a quartet.

Sherry was one live wire. She was quick-witted and a little crazy. Years in an orphanage and various foster homes and a virtual lifetime of abuse had left their mark. When I put her on the phones, she picked up the necessary information faster than anyone else *ever* before, or after, her. The first time she got stuck on a case, I said, Let's go to the welfare center and work it out there. I never had to go again with her. She became our ace advocate. I still thought we were all working on the same things, but in fact we were beginning to specialize, organically.

We also began to raise money, albeit slowly. The first major breakthrough on that front came after considerable finagling to get eight "CETA slots" to hire ourselves and others to work at DWAC. (CETA was a Carter administration jobs program that parceled out funds for public works and community organizations.)[3] Our first order of business was to secure a bigger office to accommodate the growing organization. We were moving into a whole new phase, one that accommodated individual advocacy *and* applied the issues it raised to initiate change. We would begin to write that agenda. One way or another.

Not long after we moved into our new offices, beatings of recipients and applicants by security guards escalated in frequency and ferocity at welfare centers all over the city. And they were inflicted with impunity. It became standard procedure for the guards to press charges against the victims for disorderly conduct, resisting arrest, and assaulting an officer on the heels of the abuse they perpetrated. Coupled with the threat of termination from the welfare rolls that barely tethered a fragile family to life, this action was quite effective in limiting any legal consequences for the guards.

Most victims were appropriately terrorized and disinclined to fight back. The first brought directly to our attention was Maxine. She was beaten in front of Sharon, who was at the Wycoff Center in Brooklyn assisting a third mother, Cynthia Wilcox (who also subsequently joined us on a regular basis at DWAC). We had heard of these beatings before, but none of us had witnessed one. And normally it was almost impossible to track down the victims to offer assistance. They would disappear, nameless, left to their own devices.

That day we received a call from Cynthia telling us that Sharon and another woman were being arrested at the center. Fortunately, Cynthia had the presence of mind to call us speedily. We told her to make a list of those people at the center who might later be needed as witnesses. Christine and I flew out of the office.

When we arrived at the center (getting lost and running blocks and blocks), hardly anyone was there; it had been shut down following the melee. We were directed to the police station where Maxine and Sharon had been taken into custody. At the station, Cynthia filled us in on the details while we waited for the attorneys who usually worked with us to get them out. In the meantime, Dolores, who had stayed back at the office, started calling the press, on the mistaken assumption that this was news. Apparently, various city desk editors agreed with her until they contacted "central office," who persuaded them there had been no commotion. You know, business as usual. With such responsible authorities disclaiming reality, how could we possibly have hoped to be taken seriously?[4]

Maxine—black, pregnant, and mother of one—had gone to the center to get her check, because she had not received it in the mail. She was told she didn't have an appointment, the check wasn't ready, and she should come back another day. She had no food at home and not even enough money to take the subway back. Overwhelmed, she sat down, with her eight-year-old son standing next to her, and began to cry. Her face buried in her hands, she started rocking side to side, hitting a desk with her knees in muted, rhythmic taps. This would not be tolerated, so the guards were called.

Instead of simply escorting her out of the building, and certainly without stopping to inquire whether he could help, a six-foot-tall guard confronted her, shouting, "If you don't shut the fuck up, I'll arrest you," according to a welfare mother who witnessed the scene. Maxine was unable to stop crying, so another guard ordered her into the guardroom, saying he was going to issue her a summons for destroying city property (presumably the metal desk against which she had been thudding). Within minutes, the thin walls of the guardroom began to vibrate, and loud screams from inside were heard by dozens of women in the waiting room.

Sharon Hunt led the charge to open the door that revealed the fray. One witness who later testified at the trial said, "I saw him pick [Maxine] up and throw her against some filing cabinets. . . . Then he began kicking her on the floor." All the while, Maxine's son was standing there, shell-shocked.

Sharon demanded that a female guard be sent in, for which transgression (along with opening the door, no doubt) she, too, was arrested. The charges against Sharon, but not those against Maxine, were ultimately dropped. She would be tried for harassment, resisting arrest, assaulting an officer, and disorderly conduct. The day after the incident, Maxine began bleeding and suffered a miscarriage. At the trial, even her lawyer confided to us that Maxine made a lousy witness on her own behalf, as she was obviously somewhat disturbed. She babbled, sometimes incoherently. So, despite the testimony of several witnesses who corroborated her story, and that of three guards who contradicted one another, she was convicted by a jury of six of the two lesser charges. Was this for something she did? Or for something she wasn't—middle class, perhaps white, and, certainly, composed?

At the trial it was also revealed that Maxine's welfare check had been sitting face up on the desk of a worker behind the "cage" (a protective barrier) throughout the day she was ignored, beaten, and arrested. For some inexplicable reason, the workers who had the responsibility to *give* her the check had chosen not to. All that had transpired as a consequence of that one cruel decision could have been avoided.

After the arrest, Maxine was cut off welfare for some months and lived hand to mouth, often borrowing what little money we—and her lawyer—had to offer while Sharon and the attorney worked to get her welfare grant restored. She lived in a desolate neighborhood speckled with abandoned buildings. Her own apartment had no stove, no sink, and no front door lock. What could her son possibly have done to warrant the world he was brought into?

The security guard was quietly moved to a center in another section of the city. At the time, this was about the city's only "remedy" to charges of abuse. The reason for moving the guards was simple: once a guard got a reputation for being vicious, unrest in the center escalated. We came to know this guard as Jack, a tall white man with a serious drinking problem. We tracked his course. He later lost his job, but not until he had assaulted several more women.

Maxine was first, but she was by no means last. By the summer of 1988 we were receiving as many as ten calls a week about what we called welfare center brutality. Sometimes they came from recipients who witnessed a beating. Other times they were anonymous calls from a worker in the center who just couldn't ignore it anymore. It has to be assumed that many more beatings were occurring, because we were unknown to most people—hardly a household name, even among the poor. The calls came in from every borough. It was rampant.

Late that summer, Dolores received a call from Mary,[5] who had been referred to us after a grizzly ordeal at the Lower Manhattan welfare center on West Thirteenth Street. The next day, Mary came in to see us. She was a pretty, petite, and soft-spoken forty-year-old with two teenagers of her own at home plus two more she had taken in because their family life was unhappy. During the school year she worked as a teacher's aide in a school for the deaf. After eleven years on the job, she was making less than $5,000 annually. She also had some child support coming to her, but wasn't receiving it because of three years of inept case handling at the welfare center. She had gone to the center that day to try again to get her case unraveled. If she had no income in the months when school was not in session, she often had to get welfare. The welfare had arranged to have her child-support payments sent directly to them, which was not unreasonable when she was on the rolls. Trouble was, when she returned to her job, they kept on taking the child-support payments. This was as illegal as it was counterproductive. So Mary was trying to get back what she was owed and, given the state of her finances, she found herself needing welfare yet again. She applied only for the two children who were her own.

As she was being interviewed, a worker at the next desk began insulting her. "You need money, Mrs. Whitey? Why don't you walk the streets? Why don't you suck cock?" She pleaded with him to stop, but he continued. Her own worker said nothing. Embarrassed, she got up to leave, when a phone call was made to summon a guard. Before Mary knew what was happening, she had been thrown to the floor by two guards, quickly handcuffed, and dragged over to the elevator banks. She said the beating continued outside the elevators for several minutes; at least one guard was fully out of control. She overheard one of them saying, "Jack is really going to do it this time. He's going to kill her." She also smelled alcohol on his breath.

Over a thirty-hour period, Mary was repeatedly beaten, sexually assaulted, and verbally abused. She was arrested and thrown into jail. She did not go free until her arraignment in criminal court the next day. In the interim, because she had been prohibited from taking the medication that prevented her from having seizures, she had one. During the grand mal seizure a wooden doorstop was stuffed into her mouth, leaving splinters in her tongue, lips, and palate. Afterward, every time she asked for help, she was told to shut up or they'd shove the doorstop back in. Ultimately someone must have become worried because Mary was taken briefly to St. Clare's Hospital, then shuttled back to a police detention center some blocks away from the welfare office.

In spite of her obviously traumatized condition, when her father picked her up at the courthouse, the first thing he asked her was "What did you do?" It did not even occur to him that she had done nothing wrong—after all, she had been arrested. His doubt was yet another blow. She showed us photographs taken by her boyfriend shortly after she returned home, in which she was wearing what were then called baby-doll pajamas. Every part of her body that was exposed was blotched purple, from her face to her feet.

She said she was getting threatening phone calls on a regular basis telling her to keep her mouth shut. Shortly thereafter, Mary's phone number was changed and unlisted. Still the calls came, which made us believe there was some police involvement, perhaps just a comradely gesture by the police to the security guards. (Security guards were not police but were under contract to HRA.)

As acquiescent as she appeared (always speaking in a near whisper), Mary was nothing if not brave. She had been mercilessly abused, thoroughly humiliated, and now she was being intimidated by anonymous phone calls. Her boyfriend couldn't stand the strain; shortly after we met the two of them, he was gone. But Mary decided to fight.

The first time she had to go back to the welfare center after the episode, she was shaking perceptibly. Her sense of helplessness was often palpable in the weeks immediately after the incident. At DWAC we unanimously decided this moment called for some extraordinary advocacy techniques, so we organized a few women and went to the center with her. The show of force resulted in exceptional service. In a matter of hours, the problem that had been insoluble for three years was settled.

Mary and several other victims of similar abuse all agreed to "go public." One of them was a city worker whose finger had been broken when she intervened on behalf of another woman. Another was a pregnant woman who had been thrown down a flight of stairs. We set up a series of forums, which for once garnered significant press coverage. (Journalists are partial to the juicy stuff.) At one particularly hairy city council hearing, Blanche Bernstein, then commissioner of HRA, denounced us as hysterical women who were making up the stories.

Bert Rose, then assistant president of Teamsters Local 237, which represented the guards, was next to testify. *Teamsters!* My heart sank. I was sure he, too, would deny the beatings, and there would be so many thems lined up against us that we *would* appear nuts. But he surprised us all. He didn't deny the brutality. In fact, he condemned it and went on to offer startling details.

For one, the guards were barely trained. Many were dropouts or failures of the police academy who were subsequently hired by HRA. (In more than one case, as it turned out, these guards had been expelled from the academy for having noticeable authoritarian complexes.) The only real requirements for the job were to be young and big enough to give the impression that you could, and would, hurt someone. Rose was a union rep with a mission, as we were about to see. He finished his analysis with the clincher that the guards were so underpaid that it was hard to attract more acceptable people to the job. He concluded, "The state is getting what it pays for." How's that for strange bedfellows— welfare mothers and the Teamsters?

As attention was drawn to the issue, Cindy Mann, DWAC's ace attorney with a strategically political bent, organized several other attorneys who volunteered to file lawsuits for damages against HRA, the commissioners, and the security guards. Unfortunately for Mary, so much attention had been drawn to her that she was fired from her job. It was bad enough she had let this thing happen to her; she didn't have to tell the whole world, did she? It took two years to settle her case, at which time she ended up with about $20,000. After all, how much is a welfare mother worth, anyway? Within months of the settlement, the rest of the suits were also settled out of court. Each of the plaintiffs received some, albeit little, compensation.

In between, I met once or twice with Bert Rose to talk about sensitivity training for the security guards and related matters. The union won, too. Salaries and training were upgraded. Some, but not all, of the bad apples were removed. The others in any event were put on notice.

A year after we had begun, an extensive article by Eric Effron and

Judith Levine on welfare center brutality appeared in *The Village Voice*. It had been a long haul, but we made a dent. For years after our campaign, no additional incidents were brought to our attention. We had been heard. This time, our tactics had been pretty conventional—the issue was so dramatic it carried its own momentum. That wouldn't always be the case. Concurrent with this campaign, we found ourselves taking on a number of other issues as the need arose and the opportunity presented itself. It was by the seat of our jeans that many agendas were finally emerging publicly and with a frequency that couldn't have been predicted.

Just after Maxine's crisis and before Mary's, the CETA jobs came through. Because of "nepotism" rules, it proved somewhat difficult to get slots for all of us. Dolores and Sharon lucked out fairly early in the game, when a computer spit out their names in a miraculous match to job openings we had. Christine and I were forced to wait for other funding.

With new people coming in, there were suddenly thousands of little things that had to be done, many of which turned out to be quite big things that would radically alter the way DWAC functioned. Like personnel practices. Up till this time we had run pretty much as a team, functioning largely on consensus and the drive we all shared to do something about welfare and its offshoots, like food stamps, housing, and medicaid. However, administrative requirements and practical realities no longer allowed for our "management style."

We had many squabbles over procedures as we cranked them out. We hadn't even gotten the new people yet, neither Christine nor I was about to start getting paid, and we were writing policies for the circumstances under which automatic raises would kick in. Needless to say, I was apoplectic. When we stopped haggling over them, the practices had to be certified by DWAC's legal board. This board thing was one big pain in the butt. We never needed anyone's permission when we had no money. Now, all of a sudden everything had to be flown past people who didn't even work at DWAC.

Most overwhelming of all were the new bodies. It was one thing to *think* about having full-time paid staff. But, unlike "volunteers," this crew didn't come equipped with a mission. The first day was tough, but the days afterward were brutal. Each night we spent hours preparing for the day to come. The bodies came with mouths attached and running. Some turned out to be terrific. Others were truly regrettable. Who came in two hours late every day, who was jealous of an assignment someone else got, who wanted to answer phones, who didn't. Mercy.

Fiscal records continued to be a problem. We were under a lot of pressure, from both board members and those foundation people who were considering us for funding, to do something about them. Bob Ostrow, an affluent, white businessman with a gray-white "Afro," came to our rescue. He was almost scary. When he was done, however, the Downtown Welfare Advocate Center had the spiffiest set of books any grass-roots organization ever had. He was a godsend.

While we were tackling the books, we were forced to go back to the personnel practices. We had barely finished the personnel practices before we found we'd have to amend them. One of our new recruits— until then the only male on staff—showed up with a set of guns. We fired him on the spot. Except we couldn't do that. Quickly, an amendment was drawn up that allowed firing on the spot for certain kinds of threatening offenses, like carrying guns to work. This meant getting the fastest vote this side of the Pecos from the board. Fortunately, the panic was shared and the board ratified the change almost immediately. Everything needed to have been done yesterday, if not the day before.

The only group model with which any of us were especially familiar was the family. With that as a starting point, we evolved a form of regular staff meetings that amounted to little more than weekly rap sessions. There were the usual housekeeping issues, the what-do-we-do-next discussions, the political dialogue, and the how-do-we-feel, where-are-we-coming-from. It was these last two that helped to knit the group together, but they also had risk-laden results, of which I was unaware until it was too late.

Once, we went around the room telling something biographical about ourselves. The next day Josie, a middle-aged welfare mother, didn't show up for work on time. Late in the morning she appeared in the doorway, disheveled, wearing the clothes she'd had on the day before. Cindy and I took Josie into the back office. She wept and talked for the next several hours.

During the staff meeting, it had occurred to her that she didn't have much to say about herself, either because no one had asked before or because she had never given her past much thought. Later, long-dormant memories of her childhood and her failed marriage barged into her brain and refused to leave, keeping her up all night. She remembered that her mother had died when she was very young. Apparently, her father felt he was unable to take care of her by himself and placed her in an orphanage. She couldn't imagine why he had left her with these strange people and wondered when he was coming back.

Until this time, Josie had never eaten anything but Italian food. She remembered the first meals at the orphanage as inedible, if for no other reason than that they were unfamiliar. But the nuns didn't see it that way. They forced her to swallow the food, bite after nauseating bite. When she vomited on her plate, they made her eat her vomit.

There were memories less sad but in other ways disturbing. She told us that at night she noticed the nuns placing what she assumed to be little presents under the pillows of a chosen few girls. She always imagined the reason they never placed one under her pillow was that she just wasn't good enough, no matter how hard she tried. It wasn't until she was quite a bit older that she found out they were putting sanitary napkins under the pillows of girls who had their periods. Discovering the truth did not take away the pain of those many days she'd tried to be especially good and the many nights she'd hoped and prayed in vain.

Maybe the fastest way to exit from childhood is to get married, which Josie did while still a teenager. She then had children in rapid succession. Her husband was in the service, stationed away from home for months at a time. A check was sent to her each month by the government—her husband's dependent pay. That was her lifeline. One day the checks just stopped coming. She was told that they were being sent to another address. Ultimately she was able to determine that her husband was having an affair with a woman who also had several kids (not his) and that he'd had the dependent pay shifted over to her address because he no longer wished to maintain a relationship with either Josie or their children.

The courts offered her no useful assistance in spite of her legitimate claim. She, like millions of others, turned to welfare. DWAC offered her her first paying job.

Josie's bosom buddy, Jackie Goeings, initially came to DWAC for legal advice on getting welfare benefits for two of her grandchildren who lived with her. Not long after, Jackie joined us. Josie was white. Jackie was black. At the time, neither had more than a high school education and both had some amount of difficulty learning the myriad welfare regulations they needed to know to handle the people coming in for help or calling on the phone. That didn't really get in the way of either of them, though.

Jackie was the more aggressive. She had great heart and a will hell-bent on justice. Some of us would worry that without knowing it she (like Josie) might give someone the wrong information and jam up the case even worse. However, in the end she accomplished what nobody else did—she could occasionally reap benefits for people to which they were not technically entitled. Welfare workers cringed when Jackie got on *their* cases. Knowing how dogged she could be, they'd give in before she started.

Several women came to DWAC for help, then returned to volunteer. That continued to be the best way to acquire new staff. The investment was personal from the beginning, and the commitment enduring.

They came and went. Aside from those who were unsuited to the place from the git go, the welfare mothers in particular were under extraordinary pressure, juggling kids, job, day care, the occasional lover, the sporadic batterer, the works. Even those who didn't have kids were under a lot of strain. For those of us on whom DWAC had a grip, the days were long and hot, summer or winter. There was never enough time. We were becoming a family, trading children here and there, socializing mostly with one another, working our buns off. Still, we found ourselves joking and mocking the "outside" world much of the time. It was a relentless scramble, sometimes delightful, almost always teeming with significance, twelve to sixteen hours a day, seven days a week.

It was a sight to behold. It was a rare day when someone's kids weren't there. We battled for opportunities to cuddle the baby of the moment, or check out our child appeal quotient on the closest toddler.

As soon as a kid was old enough to fold paper, she (or he) was old enough to help with mailings. We held mailing parties. Groups of staff and volunteers and kids ate, drank, and stuffed.

My own daughter had started kindergarten by this time. When asked what she did in school her first day, she replied that school was just going to children's meetings, where the kids sat around and talked. The teacher chaired the meetings. It was all very matter of fact. She had graduated from day care, and now she went to meetings like her mother. Still, she loved days off, when she could come to DWAC and lick envelopes or go out with me or one of the staff to leaflet perfect strangers. No one ever refused to take her leaflets. She was quite the budding organizer. It should have been so easy.

It would be impossible to exaggerate how consumed we were in the first year we had paid staff. Everything was trial by fire. Everything was yet to be discovered. We had no established routes to take. Hiring, firing, establishing a rapport and then having to replace weary staff, creating policies where none existed. We needed to get incorporated, get tax-exempt status, create bylaws without the slightest idea what their impact would be on our day-to-day operations. We had to raise money. And get stationary, and telephones, and a typewriter, and every conceivable item required of a real staffed operation. And we had to keep a running political agenda on the fire at all times.

Underneath the fund-raising and schmoozing and letter writing and press conferences, underneath the politicking and studying and figuring, underneath the organizing and attempts at being inspirational, and underneath the sleepless nights when plans were hatched and speeches drafted, underneath the caring and worrying, underneath all of that and then some there was the daily stream of people on the edge, desperate for a moment to breathe freely. Their questions had to be answered.

But damage control was no longer enough for us. We had to change the way people thought in order to change the way welfare families were treated. We lacked sufficient resources and know-how on many levels. The obstacles were considerable. Wanting to be heard would not necessarily allow us to be heard. We would have to force ourselves onto the political terrain, often adopting NWRO tactics. Depending on the issue and the people involved, our actions came to include anything from simple press conferences through hit-and-run takeovers of microphones at public gatherings to mass demonstrations. The city itself was becoming our real office. And DWAC was about to begin its brief run at being a fashionable cause.

Chapter 3

Challenging the Myths

[When] ideas are neglected by those who ought to attend to them—that is to say, those who have been trained to think critically about ideas—they sometimes acquire an unchecked momentum and an irresistible power over multitudes of men that may grow too violent to be affected by rational criticism.

—Isaiah Berlin

The problems DWAC helped to solve—charting a course through the labyrinthine welfare application process for those lost at the outset, unscrambling the cases of those still in need who had been recklessly cut off welfare, or stopping welfare center brutality—were not only epidemic at the level of the welfare centers but also endemic to the entire welfare system. The ways it was conceived, funded, and administered were all part of a bigger societal picture, one that had no respect for poor mothers, one that wrongly described them as pathological and foolishly prescribed a charlatan's cure. Society's picture of welfare and the people it supposedly served had less to do with reality than with myth.

One outlandish example of the madness of this perspective was embedded in food stamp rules that we at DWAC rarely tired of ranting about. In those days, because the government printed no denomination of stamp smaller than a dollar, and because stores were prohibited from giving real money change (goodness knows, a person might try to buy a bar of soap with the change, and that, too, was prohibited), every store effectively minted its own change. Some big chains, like Grand Union, gave out these aluminum coins. They were not transferable from store to store, often not even within the same chain. The A & P gave out paper slips with their logo on them. Sometimes a vegetable store would try hoisting some wimpy fruit on me instead of change, but I'd refuse that, unless they planned to give it to me at cost. I argued that they were not allowed to make a profit on my change.

Most recipients had containers with various forms of food stamp change in them. But certainly, whether they gave you a scrap torn from a newspaper with 83 cents written on it (as some did) or actual toy coins, whether the store went out of business or you moved away from it, sooner or later, much of the "change" was lost.

Through the better part of the 1970s, grocery stores made millions on that little scam. Although stores must now give real change, the original policy was much like others that still exist. It presumed the welfare mother's inability to make wise choices. Policymakers will go to absurd lengths to ensure that not even a penny is diverted from its intended purpose, at least not by welfare mothers. Because the mothers were portrayed as inferior, ignorant, deviant, mentally and/or morally deficient, an inappropriate and wasteful policy enriched the grocery stores while children went hungry.

This fundamental fallacy permeated the welfare system directly, the social welfare agencies that received huge government contracts to "help the poor," the policy-making bodies that concocted the rules, the politicians who made hay off them, and the media, which reported on all of it. Together these entities recklessly influenced public will to the point that the damage was all but irreparable.

Not to worry. The Downtown Welfare Advocate Center was going to try to change that. This was surely one case where ignorance was bliss. Ours, that is. Since we knew very little about the political process, we didn't let the enormity of the problem dissuade us from trying. We were like Sisyphus, only we were struggling up the mountain backward without even knowing it. We *did* know that the way welfare mothers were defined, the way poverty was assumed to be the product of an inherent personal pathology, had given rise to countless myths, each one fueling the next and influencing social policy.

A meeting with one of several welfare commissioners (Stanley Brezenoff) whose tenure coincided with ours was particularly illustrative. About ten DWAC staff and volunteers raised a number of issues that could have been resolved with a stroke of the commissioner's pen. To each request, he responded simply, "No." Worse, when we brought up one bureaucratically benign matter, he cautioned that if we persisted he would strengthen the negative aspects. In this case, mothers of school-age children were regularly required to appear at the principal's office to get written verification that the children were in school. Welfare officials claimed these letters "proved" the children were living at home. To the welfare mothers, the whole process was more harassment. Certainly the letters did not actually prove much of anything. They did cause untold humiliation of the welfare children, especially the older ones, because the other kids at school knew perfectly well what the periodic lineup of mothers meant. This increased truancy. The very next day the welfare kids were too ashamed to go back to school, as all had once again been reminded that they were on welfare. In addition to pointing this out to Brezenoff, we argued that if preschoolers required no such "proof," why should the older children?

Commissioner Brezenoff fired back, "If you continue to pursue this issue, we'll figure out a way to get regular statements for the toddlers as well." It would have been easy, humane, and cost efficient for him to have removed the stigma of these letters from the families. But no.

Keeping the mothers constantly responding to frivolous demands helped to keep the rolls down. It ensured that only those *in truly desperate need* would subject themselves to the endless red tape and attendant humiliation of the welfare. In other words, to prevent those who were not in serious need from committing welfare fraud, those who *were* had to be tormented. Since welfare recipients are perceived to be the dregs of society, there is no need to treat them humanely.

These were poor mother-only families—not intact "nuclear" families where one partner could spell the other or offer support of any kind—who were being tested to the limit. It was obvious to us that welfare was a women's problem. The welfare acted like the women had nothing better or more useful to do than jump to the snap of virtually endless demands to supply papers, evidence of "proper behavior," and other time- and soul-consuming documentation of their worthiness. They had no concept of what it was like to scrounge for necessities in every conceivable corner of your life. But politically speaking, the inherent child-rearing issues were virtually irrelevant. Government documents show that the vast majority of AFDC recipients are women and their children; over 92 percent of the families have no fathers (including stepfathers) in the home.[1] Most experts knew it, but they did not reconcile their own prejudices against welfare recipients generally with the actual facts of who they were, what they were about, and what their real needs were. Perfectly intelligent policymakers satisfying hot-air politicians held a wealth of contradictory information in their heads and proceeded as if it weren't even there. Unfortunately for welfare mothers, they did it well.

The myths were many and pervasive, even though the facts defy the fictions. For instance:

• *"Qualifying for welfare is a piece of cake."*
In fact, no welfare recipient gets enough. And, because of excessive red tape, many eligible people get nothing at all.

Establishing eligibility for welfare, no matter how desperately poor one is, usually takes thirty days. Reams of paperwork must be filled out and numerous documents presented for verification. Applicants and recipients recertifying eligibility are interrogated like crime suspects, though their only transgression is poverty. Often they are verbally and occasionally even physically abused.

Tens of thousands of eligible people (half of whom are children) are "churned" from welfare each month. It is estimated that nationwide some one million people are cut off each year in spite of the fact that they are still in terrible need and entitled to welfare.[2]

• *"Women on welfare keep having babies to get more money."*
In fact, there are no economic "rewards" for having additional babies on welfare. The average per capita amount of a welfare grant decreases as the number of persons in the household increases. Having more babies, in essence, makes a family poorer.

AVERAGE U.S. PER CAPITA WELFARE PAYMENTS, 1990

Number of Persons in Household	$ per Person per Month
1.	326.94
2.	185.38
3.	150.23
4.	128.06

And the most common family unit on welfare is a mother and one child. Seventy-three percent of all AFDC households have two or fewer children.

• *"Teenagers having babies is the problem."*

In fact, teenage mothers represented only 3.8 percent of the total AFDC caseload as of 1989. This is down from a "high" of 8.3 percent in 1975.

Both the rate and number of teenagers having babies have been declining for the last twenty years, and the rate of decline has been faster among blacks than whites.

Only one in three teenagers who *does* have a baby ends up on welfare.

Pregnant teenagers tend not to wed as often as they once did. Shotgun marriages are out, especially since many mothers of teenagers now know that forcing marriage on young people does not force males to be responsible. It never did. This accounts for the rise in "illegitimate" births.

Teenagers *do* have sex and get pregnant more frequently and at a younger age than they did twenty years ago. They also have many abortions; some even use abortion as a form of contraception. This is a health problem that education could change. It is not a welfare problem.

Young teenagers are more often impregnated by adult men than by males their own age. Thirteen-year-old boys are not getting thirteen-year-old girls pregnant. Statutory rape laws are rarely enforced. Our culture punishes the girls.

• *"Welfare is like a genetic disease—generation after generation."*

In fact, most children who grow up on welfare do not become welfare recipients as adults.

58

Analyzing data from the Panel Study of Income Dynamics, Martha Hill and Michael Ponza conclude, "Links between parents and children's economic circumstances do exist. However, long term dependency as a child does not cause long term dependency as an adult, at least among blacks" (the population for whom they had the most extensive data). They also conclude, "Parental attitudes and values had little effect on children's later economic outcomes and welfare dependence."

Children from welfare "dependent" families are no more likely to become welfare "dependent" than children from families who never received welfare. The most frequent precipitator of welfare receipt is a change in family composition, such as divorce, separation, or the birth of a child. Fully 75 percent of first-time recipients are the result of the creation of a single-parent household. The majority of these families are previously married female households which the husbands have left through divorce or separation. If, for instance, a woman gives birth and has no income cushion through the father or any other means, she is highly likely to become a welfare recipient for some time, especially while the child is small. This is true whether her own parents were on welfare or not.

If welfare were a lifelong "disease," there would be as many or more teenagers on welfare as children under five (because birth rates are declining). Instead, 40.8 percent of AFDC children are under five years old, 73 percent are under twelve, and only 21.8 percent are twelve or over (3.5 percent are unknown).

• *"Welfare causes dependency."*
In fact, only 8 percent of all welfare recipients are on welfare for eight years or more for their entire support.

More than two thirds of all recipients are off welfare in three years or less.

One out of four of all U.S. citizens experiences welfare for at least a short period in a decade. Only one out of fifty receives at least half their income from welfare for eight years or more.

Of those families who are described as "long term recipients," most are large. These families are most often created by the desertion of the father. It takes a larger salary and more supports (i.e., day care) for younger children to cover the needs of a larger family. As children age out of the household, their parents leave welfare on their own or become ineligible for AFDC, receipt of which is conditioned on having children in the household.

• *"Welfare recipients cheat."*
In fact, most major welfare fraud is accomplished by welfare and food stamp workers, not poor people.

Allegations of petty welfare fraud by the Department of Health and Human Services recently revealed that fewer than 2.6 percent warranted "further investigation." Fewer still were deemed "true fraud." Most overpayments are actually the result of errors made by the welfare department.

In contrast to tax fraud, welfare is squeaky clean. The IRS estimates a 20 to 25 percent error rate in payment of taxes—most of which is due to underreporting of income by taxpayers.[3]

At DWAC, we hadn't been seeing welfare fraud; we did see workers' mistakes—usually to the detriment of the families. We weren't seeing lots of very large families, but those we did see were proof beyond any question that the mothers were not only "working" but virtually killing themselves with child-rearing responsibilities. They were also poorer than all the rest. We saw very few welfare mothers who were raised by welfare mothers. The "three generations of welfare recipients" weren't hiding, they were just another mythical stereotype.

Virtually nothing we had absorbed from the political culture around us jibed with what we experienced. Reality, the facts, had to be dug up from other sources before we would be believed. Information became the most powerful mechanism for self-affirmation and the most effective tool at our disposal to change the way people thought. And that was essential to changing policy.

My introduction to the power of information came about quite by accident. One day shortly after I began to participate more actively, John Morken, the law student who'd helped me when I was having trouble with my own case at the welfare center, called me at home. He said a local television talk show wanted some welfare recipients to appear with high-level representatives of the welfare department. He asked if I'd be interested. I must have hesitated, but he talked me into it, saying he and

Diana Voelker would be willing to come to my house that evening to help me study. I consented.

They arrived laden with government reports, books, and assorted papers on the A to Z of welfare—demographics (who's on the rolls?), charts (how much do they really get?), theory (what's it all about?). Within a couple of hours, my mind's eye was bugging out: most welfare recipients were children; the majority of people on welfare nationwide were white; for every family on the rolls there was one who needed welfare but wasn't getting it (largely because of the bureaucratic imperative to keep the rolls down); and on and on. It was all there on paper, courtesy of the government.

Next day we met at the station to debate on *Midday Live!* with TV talk show host Bill Boggs presiding over the melee. Diana, John, and I sat on one side; Herb Rosenzweig, deputy commissioner for income maintenance at the Human Resources Administration, and an aide sat on the city's side. Rosenzweig was thin and dark, with a nervous quality that made him sort of tremble when he spoke. We were stocked with facts and stories. The combination was deadly. Neither Rosenzweig nor his aide was prepared. They had no concrete experience of the programs they were talking about, nor had they been insecure enough to study the night before—after all, we were only welfare recipients.

Rosenzweig seemed to give up about halfway through. The aide came to the rescue, or at least tried. He began talking about the wonderful job programs run by the city and the benefits available to recipients who got employment outside the home. This was perfect, since I'd been tricked with a paid job the previous year and had only last night learned what my "real" benefits should have been. I briefly described my experience, ending with the statement that, since most people didn't have a clue as to their rights, what little was available legally never got to them anyway.

Diana followed with her experience of the so-called Work Incentive program, during which her paperwork had been lost for months. The WIN program, as the welfare called it (or W[h]IP, as recipients referred to it), was the Keystone Kops training program of the welfare. Ultimately Diana got herself into college in spite of the program, but not without continual hassles from it. Had she not organized her own solution, she'd still have been waiting for WIP to place her.

When Diana argued that there were no real jobs behind the work programs, the aide countered that there were. He said anyone who wanted one could come and be placed. Diana sucker-punched him. "Well then, tell me what address, and we'll have thirty thousand recipients down there first thing tomorrow morning." He almost fell out of his chair. When he refused to give out an address, it was all over.

We were ecstatic. For years after, no one from the city administration was allowed to appear on any talk show with any of us, in spite of many similar requests. Now I knew why it was called the information revolution. Anyone with access to information could use it. And it was free. DWAC mined it like it was gold.

Having very real daily experiences with welfare recipients and the most up-to-date facts on the tips of our tongues, we could hold the moral and intellectual high ground in many kinds of situations. It had become apparent that virtually every day, some place in the country, some group would discuss poor people and make decisions that would affect our lives. Generally, the professionals operated with a healthy dose of myth-tainted information but virtually no direct experience of poor people. Lacking an invitation ceased to be an excuse for us to ignore key events. So when we burst into meetings, took over microphones, and started to talk, there was little the pros could do, or tried to do, to stop us. It was brazen but effective.

When we weren't using the media or disrupting policy meetings and conferences, we were working on literature of various types that would get our points across. Sometimes we made little how-to pamphlets for our members to use in welfare centers. Some of us wrote songs or chants to be used at demonstrations. Then we struck upon the idea of creating a comic book to make our information accessible not only to our members but to legislators and others who were commonly deluged with lots of paper and little time to read. The first edition was called *Children on Welfare: Families in Need.*

It turned out to be quite a dynamic public relations device. It traveled far and wide. We even made money selling it. Probably because the material was moving and the data easy to install in the brain, even some of our detractors found themselves quoting liberally from it. Now and then some talk show or newspaper would flash some material from it as backup for a story related to welfare and poverty. In this case, half a dozen words were worth a baker's dozen of pictures. Recipients armed with it could stand up to the thickest heads and hold their own, however insecure they might otherwise have been. Policymakers who wished to resist the necessary change it promoted were defenseless. The comic book more than did its job.

As DWAC grew and evolved, we became adept at turning a number of issues around, mostly because of our unique information—that supplied by the mothers coming in for help and the useful data and other written material we absorbed. For instance, Cynthia Wilcox (the woman who first notified us of the beating and arrests in Brooklyn) had a problem that prompted its own campaign. Her temporarily postponed case soon commanded a lot of our attention, in part because she had been so helpful and because it raised a number of issues that needed addressing.

Hers was a mind-boggling runaround at the welfare center, which culminated with her sobbing audibly at the public library. She had reached her wits' end searching for a solution to her crisis. A friendly librarian noticed and intervened. When Cynthia spilled out her story, the librarian referred her to DWAC, having heard about us from somewhere.

Coincidentally, the Center on Social Welfare Policy and Law (CSWPL) was working on a similar issue. We linked them with her. It didn't turn out as simply as we would have liked. Before we knew it, DWAC was off on another campaign. This was in opposition to what were called two-party rent checks.

Welfare checks in New York are broken into component parts. The first element is the rent or shelter portion of the check. The rest is referred to as the "pre-added allowance" (before rent is added). This portion is also sometimes called the basic grant.[4] The recipient receives half her rent allowance and half the "other" semimonthly. This wouldn't be such a problem if landlords were willing to accept half the rent twice each month. But no, they want theirs all at one time. So right from the start, a recipient is in a sorry spot, having to borrow from "other" to pay for rent. Except "other" is so small, there isn't enough to borrow from and feed your kids and pay the utility bill and buy toilet paper and everything else. The disadvantage created by this arbitrary division of the check causes even further trauma if anything more goes wrong. Often it does.

In Cynthia's case it did, in spades. Almost immediately after she'd paid the landlord her first month's rent, her refrigerator conked out, followed by the electricity. The landlord said he would send an electrician, but no one came. Cynthia found herself hiring neighborhood people to help her fix this and that, and soon she stopped paying the landlord his rent, using the money to make the repairs herself. She said, "I put the money into the house."

A dispossess notice followed. She contacted her landlord, who said he would make repairs if she paid him what she owed. But she had no money left with which to pay. When she took the notice to the welfare, they responded by giving her an "advance" on subsequent checks to pay the back rent. The "advance" meant that she was borrowing from herself, so her subsequent welfare checks were reduced. The welfare "recouped" the difference.

Cynthia had been a "bad girl" by withholding her rent, so she was put on two-party checks for future payments. These are forms of vendor payments that have to be endorsed by both the recipient and the landlord in order to be cashed, thereby restricting the use to rent. (If the recipient fails to turn the two-party check over to the landlord, she is commonly put on direct vendor payments and the rent goes to the landlord without being buzzed by the recipient first. As a practical matter, two-party and direct vendor checks have the same effect—they prevent recipients from using the rent as leverage to get landlords to behave responsibly or from using the money to make essential repairs themselves when landlords don't.)

Why should her landlord make repairs? He hadn't before, and now he was effectively guaranteed the rent no matter what he didn't do. Cynthia called the city building inspectors, who made a total of six documented visits to her apartment, citing numerous violations. Things went from bad to worse. One of Cynthia's children landed in the hospital. When the baby recuperated, the doctors refused to release her because they had become aware that there was no heat or hot water at home. The government, which had intervened inappropriately by putting Cynthia on a two-party check and recouping her, was now dishing out hundreds of dollars in medicaid expenditures each day they kept her baby in the hospital.

Cynthia tried to move but was effectively prohibited from doing so by the two-party check, which was not transferable. The entire case history is so convoluted, yet it's not unusual for people on welfare.

Wouldn't you know, just about that time the city became more enamored than ever of two-party checks. That was how a case like Cynthia's would end us in another campaign. The welfare commissioner in 1978, Blanche Bernstein, proposed a demonstration project in which all the recipients in a given area would be put on two-party checks. Bernstein argued that welfare recipients lived in the most dilapidated housing because of rent arrears. The theory was that if recipients were forced to pay rent, housing conditions would improve. There was no evidence that this was the case; in fact, there was considerable evidence that the problems recipients experienced came more from *paying* for uninhabitable housing than from withholding rent. Slumlords could feel confident that their money would come despite their properties' state of disrepair. The odds were pretty much in their favor. A "notice of eviction" would bring the laggards into line and often, as in Cynthia's case, result in back payments without the landlord living up to his end of the bargain.

In the abstract, two-party checks and other vendor payments make a certain kind of sense, especially if you subscribe to the theory that poor people, unlike other Homo sapiens, behave in ways that are contradictory to their own self-interests. For instance, they don't pay the rent because they drink it up on Saturday and wait patiently till Monday for the eviction notice. Trouble with this theory is, behavior that would result in a life-threatening condition—homelessness—is no more common among poor women than it is among any other part of the population. Besides, we didn't oppose two-party checks where such behavior could be proven. Our opposition was to their generalized, indiscriminate use. Cynthia used her checks in "the best interest of the child" (a key principle in welfare) by making essential repairs. She even went through all the motions with the housing inspectors. The welfare responded by being as stupid as the landlord was corrupt. The only protection recipients had in such cases was their own ingenuity, a weapon that would be eliminated from everybody in the demonstration area if Bernstein's project went forward.

All the mothers like Cynthia in that neighborhood needed help. Could we walk away saying we were too busy being good organizers? We just added this campaign to our already overloaded schedules and kept on going.

Not only was Cynthia's case an example of the lunacy of two-party checks but in many ways it was the perfect example of how the welfare state has deteriorated. It would have cost very little to have given her the money she needed to live on, leaving her to manage it well, which she amply proved she could. Instead, the government proved repeatedly that the bureaucracy was not equipped with the necessary elements to make rational, individual decisions in the interests of either the families or the state. While she was denied the one thing she needed most, Cynthia and her children were given an array of services costing taxpayers a veritable fortune.

She took up untold amounts of time with welfare center personnel as well as housing inspectors. She utilized hospital workers—doctors, nurses, dieticians, and aides when her baby was sick and even when she was healthy (because they wouldn't discharge her). Cynthia went to the public library and tapped the services of the librarian as well as the law books. She was referred to us and was helped by a CETA worker and several others who were paid by tax-exempt foundation dollars. We sent her to the Center on Social Welfare Policy and Law, which was directly funded by federal treasury dollars. Subsequently, Brooklyn Legal Services, also federally funded, filed an action in Brooklyn Supreme Court on her behalf, taking up countless judicial workers' time. And all along, all she wanted was her welfare check and a fair shot at forcing accountability on a recalcitrant landlord. At the end of this journey, Cynthia moved to another apartment. This one was infested with mice and roaches, often had no heat and hot water . . .

If Cynthia had been asked what she wanted or what she needed, her answer would have been more money and the freedom to choose. What she got was a fortune in service workers, none of whom could deliver what she needed in the final analysis. The welfare *state* has gone berserk. The U.S. Treasury forks over billions of wasted dollars while welfare recipients bear a horrendous burden.

Cynthia's case and others like it provided grist for the series of meetings regarding the proposed demonstration project that ensued. Henry Freedman and Tim Casey of CSWPL were our lawyers. Initially Henry resisted representing the issue from *our* point of view. We argued that if the mother didn't have enough money to cover essentials, she should be allowed to decide how best to spend what she *did* have. After all, a child can starve to death in a few days. It usually takes months to get evicted. Henry thought it would be politically disadvantageous to raise the issue in that context. We insisted. Henry caved. This was rarely the habit of legal services. By that time, I was so accustomed to lawyers going off on tangents that I was actually surprised when CSWPL relented.

Typically, we met with government bureaucrats and politicians (to convince them to oppose the project) or with representatives of third-party institutions, like the social welfare agencies we hoped would apply additional pressure. In these meetings, we evolved a sort of political art form without ever discussing it as such. Before each we would go through a quick rundown of the group at hand, their positions with respect to the issues, and any new information that may have come to light. Then we'd go in. Henry usually led off, and I would butt in, playing the recipient "role" as necessary. Tim and Christine would fill in pieces we left out. We were all pretty facile with facts. DWAC's "job" was to ground people with our true-life tales. No one wants to feel responsible for the tragedies caused by foolish policies.

Among the most memorable of these meetings was one held at the Community Service Society (CSS). Assemblymember Oliver Koppell was there from the West Bronx to urge support for the city's proposal. Koppell cavalierly cast aspersions on welfare recipients as he made his points—they don't pay rent, they're irresponsible, they can't make rational decisions, and so on. It was not uncommon for white liberals who would mull over every thought for racist content to revile poor people with impunity. Suddenly Tim pounced on Koppell. He said he would not tolerate any more bigoted talk directed at welfare recipients, adding that he himself had been raised on welfare. I was surprised by the biographical fact, as I'm sure the others were.[5] I appreciated Tim's indignation at the slurs piling up.

I asked Koppell if he would use his rent money if he didn't have money to buy milk for his baby. He said of course he would, but the basic grant wasn't his concern or his responsibility to take into account when negotiating public decisions. In fact, because he was a state legislator, it was absolutely his responsibility, and his colleagues', to set welfare benefit levels. Problem was, until the grant met actual costs, mothers would be forced to choose between essential items of need. "Heat or eat" was the common parlance for this dilemma. The Community Service Society signed on with us in this campaign.

Among the influential individuals who supported our position on this project was City Council President Carol Bellamy, until then a frequent target of DWAC hit-and-run actions. Bellamy was generally regarded as a liberal when we started going after her. She was the most prominent elected woman in the state. She had demonstrated repeatedly that she was ignorant of poor women's issues as we defined them. She had made the regrettable mistake of saying she agreed that welfare benefits were too low but that it was not "politically feasible" to support our quest for grant increases. We would try to change her mind. She may have been unaware of *why* she was chosen, but she was certainly aware *that* she was chosen.

After months of surprise confrontations at conferences and other public appearances, Bellamy came around. We pressed her to hire someone whose specific job would be welfare issues. She hired David Tobis. Probably so she could avoid looking like she was capitulating, he was first assigned to the two-party rent check debate rather than the welfare grant increase. He undertook a study of buildings where there already were large numbers of two-party check arrangements. We had argued that these would demonstrate whether landlords who had the effective rent guarantee were providing better services than those who didn't. The results of Tobis's study were surprising. Landlords with the highest rates of two-party checks in their buildings had exceptionally high rates of building code violations *and* the highest rates of tax delinquency—just the opposite of the outcomes predicted by HRA. It was fun to watch them swallow that canary.

Blanche Bernstein, who'd submitted the demonstration project to what was then the Department of Health, Education and Welfare (HEW), wrote a chapter on the two-party check episode in a book called *The Politics of Welfare*. She said that CSWPL and DWAC spearheaded the opposition. She was right about that. Where she was wrong was in her analysis of the project as well as in her assumption that DWAC was a subsidiary of CSWPL. She, like so many others, made the mistake of underestimating us because we were welfare recipients.

We soon began working to have Bernstein ousted. She probably attributed her forced resignation to other, more powerful groups. In a sense, that would be correct, but we were going to those groups and politicians either straight up or through hit-and-runs to get them to demand her resignation. Third-party pressure tactics would prove to be of substantial benefit for a time, even though they were creating the conditions of our own demise, as we would find out.

When the whole thing wound down many months after, we came out ahead. The Department of Health, Education and Welfare rejected the city's bid for the demonstration project and changed the regulations governing two-party checks. As a result, if a mother like Cynthia could prove she'd spent the money in "the best interests of the child" even though she hadn't paid rent, she could not be forced onto a vendor payment of any kind.[6] Implicit in this change was the concept that welfare grants might not *be enough* for essentials. If so, it was inevitable that mothers had to choose. This was the idea we most wanted to convey, the one Henry Freedman had been convinced would never fly. It was also the one most strongly linked to our goal of raising welfare benefits generally.

Without realizing it, we had turned the two-party check issue into a dialogue on the inadequacy of the welfare grant. We had met with dozens of people, produced reams of paper, and convinced a lot of power players not only that the proposal should be rejected but that the welfare grant was inadequate.

These events and some others brought us to the attention of some heavy hitters at HEW. A group of suits came to New York to meet with us at our offices. We lobbed information like hand grenades—systemic abuses, brutality in the centers, endless red tape, and more, replete with the proof. The two-hour meeting was punctuated by Sharon Hunt's antics with the telephone. Every few minutes she picked it up and dialed a number that was supposed to access an administrative process ("fair hearings") for recipients to resolve disputes with welfare centers. She extended the receiver across the table so they could hear. Without fail, the line was busy. The number was useless.

I always worried about things like that, figuring this would be the one time the welfare workers would do something right. But, although the workers did try to mask their contempt when they knew important visitors were on the scene, they just didn't seem to be able to pull it off. My favorite such occasion was when Congressmember Stephen Solarz wanted an inside view, and CSS Executive Director Bert Beck asked me to accompany them. To be more accurate, I was extremely busy that day, and staff at CSS had to bully me into dropping everything to rescue Beck. No doubt he hadn't been on the inside any too often. Anyway, we went to the Lower Manhattan center, which was closest to CSS. I acted as a guide and raised issues like the need to increase cash assistance and decrease the red tape.

Midway through the conversation, a welfare worker came over to tell us we had to leave. We were sitting at a table set up for the use of advocates from the community. I told her we had a right to be there. She got increasingly huffy, then went to get a supervisor, who soon appeared to dismiss us. When Beck and Solarz (who had been silently observing up till then) revealed their credentials, she turned into butter.

When we resumed, I told them that discourteous workers were the norm not the exception and that people were made to wait absurdly long hours to be seen at all. Solarz wandered off momentarily to ask a woman with two small children how long she'd been waiting. I thought, With my luck she just got here ten minutes ago and some worker's going to call her name right now. No such sweat. She looked up at him and asked, "What day is this?" When he said Wednesday, she said she'd come in for the first time on Monday and was still waiting. That was one of the perverse things about our work: every day we'd kill ourselves to make things better at the centers, but on a day like this, we ached for things to be just the way they usually were—dreadful.

Lower Manhattan was a family center, and Solarz was willing to concede at least to me that it was reasonable for mothers to care for their children at home even on welfare. He had reservations regarding people who were single and on "home relief" (general assistance in many states). He asked why they shouldn't or couldn't get jobs. Again, I worried that something would go right for a change, but I asked him if he wanted to visit the Waverly center just next door, which served single adults and childless couples. Of course he did. We went. At first I said nothing, but I was relieved by the sight. Who was in a wheelchair, who had a broken arm or leg, which one was nodding out on junk, all looked poor. After he surveyed the scene, I asked him, "Which ones would you employ?" He looked at me but didn't answer.

The question of jobs versus income would never go away. Though it was less critical in the early 1970s, by the late 1970s you had to be prepared to answer it twenty-five ways. In part this was a consequence of an unfortunate crossover commonly made when people thought about a male model of poverty, even though the problem of welfare was predominantly a women's problem. And no matter where you stood, men were calling all the political shots.

At the level of the federal government, the presidents and their men, not to mention Congress, became increasingly enamored of the idea that welfare mothers needed jobs outside the home, first and fore-most. At the level of social welfare agencies (both private and public) that would get government contracts for "job training" and whatnot as-sociated with the job issue, dollars were a powerful motivating force. They upped the ante by dragging the age-old issue of "dependency" back out of storage. So-called progressives, who only a decade earlier had conceded that structural changes in the economy meant that well-paying jobs were going bye-bye in large measure, ran away from income secu-rity and foolishly fell back onto a "full employment" standard. Certain segments of the women's movement went off half-cocked by supporting jobs for welfare mothers—even against their will. They believed only jobs would liberate us. No amount of reasoning would put a plug in any of them. (Other segments of the women's movement, however, re-mained rational.)

Certainly most of the women we came into contact with were not in need of jobs, nor were more than a few looking for them. Some did decide to go back to school or on to college so they would be able to get better jobs when the time came. Commonly, these women would argue that they had made a "sacrifice" for the baby by being on welfare and now it was okay for them to start working toward solving their own needs. However, true to welfare's contradictory form, if a mother

71

wanted to go to school to enhance her job options, she could only go to an "approved" program. No four-year college programs were on the approved list. If she chose a four-year college and got caught, she would lose child-care and travel subsidies and could be forced into an "approved" program such as beauty school, a workfare slot, or home health aide training.

There were no jobs with livable wages for most poor women anyway. The job training programs tended to do more harm than good. One woman in a New York City program was hospitalized for acute appendicitis. Two days later, she called from the hospital to inform her supervisor. Upon release from the hospital, she found out her case had been closed for failure to report to a work assignment. Her children, who should not have been cut off even if their mother deliberately failed to report, also lost their benefits.

For every recipient "shown off" to the media as a demonstration of how good the programs are, hundreds more were used as indentured servants or simply shuttled from place to place without hope of getting any job. Their children, in whose behalf all this effort was presumably expended, were often turned over to inadequate child-care programs or worse. The work programs have always been costly in human as well as fiscal terms, yet when women did obtain waged work, it tended to pay just as poorly as welfare if not worse. As Johnnie Tillman put it in 1972,

> We always have a lot of programs—poverty programs, Model Cities programs—and they all are geared around the poor. But nothing is actually filtered down to the poor. There are a lot of jobs created for other people, and when we do have an opportunity to participate in jobs, we have the lowest paying ones. Most of the jobs throughout the programs are no larger than a welfare check.[7]

That has not changed to this day.[8]

Many women who wanted to work outside the home nevertheless opted at least for a period to take care of their children personally, even if that meant they had to be on welfare. Irrespective of the specific reasons for being on welfare, everyone needed more income. Even if you received every penny you were entitled to, it wouldn't be enough to live on.

No other demographic group in our society is more often poor than single mothers. Three out of four female-headed households are poor or near poor. Three out of five live below the poverty line. One in two is on welfare. Hispanic single mothers with minor children have a poverty rate of 80 percent. The poverty rate for non-Hispanic black women is 52 percent and for non-Hispanic white women 43 percent.[9] Let's face it, *children are poor because their mothers are poor.* Knowing this, DWAC would argue that income, regardless of the mother's relationship to the waged labor market, must be increased—both for those with no outside source of income and for those whose paying jobs did not get them and their children out of poverty.

But even men close to us found it hard to accept the terms of our stand on income and jobs. One meeting was particularly illustrative. It was set up as a briefing on welfare rights for a group who called themselves "change-oriented foundations." Shirley Smith, head of Ohio Welfare Rights, Hulbert James and Bert Deleuw, both formerly staff of NWRO, and I were asked to participate.

The four of us met early to discuss our presentations and plan a strategy of sorts. We all agreed to stick to the subject at hand: welfare rights, and not the favorite subject of the men, jobs. They said they would save their jobs campaign pitches for a more appropriate occasion. It did not turn out that way.

Shirley was the first presenter. She stuck to a welfare rights agenda as expected. When my turn came, I did, too. I ended with a catchphrase I borrowed from the ancient Greeks: "There will be justice in Athens only when the uninjured parties are as indignant as the injured parties."

Shirley and I were the only two welfare recipients and the only two current leaders of welfare rights groups present. So when Hulbert and Bert moved on to talking about jobs, I'd hoped at least somebody thought privately that something must be wrong with the picture. The men had a way of ignoring the women that had been built into the welfare rights movement of the 1960s right from the start. It was just one of those things that men did. After all, it wasn't politically *smart* to emphasize "handouts" for people who "did nothing." That's how they saw it. Hulbert was an absentee parent himself. As I understand it, he had several children down South, and he certainly didn't do much with respect to their upbringing. Bert had no children at the time, and that was pretty easy, too. So it was to be expected that each readily dismissed child rearing as work. And with the CETAs amassing nationwide, they could point to a new group ready and waiting to be organized—the sainted *"working"* poor.

The plantation ideology was inescapable. Whether it was professional organizers, legal services lawyers, church representatives, or for that matter the hordes of social workers and theorists speaking in behalf of poor women or studying us, the result was a lot like white slave masters pitching the value of slavery to black slaves. Poor women kept saying, We need more money and a better way to make rational choices about the care of our children. We did not say we needed more work. Everyone else said that.

That is not to say that some poor women wouldn't have opted out of household labor in favor of other work sooner than they now do if it were more lucrative and offered some relief from the daily burdens associated with parenting. The point is, a rational basis for making that choice was simply not there, as there was no economic security guaranteed to poor mothers no matter what they did with their time. In fact, since we tended to be paid the lowest wages in the job market, the virtual guarantee was that we would remain poor no matter which choice we opted for. College-educated white women earned less in the labor market than males—black or white—with only a high school education.

Even the search for a paying job is often untenable. Seeking and getting an interview for a job are clearly two different things. Assuming the interviews are granted, welfare mothers lack sufficient resources to travel from interview to interview, much less dress properly. Believe me, I know.

Once, when I was invited to Albany to make a presentation before the Democratic Study Group of the legislature, Cindy Mann (our lawyer) insisted on taking me shopping. It was her professional opinion that I needed to dress differently. I never really bought clothes. (Cindy herself dressed quite casually, but she kept a presentable outfit at DWAC in the event she had to play lawyer on a moment's notice.) We went to a "discount" store where they sold *very* expensive clothes at *merely* expensive (to me) prices. There Cindy picked out not one, but two suits for me. These would go fine with the leather briefcase a group of welfare lawyers had bought for my birthday the year before.

She was right. As I walked the halls of the legislative office building, I noticed a palpable difference in the way people looked at and spoke to me. Likewise, when I made my presentation for the study group, I was quite surprised by the deference paid to me. (If I'd've known that, I'd've copped a suit a long time ago.) Had I still been on welfare instead of in my current paying job, I wouldn't have been able to consider buying one, much less two, good suits.

Still, there were many women who got off welfare to work at jobs that didn't pay enough to change anything about their material condition. They lived in the same neighborhoods, the same dismal apartments. I knew several who had gotten off welfare when their children turned school age, only to return when the children entered puberty and the local drug dealers became such a menace that the mothers were willing to subject themselves once again to the constant humiliation and limitless abuses of the welfare, the lesser of two ghoulish evils. To me, these were true heroines. They braved the wilds of ravaged neighborhoods and withstood the scorn of a whole generation of Americans who in chorus proclaimed them lazy and illiterate.

In spite of what ought to be obvious hazards associated with sending poor mothers off to low-paying jobs without appropriate child care available, welfare administrators nationwide continue to be utterly devoted to helping women off the dole and into jobs at places like McDonald's, where the midnight shift is called the mothers' shift and the challenge is all in the feet.

The much ballyhooed job and training programs cause tens of thousands of people to be cut off the welfare rolls for real or perceived transgressions—like having appendicitis without permission. Others participate fully, in spite of often totally inadequate or incompetent trainers. Usually they continue because once in, it is all but impossible to get out. One mother of a two-year-old, initially attracted to the "opportunity" hype surrounding the "job clubs," volunteered. (*Job clubs* was one of the many silly names used for variations on training programs for welfare recipients to get help obtaining paid employment.) At one training session, she was told to stand up and turn around slowly, during which time the male teacher leered at her and made lurid comments. After she sat down, the question was posed to the class, "What do you do in a situation like this?" Most of the women thought they were not obliged to put up with that behavior from an employer. Wrong. They were informed that they were to do whatever they were told to do to get and keep a job. That was "real life."

After the sexual harassment training, she wanted out. But the welfare wouldn't let her out, even though she had not been a mandatory participant. The welfare claimed that a nonmandatory participant automatically relinquished her right to be a full-time parent, no matter how young her child.

From her perspective, the job club was ludicrous. Participants were given a phone book and told to start at *A* and place cold calls to prospective employers. This, of course, was not terribly productive. Next day she brought in a newspaper with the intention of going through the help-wanted ads. She was stopped. The object lesson was that to keep a job, one must do anything asked of one, no matter how ridiculous.

One mother in a "nontraditional" training program in Baltimore became an apprentice on a construction job, earning $3.50 per hour. She described her day-to-day life to me:

> I get up about six in the morning. I get myself together, then I get up the kids and get 'em ready. Depending on how tired I was the night before, I might have to plait my daughter's hair. Then I get breakfast and we eat.
>
> My job starts at eight, but they don't have to be to school till nine. So I take the kids to my cousin's (I pay her to get them to school). Then I go to work. I start worrying about three o'clock 'cause I know school's out and they'll be going home alone. I'm done work at four. I go home quick as I can.
>
> Then, if I don't have to go shopping, I cook dinner. After dinner I help with their homework while I do the dishes and clean up some. When that's over, it's usually time to get 'em in the bath and ready for bed. If I can, I like to plait my daughter's hair, but if I'm too tired, it waits till morning. Then I take my own bath. Then I'm finished and I go to bed myself—usually by ten o'clock. Next day I just do it again.

She spent her weekends on housecleaning, laundry, and grocery shopping. On Sunday afternoons she often took the kids over to her mom's for a visit. At $3.50 per hour, getting paid for 37.5 hours a week, 52 weeks a year, she would have received $6,825 per year, or about $2,300 less than the poverty line for a three-person family in 1986, when I interviewed her. According to the people who ran the program, there was little hope that at the end of the year she'd be placed in any job making over $4.00 per hour, which translated into approximately $1,300 less than the poverty line.

At DWAC we were not opposed to help for women who wanted to get paying jobs, but we did want help to *be helpful*. We also wanted women to have a choice as to whether and when to leave the welfare rolls. When a woman on social security makes that decision, she makes it on her own. When women with husbands make that decision, the state does not intervene. Their decisions are organically linked to all kinds of issues involving their families. No one stands looking over their shoulders or pushing them into an abyss "for their own good." Why, if the welfare job and training programs are so hot, aren't other women in need allowed to join them?

We started out as aliens, and in a sense we stayed that way. Poverty was an enormously powerful barrier between us and most others. A few individuals representing various agencies and political players remained loyal. Most profound and confounding, though, was the stigma of welfare. Almost no one looked at it from any other than a male model of poverty. We argued ad infinitum that we already had jobs, we simply weren't paid for them. We might as well have been speaking in tongues. I learned a fail-safe trick from Robert Theobald, a futurist and enthusiast of guaranteed income: I'd ask an audience if anyone thought full employment in the real sense would ever come to pass. None would raise a hand. You could bet on it. Still, the popular notion of forcing mothers into jobs was gaining ground.

Thoughtful people could understand that even if we were to agree on the job question, there simply weren't the jobs with adequate wages—nor the child care—available for the millions who would need them. Few could follow the logical extension of that: one way or another, there would always be a large number of people who would, without some form of income maintenance, be totally bereft of any income with which to obtain even the most meager of necessities.

And, in part because there appears to be no end in sight for women being the primary caretakers of children (and the elderly), women will continue to bear not only the poverty but the merciless ill will it generates. Under the circumstances, welfare rights—income rights—in some form would continue to be required if only to slow the rate of political regression that had been going on at least since the late 1960s. Better yet, income rights might someday simply eliminate welfare as we know it.

The underbelly of the mythology is racist and sexist. The prevailing (mis)wisdom is that welfare recipients and other poor people are de facto inferior or otherwise damaged goods that may be reparable if only enough [social] workers are set to the task. The alternative is that they are the cumulative result of an economy that cannot or will not accommodate them in the marketplace or that they are often victims of circumstances beyond their control. The numbers tell all, and the evidence is overwhelming. The vast majority of welfare recipients are women, and they are disproportionately people of African-American descent and other peoples of color. The median income of mother-only families of any race is lower than that of men of all races.[10] The rate of unemployment among black males is much higher than that of whites, and the gap has increased in recent decades.[11]

To accept these rather extraordinary economic and employment differences among people of different races and genders is to accept the notions that nonwhites are inferior to whites and women are inferior to men. It wasn't long ago (as Gloria Steinem describes in amusing detail in *Revolution from Within*) that so-called scientists were attempting to prove these principles of inequality through craniology—the now discredited study of skull and brain characteristics among different groups of people. Most particularly, they wished to prove (and claimed to have proven for some time) that the brains and skulls of blacks and women were smaller than those of white men. This, they concluded, was evidence of the intellectual inferiority of women of all races and black men compared with white men. Almost concurrently the "science" of eugenics (through much of the latter half of the nineteenth and well into the twentieth century) attempted to show that poor people were genetically inferior to others (think southern European versus whiter northern European descendants here).[12] The problem was not the system but the people themselves, and "scientific" evidence proved it. It is not surprising that white men dominated both these fields.

At DWAC we took racial and gender equality as a given. We did not take it upon ourselves to fight for improved job and training programs. Under the current economic, social, and political circumstances, we saw them as an oxymoron. Our job was to disseminate information, to educate, to change political and public will. Our central goal was the one welfare mothers wanted: to raise cash benefits even in this climate of social regression. The reasons *why* were covered in the comic book. *How* was a whole 'nother elusive problem.

Chapter 4

Upping the Stakes

The white liberal was monopolizing the civil rights struggle of the Negro and he was allowing in only those Negroes willing to get along with him. —Adam Clayton Powell

The truth must not only be the truth; it must also be told.
—Malcolm X

By the late 1970s, DWAC had established a reputation as the most active welfare rights organization left in the state. But it was our inexperience, not our skills that kept the social policy movers coming toward us. We must have seemed like easy targets. The organization was being pulled in opposite directions by the array of social welfare professionals, organizers from other parts of the country, local politicians, foundation executives, church leaders—all lining up to assist or destroy as the case might be everything we were trying to accomplish. It was bewildering how suddenly DWAC appeared on the political map.

Some social welfare professionals spent a fair amount of time trying to convince us that they wanted our input. These people were usually from private nonprofit service agencies with large foundation grants, tax-exempt trusts or endowments, and/or government contracts. At the time it was politically uncouth for such organizations to act in our behalf without involving at least some poor people in the discussions. It was called "maximum feasible participation," a legacy from the Great Society. Besides, it was all but impossible for these groups to get funds for their activities without such involvement.

The first time I went to Washington, DC (courtesy of the national Legal Services Corporation), I had been asked to represent New York's welfare recipients at a meeting on President Carter's proposed welfare reform. At least two weeks before the meeting, the bill accompanied by assorted analyses was sent to all attenders—lawyers, organizers, and poor women.

For most of the first plenary session, I sat bored stiff and homesick while dozens of enthusiastic young things calling themselves lawyers asked endless questions about the obvious. Then the tenor of the meeting changed dramatically. From somewhere in the back of the room, a sweet voice with an exaggerated drawl indicated that as a representative of those upon whom this reform was about to be inflicted, she had had enough of the drivel that had taken up the last few hours. Johnnie Tillman wanted to start talking about what to do to stop it. She was president of the National Welfare Rights Organization in its heyday and had just sliced through the bull in a flash.

Then, Rosa Maria Zias Negron introduced herself in a fairly thick Hispanic accent. She wanted to know just who was in the room. She also said she was a welfare mother and had already read all the junk that had been sent in the mail, and she didn't need any help interpreting it. The lawyers were wasting valuable time, and they should have done their homework.

Nezzie Willis from Chicago piped in. She said the lawyers didn't have to live with the results of the proposed "reform," but her kids did, and she didn't want any part of it. She, too, wanted to reframe the discussion.

When the introductions finally took place, it became evident that only eight welfare mothers ("representatives of the poor") were present, compared with 150-odd lawyers and a smattering of other professionals. What seemed like a colossal waste of time suddenly turned into an interesting debate. These women also headed welfare rights groups, were as smart and had every bit as much political savvy as anyone at the conference.

All the lawyer talk implied the legislation was all but inevitable. In the lawyers' view, it was necessary to conceive of the million and one legal ministrategies for challenging minutiae related to the overall proposal. Occasionally one of them would get defensive about the attitudes of the recipients. Finally, one welfare mother piped in, "Look, if the shoe don't fit, don't wear it." We weren't angry at every last lawyer in the room, but it had become clear that any number of them had little concern beyond their careers, and that simply wasn't enough.

To us, any bill that didn't increase welfare benefits off the top was suspect. This one did not propose making up for the dwindling purchasing power of welfare benefits at all. Worse, Carter was proposing a uniform federal benefit level *lower* than that in all but twelve states. Recipients in those twelve states might benefit, but at the expense of the vast majority living on the edge as it was. (States would be allowed to subsidize their own grants but wouldn't be required to over time.) On the cash assistance issue alone, the bill was a clear loser. The welfare mothers were flat-out opposed to it.

It also had strong forced-work components and any number of insidious regulatory changes. The lawyers were quick to point out its positives, like the fact that it mandated AFDC-U or welfare for two-parent families in all states. That wasn't a particularly large population in waiting, however.

Besides, we had all just been through the food stamp debacle brought to us courtesy of the Carter administration and the food law advocates that ended up cutting food stamps to most of the country's recipients. (I'd learned sometime back to watch out anytime someone important said poor people were going to cash in on this or that. The first time, I read in the paper that food stamps were going up. Then I got a notice in the mail saying I would have to pay three dollars more in cash for two dollars more in food stamps. Now *there's* a deal.) Recently, the "purchase requirement" on food stamps had been eliminated after ten years of negotiations "in our behalf." This sounded good, but when most people ended up with cuts in the stamps remaining, the joy was short-lived.

So we were more than a little sensitive about being helped and all. It certainly led to some lively and—for the recipients at least—powerfully affirming debates. After much poking, prodding, plotting, and pouting, it was agreed that additional funds would be raised by the hosting groups for a follow-up meeting in which a more active, grass-roots strategy would dominate the agenda.

Each night when the lawyers went off to bed, the welfare mothers retreated to our own circle. Somewhere between midnight and 3:00 A.M., we held our own informal conference. Ideas flew. War stories—and gossip—were traded. Advice was doled out diligently, especially to me, the new kid. Occasionally egos, easily bruised from years of self-flagellation and systemic punishment, clashed. One or another of the women would bale the rest out. We may have been stranded at sea without a life raft, but at least there was a "we." For me, that was profound. Discovering the existence of these other women was wonderful. We had a coherent worldview quite unlike any in textbooks. In each case it had evolved out of personal experience, different only in relatively minor details, despite the geographic gulfs that separated us.

The minutes of the meeting, which I received in the mail afterward, were remarkable, too. The conference had been transformed by eight women. Except for the mention of our names (and, of course, our status) in the list of attenders, nothing in the minutes would have suggested we had been there at all.

The follow-up meeting was called. Though this was the result of agitation by the welfare mothers, the dominant force—those who controlled the resources—was the male organizers. They wanted us to mold the agenda around the struggle for "jobs." At the time, welfare mothers were still allowed to *say* what they wanted, thought, and felt, even if nothing was done about it. So, without hesitation, the women argued the response to welfare *de*form should be what our legitimate concerns were, unmodified by anyone else's political spins: we would discuss *income*.

Throughout these years, the money and power even for little things, even for progressive, liberal things, even for poor women's things, rested with men. We wrestled a compromise. Those who wanted to work on a strategy for "jobs" would go to one room; the rest of us would go elsewhere.

As the majority of participants, the welfare mothers had a large group. None of the men, including those who had been organizers with the National Welfare Rights Organization, bothered to attend our workshop initially.

The welfare mothers managed to forge a consensus in spite of the others. We wanted to plan some kind of national demonstration, but none of us had the funds to pull it off. We settled on a day of demonstrations that would be held in the states we represented. Our demand would be "Less red tape, more money."

The "jobs" workshop, having no constituent representation, got nowhere. The rifts in the original welfare rights organization were becoming more evident. Professionals, mostly middle-class and largely male, generally dominated a group of poor women. But when the men couldn't be captains, they simply didn't play ball, or they played it with considerably less heart than when they controlled it. Unfortunately, without their full-fledged support, the women were never able to loosen the philanthropic purse strings that would stabilize their organizations. When the women opted to dump the male leadership, the end was inevitable. Worse, it would be perceived as the failure of the women, not the result of essentially insurmountable odds.

Carter's bill managed to attract enough opposition to die in Congress.

The women at DWAC had gotten a much needed morale boost from these meetings. We reaffirmed our commitment to raising welfare benefits in New York State. The pros said we couldn't succeed because of the obvious retrenchment from issues of economic justice at all levels of government and society. We didn't see it quite that way. What we saw was an army of social welfare professionals who, with all their practical experience, had simply stopped raising the issues that counted most to poor people as their own organizational budgets and personal salaries climbed. Could it be that they had gotten just a little too practical? Was it possible that, as many of them reached the apex of their funding under Jimmy Carter, they became a tad too comfortable? Were they reluctant to risk irritating those in control of funding for their organizations?

In any event, we knew that increasing welfare benefits was the single issue recipients were most concerned about and would rally around. We began to put a number of tactical maneuvers into place. The comic book was one. Demonstrations to bring as many poor people as possible to the process would be expanded. We started a membership organization with chapters in every borough of the city and in cities and counties around the state. To support upstate organizing, we set up an upstate office. We would ask and, if necessary, hound every public official, every influential agency or person to support the grant increase. We could and did dog Governor Carey, a long-term holdout, at any number of public events in the city and elsewhere. We would find as many ways to advance our position in the media as humanly possible, despite the overwhelming bad press the subject of welfare usually generated.

A document surfaced that helped heat up the debate. We called it the Smith Study. (Smith was a prior commissioner of the Human Resources Administration, and the study had been done during his tenure.) Blanche Bernstein was at the helm when it was deep-sixed. She decided to bury rather than release it because it demonstrated quite convincingly how intolerably low welfare benefits in New York had fallen as well as how ridiculous the original standard of need had been with respect to actual prices of goods and services deemed "essential."

The Smith Study was valuable to us for several reasons. First, it outlined the precise methodology originally used to establish the grant in New York State. This made it possible to apply the Bureau of Labor Statistics consumer price index to each element in the grant to determine the gap in purchasing power between the original standard and its current value. It also helped undergird a class action lawsuit to raise benefits that was coordinated by Cindy Mann. Politically, it was a gem.

When the so-called standard of need was set in New York in 1970, it was pegged to what was called the Bureau of Labor Statistics Lower Living Standard (BLS-LLS) for a family of four in 1969.[1] Some logical items of need, like money for rent, were removed from the BLS-LLS because that would be covered by a separate rent allowance. But in modifying the BLS-LLS, the state made some changes that were hard to justify. Among them:

• They eliminated any dollar amount whatsoever for books and newspapers, recreation, food away from home, and so on. (They did not increase "food-at-home" to make up for the food away from home subtraction. Apparently when nonrecipients were dining out, welfare families weren't expected to eat at all.)

• They grossly underbudgeted other essential items, such as utilities and educational materials. Recipients were budgeted for 75 kilowatt hours of electricity, but average consumption was 225, without luxuries like washing machines.

• When they were "done," they reduced the already absurdly inadequate sum by an additional 12 percent.

With the study we could show the press, the courts, the legislature, and anybody else who wanted to know what was required for recipients to "stay in place." The Smith Study then settled the question of what our demand would be as we sought the increase. We would ask for parity with the past.

By this time, the basic grant had lost almost half its purchasing power due to inflation. It therefore failed to meet the state's own definition of need. Recipients were budgeted $4.23 for telephone services, but the minimum monthly bill in the state at the time was $8.96. A family of four was budgeted for thirty-five trips by bus or subway in 1970. Because the grant was raised only once in nearly ten years (from 1969 prices to 1972 prices), by the late seventies families were limited to fifteen trips. The price of dried beans was just over 20 cents a pound in 1969. In 1979 a pound of beans was going for nearly 70 cents. Each element of the grant, all considered "essential" in 1970, was chopped in half or worse.

As we worked to stack up support, we began to notice that some of the more powerful social welfare agencies appeared to be disseminating totally erroneous data on the gap in the purchasing power of the basic grant. Needless to say, they claimed the gap was considerably smaller than it was.

Among the more influential of these agencies was the Community Council of Greater New York (CCGNY). They manufactured studies and data that were used by most of the other human service agencies in the state to support various stands on a host of issues, not the least of which was welfare benefit levels. The council's funding was almost wholly derived from government contracts, although they were not a government agency. Traditionally, using their statistics, CCGNY would bring together a coalition of the major social policy brokers in the city and state to lobby "in behalf of the poor." Although their power never measured up to that of the major charities, like the Federation of Jewish Philanthropies or Catholic Charities, the council was influential in setting the tone and marking the line for many joint lobbying efforts by the agencies with which they worked. Their data were also gospel with most of the city's major media, including *The New York Times*—"the newspaper of record."

At first we gave CCGNY the benefit of the doubt—perhaps there was some unintentional error in their analysis of the grant. After releasing the Smith Study and the updated statistics to the press, we went back to CCGNY. Again they demurred. If they hadn't been the all-but-official arbiter of welfare data as reported by *The New York Times* and others, it wouldn't have mattered so much. But because they had significant influence by virtue of their hegemony with the major media, the other agencies, and politicians, any departure from their statistics by us would be ignored or presumed to be incorrect.

The direct approach wasn't working. Opportunity knocked soon enough. The council was holding a legislative day, with state senators and assemblymembers in attendance. DWAC was asked to make a presentation. The council began by handing out papers with their analysis of the welfare grant, which supported raising welfare benefits and argued that a 15 percent cost of living increase would nearly restore its purchasing power.

When my turn to speak came, I said I didn't understand how the council had derived these numbers, because they made no sense. I reminded everyone that the press had recently blasted the 100 percent increase in prices over the last decade, during which time the basic grant had been raised only once, by 11.85 percent. Consequently, the basic grant was worth about half what had been intended when the state set the standard for meeting "absolute need."

Various legislators reacted. One said it was obvious to anyone who had been alive during the last ten years that inflation was far more dramatic than CCGNY's presentation indicated. It was common knowledge that the 1970s had produced several years of double-digit inflation. Another legislator concurred, saying he didn't know why they had compromised the data and our (welfare recipients') interests in the process. He said it was not CCGNY's job to do that; it was the job of legislators to do the compromising. Another said it was difficult selling his largely affluent constituency on welfare benefit increases, and he needed the most dramatic presentation of the facts that he could get to pull it off. So went the others, in turn.

Right then and there, DWAC stopped being the darling of New York City's social welfare elite. The council in general, and Susan Kinoy, who had organized this event, in particular never forgave or forgot. After all, she had even held a fund-raiser for DWAC at her apartment (at which approximately $1,500 was raised), and now her organization was shamed. We had been stuck with little choice, since CCGNY had torpedoed every attempt to straighten out the statistical inconsistencies with which they blanketed New York. Fifteen hundred dollars was helpful, but it couldn't buy our disloyalty to other poor women. No amount of money could do that.

Still, it was unclear whether the council had made errors or was intentionally falsifying the numbers. Soon we found out. A meeting was called a few days later for the professionals to go over the stats and come to some agreement on them. Dan Wise, who had replaced Mike O'Conner at Community Action for Legal Services (CALS), recommended that I attend, even though DWAC was clearly not invited. Several of us had pocket calculators and copies of the most recent consumer price index and other related documents. Nervously, Dan lead the way. It was not his style to be confrontational, or for that matter particularly brave, but he was committed to the facts. We went through each element of the grant, how it was constructed, and what the appropriate numbers would be if done correctly. Most people at the table could easily see that CCGNY's numbers were way off base. At each juncture, the council had to renounce their data till we had won on all counts. Pitifully, their statistician was forced to proclaim mea culpas all over the place. However, I got the distinct impression it wasn't her fault. Something else was behind this. In any case, the group instructed the council to issue revised data in view of the egregious errors. Round two of the data fight went to DWAC.

Just before the meeting adjourned, Nick Bollman, a true silver tongue from CCGNY, made a proposal. He said it was obvious no one could possibly live on the welfare grant as it was, so he felt some assessment, however hypothetical, needed to be made of recipients' black market potential through such endeavors as prostitution and numbers running. These, he said, should be factored into any data on recipient income "to be fair." One of the other men in the room stood up and lectured Bollman with evident disdain. He said if we ever tried to factor in the graft of some politicians and police against all the others, we'd be strung up by the thumbs. He would not go along with any proposal of the kind and hoped he never heard another hint of it. Then he left the meeting. It was a rare moment.

Nick Bollman and CCGNY were shot down again. To recoup his faltering image, Bollman turned to ask if I thought I could get recipients to a demonstration in Albany to raise welfare grants. He said they would get up the money for buses if DWAC wanted to organize the people. I agreed.

In spite of all that had gone on, we had to go forward with some kind of direct action if welfare benefits were going to be increased, and Albany was the place to do it. We might as well take Bollman up on his offer, even if working with CCGNY was dealing with a school of piranhas. We didn't have much choice.

The following Saturday the council released their newly revised data at the annual conference of the Black and Puerto Rican Legislative Caucus. The new literature on the welfare grant was supposed to reflect the consensus of the group session earlier that week. Sure enough, the numbers had been changed. Only once again they were wrong. They came out approximately where they were before. A different but equally invalid route was taken to get there. Now it was certain there was no accidental miscalculation. They were deliberately fudging the data.

Most of the rest of the social welfare community stayed lockstep with the council on this, in spite of continued and repeated efforts by DWAC and others to demonstrate and solve the problem over several years. It wasn't long before Susan Kinoy appeared to have started an all-out assault on DWAC. She confronted foundation staff who supported us financially, and she helped set up a phony welfare rights–type group that worked out of the council. It never produced any notable work product and rarely had more than four or five actual recipients involved. Its primary function was to establish a paper trail that would make it look like CCGNY worked closely with a group of recipients. (The staff director of this group, paid for by the council, was a former DWAC employee. We had long since let her go. Though she had never been on welfare, she resented the way DWAC elevated recipients to speak in public, so she was always difficult.[2] The council doubled the salary we had been paying her.)

In spite of objective attempts to destroy DWAC, CCGNY was forced to continue dealing with us, at least publicly and superficially. One reason was the New York State Health and Welfare Coalition, which was a statewide group CCGNY had activated some years previously. The organization was cochaired by welfare mothers—a white woman from Schenectady and a black woman from White Plains. In theory, it was composed of social welfare and church organizations who would generously work with welfare groups to advance the recipients' positions on issues. DWAC's participation gave it New York City recipient representation, which it otherwise didn't have. (The council hadn't started their own welfare rights group until shortly after DWAC began attending some of the Health and Welfare Coalition meetings.)

My experiences at the meetings in Washington of various entities had made me suspicious of do-gooder liberals, who all claimed to want the "maximum feasible participation" of poor people in their affairs. But I had run into none ever so explicit in their stated intention of existing solely as a vehicle for the political expression of poor people as this so-called Health and Welfare Coalition.

Even if they meant what they said, professional social worker types had an irritating habit of asserting their superiority complexes in every meeting, as if they knew something significant that we didn't. To some extent that was true—like, for instance, what their real agenda was. But the bigotry went deeper. One common insult was the tendency to exclaim that we needed to do thus and so because "welfare recipients can't speak for themselves." They might as well have said the bimbos in this room who are poor, much less those outside this room they are supposed to represent, don't really exist. Now it may not have been intentional, but an element of self-importance often marred their attempts at camaraderie. When it did, recipients in the room would catch each other's eyes rolling in their heads.

Everyone claimed to want this statewide demonstration to take place, and since recipients we worked with in the city were fired up for it, we continued to organize it. But a blowout was on its way over what position the Health and Welfare Coalition would take on raising the welfare grant. The recipients all agreed we should call for restoration of purchasing power for all the goods and services it was supposed to cover. That didn't seem too extravagant—after all, the state had set it. The trouble was that demanding 100 percent of the so-called standard of need meant virtually doubling the grant. Jim Cashen from Catholic Charities led the opposition.

The social-welfares were in bit of a pickle. According to the coalition's bylaws, the professionals were obligated to support the recipients' position. The odd thing about their recalcitrance was how different it was from their normal lobbying positions on other items. When they lobbied for funds for *services* to recipients (monies for themselves), their habit was to ask for *more* than they expected or even needed, as a sort of bargaining chip. All we really wanted was to present the most accurate posture that could be defended. We were saying that the welfare grant should be made to keep pace with inflation. We weren't asking to get ahead, simply to get even. Nor did we have any unrealistic expectations. We never thought the legislature would double the grant, but it only seemed right to *ask* for justice.

It would have been irresponsible for welfare recipients' leaders to go back to the people we represented saying, We've decided to ask for half what you need to survive on. Imagine the military asking for less than they thought was necessary, or peanut farmers lobbying for subsidies at half the rate they were getting ten years ago. This was standard lobbying procedure—not some far-out, crazed posture of ours.

But Cashen and representatives of the other agencies whose funding came largely from government contracts would not budge. The recipient cochairs were incensed. Feeling used, no doubt, they announced their resignations on the spot. There was a pattern emerging in all of this. Once again, the do-gooders had proven their mettle. They were always claiming to want our participation, but, when push came to shove, what they really wanted was for us to produce bodies for show. On the surface, these organizations existed for the benefit of poor people. When we tried to make them meet their stated objectives, the neat little charade of a coalition began self-immolating.

I had thought it would be so easy. I thought everyone would take the same position because it was right and the data supported it and, besides, it was our lives not theirs. It never occurred to me in the beginning that more was at issue than just helping poor people. I could have understood it if they were conservatives who opposed any welfare spending, but these liberals had a profound hidden agenda. Still, the demonstration would go forward.

On March 14, 1979, over 2,000 people—largely women and children on welfare—converged in Albany. They had come from as far west as Buffalo, as far north as the Canadian border, and as far south as New York City and Long Island. As we assembled outside the Capitol, it began to drizzle. Many had umbrellas with them; others had only the black cloths that had been distributed for the "funeral." They lined up and began a procession past the child's coffin that had been placed on a low step of the capitol building. The priest stood in black robes beside it. As each person reached the coffin, she flung her headpiece on top to "bury" it.

Behind, a couple steps up, a string of children standing side by side held up the nearly block-long black banner that read in white letters: Welfare Budgets Are Killing Our Children. Some of the kids were so small only their heads from the eyes up and their hands could be seen. They looked like baby bandits all wearing the same bandanna. That picture appeared on the front pages of several newspapers a day later.

Over the next few hours, small groups of people from various districts went off to lobby their legislators personally. They had been studying their fact books. They were ready for this.

That evening the demonstration was on all the upstate television stations, and the next day it was in all the papers, including the New York dailies. We got word that a couple dozen legislators were introducing a bill to increase welfare benefits that very day. That was a couple dozen more than we'd had behind us the day before, but the governor, a Democrat, was opposed. Without his support the bill would go no-where. Surprisingly, the Republican leader in the senate had been quoted as saying, "We can't be Scrooges forever," in support of raising benefits. Still, it wasn't the kind of issue horse trades are made of, unfortunately. It would take a lot more to win.

On March 27, 1979, *The New York Times* reported that Commissioner Bernstein had resigned. That same day they reported that we had filed a class action suit against the government for failing to raise welfare benefits to keep pace with the inflation of its own proclaimed standard of need. Cindy Mann and several other lawyers organized by her argued that the state had violated Article 17 of its constitution, which requires the aid, care, and support of the needy. Once a legislative session was over, it was difficult to generate activity to keep the press involved, an essential element in achieving the desired results. The lawsuit was one of our means to be heard, whether or not we won it.

Most of us had started out with a direct personal stake, as welfare mothers who stood to reap the benefits of increased welfare grants. Now, as paid employees, we felt that the pressure was actually heightened, because so many other recipients placed their faith in us. So we were frantic to come up with a new strategy for sustaining and elevating the debate.

Until a strategy that would involve more of the people who had come to Albany was settled on, we could continue with hit-and-runs, which we did. The governor was to receive an award for his efforts in behalf of racial justice from one of the many prominent Catholic organizations in the state. Cindy had a plan. She had secured tickets to the $150-a-person event from an anonymous benefactor. Christine would carry a briefcase with a hidden sound system and pull it out at the moment I signaled. Several lawyers would be available to get us out of trouble. In a pig's eye.

Unfortunately for me, Cindy had thought of everything, down to the simplest detail. All I had to do was risk my hide, psyche myself up like a circus performer about to be catapulted from a cannon, and think of something pithy to say on the way out. Clearly I was not likely to be invited up to the podium to continue barking at the governor.

Things went without a hitch as Christine and I took seats at one of many tables for ten. Finally the keynote speaker, Bayard Rustin, was introduced. The cooing and applause of the crowd told me he was much venerated. He was not the ideal candidate to step on. This was going to be trouble. He finished his rather dull speech to a thunderous chorus of cheers. The governor walked briskly toward the podium, reaching for Rustin's hand photo-op style, then stood at the mike to give thanks. That was our cue. There would be only a heartbeat between when the smitten crowd would stop clapping and when the governor would start talking.

Christine instantly yanked the sound box out. In the same smooth motion, she handed me the microphone, turning the machine on with her other hand. I rose and immediately started talking. "You can't have racial justice in the absence of economic justice!" No more than a couple of sentences about the welfare grant had zipped through my teeth when the sanctimonious audience booed, hissed, and clanged on glasses with assorted silverware. I'd never seen anything quite like it—people in evening gowns and tuxes acting like riled hockey fans.

Then this giant-size male grabbed me, and another one pulled the mike out of its socket, grabbing at Christine. I whirled around. I jerked the tie of the man hassling me so his head was almost level with mine. I wouldn't let go of his tie, and he probably thought it would be uncool to break my arm, which I'm sure he could have done. We moved, in concert, into the hallway.

Tim Casey was strongly urging them to let go of us. Cindy also started in our direction. Among the people I'd noticed on the dais was Councilmember Mary Pinkett, who had been at the opposite end of the room. I could see her making a beeline toward us as we continued the fray. She was coming to the rescue. She had a formidable look on her face as she stepped in to insist that we be let go. Unfortunately for the security guards (and probably because she was black), one of them said to her something like "Are you one of those welfare mothers, too?" Well, that just made her blood boil. Besides, she was more than a little well dressed and had announced her status the second she caught up with us. He either didn't believe her or didn't hear her. She had to repeat that she was a city council member and demand our release a second time. When they realized what a potentially volatile situation they had on their hands, they agreed to let us go. Thank you, Mary!

The next morning *The New York Times* covered our hit-and-run for the first time, though reporters had been present at many others. It was

just a snippet headlined "Woman Berates Carey as He Receives Award."
An editorial on NBC TV news in New York City shortly thereafter cited
the incident and recommended a raise in the welfare grant. The Catholic
Interracial Council, which made the award, vowed to see DWAC go
down the tubes. We were worried about the repercussions of the action
because we were under consideration for a major grant, but we never did
make political decisions based on money. Two days later the Downtown
Welfare Advocate Center was voted the largest grant in our history—
some $90,000—by another Catholic organization, the Campaign for
Human Development. People could give us financial aid or not, but they
would not control us. We were all too "catholic" for that. It was our
strength—and weakness. Enemies are easily made. And kept.

We needed another handle and an effective strategy. I decided to scour
the welfare rules and regulations of New York State, known generically
as Title 18, praying for something to pop up. Anything. It did.

    Buried within the reams of technical drivel was a provision for
special grants to family members on AFDC in the event their clothes had
been destroyed by "flood, fire or other like catastrophe." *Catastrophe* was
the key. President Carter had recently declared inflation a catastrophe.
Journalists of every ilk trumpeted the bad news. There was the unusual
concurrence of high inflation and low employment. They coined a new
word for it: *stagflation.* If everybody else thought it was a *catastrophe,* who
were we to differ? No one was hurt by it more than poor families, who
faced ever-rising costs and government cutbacks at every turn.

    We could adapt an old and highly effective model used by the
National Welfare Rights Organization in the late 1960s. In those days,
"special needs" grants proved pivotal in mobilizing recipients all over the
nation. At that time families were entitled to these "special grants" every
couple of years if they knew to apply for them. NWRO had organized
throngs of women to apply. Once the money was in their hands, recipients were sold on group action. It was a huge mobilization. However,
it was largely their success that led to the modification in the current regs
applying more stringent criteria—making it much harder for recipients
to get the grants. They were no longer available on a regularized basis.
Some catastrophe had to hit to make a family eligible. Even when a

family met the criteria, the department was stingy about giving out clothing allowances.

I flew the idea by Cindy, who had a good head for legal strategies useful to community organizing. At first she said that, legally, the kind of catastrophe the regulations intended would not include inflation. But the word *catastrophe* in relation to inflation had come out of the president's own mouth. Yvonne Lewis, another lawyer who worked with us, thought it was "arguable." The idea appealed to recipients who belonged to what had now become the Redistribute America Movement (RAM), a membership organization staffed by DWAC. It would allow us to keep the heat on about getting more money for recipients—one way or another. Plus, a decision to give clothing allowances did not require an act of the legislature. It could be made administratively by the welfare commissioner (as had recently happened in Massachusetts) or even any welfare center director. At least theoretically.

Rhoda Linton, who had been largely responsible for developing NWRO's campaign, was quick to send a comprehensive packet of materials. Fortunately, the original sign-up sheets for the special grants required only minor modifications to suit the current regulations. We made the changes, put the name "Redistribute America Movement" at the top, and duplicated thousands. The right was in the rules and regulations. Putting it into practice would have to be established politically. The better part of the fall of 1979 was directed to this end. We just had to wait for the opportunity to spring the action on the appropriate target.

We settled on a small test run. While the kinks were being worked out, we would organize some current recipients to participate. To do that, staff members would go door to door, holding minimeetings in kitchens and living rooms of our members.

Stanley Brezenoff was appointed by Mayor Koch to replace Blanche Bernstein after she was forced to resign as the head of HRA. *The New York Times* had recently done a feature story on him with bold headlines proclaiming him a "Hands On Man." In fact, he was Bernstein with a smile—infinitely more treacherous.

Brezenoff may have thought he was well rid of us after his stone cold performance at our first encounter, when he had denied us everything including the elimination of the irritating school letter. Not. We had set up a "Welfare Task Force" with Ruth Messinger, a city council member, some time before. The successful reception of the Children on Welfare Factbook, the sporadic press engendered by our work against brutality in the welfare centers, the various maneuvers over our lawsuit to raise benefits through the courts, the demonstration in Albany, and the two-party rent check ordeal gave this Welfare Task Force a continued raison d'être. It came to include an invitation by Ruth to Commissioner Brezenoff to attend one of our meetings. The deal was as usual—DWAC supplied the recipients and issues, and Ruth accessed officials, to some extent the press, and significant others.

Early in the morning one winter day in 1980, the test run began. A small group of us arrived before the task force meeting began. We sat at the far end of the room, facing the door. Ruth smiled hello when she came, taking a seat opposite us at the front of a huge conference table. Then, about a dozen at a time, more recipients filtered in, usually with staff organizers or attorneys. Perplexed, Ruth again looked over at me. She was getting apprehensive.

Brezenoff and his entourage rode an elevator up with a few more recipients. Our people scattered around the room as he and his staff took seats on either side of Ruth. We knew at some point the elevators would be shut down to stop the flow as it became apparent that an action was under way. About 150 people got in before that happened. We jammed the perimeter of the room. Ronnie Gray, one of the few male staff members ever at DWAC, had positioned himself near the door, virtually behind Brezenoff. He encouraged a woman with a baby carriage to stand in front of the now closed door. Ruth pulled herself together and calmly introduced Brezenoff.

It wasn't long before he was interrupted by a recipient waving an "application" form at him. She was followed in short order by another and another and another, each making her way forward to hand him the forms. Or rather, to place them on the table in front of him. He refused even to touch one. As they "applied," many women spoke, one more moving than the next. A mother told of her baby freezing to death in a heatless apartment last winter. Weeping, she said if she had had more blankets or more winter clothes her baby might still be alive. Brezenoff snapped.

Jumping up, he started shouting. Ruth stood up to calm him down. Throwing off her arm, he pushed her back down. He howled that he couldn't do it and the people who'd brought the recipients there knew perfectly well that he couldn't. Cool as a cucumber, Yvonne countered effectively. She stated that she was an attorney, had examined the regs and the request forms. She said that not only were they perfectly legal but it was in his power to grant the requests. It was quite clearly at his discretion.

More recipients spoke, bolstered by the others, the rising temperature of the meeting, and Yvonne's statement. Brezenoff had had enough. He moved as if to go out the door, when Ronnie stepped behind the baby carriage. A bodyguard or staff member must have moved an instant before, because the door opened. Faced with the baby and the carriage, Brezenoff hesitated. Then he jumped right over it, managing to get past Ronnie. As providence would have it, shutting the elevators down to keep more of us from coming up also prevented him and his entourage from going down. He dashed into the men's room to wait. When he came out, he was completely surrounded again. An elevator opened. He and his staff pushed their way on. One of his aides said to him, "You could have done it, couldn't you?" Just as the doors were closing, he told her to shut up and get on the goddamned elevator. Everyone within earshot heard it.

I'd barely made it back to the office when I started getting the wailing calls. Nick the silver-tongued Bollman from the Community Council of Greater New York called. Shame on me. How could I do that to Ruth? Ruth called, too. Both Cindy and I tried to convince her it had been in her own best interest not to have known about it—it was her defense, in fact. That Brezenoff could have agreed to the clothing grants was not, apparently, on the minds of any of the callers. I worried that Ruth would never forgive me. She never did.

The DWAC debriefing was telling. We had discovered a number of things. For one, recipients were down (as in up) for this campaign. Also, there was some room in the law that we could utilize to our advantage. Perhaps most pleasing, Stan the hands-on man could be rattled. Much fun was had at his expense, as people rehashed his athletic prowess in jumping over the baby carriage only to be stuck with all of us following him to the elevator bank. Too bad the real story was barely reported. It would have made great copy—or a terrific cartoon.

One thing was clear, in any event. This clothing campaign was going to happen. As we moved into February and began spreading the word to upstate chapters, we found almost equal enthusiasm everywhere.

Except for White Plains. Marcy May came back from a meeting there with just a tad of bad news. It was a tad that would throw us into a tizzy for the next several weeks. It wasn't that they were opposed to the clothing campaign, but somehow they had gotten the idea we were going to do another mass demonstration at the capital. They had already started working on it and were in no mood to bargain it away. Without New York City and the DWAC staff to coordinate it, it would be a bust. And, anyway, DWAC shouldn't be telling the chapters what to do—that should be the job of the statewide committee. We would have to drop everything and turn our full attention to a monstrous undertaking almost none of us wanted even to think about. But it would have been political suicide to cross our own steering committee. We were stuck.

Shortly before the mass demonstration, a small group of us decided to make a trip to Albany. We made a special appointment to meet with the Black and Puerto Rican Legislative Caucus. The legislators made responsive statements, sometimes asked questions, and seemed quite supportive. After all, most of them were from districts where large numbers of recipients lived, as they were well aware. I had figured out that if they were willing to hold firm, they were a big enough group to shift the balance of power in the assembly, thereby making it impossible for Speaker Stanley Fink to settle the budget bill (without which the state would come to a virtual halt). In other words, they were all Democrats and mostly assembly members. Without them, the Democrats would not have enough votes to carry a majority against the Republicans. Fink would stall the vote. This would disrupt the budget process, and the leaders would have to capitulate on the welfare grant increase. The caucus hemmed and hawed some. I think they were thrown off balance by the challenge. (Put your vote where your mouth is.) Maybe they were annoyed because of some past faux pas of mine. This was the kind of thing I could only barely fathom—the grant increase was for poor families, for God's sake. It should have been outside politics. Finally, murmurs of agreement bubbled up, and the chair concurred. Sort of.

Seven weeks of brutal work later, we held another demonstration in Albany. After the rally, participants departed for the offices of their local legislators. By the end of that legislative session, an increase was passed in the assembly but died in the state senate. Ironically, the then senate majority leader, Warren Anderson (an upstate Republican), was still *publicly* calling for the increase, but Speaker Fink and the governor (both Democrats) were holding out. Truth was, this was all one bald-faced charade executed by the leaders.

In the puppet show that passed for politics, the majority leaders of each house along with the governor controlled virtually every vote on every bill of consequence. If it didn't get approval from any one of the "Big Three," even a popular bill would go nowhere. Minority leaders had some say, but usually not much. Bills might be introduced, but unless they were relatively benign, they never made it out of committee to be voted on at all. Even when a bill was finally allowed to hit the floor, the stonewalling could go on indefinitely—until all the guys at the top said go.

The assembly bill was allowed to pass, no doubt because it was advantageous—and safe. The assembly was dominated by New York City legislators who were accountable to a liberal constituency. This had finally become a very public issue. Fink could afford to okay letting the bill out of committee so they could "vote their conscience," knowing the increase wouldn't fly in the senate until Anderson put his foot down for real (which he clearly hadn't). Even if he had, without the governor's express backing, a bill could be vetoed—meaning war. The top men were executing a political Punch-and-Judy show that would protect each of them from the wrath of the others—and their constituents. In effect, a big money bill was a big dead bill till the Big Three agreed. That hadn't happened yet.

When the budget bill was passed without a welfare grant increase in it, we also knew the caucus hadn't held out. I was so naive. Until then, I had no idea what the power of the governor and the majority leaders over the rest was. I hadn't known how easy it was for them to withhold committee appointments, staff, and plain old pork barrel bucks "for the community" that got the same tired people elected every year. I was learning fast. Democracy? Well, maybe.

Back to business as usual, we soon found that the clothing campaign was bound to keep government officials hopping, even if the press didn't know what was going on. To everyone's surprise, women all over the state were signing up to join the campaign. In addition, when they joined the campaign, they joined RAM, which mushroomed to an official membership of over 5,000 in a few short months. In some locations, recipient leaders would staff their own sign-up tables, helping other mothers fill out the forms, giving them instructions for follow-up, and collecting dues. In dollar bills and dimes, nearly $10,000 was collected during this period. The leaders would come to the office and empty out their pockets with an unmistakable pride and sense of ownership. Others would be running the mimeo machines night and day to keep up with the demand. RAM was their organization, and they knew it now, like never before.

Clearly the volunteers didn't have money to be riding the subways back and forth from Brooklyn or the Bronx, nor did they have baby-sitting or lunch money when they worked for several hours. For those whose time and work merited it, we devised an "arrangement" to cover personal expenses each day. They would submit expense vouchers, and at the end of the week they'd be "paid." Not a wage, but something that said we took their work seriously. It became competitive. The ultimate competition was a shot at a real paying job at DWAC when one opened up. Starting salaries were $10,000 annually. To a welfare mother, at first that seemed like a lot. Once they had to live on it for a while, most could see, what it meant to be a low-wage worker. Moneywise, after taxes and FICA, it wasn't much better than welfare, and the additional saga of sustaining reliable child care was punishing. After Reagan came into office, regulations were altered to make it even more difficult to live on the income from wages unless the job paid a good deal more than DWAC had to offer. Nobody ever stayed for the money. It was this family feeling coupled with a sense that the work was important that kept us all there.

Some of the mothers went back for their general equivalency diplomas, so they could graduate from high school; others started college. When their personal conditions, like quality child care, are right and they are asked to learn and do something that gives them pride, poor women will jump at the opportunity like anybody else. We didn't set out to be a job training program—hell, we didn't even believe in them. But we were also that.

For the first time we faced the unlikely situation of having too many participants. Without computerized equipment (not even a word processor), putting out a mailing was a three-week venture. Every piece of mail had to be hand-folded, addressed, stamped, and so on. The hieroglyphics of some of those who had joined required a special pile, from which each of us would try to pull out some approximation of a name and address, ultimately giving up, passing it to the next person for a go. If organizations can exist in heaven and hell simultaneously, this was it.

We had to slow it down, so we reduced the times and locations for joining and concentrated on the next steps. Beginning on September 15, 1980, recipients from all over the state would submit their applications for clothing grants at their welfare centers. Since there were so many centers in New York City, we would hold seventeen demonstrations through the week, starting with a kickoff that Monday in Manhattan, which drew over a thousand recipients. The police seemed to be as overwhelmed by the numbers as we were. What we didn't yet know was that similarly extraordinary numbers of women had shown up in twelve cities that day.

On a flatbed truck, Karren Thomas, a welfare mother now on staff, stepped up to a microphone and spoke to the group of mostly African-American and Latina women. She told of going to her welfare worker after her pipes burst during one heatless winter. First the water turned to ice. Then it melted and flooded down her walls, ruining most of her kids' clothes and what little she had in the way of furniture. Her worker refused to give her a clothing or furniture replacement allowance, saying the damage was not caused by a flood—it was just "cascading water."

Another RAM member spoke. "It rains. It gets cold. The seasons change, but our checks remain the same." She went on. "I know a lot of y'all spent your rent money, utility money, and sold your food stamps to buy school clothes for your kids. We need a special grant to buy our kids clothes, because our kids grow!" It was commonly known that welfare mothers had a heavy investment in keeping their kids in school. Most of them felt that education was the way out for their children. That meant they would reach further into that deep deep hole to obtain school clothes, often no matter what they had to sacrifice. The mothers felt their children would be too ashamed to go to school if they had to go in clothes that were raggedy or didn't fit.

By accident, I started a riot that day. The center's doors were barricaded, and no one was being allowed to enter. If the recipients couldn't enter, they also couldn't submit their applications. Negotiations between welfare center officials and our lawyers were stalled. I happened to be at the mike and foolishly blurted out, "Well, if they won't let them in, then we'll all go in," at which point I jumped off the soapbox and moved toward the door. Suddenly this mass was moving as one, and with force. Almost as quickly as I'd started it, I realized how potentially dangerous this was, especially for the people closest to the door.

I learned one tough lesson that day: it is much easier to start a riot than it is to stop one. Pulling back through the crowd to get to megaphones and microphones, a number of us called on the women to return. A few people were hurt (including Cindy Mann, who was up front negotiating when I screwed up). The matter was also settled. Those with forms who belonged to this center could enter three at a time and submit their applications.

Almost every newspaper in the state, with the exception of the New York City dailies, carried the story of its own local action. This was especially important since it was the upstate legislators who were least likely to favor raising the welfare grant. Now they had a clear picture that recipients everywhere were becoming engaged. Most of the recipients upstate were white. County party leaders did not believe they would come out on their own. For that matter, legislators, like most others, thought that most welfare recipients were black. But thousands of poor women upstate surely did come out. Something was brewing. DWAC and RAM were a rare concoction.

The mettle of DWAC was about to be put to the toughest test yet. The Downtown Welfare Advocate Center had to coordinate sixteen more of these actions in the city through the remainder of the week. To fit them all in, two or three were scheduled in the morning and again in the afternoon. Staff were divided to cover each. Where larger crowds were expected, more staff, more bullhorns, more placards, more of everything would go.

From my first location, I called our office to see how the others were doing. I was told they were fine but there was a recipient on the phone at a center not on the schedule who was trying to submit her application alone without success. I called her center director and said I had several hundred people only minutes away who would be delighted to come over to help the woman out. I reached Stanley Brezenoff's assistant and told her the same thing, suggesting she jack up the center director in question and any others throughout the week. She did. The woman submitted her form and got a receipt. I did get a mischievous kick out of the bluff. In fact, it would have been very hard if not impossible to move several hundred people to another site. But the welfare didn't know that. In the weeks to come, many women reported that all they had to do to get proper service on any snag was to pull out their RAM ID cards.

By Friday, having sung and chanted and marched and revved up crowds twice a day every day, we were all hoarse and dead on our feet. It was without question the most physically demanding week we'd ever worked. And still nobody had anything to show for it. The welfare officials had thirty days from the date of application in which to make a decision. So, thirty days after the application action in Brownsville, one of the most bizarre locations in all New York, we went back to collect.

Generally, Brownsville is a sea of cement in Brooklyn. It has high-rise projects as far as the eye can see, with barely a tree or shrub, much less a patch of grass to be found. Of Brownsville it is said that small children often mistake rats for cats, having never seen the latter. Brownsville borders East New York, perhaps the poorest and most tragic area of the city. The smaller houses there are scattered among the rubble of houses that used to be. On one occasion, I saw a "house" that was really only the remains of three walls and a partial roof (no windows, none necessary). A small load of laundry, including children's clothes, hung on a string crossing the open space from one wall to another. On the "floor" was a double mattress with sheets on it, one chair, and nothing else. Whoever lived there wasn't home. Still, they lived there, so they would not have been called "homeless" by any official definition. Our largest chapter of dues-paying members came from here—over 800 families.

The Brownsville welfare center is situated in the no-man's-land between Brownsville and East New York. It is near nothing. Most of the block is parking lot, strewn with the blight of piled-up scrap. Quite a distance away and catty-corner to the center was a run-down bodega with the only working public telephone for blocks. When recipients were in trouble at this center, they had to make the trek rain or shine, snow or sleet, to the bodega to call for help. That is, if they had a dime and until the bodega went out of business.

We gathered a few blocks away at 444 Hopkinson Street, where one of DWAC's official board members, Joe Francois, then ran a community center. He often let us use space there, in spite of the risks (such as withdrawal of his agency's government funds, which did happen only months later).

That morning cars looking like unmarked police vehicles were parked across the street. A few white men in suits milled about them. Occasionally a regular police car would swing by. In all the times I had been in the area before, I couldn't remember a single police car anywhere in sight. Nor had I ever seen a white man there in a business suit.

We would not be taking the Brownsville center by surprise. If we could get into the building, we could stage a sit-in; if not, we'd be restricted to a picket, which would carry the force of a smirk behind someone's back. We headed to the center. Police were ready and waiting to stop us. We picketed, sang songs, chanted "Clothe our children now!" and tried to be cheery about the whole strategic botch-up. It was back to the drawing boards. Staff tried not to look dejected. Everyone vowed it was not over yet.

We learned later that, on the same day we demonstrated at the Brownsville center, one of our members had committed suicide. The welfare had failed, again, to send the correct amount in her check. Like others who had been through it just too many times before, she had been pushed too far. She climbed onto the roof of her six-story building with a pint bottle of rum, telling her neighbors she was going to jump when she finished it. In the end, whether she jumped or slipped, she left behind six children.

* * *

We would have to spring a takeover where we would not be expected. We let it leak out that we were planning a sit-in at Stan Brezenoff's Central Office. A number of us agreed to get arrested if we could wrestle no concessions from Brezenoff.

Some 300 women and children gathered at a church within walking distance of Central Office. Those of us who were to be arrested gathered elsewhere. We would come from different directions; those to be arrested would go in a side door. The rest would walk straight ahead toward 250 Church Street. The women marching toward them could see that the police were well prepared at 250, complete with barricades and billy clubs. Somehow both our groups reached the correct doors at about the same time—not at 250, but at 241 Church, across the street on the corner before and some distance away from Central Office. All of us were inside the building before the police could move their gear. It worked. We had taken over the EAU (emergency assistance unit) that was most renowned for its consistent failure to help families in need. This was the after-hours center, where families with no resources were supposed to go if they were in dire straits after 5:00 P.M. DWAC had fought many individual battles because of this heartless place.

For now the center was in our control. Sweet. A hand-lettered sign was taped to a window. It read, "THE PEOPLE'S WELFARE CENTER." Father Robert Chapman, archdeacon of the New York City Protestant Episcopal Diocese, and authors Frances Fox Piven and Richard Cloward arrived to go to jail in solidarity with us if it came to that.

Negotiations between us and Brezenoff went nowhere. We were told to leave or be arrested. When it was time, those of us who would not leave huddled in a circle. The others filed out to the sidewalk. At almost the precise time the police were supposed to arrest us, Edna Blue, a RAM leader and self-proclaimed minister, opened the Bible she carried to special events and started praying out loud. The rest of us joined hands. Edna was either seriously slick or dead serious. It soon appeared that her pleas to God to keep these policemen from making a grave error were being answered. The cops had turned to stone. When Edna stopped praying, Father Chapman started another prayer. Shortly we all began singing hymns. The police didn't move. We had to stop singing so they would arrest us and we could get it over with. Cheering and crying women flanked our way to the paddy wagon.

Political arrests are often different from criminal arrests. Several of us had been through this before. We tried to prepare the others. Since we had done nothing violent, we were treated with relative civility. Most of the approximately twenty of us were put in a single holding cell after our names were taken and our possessions confiscated. (The men were separated from the women.) There were already two women in there—one for shoplifting a great pair of boots, the other for prostitution.

There were wooden benches fixed to the gray walls on either side of the cell where some of us sat. There wasn't enough space for all of us to sit at the same time, so the younger ones rotated. Periodically other women were thrown into the mix for alleged street crimes. The women who had been brought in on their own could tell we were together for something unusual and guessed it was political pretty quickly. When we told them specifically what we were there for, they cheered, even looking out for us if a guard was bitching.

Hours after the arrest, they began what seemed like a deliberately dragged-out process of letting us go, one at a time. One thing about jail—once that door slams shut, they can choose to do whatever they please. Even if you felt confident about *going* in, *being* in was altogether different. Inside, the full conceptual force of incarceration whacks you in the brain.

We were all out by around midnight. The air was crisp but not biting. It was October 10, 1980. Less than one month later, Ronald Reagan was elected president of the United States.

Periodically for months afterward we would gather at a courthouse to hear our cases postponed and, ultimately, adjudicated. We all received ACDs, adjournments in contemplation of dismissal. That meant we were supposed to keep out of trouble for six months. Accomplishing this, our cases would be dismissed and expunged from the record. But they never were really expunged.

We had hoped having two authors (Piven and Cloward) and Archdeacon Chapman with us would attract the press, but we were curiously ignored. That is, until Chapman took it upon himself to write letters to the newspapers about the incident. They were printed. Toward the end of his explanation of our objectives, he wrote,

This "Great Society" considers us so notorious for demanding clothing for poor children that we required handcuffing, finger-printing and photographing.

Perhaps the time is now for a little in-depth reflection upon the human cost of our dollar centeredness. "Later" could be too late to redeem the society we were meant to be, and under God, still have a chance to become.

Stanley Brezenoff was forced to respond by letter to the papers. As expected, he denied having the power to grant the clothing requests but went on to say that raising welfare benefits through the state legislature would be the city's highest priority next legislative session. He blinked.

Now we started racking up supporters almost as fast as RAM had grown. Ultimately, it would be these third-party interests who would move the legislature. There was barely a politician, union leader, social welfare, civil rights, women's, or church leader in town who wasn't on record favoring the raise. I even caught Carol Bellamy ("it's not politically feasible to support you") on the TV news saying raising welfare benefits was the most important issue in the city! We had made the impossible feasible. In fact, in politics almost nothing is unfeasible. It just takes work and vision. Lots of it.

Those still hedging raised concerns about how an increase would be paid for. Somehow, we would have to come up with an answer, now more than ever because of Ronald Reagan's ascendancy to the White House. Talk about cuts in social programs was relentless. David Stockman, Reagan's choice to head the Office of Management and Budget, became so notorious that Isabelle made up a song just for him. Sung to the tune of "Davy Crockett," it began,

He was born 'neath the sign of the treasury
Biggest mess in the land of the free
Cut him some fat when he was only three
And punished the sins of inefficiency.

refrain:
Davy, Davy Stockman
Prince of the OMB.

A couple verses later it ended,

Champion knight of wealth and greed
The Trojan Horse is Davy's steed
A horse that big has to have a lot of feed
So they grind up the bones of those in need.

With the collapse of the direct action approach to the clothing campaign, we were forced into a paper box. Under Cindy's supervision, we flooded the state with administrative challenges requiring an individual hearing for each denied request. It would cost the state at least three times as much to do these hearings as it would to give the clothing grants out. No doubt the welfare officials saw it as a short-term expense to avoid the inevitable barrage of additional requests that would follow in the event they capitulated.

This was not the stuff that makes for much citizen participation. Too dry. We hit upon another strategy. This time we would evolve a number of creative variations, sometimes quite embarrassing to those they touched. The genesis was in a song brought to DWAC by Deborah, a former welfare mother and head of our upstate office. It was sung to the tune of "Camptown Races." It was easily picked up and had a catchy refrain:

They call it tax abatements but it's welfare,
welfare,
They call it tax abatements but it's
welfare for the rich.

Welfare for the rich, welfare for the rich, oh
We don't wanna pay no more welfare for the rich.

In place of "tax abatements" any number of variations were substituted as people thought them up, like "business lunches" "corporate bailouts," "interest deductions," and so on. Welfare for the rich became the rallying cry for the next phase of our campaign to raise welfare benefits. We put it to use for the first time around Christmas of '81. A group of New Yorkers, some rich, some middle class, some poor, gathered in front of Tiffany's (on one of the most posh blocks in the world), to take a bus trip through welfare areas.

Tiffany's had recently received a multimillion-dollar tax abatement in exchange for a promise to "create or retain 6 jobs." Two welfare mothers lugged a sizable baby doll frozen in a block of ice into the store, where they were met by a representative. Cameras clicked like lightning gone haywire, recording the dripping object and the players. The women said, "This is what we get when you get tax abatements." The representative said he was not authorized to accept anything on behalf of Tiffany's. The women retorted that they were authorized to give it on behalf of RAM, and they thrust it toward him. Reflexively, he reached out for it. They quickly let go. There he was, standing with a frozen baby doll dripping on that splendid floor in front of all those cameras.

After the "show," the group boarded a bus for a tour of welfare neighborhoods. Traveling down Fifth Avenue, we continued passing luxury tax-abated buildings. Not one picture or word about the event appeared in any of New York's dailies, not one second on local TV, even though the reporters fought one another for position and Gloria Steinem gave a send-off message in front of Tiffany's. This was not news, apparently. Most people were too busy shopping. Besides, lots of them were knocking off checks to charities to lower their taxes by December 31, as if that would somehow help.

Our next hit was Donald Trump. An even more stupendous tax abatement went to him for the development of a luxury hotel. It was the most generous tax deal to a single company in the city's history. It not only involved city approval but utilized a state entity—the Urban Development Corporation—which was originally passed off as a vehicle for the production of low-income housing. Not surprisingly, there was solid evidence that the Trump family fortune had been very very good to Governor Carey. (Carey received $102,000 in campaign contributions from the Trumps for his 1974 and 1978 campaigns. Trump was also the coguarantor of a $300,000 loan to kick off Carey's campaign.)

So, on March 10, 1981, a couple went to register at the luxury

Grand Hyatt Hotel, claiming the taxes they paid entitled them to the room for free. Concurrently, we were outside chanting, "Donald Trump owns the Hyatt, but the people had to buy it!" As the demonstration progressed, a stretch limo pulled up in front. Tim Casey, wearing a Ronald Reagan mask, popped his head out the sunroof (Nancy popped out beside him), waved to the crowd, and started talking about privatizing social programs. There were no free rooms that night, but the six o'clock news carried the demonstration live. Press coverage to which people like Donald Trump were obligated to respond on camera was essential to changing the way people thought—about welfare, about the uses of their tax dollars, about the whole boondoggle shared by politicians and some of the least needy people in the world.

Once we started running the line that tax abatements were really a form of welfare, we were on another roll. For some reason, it appealed to a completely different set of people. It contrasted both with the posture that a welfare increase would be fine "if only the money were there" and with the rhetoric of "cutting the fat" while actually giving enormous tax breaks to millionaires.

Our May 1981 newsletter, "The RAM's Horn," carried a one-inch-tall headline: WE WON! A welfare grant increase was passed. The text explained the details of the increase and described many of the efforts that had been put into moving that agenda.

At DWAC, we were actually a little less sanguine about the victory. It had taken us three years. We had achieved only a 15 percent increase, in spite of the ravages of years of unabated high inflation.[3] (Nonetheless, 15 percent was more than before, and, to poor people, almost any amount more is helpful. In the aggregate, it would amount to hundreds of millions of dollars, as it would be sustained year after year.) The courts rejected our lawsuit by arguing that it was not justiciable because welfare was the legislature's responsibility. (The lawsuit had, however, elevated the debate as it garnered considerable additional press coverage, including a substantial and largely favorable article in the *Law Review Journal*.) The social welfare institutions had quite clearly sold us out, ensuring the increase would be minimal. No doubt their government contracts were safe, for the moment. Foundation directors were calling DWAC about distraught board members who were appalled at our antics, mostly with respect to the governor. Some of them even received complaints about us from the social-welfares, like Susan Kinoy, who would have known complaining was as good as telling them to stop funding us altogether.

Little did they know that the future held more. Demonstrations were planned in Saratoga Springs, where a good number of the very wealthy ("horsey set") summered each year. Governor Carey was a regular, too. We aimed to disrupt the Fasig-Tipton annual yearling auction. The tax loopholes generated by that event alone would set off a chain reaction of tax shelters so big they could feed all the poor children in the county for years. Horse purchasing, owning, breeding, and even putting out to pasture were tax shelters beyond the pale.

The town's mayor attempted to abridge RAM's right to assemble, guaranteed in the first amendment of the Bill of Rights, claiming the wealthy would be upset. Like those of many small towns, Saratoga Springs's "government" was too ignorant to be more subtle. We had to obtain a court order for RAM to exercise the basic right of all Americans, rich or poor. Not only did the town lose in court but the whole debacle boomeranged, generating media coverage all over the state before and after the action. It also taught us another lesson about the media. This odd event was covered in such prestigious publications as *The New Yorker*. It was even covered in the sports section of *The New York Times*. Quirky worked better upstate, especially where the very wealthy (out-of-towners) and the very poor "communed."

Another demonstration was held at Mobil Oil's headquarters in New York City, asking them to give us their two cents (on every barrel of crude, that is) to build housing for poor families. All the talk of public-private partnership, not to mention their obscene earnings and profits that year, was giving us new ideas.

I for one was beginning to see the links in the political food chain from the poorest to the most affluent. The experience had been punishing, brutal, from that first Christmas alone to the last moments on the torture rack that passed for participatory democracy. I had picked up the rock; now I had to look under it. There was much more to know, to learn. I was exhausted from the ordeal, and, given what I now understood about politics, I wasn't so sure DWAC as it was constituted was the best way to effect change. The price of entry had been too high, and we could only occasionally and only by force sit at the table where the social agenda was written. I resigned as DWAC's director.

What DWAC continued to do best and had always done well was respond to poor women in crisis. Each success—and there were thousands every year—meant that some family on the brink of disaster was at least temporarily pulled back from the edge. We helped them access an income, however small, that would allow them some relief, some measure of independence from the ever-intrusive welfare state, and the ability to go on together. And because we engaged them in the process of resolving their problems, instead of just doing the deed, we left them with knowledge and at least a little more power than when they came to us.

On our end, the knowledge gained from the women who came to us for help allowed us to keep track of the patterns of crises, honing all our sensibilities to continue to bring an alternative voice to state and sometimes national attention. DWAC still scored an occasional victory injecting the views of poor mothers into the public arena. The means might change; the message remained intact. Like NWRO, we had left a network of poor women who were politically active in cities and towns all over the state, loosely connected to many similar groups across the country. This network shared a politics that is distinctly different from the dominant themes of the right, left, or center in U.S. social policy. The people who wield the power to respond have yet to give credence to that voice.

Could we have done things differently? Maybe. In retrospect, it's obvious that the kind of direct action mode we operated under could not last forever, if for no other reason than we never could have sustained the funding needed to keep going. We were always in the unenviable position of having to bite the hand that fed us. Yet, before we started functioning in that manner, we were little more than human Raggedy Ann dolls, drooping for the advantage of social welfare agencies as they saw fit—the pitiful version of "maximum feasible participation." We had evolved from a group whose primary function was helping individual families in need to a more comprehensive political operation that sought to insert our views into the public arena, to get at the underlying issues—especially income in the larger sense. We wanted to sit at the table to write the agenda, and for the life of me I still can't think of another way we could have gotten closer—at least in the beginning.

Could we have compromised? Could we have modified our numbers, or twisted the meaning of this or that to satisfy some third-party interests, or asked for less for our constituency? Not on our lives. Once we started getting paid, we no longer had a right even to consider compromising the interests of welfare families, period. What's more, it was absolutely essential to us to have our members feel that we were firmly, permanently on their side. There was a place called home in it, a place with respect. In any event, once a community group starts that game, they cease to exist except at the will of the power brokers.

We were also stuck in a particular moment historically. Mass movements per se had largely dissipated, but the style of organizing was still evolving out of them, and foundation funds were often tied to that style. Though we didn't make decisions based on money, foundations meddled in our affairs with impunity. There was a group that thought of itself as promoting grass-roots organizing, and they wanted DWAC that way. There was a distinct vogue about it. There was another that wanted the opposite—the studies, the research, the direct service. Both seemed to want leadership development.[4] We could do all those things and did to one degree or another. But as the politics heated up, most of even those who wanted us to sustain the organizing momentum found they could no longer fund it, for reasons none would ever quite explain. One thing is certain: our consistent refusal to run a "jobs" agenda or register voters when that was the funders' fancy didn't help. Worse, writing articles on such subjects as the futility and crass manipulation of poor people inherent in the voter registration strategy did not smooth things over with those who promoted and poured millions of dollars into it. We insisted on reflecting the positions of our constituency, in spite of the opposition of liberals who without us could call the policy shots and be praised no matter how foolish or greedy they got.

Despite all our efforts, income would continue to be, and still is, the major issue. But it was obfuscated by the myths—especially the one that implied that welfare recipients were living high off the hog without "working." We were neither living well nor being ladies of leisure. As aggregate spending "in behalf of poor people" climbed and was absorbed, in part, by the not-for-profits, the din of disapproval made it increasingly difficult to overcome the obstacles. In the end, it was those who "spoke for us" who took not only the money but the words right out of our mouths, or, more accurately, the mouths right out of our faces.

Our experience with elected officials exposed a crude dynamic of political trickle down—from the executive to the legislators (pork) to the agencies that give and receive government contracts. By observing the symbiotic process in reverse, we could see the returns—support of politicians by the major social welfare institutions through prestige (awards and so on), campaign contributions of money and workers (directly or indirectly), and votes. Make no mistake: all this is not unique to New York.

The do-good institutions have a prodigious stake in preserving the status quo, even while pretending not to. If we had continued to accumulate knowledge and power, we might have exposed them for what they were; we would have demonstrated how little their programs accomplished, how readily they fudged statistics and altered issues for their own political ends. Bottom line, as long as we existed to interpret our own needs and aspirations, many of the not-for-profits were superfluous. We were dangerous.

PART II

Filling the Gap: A Charitable Deduction

The toughest adversaries of welfare mothers who organized for their rights were often those in the "not-for-profit" charity organizations. These functioned in a kind of vulturine relation to poor people. Their very survival depended upon the existence of poor people. In theory, they were "allies." In fact, as agents of the status quo, they couldn't sell poor women out fast enough. (Or buy some, advertise them in their promotional literature, and parade them around like tamed savages, living testimony to the power of social work.) Sometimes they were even well intentioned. Class and cultural barriers combined with their paychecks made it all but impossible for most to understand poor women at all, much less to represent their interests. Active welfare mothers who tried to hold on to their own agendas without getting walloped by the "helping hands" were universally skeptical of the do-good agencies. They had all been "helped" at least once too often. The money in the other person's pocket tainted their relationships, as one's well-being was predicated on the other's lack thereof. A welfare mother and activist from Minneapolis dubbed one of her group's functions as "non-profit prevention work," as if she were talking of rape or disease "prevention." I heard stories of deceit by the charities from poor women across the country— California, Massachusetts, Illinois, New Mexico . . .

Why did these things happen like a recurring nightmare shared across great geographic spans as if by magic? Because, except to poor people themselves, poverty is megabusiness. In the guise of "serving the poor," a triad of interests converge. First, there are the mediating institutions, the so-called not-for-profit agencies. These are the giant charities that have multimillion-dollar endowments and real estate holdings, and

119

that get the lion's share of tax-deducted charitable dollars and human service government contracts, as well as the thousands of smaller ones that vie for a cut, often in the hope of becoming one of the giants. These tax-exempt entities overtly and covertly influence government social policy "in behalf of the poor" through "public interest" advocacy for programs they want foundations to start and the government to sustain. They exist outside government, have their own boards of directors, their own "constitutions" (known as bylaws), and their own missions. (DWAC was a small nonprofit corporation, albeit one of few made up of, and run by, poor women.)

Second, the for-profit corporate sector and wealthy individuals who inherited from their ancestral prototypes fund nonprofits either through the foundations they originated, like Ford and Carnegie, or directly through active, current donations. In addition to lowering their tax burdens, a primary objective is to affect public policy to their perceived advantage, *including to spawn future government spending programs.* This is usually accomplished by "seeding" (giving initial money to) nonprofits that will produce "studies" that support their contentions and run "models" based on the studies. (The process can also be initiated by the non-profits, whose fund-raisers convince donors of the merits of their programs.)

The third element in the triad is government. The models I just described are meant to be copied by other nonprofits around the country, at some point creating a sufficient mass to convince government to take over their funding in whole or in part. This creates an even greater incentive for additional nonprofits to adopt some variation on the model. The competition for government contracts soon becomes highly political, and the model, which may or may not have been a good idea in the first place, is long forgotten. Among the government monies recently taking this route are those for "drug treatment" and those for fighting "hunger and homelessness."

Elected officials and their surrogates (the agency bureaucrats) who distribute the money nationwide become powerful in direct proportion to increases in the amounts of money they control. The nonprofit corporations interface with government through rotating staff positions (depending on who is in office) and with profit-making corporations through interlocking directorates and sometimes staff positions. To complete the circle, the corporate sector endorses and funds the campaigns of politicians who have been helpful along the way. The nonprofits create awards and covertly provide troops to aid in future political campaigns, a very significant element in the larger picture.

The entire process is represented as filling an essential social gap that government has heretofore missed. For instance, knowing welfare benefits were too low for people to live on, instead of lobbying to raise the grants, these shakers and movers of public policy developed a nationwide network of soup kitchens and food pantries. Poor people have no say and are left out of the process but live with the consequences—good, bad, or irrelevant. Collectively, along with AFDC, social security, medicaid, and other government-administered entitlement and service programs, the programs of these independent concerns constitute the "welfare state" (distinct from small-*w* welfare, or public assistance per se). The media wrap it up for the others by sloppy reporting and out-and-out endorsements or acknowledgments of the agencies, pols, and "benefactors."

The welfare state is not new to the late twentieth century, but the nonprofit service sector has never been richer (in terms of share of the gross national product and jobs), more powerful, or less accountable. It is the only significant power bloc that is essentially unregulated, in spite of the fact that most of its money comes from the government, through either direct service contracts or tax expenditures.[1] Its influence over public policy has mushroomed since the 1960s. It has become a veritable fifth estate. Taxpayers foot the bill. Poor people suffer the consequences.

In recent decades, this fifth estate has been costly in human as well as fiscal terms. The boulder that propelled the avalanche certainly preceded the Reagan administration, contrary to the claims of most liberals. The tendencies had been in play through most of the 1970s. A few of the actual cuts facing recipients that came out of Reagan's White House were proposed in Carter's failed welfare reform bill.[2] Some nonprofits were hit by federal cutbacks under Reagan, too. But for the most part their budgets were sustained or even increased by a combination of local government grants; foundations, which helped fill the newly perceived gap; and donations by individuals with the money to make a difference. Contrary to popular belief, in the aggregate, nonprofits actually experienced increased funding, in excess of the rate of inflation, even during the Reagan administration.

The point is, that "Ominous" Budget Reconciliation Act of 1981 engineered by our boy Stockman was really a reshuffling of the deck. In the now infamous *Atlantic Monthly* interview by William Greider, Stockman revealed that the scramble to preserve special interests in the budget process was comparable to "pigs at the trough." He said the only ones unable to get there would lose out—the poorest people. Lose we did. Whether trough or table, we weren't sitting at it; we weren't writing any part of our own agenda. Neither Democrats nor Republicans, liberals nor conservatives, mainstream nor fringe were listening to us. When it was over, tens of thousands of welfare recipients were cut off the rolls, hundreds of thousands had already minuscule grants and food stamps reduced. Millions were thrown into turmoil by barbaric administrative requirements to jump through more hoops than all the trained lions ever on earth put together on the same day could have managed.

Federal cutbacks to states became yet another excuse for state and local governments to reduce cash benefits to welfare recipients. The endlessly documented result was a dramatic retrenchment from economic justice and the concomitant surge in poverty (both depth and rate) and homelessness. What money states did get, they wanted to distribute equitably among the social welfare agencies—not to poor people.

During these years, I was there, a virtual double agent for poor people in every conceivable position that would allow an insider's peek at some aspect of the welfare state. After DWAC, I worked in a foundation, followed by a stint as a special assistant to the New York State commissioner of the Department of Social Services, the state apparatus that oversees the administration of welfare, medicaid, and so on, and service contracts that are parceled out to the nonprofits. Subsequent to that job, I set up a subsidiary of DWAC, called Social Agenda, which was motivated by a continued desire to advance the positions of people who experienced poverty in the public realm. I also spent time on a fellowship, which landed me in the middle of an enlightening experience with the New York State legislature. Before and after that I was a consultant for a number of social welfare agencies.

Chapter 5

City Silos and the Pop-Tart Connection

*What experience and history teach is—that people and
governments never have learned anything from history, or acted on
principles deduced from it.*   —G. W. F. Hegel

The rise of food banks and soup kitchens in the 1980s was part of the
nation's eroding commitment to provide an adequate income for all
families. This reintroduction of commodity distribution was a step backward from food stamps, which in themselves were a retreat from income
relief. The commodity programs first emerged during the Great Depression, when farm prices dropped so precipitously because of overproduction that farmers could get less for their produce than they'd paid for the
seed.[1] This had been happening for decades as farming methods produced abundance. But it wasn't until unemployment spread like wildfire
after the stock market crash of 1929 that the interests of farmers were put
together with those of people who had no money for food. Local
governments began purchasing commodities; shortly thereafter a national program came to be administered by the U.S. Department of
Agriculture.

By the late 1960s the program had a well-documented, horrendous, and sometimes hilarious track record. There were many and apparently insurmountable difficulties. For one, items distributed depended entirely on the vagaries of the market. If honey were overproduced, it would become a commodity. Many people who had no use for honey would get enormous containers of it, with virtually no hope of consuming all that sugar. Peanut butter came in huge quantities, too. It is nutritious but difficult to eat much of in the absence of accompaniments like bread.

The commodities program was erratic in every sense. Most poor people received nothing at all for varying reasons. If a family without transportation lived far from a distribution point, they couldn't pick up what little was available, and so on. The program was finally iced because it served too few of the truly needy, gave too little to those it reached, and offered unusable items to others.

Except for institutional purposes, such as milk to schools, food stamps replaced commodities during the Nixon administration, in 1974. But poor activists didn't want them—they wanted cash. Indeed, in the years preceding their introduction, the National Welfare Rights Organization (NWRO) campaigned against food stamps because of the inevitable stigma attached to them and the complications that would and did arise in their administration and daily usage. Increased cash assistance would have eliminated all that, and the need for yet another bureaucracy and more red tape.

The stamps had advantages over commodities, however. Families with food stamps had at least some choice in their acquisition of food. The stamps would also be more effectively distributed among poor families. In spite of the stigma attached to food stamps, the initial red tape they involved, and the minuscule quantity each family received, most people were not sorry to kiss the commodities program good-bye. Absent more income assistance, food stamps were better than nothing and better than government surplus. For the time being, wide-scale commodity distribution was essentially over.

Still, poor activists often continued to be at odds with food program advocates when it came to food stamps. The endemic conflict came to roost during one meeting in Washington toward the end of the Carter administration. By this time, increased cash assistance seemed light-years away. The participants were a larger than usual mix of welfare recipients combined with advocates and lawyers from the Food Research and Action Center (FRAC) and the incipient National Anti-Hunger Coalition. We were to be visited by two or three congressmen, each of whom supported a bill to cut our food stamps less than some other politician proposed, as if cuts were a fait accompli and now they were dickering over the price. FRAC advised us to be nice. I didn't see it their way. Why be honey-tongued with someone who was introducing a bill to cut food stamps—for the second time in the Carter administration—for most recipients?

I can't remember exactly what I said. I do remember the fallout. With a patronizing air, Jeff Kirsch from FRAC stepped in to apologize for my bad manners. Roxanne Jones, a former NWRO leader, (now a Pennsylvania state senator)—petite, black, and to the point—interrupted Kirsch—white and male. She set off a chain reaction of welfare mothers. Spewing acid. He should never, *never* have contradicted a welfare mother in front of an outsider like that. These guys were, after all, talking about *cutting* what little we already had, and the idiots running the show wanted us to thank them! I guess Kirsch figured he could get away with it because I was white. He never did fathom the common ground we welfare mothers shared. He wasn't the first. He wouldn't be the last.

We proposed organizing to stop the cuts. We asked for assistance from FRAC, which at the time was heavily funded by the government. A resounding no accompanied claims that they weren't allowed to organize or assist any groups engaged in political organizing. As it happens, agencies like FRAC and the Legal Services Corporation reached the pinnacle of their federal funding under Carter. Crossing the line on this and similar issues could have cost them some real bucks. Whether it was food stamps in this instance or welfare benefits in others, "our lobbyists" were funded by the same Congress that was proposing and cutting our benefits. Imagine the tobacco companies hiring the American Cancer Society to lobby for them. Once again it became eminently clear that without our own voice, we were at the mercy of a crazy arrangement.

We couldn't count on the FRACs to voice our interests. When the commodity distribution issue started to unfold, we knew right where all of them would be standing. Under whichever money tree was dropping coconuts. In the meantime, there was work to do.

On May 9, 1980, DWAC did its part by sitting in and liberating lunch from the cafeteria of New York's branch of the U.S. Department of Agriculture. Demonstrations of varying kinds were also held in Atlanta; Chicago; Springfield and Pittsfield, Massachusetts; Philadelphia; Baltimore; Baton Rouge; Phoenix; Great Falls, Montana; Wichita, Kansas. The lack of help from FRAC had not impeded our objective. Food stamps were temporarily in reprieve. There is no doubt that FRAC took the credit for "speaking out for the poor."

The Rise of a Tyranny of Kindness

It was in January of 1977 that Philip Toia, then commissioner of the New York State Department of Social Services, called for a return to the soup-line concept of welfare. He heralded it as the cheapest way of feeding the poor and claimed it would reduce public assistance expenditures. Soup lines were a throwback to the Great Depression, when people with neither food nor money stood in long lines to be fed from huge caldrons. Toia argued that part of the responsibility for human services being handled by government should be turned over to voluntary agencies. His speech was made at a meeting of the New York Public Welfare Association in a Syracuse, New York, hotel. It was an awesome charge.

The lack of outrage among the roomful of concerned charity types was deafening. Maybe they all had calculators in their heads telling them how implementation of this plan would position them for increased government contracts. Or maybe they worried about putting the contracts they already had at risk if they balked. It was probably some of both.

As the word spread, it would be hyperbole to say that opposition from the panoply of professional good guys was muted. Toia's statements dramatically marked the retreat from issues of social justice that was brewing even before the election of Ronald Reagan. Acceptance of the principle by social welfare gurus all but handed Reagan carte blanche on poverty issues.

The cuts that hurt poor people occurred at the same time that a liberal-conservative consensus was developing on the propriety of and need for more volunteerism and charitable acts. Without understanding the consequences or even imagining the hidden agendas at work, many liberals especially were ready at the starting gate. Soup kitchens and food pantries began popping up everywhere. Politicians loved it. Particularly the cost savings part, which was never uttered in public again. Television news producers were thrilled. Potential volunteers loved it, especially on Thanksgiving, when they, the politicians, and the journalists suddenly infested soup kitchens like maggots in garbage. It should be renamed I Love the Poor Day.

Trouble was, the entire food movement was based on a false set of assumptions. We tried to insert our views. It was senseless to treat the problem here the way it would be treated in countries where there simply was no food at all. In the United States food was and is in everyone's refrigerator (if they aren't poor, that is). It is in grocery stores everywhere. You cannot go out to dinner in any of thousands of restaurants and imagine that food scarcity has been in any way a problem here. Ours is not a nation without food but one of vast, embarrassing abundance. The issue of individual families' poverty could not be solved by returning them to the stone age of breadlines. Establishing institutionalized begging sites was never a solution. It wasn't food that was missing. Poor people lacked the normal means of access: money. Anything other than that would become a means of further separating the haves and the have-nots. Anything else would be a moral heist of poor people and a helluva waste of time and resources.

A mass movement of many kinds of people quietly but quickly emerged. If there was one thing they agreed on, it was the need to evolve a secondary or discard distribution market for poor people. The sheer diversity of interests that became entangled was mind-boggling. The only people who didn't cash in, the only ones absent from the debate in any public way, as ever, were poor. It was not for lack of trying. We were the tree falling, alone, in the forest.

The advocacy that produced the nightmare stemmed from two major strains—"food" advocates and environmentalists. The former were motivated initially, at least, by the naive and arrogant notion that they could somehow "feed the hungry" if they just pulled their acts together. The latter were aroused largely by a concern for the environment. To them, it was obvious that overproduction of all kinds of goods on a grand scale was environmentally unsound—at a minimum, depleting scarce landfill space. Both strains converged on the idea of getting leftovers to poor people. Some of the lay advocacy community lauded the dual principles of "sparing the environment" (by pawning off what would otherwise become garbage onto poor people) and "feeding the hungry." There were also those who saw dollar signs floating in this one—fat tax write-offs for the corporations, grants for the local programs, a ride to the moon for advocates of the sorry developments.

There were as many ideas on ways to help as there would come to be ways to fund them. Groups in the western part of the nation were charmed by the notion of "gleaning" and advocated a return to the ancient practice of allowing poor people to scavenge (glean) the fields for leftovers once the salable and edible crops had by and large been harvested. As one who had "gleaned" from grocery store garbage bins before locks were put on them, I knew where they were coming from. For that matter, when I lived upstate, I even gleaned from the better garbage *dumps*.

Nonetheless, I could see this was not a reasonable "solution" for the mounting millions living on the edge with fewer and fewer resources to fall back on. It couldn't, wouldn't, and ultimately didn't work for the huge majority of poor people, especially where there were no farms. There weren't even your usual grocery store throw-out bins in the poorest neighborhoods. The "corner grocery" sold the same old stuff till the smell roiled even the rats.

Middle- and upper-class people lobbied, raised foundation funds, sponsored walkathons and celebrity events, placed public service announcements on TV, and bought ads in such small-town papers as *The New York Times*. All this and more they did to help. Had half those resources been put to work for income security for a decade, by now there would be less poverty, even if the goal of guaranteed income were not yet in our grasp.

The nationwide banzai of the discard market exploded in the early 1980s into a demand that the government release food stored in silos around the country. These were products kept off the market to prop up farm prices. The advocates argued that it was wasteful to maintain these commodities with "hungry" people in every corner of the nation. Maybe so, but before the advent of food stamps in 1974, this method of distributing food had been standard for years. Soon the far greater shortcomings of the commodities program would once again become all too apparent.

Now that commodities were to be reintroduced on a grand scale, a new cast of characters emerged. Sweet young things, usually white, played right into the hands of behind-the-scenes power brokers. With the media almost lockstep beside them, they fought vigorously to "introduce" commodities to the "hungry." The advocates had little to no awareness of the historical underpinnings of the commodities programs, no real communication with the people they sought to "help," and usually no real idea what poor people would say if asked. In places like New York, where organized groups did exist, they were ignored.

By 1981 the hunger advocates were rewarded with the birth of TEFAP, originally the *Temporary* Emergency Food Assistance Program (changed in the 1990 farm bill to *The* Emergency Food Assistance Program). This program first became the bureaucratic conduit for big, orangey yellow, cheese-looking stuff transported to locations across the country. Often those who accepted it were ill prepared to distribute it. Sometimes whole loads would sit unrefrigerated in hot weather for days, just waiting for the local Community Action Program or church group to get their act together for the distribution. The stuff carried a cigarette-like label warning people with high blood pressure and heart disease of the dangerously high sodium content. African Americans are disproportionately represented in the ranks of the poor. It was well known and documented that they also have greater rates of high blood pressure and heart problems than whites. Getting a five-pound block of this stuff with worms in it was not unheard of. People would not notice until at least some of it had been consumed.

Needless to say, DWAC and RAM were not amused. At least not until the Cheesettes made their debut outside my window one tranquil January night in the early eighties. It was my birthday. Startled, I heard a megaphone. "Give me a *C,*" and a crowd shouted "C." "Give me an *H,*" and "H" responded. I went to the window, and there were staff and members of DWAC and RAM dressed in cardboard boxes painted orange with green letters, shouting and dancing. When the neighbors started complaining, the Cheesettes bumbled upstairs to my living room singing a medley beginning with "If it says surplus surplus surplus, on the label label label, you don't want it want it want it on your table table table." Gripped by a sort of tyranny of kindness, do-gooders all over the country were mobilizing to bring someone else's garbage to our tables. At first we joked about the scheming advocates. We referred to their efforts as the "Table Scraps Are a Right" (TSAR) campaign. We thought we were exaggerating. We were wrong.

Corporate Greed, the IRS, Desert Share, and the Garbage Barge

The discard market for products that couldn't be pawned off on the general public was shot from a cannon. It is now a highly organized system. At the top is Second Harvest (SH), a national cartel located in Chicago. It is a not-for-profit corporation controlled by some of the biggest consumer product manufacturers and distributors in the country, among which are Kellogg Company, the Stop & Shop Companies, McDonald's Corporation, Monsanto Agricultural Corporation, Procter & Gamble, and others. Second Harvest claims to distribute literally tons of food donated by corporations to approximately 200 food banks. These city silos supply the soup kitchens and food pantries that popped up all over the United States during the 1980s. These, in turn, developed their own institutional base. At the beginning of the decade, barely a handful existed. By the end of the decade, there were in excess of 40,000. They were among the true growth industries of the eighties. All people alive at the time and over the age of ten had to know about these developments to some degree or another, even if they didn't comprehend their significance.

Soup kitchens provide actual meals, usually cooked, nearly always to men and some single women, rarely to children and families. Funny, even in poverty and without "wives," homeless men would get (a) the most actual food and (b) cooked food—free of charge. For that matter, more of the "nutrition" *money* has been targeted to places serving single men (or the elderly) than to poor families. That's why, try as they might, TV journalists in whatever city always report increasing numbers of children coming into the soup kitchens while cameras pan a sea of mostly men. (They are searching out a kid to photograph on some holiday.

When and if they find one, the cameras pause.) It's called objective journalism.

Food pantries, by contrast, carry mostly uncooked items—given to families on the presumption that they have cooking facilities available. (Many don't have working appliances or have their utilities cut off. They are not asked about this.) Pantries far outnumber soup kitchens, as women and children weigh in heavily on the poverty statistics. As often as not, the smallest ones are operated by unpaid volunteers, frequently poor themselves. The pantries receive the least funding or product of the network. At each level of the discard market, the players calculate and pursue their interests, using economic and political power to achieve their ends. Poor people are the shills, otherwise irrelevant to the process and exempted from the real dividends.

Second Harvest also reaps the benefits only cold cash can deliver. Most corporations on the board give hefty cash donations to SH. These, plus government contracts, individual contributions, and other grants provide SH with about $14 million annually to operate.[2] The cash is used to pay for salaries, rent, computers, accountants. Second Harvest assists the corporations by taking products they cannot sell because they have reached their pull date; have been poorly packaged, short-weighted, or overproduced; or are market failures or otherwise damaged. Before the meteoric rise of SH, most of these items would have been dumped at the corporations' expense. Now the corporations get a tax break for much of what is actually garbage, while spreading transportation and environmental hazards to other places. It is most certainly in the interests of a variety of corporations to see that SH thrives.

This is how it works: Corporation X overproduces meat tenderizer and is unable to sell it to the supermarket chain that usually buys it. Before Second Harvest came along, X would have dumped it, because it was taking up space needed for new products. Now they give Second Harvest a call. An employee there checks the computer for a food bank (city silo) that will pay a nominal fee to SH for it; hopefully, this will be the bank closest to the source. They give the bank a call and tell them X has a truckload of meat tenderizer that needs to be picked up. This food banker is reluctant to take it, especially since he knows it will be hard to hawk to the food pantries and soup kitchens in his area. But he caves. He then sends truckers out to pick it up. He calls other banks on the East Coast in the hope that a few will take at least some of it off his hands. He manages to get rid of about half, trucking it out to the other banks.

The rest is unloaded and stored by the food bank and is listed on the inventory sent out to the Ks and Ps. The kitchens, which serve prepared meals (primarily to single men) can use a little, but not nearly enough to get all of it out of the warehouse. Although the pantries realize that people coming to them for food have no use for it, a few agree to take some. (The pantries distribute mostly dry goods to poor families.) It is bagged for distribution anyway. Of course, there is no meat in the bag.

Six months pass, and the banks have cases of meat tenderizer left over. Finally, they dump it. Up and down the East Coast, landfills are paid by the food bankers for the right to throw away Corporation X's garbage. In fact, a good deal of the "second harvest" is dumped by the banks off the top. This takes up valuable local landfill space and passes the direct cost on to the food bank. The entire financial burden is ultimately carried by taxpayers one way or another. The corporations win coming and going.

Second Harvest is not a warehouse of any kind. Second Harvest is a set of polished offices with computers that unite donated things with warehouses that will take them. Not infrequently, corporate donors toss SH items that are of no use even to the discard market. If Second Harvest or any of their subsidiary food banks cannot unload the items, the trucks holding them become like the infamous New York City garbage barge, moving along with unwanted cargo, normally known as garbage. A little muscle gets it unloaded bit by bit, "as a favor" to SH.

Second Harvest claims to have received the equivalent of $404 million in cash and kind donations in fiscal year 1991. If this is true, it makes this relative newcomer the third largest charity in the nation, ahead of even the American Red Cross. Second Harvest arrived at this total by valuing every pound of goods received at $2.10.[3] Of course, that's preposterous, but it sure leaves a lot of room for creative book-keeping for the nonprofit itself, and the corporations dodging taxes.

John H. Bryan, Jr., put it most succinctly in his 1986 keynote address to Second Harvest's annual conference. (Bryan is CEO of the Sara Lee Corporation and chairman [sic] of the Grocery Manufacturers of America, both of which have seats on the SH board.) According to the glossy, multicolored annual report,

> Mr. Bryan spoke of three long term benefits to corporate social involvement, the first and most obvious being tax incentives. Another is the need for a business to support a community from which it draws its work force. Third is a concern for corporate image. Said Bryan, "I am struck by how strongly Second Harvest satisfies these motives. I doubt that any charitable cause could better serve the motives of corporate giving."

Corporations are not the only donors of unused stuff. In a moment of misplaced generosity, the General Services Administration announced that $3.6 million worth of the surplus from Desert Storm would be turned into a Second Harvest bonanza. From the aptly named Operation Desert Share, at last poor people get a cut of the American pie, the bounty of military procurements. This time the military will do the shipping. Second Harvest's task is to match goods and banks and to sell themselves to the media and, by extension, to potential donors once again. The bucks won't stop there, however. Operation Desert Share is slated to provide up to $300 million worth of food to charities across the nation. To boot, many of the corporations benefited by selling the goods to the military in the first place.

How Nutritious Is a Can of Low-Cal Soda, Anyway?

Nutrition, in fact, appears to be irrelevant to this discard market in spite of slick literature that drips with charitable impulses. Donors are led to believe SH plays a major role in feeding the hungry nationwide through the gathering of donated food. Nutrition is assumed. But much of what gets distributed is not food at all. Like any big industry, the cartel has its secrets. Sometimes they can be ferreted out. Close inspection of their annual reports gives up a few. For instance, in small type, an apparently random list of items distributed appears under the heading Food Groups by Pounds.

In 1986, the largest single category on the list of donations to SH,

Food Group	Pounds
Beverages	8,215,185
Juices	7,261,358
Dough Products	9,885,681
Cereals & Grains	9,035,805
Dairy Products	4,195,748
Non-Dairy	301,761
Desserts	6,762,954
Fruits & Vegetables	14,650,606
Soups	1,286,852
Meals/Comp. Entrees	5,807,909
Snack Foods	16,395,103
Pastas	1,942,430
Misc. Food Items	6,434,796
Spices/Condiments	10,660,021
Meats/Fish/Poultry	695,235
Non-Food Items	17,103,163
Crackers & Cookies	7,928,820
TOTAL	128,563,427

printed near the bottom and labeled "Non-Food Items," consisted of 17,103,163 pounds. "Meats/Fish/Poultry" appeared at 695,235 pounds, directly above "Non-Food Items." A careless reader might confuse the two. But make no mistake, the ratio of nonfood items to meat/fish/poultry was almost 25 to 1. Fruits and vegetables combined also weighed in at less than "Non-food," 14,650,606 pounds. "Desserts," "Snack Foods," and "Crackers & Cookies" weighed a whopping combined total of 31,086,877 pounds, although they were divided into three categories, dispersed through the list. Snack foods alone (for some reason distinguished from crackers and cookies) was the second most plentiful bounty distributed by SH in 1986. "Spices/Condiments" outweighed three other categories combined: "Pastas," "Soups," and "Meals/Comp. Entrees." The list was organized by neither weight nor alphabet. It was certainly not organized by types of goods. If anything, it appears to have been organized to obscure the facts.

In 1989, SH employed slightly more sophisticated, though equally random, reporting methods. The year-end report used percentages instead of pounds as the measuring device. Nonfood items were broken into three separate categories, so the total didn't stick out. Combined, they were 9.9 percent, coming in only slightly above "beverages" at 9.1 percent. This time, "Snack Foods, Cookies" was the biggest category, at 13.8 percent, again distinguished from other junk foods. To be fair, cereals and grains were not far behind—13.7 percent. I suspect Cap'n Crunch, Cocoa Puffs, and other heavily sugared cereals counted for some measure of this category.

By the 1990 annual report, Second Harvest was back to measuring in pounds again. This time the largest single item was listed as "Cereals and Grains," at over 36 million pounds. But sweets, including sodas and snacks when combined, exceeded that sum. "Spices, Condiments, Sauces" outranked "Fruits and Vegetables" again, and "Personal, Health, Beauty Care" items weighed in above the discard market staple—pasta. Household products trounced protein foods.

Inventory tapes sent out monthly by the local food banks are even more revealing. For months on end (until shortly after it was published in newspapers), New York's city silo, Food for Survival (FFS), and others carried "microwave browning spray" purportedly supplied by the Second Harvest system. The Food for Survival inventory sheet read, "Buy one, get one free." Meat marinade appeared frequently also, but virtually no meat. Lo-cal sodas and seltzer scored big time. And assorted Gummy Bears candies appear to have been easier to come by than any foods rich in protein. The single most consistent actual put it in your mouth, chew, and get some benefit from it food is pasta. It is the only item on the Food for Survival list that usually appears with "Quantities Limited" beside it. I have never seen any form of pasta sauce on the lists. Unless meat marinade qualifies.

On June 11, 1991, a Food for Survival press release announced the donation of 500,000 jars of baby food by Beech-Nut Corporation. The release did not say the jars were past their pull date. The inventory sheets didn't mention it either. On August 21, 1991, the only meat or vegetables on the list were in the jars of baby food. Fruit could be found in the baby food, in the dessert section as frozen fruit bars, and in the snack section as "Fun Fruit Snack." Some produce, however, wouldn't show up on the inventory lists because it can be donated and must be moved on a daily basis from major markets with leftovers. Food for Survival also gets huge grants to handle government surplus. The quality and consistency of food the government purchases are often far superior to that proffered by Second Harvest. Even so, the options are limited. Dry milk, applesauce, green beans, apple juice, and pinto beans were the only state surplus on the inventory list for August 21, 1991.

One former employee said approximately 60 percent of what Food for Survival gets from Second Harvest is dumped. Bill Bolling, director of a food bank in Atlanta, says 40 to 50 percent of SH product is dumped. There is some internal logic for accepting it, according to Bolling. Often a corporation, directly or through Second Harvest, will offer a bank large quantities of assorted goods at a time, which the bank will take knowing they will have to dispose of some amount of the delivery. Bolling says the rest is usable, and, if he turned down the lot, the food bank might end up with nothing at all.

Recently, on a radio call-in talk show in St. Louis, I said that the numero-uno ingredient distributed by food banks was sugar and that meat or protein foods were all but nonexistent. A board member from the St. Louis Area Food Bank called, in defense of the donations given by the corporations to food banks like hers. "If a butcher makes a mistake cutting a piece of meat, he can always turn it into some other sellable thing, like hamburger. But if you short-weight a box of Cocoa Puffs, there's nothing to be done except throw it away or give it to the poor." I asked whether her primary motivation was feeding poor people or protecting the environment. For a moment she hedged, then acknowledged that, as an environmentalist, her first concern was getting rid of garbage. By passing it on to poor people?

On a similar show in Cincinnati, a woman who said she had taken a needy friend with five children to a pantry called to say she was shocked to find cottage cheese in the bag three weeks past date. The bread was moldy throughout. There wasn't enough to feed the entire family any real meal, but they were, she said, "grateful for what we got."

The city silos even developed their own language. Take food. True, mothers complained, what good is a box of spaghetti with nothing to put on it? Or cereal but no milk? Pop-Tarts were commonly derided. How about Hamburger Helper but no hamburger? And odd little items like mint jelly that nobody liked. When the Reagan administration announced ketchup would be counted in the school lunch program as a vegetable, myriad discard market proponents wildly (and appropriately) trashed the idea. Every television station, newspaper, every medium outside of Mars seemed indignant. Maybe they think mint jelly is a fruit. Protein is as rare at a food bank as pig's snout is at Le Cirque. Actually, the discard market almost universally warehouses many items of dubious nutritional value like microwave browning spray, MSG, and hair conditioner. With the dirty secret slipping out, insiders have taken to calling inventory "product." The word *food* is spoken only to outsiders, like donors. I've yet to see the invitation to give money to a food bank leave out the word *food,* substituting "product" in its stead.

One might ask why those who produce the garbage are not required to stop producing it. Or one might suggest that short-weighted boxes of Cocoa Puffs be sold at a lower price to those who want them—in grocery stores. Or one might ask how a tax deduction can be taken on something that can't be sold. If it can't be sold, it has no value. (At least that's what they tell us when we demand that women's labor be counted in the gross national product.) The American taxpayer is footing the bill through tax deductions for these mistakes now slithered into a sophisticated IRS dodge courtesy of places such as Second Harvest.

Turning a Head of Lettuce into an Ounce of Gold

You can give a mother 50 cents to go and buy a head of lettuce (on sale). Or you can send a head of lettuce through this crazy system and keep increasing the original price as it moves both literally and figuratively through layer after layer of do-gooders. Forget the human cost, the obligation to eat or obtain food for your children at institutionalized begging sites.

Hypothetically, a store decides the lettuce is too wilted to sell. Instead of throwing it away, it "donates" the head to a food bank. The store gets a tax deduction (tax expenditure) on a formerly valueless product. The food bank, which "handles" the product, has salaried staff, trucks, and equipment, paid for either by government grants or by donations from some other source, on which that source gets a deduction.

Let's say the lettuce was "valued" at $0.50 for tax purposes. According to a food banker in Rochester, produce costs him approximately $0.40 a pound to "handle." Now the head costs $0.90, without factoring in the tax expenditures the very existence of the bank creates. He, in turn, sells that head of lettuce (which happens to weigh exactly one pound) for $0.12 to a food pantry—we're up to $1.02. They, too, add an operational cost. We could be up to $1.42 now. The layers of government bureaucrats who are paid to oversee the myriad programs operating this way add yet more. This head is beginning to cost perhaps triple the original store price, but since it was deemed unsalable in the first place, just how much *is* it worth?

If, by the time it reaches the pantry, it is determined to be unsafe for consumption, it is dumped. The garbage must be hauled and a fee paid to the refuse removers and the owners of the landfill. This, too, is on the government tab, both for the carting cost and because the pantry's tax exemption takes a cut off the dumping bill, which may not have sales or service tax. The denizens of this discard market proudly proclaim that hundreds of millions of pounds of product move around the country via this route. One thing is certain, a poor mother shops just like anyone else (or more frugally) when she gets a chance. No head of lettuce would go home in her bag if it cost three times the price she could get it for just next door.

It gets even crazier. Sometimes a donor will pass product through the Second Harvest network, even though it could be (and once would have been) donated locally. Second Harvest pressures donors to deal directly *and only* with them. Second Harvest "locates" the food bank closest to the source. The bank pays Second Harvest. Then local pantries and kitchens who want the product, must pay the bank for it, when in the past they might have gotten it for free.

Thanks to the "user friendly" Second Harvest system, formerly free "product" now has value added at every level as it takes a journey, albeit mostly by computer, halfway around the nation only to return home. And every ticking minute of every worker's time and share of overhead costs from the moment SH gets that call is charged to all of us. The real beneficiary is the system itself, and the tens of thousands of people who have become employed through this secondary market—each with a stake in its preservation. Especially the upper echelons. Food for Survival's executive director, for instance, is paid over $60,000 annually, not counting health benefits, pension, and other perks of being an executive. Not bad for the starvation industrialists. At any given point in time, there are thirty-five to forty people on the staff of this single food bank.

Expanding the Donor Base

Second Harvest entices new companies to donate with Madison Avenue–style publications detailing the advantages that will accrue to them. One of these is a glossy, multilayer portfolio within a portfolio called "The Benefits of Donating." The middle has the usual well-crafted hype, advising companies of the value of giving unsalable merchandise to SH to feed the hungry. "Donors contribute product to Second Harvest for a variety of reasons, such as labelling errors, product formulation errors, warehouse damage, overruns, and products that are discontinued or approaching code dates." In other words, *Second Harvest attempts to acquire solely those goods that would otherwise be dumped.*

In donor profiles, SH proudly records one company's history with them:

Kroger is a growing, high-profile national retail supermarket chain with nearly 1000 stores in major metropolitan areas in seventeen states. . . .

Commitment: Kroger accepts a position on the Second Harvest board of directors in 1982. By 1983, Kroger implements a "Donate, Don't Dump" company-wide policy concerning surplus product by its stores. . . .

. . . Late in 1985, Kroger Company uses its resources as an experienced marketer to raise the public's awareness of hunger and foodbanking. . . . The program garners extensive national and local attention through advertising, public service announcements and

in-store promotional materials. In June of 1986, the promotion earns
Kroger an award from the prestigious President's Citation Program
for Private Sector Initiatives.[4]

Is it mere coincidence that tax-deducted corporate donations virtually
quadrupled from 1975 to 1985?[5] An IRS-driven garbage market is one
sick way for hardened capitalists to distribute essential goods, but that's
just what we have. And neither the IRS nor any other government
agency keeps any real track of these transactions in the aggregate.

In the back pocket of the glossy is a sheet labeled "Tax Benefits."
Second Harvest through all previous pages has invited corporations to
donate those items they would have had to pay to dump. Now they tell
them the bonus: at a minimum, the garbage turns into platinum as
"donors" are allowed to double the cost of producing it for reporting to
the IRS. Even this come-on was sweetened by the Tax Reform Act of
1986, increasing the potential deductible yet again, primarily by changing some very modest paperwork connected to inventory costing rules.
And that's if they play it fair and square. Overestimating the quantity and
quality of the donations is endemic. Since Second Harvest is valuing the
dubious donations at $2.10 a pound, the corporations could be doing it,
too.

Procter & Gamble knows a good thing when they see it. Their
designated spokesperson, James Berger, listed the benefits as "savings in
transportation expense" (the food banks have to pick donations up
wherever they are, at the company's convenience), "disposal savings,"
and "of course the tax benefits." Procter & Gamble's way of computing
the deduction hinges on the fair market value, or what the product *could*
be sold for. Though some food bankers readily admit to dumping large
amounts of Second Harvest product when they first receive it, there is
a technical catch. If the company admits they are donating totally unmar-
ketable products to SH, they have to dance around this fair market value
issue, in the unlikely event that the IRS ever stops to take a look at this
system.

Procter & Gamble does the donating business with Second Harvest
alone. Both institutions are nationwide, which makes it easy for P & G
to get pickups wherever the excess product is. Second Harvest is clearly
discreet; P & G is also confident that Second Harvest will be careful to

keep seriously damaged goods from going out to people. Why would that matter, unless Procter & Gamble is not so careful about what they donate? Incidentally, Berger works with Frank Smith, vice president of P & G's *Chemicals Division* and a board member of Second Harvest.

Berger said that among other donations are samples used in market and research testing that are left over when the project is done. Surely these items were never intended for sale to anyone at any time. Sounds like potential garbage to me (and potentially dangerous), but it can't be called that or it wouldn't have a fair market value and couldn't be written off as a tax deduction. Second Harvest rarely turns down any of P & G's potential donations. According to Berger, 95 percent of the time they can be convinced to take whatever it is.

Procter & Gamble needn't worry, though. The IRS doesn't audit to determine if the donations are in fact food and in fact edible, or at least usable. All SH products are logged in as donated goods. Second, lists of inventory show many nonfood items, useless items, and overproduced items from banks accepting SH product. Third, Don Roberts of the Public Affairs Division of the IRS says that unless a corporation claims a deduction for individual items valued at over $5,000 each ("like a painting"), the IRS would never audit its charitable deductions. In the discard market, none of the individual donations is worth more than $5,000. (Except for cash donations given for things other than food, like the $50,000 Second Harvest gets annually from Procter & Gamble.) All are for cans of this and cases of that, or even pallets of something that might be totally infested upon receipt, which prompted the donation in the first place.

Procter & Gamble doesn't have to worry about damaged goods hurting someone either. That's been covered by the "Good Samaritan Laws" passed in the early 1980s by every state and Washington, DC. These are safeguards against lawsuits in the event that a donor's product injures someone. A publication by Share Our Strength says, "Second Harvest is currently working on developing a national Good Samaritan Law that could serve as a model for improving state laws." Just in case.

Berger smartly addressed the issue of nonfood items by naming the ones that many mothers would welcome, like baby diapers (Pampers and Luvs), toilet tissue, Tide, and Cheer. He argued that if mothers get items like these free, they can then spend their other money on food. (What other money?) I have never seen any of these choice articles on a food bank inventory list, but it's certainly possible somebody somewhere gets some. As for no-cal soda and the like, Second Harvest can't always get what they want; after all, companies only donate what *they* choose, according to Berger. In other words, things they don't need, won't sell, and don't want to pay to throw away.

Pilferage

One issue that does concern Berger apparently also concerns some of the other donors—goods that come back into the primary market. When Second Harvest distributed a questionnaire to a conference sponsored by the Grocery Manufacturers of America, attenders were asked to rate Second Harvest services. Fifty-eight responses were returned. Second Harvest was rated 100 percent on courtesy and cooperation and another 100 percent on "assistance with product recall." At the bottom of this list was "product re-entry prevention capabilities." Second Harvest scored only 84 percent on that. They dropped from A+ in genuflecting to B in keeping the stuff from being resold elsewhere.[6]

Given that conference goers tend to be soft on their charitable interests, assume that the 84 percent positive rating represents a conservative estimate of the suspected filching—16 percent. If so, of the 476.40 million pounds of "food" SH takes credit for having distributed in 1990, more than 76.22 million pounds may have been diverted into the black market.

Institutionalizing an expensive distribution apparatus certainly does not prevent pilferage. Some paid workers at the sites skim the cream, as it were, for themselves. Workers virtually everywhere take something home, even if only a sample of this or that, but this or that was not intended for them. True, many aren't paid much and some at the level of direct service not at all, but many didn't need either the money or the free products. At one New York City Council hearing, it was reported that donated food was surfacing in restaurants. Toilet paper has been sold by the case on the crowded streets of Chinatown. In Chicago it was reported to have landed in grocery stores, too. In Cincinnati one felon claimed to be running a food program for former prisoners. Each week he ordered cases of various goods, promptly picked them up at the food bank, then sold them at a flea market. This is true even in the for-profit world, where almost any warehouse worker could tell you stories if so inclined. This system must be awfully tempting for the corporations, the bankers who sign off, even the handlers who might wink.

Fooling about Feeding the Poor

At the top, everybody's winking in some way. After all, Second Harvest claims an incredible, downright ludicrous, cost-benefit ratio. "Approximately $162 worth of food was distributed for every dollar expended." Not likely. Much of it isn't food, much of it ends up in the dumps, much of it is stolen, the weighing is often rigged, and the valuation excesses and tax deductions are not taken into account in this figure. Second Harvest also claims to have distributed "476.4 million pounds of food to 42,000 agencies across America" in 1990. (This poundage includes donations directly received by local banks, which is more than half the total.) It also includes the other "product"—the nonfood items and lo-cal soda—by weight. And stuff that gets dumped. Also, SH food banks distribute goods to nonprofits that serve not poor people, but a more middle-class population. Even taking them at their word, *still* they would only be donating 15.8 pounds of product for every poor person in the country, annually. Who would that keep alive? So any realistic evaluation of the importance of this cartel would have to leave some big question marks, especially since it costs billions to run all of the programs spawned by the system. (It would take years and a census squad to compute the actual total with any certitude, if it ever could be done.)

Besides the handful of adults—mostly men—who frequent soup kitchens, the number of so-called meals available through this private system is so restricted, there is barely a soul alive because of them. As Christina Walker, a longtime food distribution activist in New York, says, "They could close them all down tomorrow and no one would starve. They [the garbage advocates] have learned how to tell the big lie, and they do it all the time to raise funds." Because some of what is distributed is in all likelihood poisonous, the opposite is likely.

Managing the Managers

After the cheese stuff was done and the butter ran out, there wasn't much left in the rural silos. In the meantime, one by one, city silos—food banks—were becoming established. With walk-in refrigerators and freezers, sophisticated offices, and sprawling space for dry goods, these massive warehouses receive donated goods to be dispensed (for a modest price) to the direct givers—the soup kitchens and food pantries. There are over 200 city silos spread around the country. New York State alone boasts 7. The city silos are not volunteer operations either. The budget for just one can run into the millions, annually. Again the budgets are generally *not* to *buy food*.

In fact, Second Harvest discourages food buying among its member banks. (Not all food banks are part of the SH system.) They argue that buying food puts the network in competition with itself. So, except for the fees paid to Second Harvest, food purchasing is verboten. The money pays for employees—executives, secretaries, comptrollers, bookkeepers, laborers, truckers and trucks to move the items, whopping rents, refrigerators, freezers, everything to institutionalize a crisis mode. Even public relations specialists and fund-raisers are hired by the banks. Glossy pamphlets to aid and abet the projects do not come free. The same advocates who wailed about the costs of storing commodities in real silos didn't so much as splutter over these expenditures. For most, they had become *their* bread and butter.

One of the country's most "successful" food banks is New York City's Food for Survival. The local sites to which they are supposed to deliver complain that deliveries often take place on days when they aren't open. With a budget of over $3 million dollars, this fully computerized operation replete with beepers for drivers ought at least to be able to coordinate their deliveries. Food for Survival's biggest success has been in raising money—mostly through government contracts—not in providing services.

As far as management goes, the story internally nicknamed Turkeygate tells it all. In the 1991 holiday season, a sort of share the wealth scheme was dreamed up by Food for Survival's director, Lucy Cabrera. Because

FFS almost always has hundreds of thousands of dollars more than they need to operate, they would purchase thousands of turkeys and distribute them free to the Ks and Ps in a display of largess. According to former employees, some of the turkeys were bought *wholesale* at $0.89 a pound. Virtually every retail grocer in the country was selling them for less. Inexplicably, FFS also acquired some smoked turkeys, for $1.19 a pound.

It gets worse. Some of the turkeys were refrigerated, with the intention of distributing them first. Others, to be given out later, were stored in a huge walk-in freezer. Apparently, workers began distributing frozen turkeys while fresh ones were left to sit in the refrigerator. By the time the costly blunder was discovered, the frozen turkeys were gone and the refrigerated ones were spoiled or near spoiled. Those that could not be pawned off fast on local operations that had the wherewithal to pick them up themselves were dumped. No public announcement was made about Turkeygate.

New York City government's bone "to the poor" is lovingly referred to as EFAP—Emergency Food Assistance Program. This program began with a $450,000 appropriation in fiscal year 1984. In 1991 the city budgeted $1,980,000 for wholesale food that was stored and distributed by Food for Survival to the Ks and Ps exactly three times a year. You might think that since virtually all the sites designated for the three EFAP deliveries are already sites for other programs, which FFS also handles, it wouldn't cost much to tag on the EFAP product. Nonetheless, nearly $900,000 went from EFAP to FFS for administration, or what the city prefers to call operational costs. For every two dollars' worth of additional food FFS distributes to sites already in their computers and on their routes, the city is charged one dollar more for the service. At each level of the discard market, the players calculate and pursue their interests, using economic and political power to achieve their ends. Poor people are the shills, otherwise irrelevant to the process and exempted from the real dividends.

Local Food Barons Managing the Poor

At first, getting the cheese was easy (by red tape standards). Previously, a family merely had to show up. Once diversification and salaries came into the game, the pantries (followed in short order by the soup kitchens) started imposing restrictive practices, which they could be ruthless about. In government terms, for all practical intents and purposes they have been totally unregulated, concerning what they give out, who gets it, and how. So, from what authority did their rules flow? Themselves.

Many of these places act more like the welfare department than the welfare itself. Screening. Forms to be filled out. Lists of undesirables who are not to be helped are kept by some and passed around. Severe restrictions were put on how often people could come to the pantries (most frequently reported: three times a year), no matter how bare their cupboards. Referrals are often required. Some soup kitchens insist on authorized ID cards. The big ones give out numbers to people as they line up, allowing only a few in at a time. Rain, wind, snow, or sleet does not change the regimen—the rest wait outside. Most kitchens open for only one meal a day, and rarely more than five days a week. Many open for one meal one day a week. Some pantries open no more often than a few times a year, when government stock arrives.

I was almost as naive about these operations as anyone. For quite some time I actually believed that what was being stored and distributed was a massive quantity of wholesome, real food. The question I asked then was Why not just let poor people go in and take what they need? The flip answer was always that someone would hoard and someone would sell the stuff; stealing would be rampant. Poor folks just can't be trusted—not like someone with a salary well above the median. When did "honesty" become a class trait?

Repeatedly poor mothers would say, Just give me the money and I'll feed my own kids. For many, transportation expenses to a site cost more than the value of the food itself. In other cases, the "food" was inedible anyway. One common reaction to the notion of giving mothers the money directly has always been "If you give them the money, how will you know they will spend it on food?" In light of the monstrous developments in this discard market, I'd have to ask that question of them. For that matter, if you give the *hunger activists* the money, how do you know *they* won't spend it on their Christmas parties replete with booze? (I've been invited to many paid for by taxpayers over the years. Almost all nonprofits have a direct or indirect entertainment budget.

146

Poor, or rather "hungry" people, as the industry likes to call them, are not invited.)

Instead, poor people get shafted on the taxpayers' dime. The discard market acts as if the tightrope they dangled *product* on were really a lifeline. By its own inflated accounting, however, in New York the actual meals served per poor person barely tallies one every two months. The meal count can include hair conditioner, deodorant, and Snickers tacked on to lesser quantities of pasta, as everything is counted in pounds or dollars' worth. Then it's divided by some magic number to produce numbers of "meals." Hell, they're using a noose, squeezing resources that could have helped more directly, more humanely, simply, and usefully.

Some Power Dynamics

Like greedy, grabbing customers at a huge closeout sale, the advocates and distributors fight among themselves and with anyone perceived to stand in their way. They start out by jointly pursuing a new funding program. When it comes, they fight over shares. In New York City, as in some other big cities, there is a coalition linking the service providers with the advocacy operations. Self-interest overshadows concern for poor people. Like others in the industry, they perform the requisite rituals for ending "hunger," then move on to the stuff that counts—like getting a bigger cut of the food money for refrigerators or salaries, quicker reimbursement on government contracts, less paperwork. Even when they attempt to confront the contradictions, sooner or later they get back to basics, like the efficacy rather than the ethics of using slave labor from the welfare department's forced-work population. ("If we all had enough funding, none of us would have to use workfare labor anymore.")

The misnomer for our coalition is the New York City Coalition Against Hunger. Meal counts are a big issue here. The coalition asks the soup kitchens and pantries to tally the number of meals served. The higher the number, the bigger the claim they can make on the public purse. The coalition knows it doesn't get an accurate tally, but a self-designed magic formula to factor in underreporting (but not overreporting) allows them to claim ever-increasing numbers of meals served. The coalition boasts some 600 member organizations.

The powerhouse behind the discard market in New York is Kathy Goldman, a purported red diaper baby gone totalitarian. She runs an advocacy operation called the Community Food Resource Exchange (CFRE), which gave birth to many of the other city institutions involved in the same game. Though Goldman probably operates out of misguided good intentions, the consequences of her success (and that of others like her around the country) have been largely devastating to those living in poverty.

One of her pet projects before the creation of CFRE was the much derided summer feeding program. It was one of the programs that got the biggest laughs at welfare rights–type meetings. Women did not want to trot their children halfway across town for lunch when they could have fed them at home. From the early years on, it was riddled with scandal, money going thither and yon, food rotting in the noonday sun. Goldman was first introduced to me as the champion of the summer feeding program. She was supposed to be an ally, but from the start I knew anyone who could have thought up that boondoggle without showing a hint of remorse or at least embarrassment would be trouble. I had no idea how much. The Community Food Resource Exchange wasn't even born yet. In years to come, DWAC would attempt to "educate" her, but she put up a powerful resistance.

One thing Goldman surely had little time or patience for was talking to and understanding the people to whom she seemed to have dedicated her life. I would hazard a guess that to this day she has no idea how ridiculous the summer feeding program is, how few of the poor it actually feeds, how much of the money allocated for it has been let's say diverted. (In May of 1991, the General Accounting Office issued a report examining the summer feeding program. It begins, "Most private sponsors, for example, churches and C.A.P.s were excluded from the program in 1981 in part because of mismanagement. In 1989 they were again given contracts." The report continues, "The 10 private sponsors we visited all made errors. . . . One common observation was low participation and overrepresentation of meals served vs. recipients visible."[7] *Mismanagement* is a word the government uses a lot to mask out-and-out fraud they cannot or do not want to prove.)

The contracts to distribute the food have always had considerable political and, of course, if "administered appropriately," financial value. Throughout her career Goldman has glossed over the self-aggrandizing power dynamics of "feeding the hungry." Her continued work was so familiar that Mayor Koch nominated her for a national "antihunger" award given annually by the Pillsbury Company (a sometime board member of Second Harvest). She won.

Some advocates and distributors set out to destroy competing operations in the funding sweepstakes. Among them, as the self-anointed monarch of the feeding programs in New York, Goldman would abide no competitors. When the Coalition for the Homeless, for instance, acquired a large grant to operate a similar program out of Albany without her imprimatur, she lost no time gathering forces to oppose it. It went out of business shortly. Fortunately, it was worthless *and* essentially harmless. Its demise was irrelevant—at least to poor people. When something worked to her advantage, though, she could go the opposite way. During New York's Hands Across America debacle, she coalesced with a vengeance with virtually every element of her ilk to steer the money away from a poor people's agenda and into the hunger crowds' coffers.

Others cultivate key legislators and powerful bureaucrats as adroitly as lobbyists anywhere. In Albany, New York, one of the most creative is Russell Sykes (formerly of FRAC, where he earned his "pin" stripes). He leveraged a sole source contract from the state Health Department for a toothless operation called the Nutrition Consortium. In turn, the consortium would dribble out bits of a half-million-dollar grant to smaller groups around the state willing to be kept in Sykes's political orbit. It was supposed to be an "outreach" program. It pushed paper back and forth. The post office scored big on that one. As for the "hungry," the deal was neither tasty nor nutritious.

Sykes did not attempt to conceal his desire to wipe out the Hunger Action Network of New York State (HANNYS), a shoestring operation with aspirations slightly more energetic in defense of poor people's interests. As a consequence of HANNYS's objective attempt to organize poor people into their work, they became more aligned with poverty issues over the years. This posed a threat to both Sykes and Goldman, who sullied themselves throwing mud at HANNYS. In one sense, HANNYS is the statewide version of the New York City Coalition Against Hunger, as both are stellar examples of groups where good intentions coupled with serious ignorance had run amuck. The Nutrition Consortium appears to be particularly impotent. Sykes's control was so tight that even when he moved from one organization to another, the consortium moved with him. These conglomerates have paid staff. Only one distributes any food.

Christina Walker, former director of the Food and Hunger Hotline who also sat on the board of Food for Survival, put it this way:

> Just in the four and a half years that I was at the Food and Hunger Hotline [she resigned in 1990], I could see it happen at a very accelerated pace, what must have been under way even before, which was this very serious institutionalization [of the discard market]. It had gone beyond the institutionalization stage, it was at the stage where defenses were being built; the moats were going up and being filled. And people were going to fight tooth and nail.
>
> The first two years I was there I ran around saying things like we can't institutionalize, or in ten years there'll be a disaster, we have to examine our own participation. . . . Two years later I just shut up. The battle was over before I even got there.

An Example of the Government Funding Process

As I moved on to work at the State Department of Social Services in 1983, the monster kept up with me. One of my first assignments of significance was to participate in the distribution of several million dollars for food for the poor, which was to be pumped out through the Federal Emergency Management Agency (FEMA, pronounced "feema"). It was supposed to be a quick-turnaround, one-shot deal authorized by Congress and the president. We were on a hot deadline to get it out to the groups who would use it to help the broadest diversity of poor people, the largest numbers, and, as I tried to impose, with the best record of helping swiftly and with dignity. Nancy Travers headed the newly created Homeless Housing Assistance Program (HHAP), which was thrown the FEMA bone to divvy up as its first assignment. I was on loan because only one other professional was in place in her department. It was unclear to me how Travers landed the HHAP job. One thing shortly became absolutely evident. It was not because of her expertise in matters pertaining to poor and homeless people.

The task was monumental given the deadline and certain federal rules. For one, we had to send out a request for proposals (RFP) to groups that might be interested in receiving money to do the job. So an RFP had to be created where none had existed, replete with instructions, guidelines, application forms. A notice of the RFP had to be widely published in newspapers. The proposal deadlines meant the nonprofits would have to work quickly; summer and vacations loomed not far off. Groups called in to complain that the deadline was too close. We could do nothing about that. They called and wrote to say they didn't like the restrictions on the money. This money originally could not be used for equipment such as refrigerators, stoves, and trucks. No salaries could be covered by it either. The money was to trickle down without institutionalizing another bureaucracy to handle it. It was as if somebody in the Reagan administration had come up with the perfect foil for the braggadocio "homeless" and "hunger" volunteers, knowing sooner or later the organizations would balk if funds were released to "feed the poor" without a cut for themselves.

Almost the second the RFP was on the table, the lobbying began. Unofficially, that is. The phones rang constantly. Travers took calls from selected heavies, such as congresspersons. Otherwise, she spent a good deal of her time working with a county-by-county map of the state. For New York City, where two thirds of the poverty population lived, there were lists, neighborhood by neighborhood, including some where virtually no poor people lived. The lists were sort of a who's who in the charity business. That is, those already interfacing with government. (Other than those like DWAC, that is.)

On the deadline date, floods of papers cascaded into our offices. Travers had assigned me the task of drafting an evaluation form. By now, I already had an attitude about the discard market. I could almost care. On May 31, 1983, I sent her the following memo:

Given the speed with which these proposals will have to be evaluated, I'm inclined to suggest the Atlantic City model for our evaluations. To wit: assign each a number and color, give the roulette wheel a few spins and award the first fifty winners some money. However we decide to do it, effective dispersal will require more luck than perseverance on our part.

It ended,

Another function of the time factor as I see it is that only successful paper pushers will have much opportunity to access these funds. Less sophisticated community groups which are often as able (and more sensitive to their neighbors) to distribute necessities will have limited ability to control any of this emergency money etc.

Ms. Travers did not appreciate the humor. Then again, I didn't know how close I was. First we triaged much of the junk. All actual poor people requesting funds were automatically denied. They were advised, usually by me, what they could do, where they could go for help while decisions were made for this trickle-down money to make its way to them. Could the money have landed, *by design,* in the pockets of poor people? Of course. In the end, almost none of it did. Some of the junk found its way back into the piles of fundables, no doubt for political reasons.

Turns out nobody does much for nothing. Almost all those good things churches and charities brag about are paid for by government, usually on a per capita basis. One proposal from a large New York City agency was almost entirely blank, with only a note explaining they were busy but requested funds and said they would do the right thing with the money. When the final decisions were in, even the phantom application was there on the list with a fat contract. No small, community organization could ever have been so brazen and succeeded. More often than not, though, it is the small local groups that are most sensitive to the community, overworked, and, by God, underpaid. (The usual suspects—Catholic Charities, the Sal[i]vation Army, the United Way, and others in various parts of the state—all got a cut of the loot.)

Such and such a county had to get X amount of money even

though they didn't have any respectable service agency except the welfare department itself to distribute the food. I tried explaining the futility of that to Travers. The departments would save money for all other items of need—i.e., clothing and utilities—while using the FEMA funds as a dodge from processing welfare applications. Local governments had an additional incentive to use the FEMA funds this way as these were 100 percent federal dollars, unlike AFDC dollars, which in New York are 25 percent local, 25 percent state, and only 50 percent federal.

Sure enough, that's exactly what happened, and worse. Not long after the FEMA funds started flowing into every county on a regular basis, welfare offices all over the place began denying applicants' benefits until they had "exhausted all available resources." This meant the pantries and kitchens, too. So welfare eligibility determinations were directly affected for countless individuals and families in desperate need. Some of these, without money to pay rent, ended up homeless.

Organizations on the receiving end obtained obvious benefits— especially as the funds grew and changed to their advantage. The "giving" side was a power-building apparatus for the administration, the state agency collectively, and Nancy Travers personally.

That was round one. The feds were inclined to believe that states' reporting had been shoddy, that they could not account satisfactorily for funds they distributed. So the following year, the job (which had in part been done by the charities even before) was turned wholly over to an "Interagency Council on the Homeless," with FEMA chairing and entities such as the United Way, Catholic Charities, and "reputable" others pulling the strings both in Washington and at state or local levels. One self-propelling bureaucracy produced another. Having been privy to at least some of the reporting done by local operations to New York City's interagency council, I can tell you that the idea that the problem of misreporting has been solved is downright laughable.

The "one-shot" FEMA deal begun in 1983, like the 1981 Temporary Emergency Food Assistance Program, continues to this day. The FEMA-guided budget went from zero dollars in 1982 to $134 million for 1993, $50 million of which is now for "administration" to states and localities. No, Virginia, there isn't a free lunch.

In New York State, SNAP (State Nutrition Assistance Program) grants flowed from Albany in November of 1984. Thanksgiving was coming, and the governor thought he would look good by loosening the purse strings on soup kitchens. A million and a half dollars quickly followed. The 1990–91 budget for SNAP was $10.8 million—over seven times the original budget. It also split into categories for various populations and purposes, each with different overseers. In the beginning, nearly all the money was designated for the purchase of food. Like a precision drill team, relevant groups in the state advocated first to establish the program, then to expand it, then to split the money into smaller food shares and larger administrative shares, or "operational costs." In the last state budget, Kathy Goldman's Community Food Resource Exchange was granted $410,000 from this pot; only about half was designated for food.

The Horizontal Spread of the Discard Market

Another distinct prototype soon to be mimicked in city after city started in 1982. The first so-called prepared and perishable food program (PPFP) called itself *City* Harvest (no kidding). Hunger was in, poverty out. Waste disposal was as hot an issue in New York as elsewhere. This gem of an idea would bring leftover food from restaurants and Wall Street luncheons to underfed people on the streets. Because it was prepared and perishable, it had to be moved in a New York minute. That was the theory at least. City Harvest would pick up the excess food from some of the finest restaurants in the city and distribute it primarily to operating soup kitchens. For reasons unknown, the concept hit New York like lightning. Between the news coverage, the page 6 gossip following glitzy fund-raising events, and the general scuttlebutt among nearly everybody in social welfare, it was hot, hot, hot. Corporate donors, foundations, and individuals tripped over one another to give City Harvest money. It was truly the TSAR (Table Scraps Are a Right) campaign come to life.

City Harvest's founder, Helen Palit, is the self-proclaimed originator of the concept, which has spread to at least eighty cities and counting. The hype is dynamite. Around Thanksgiving, full-page ads aiming at dollars start appearing in *The New York Times*. Each of these costs thousands of dollars, as *The Times* ad department claims to charge City Harvest like any other advertiser. (The ads do not show up as fund-raising expenses in City Harvest financial accounts to either government sources or any others. Loopholes in reporting laws allow them to count anything that has the least bit of educational value as program expenses. Even those letters you get in the mail asking for your dough during the holiday season can usually be written off as program and not fund-raising expenses. That way, when you're trying to figure out how much money an organization spends getting money as opposed to doing the good works it claims to do, you can't tell.)

Television ads have now been added to the mix. The ads cleverly lure potential donors into thinking City Harvest, too, plays a major role not only in "feeding the hungry and homeless" but also in stemming the onslaught of garbage. An environmentalists' dream come true. A match made in heaven—poor people and garbage. To the extent that any garbage was kept out of landfills because of City Harvest, it was in the form of biodegradables. Helen Palit, a mercurial self-promoter, never hinted at the amount of nonbiodegradable materials City Harvest hypocritically produced for the city's sanitation department.

For instance, one queer habit of City Harvest described by former employees was the use of extraordinarily thick plastic FDA-approved food handling bags as waste basket liners at every desk, to be thrown away each time they filled up. It is not possible to purchase bags as thick as this at any ordinary retail store for any purpose. Besides, City Harvest didn't use any kind of food bags for food. Nonetheless, if the truth be told, 172 cases of these were purchased, even though City Harvest had no sensible use for them at the end of July 1985, according to the organization's documents and statements of former employees.

You see, City Harvest, like hundreds of others, was the recipient of FEMA funds, which had to be expended and accounted for by July 31, 1985. As of July 25, 1985, they still had nearly $12,000 sitting in an account. If City Harvest wanted more, the money had to be spent—at least that's the logic nonprofits always give for these year-end excesses. So taxpayers effectively bought nearly $4,000 of plastic, headed almost straight for the dump, in behalf of the appreciative "hungry." By itself, $4,000 worth of plastic bags may not seem like much, but when thousands of organizations are playing the same game, waste is endemic. A check dated July 31, 1985, for $11,711.33 was made out to Keppler Bros. for "FEMA supplies" and signed by Helen Verduin Palit. The other items supposedly purchased with this check apparently never arrived at City Harvest. The rest of the money seems to have been artificially accounted for, with the aid of the Federation of Protestant Welfare Agencies, which handled shaky FEMA accounts for quite a number of discard market organizational "clients."

Deadly?

Far more serious than the numerous financial indiscretions at City Harvest and other misrepresentations perpetrated in *The Times* and elsewhere is the question of potential food poisoning of those who do end up eating at least some of the goods. It's about what are called bacteria and how they multiply. City Harvest's food brochures state that the "entire operation is run in strict accordance with New York City Health Department Guidelines." Not quite.

New York's health codes specify a maximum temperature of 45 degrees for refrigerated foods and a minimum temperature of 140 degrees for hot foods; in the area between, bacteria grow like crazy. As of August 1991, City Harvest had no refrigerated vehicles and no capacity to ensure appropriately heated temperatures when required either. Because pick-ups may stay in the van or truck for hours before being delivered, the hazards could be great. Let's face it; if a street person dies, he doesn't get an autopsy the next day to determine cause of death. On a sweltering summer day, it wouldn't take long for soup fixins to become deadly weapons. Even in winter, vehicles shifting between warm and cold would keep temperatures vacillating and poor people at risk. No risk to donors, though. The Good Samaritan Law has them covered.

Besides, they're given every reason to believe City Harvest's practices are safe. For one, City Harvest tells them that all "drivers must successfully complete the Health Department's Food Handler's Course," another bit of a fib. To be certified food handlers, participants are required to take a fifteen-hour course and pass a test. City Harvest drivers take neither the course nor the test. At most, some of the drivers attend a three-hour lecture by health officials. City Harvest vehicles aren't even inspected. These are the good guys. They are taken at their word.

City Harvest normally took credit for a great deal of poundage they didn't actually have much to do with, padding the stakes in both pounds and costs per meal—the more pounds, the less cost. The lower the cost-benefit ratio claimed, the easier to raise money for the operation. For instance, when a driver makes a pickup, in theory he weighs it, but in practice he just signs the donor's written declaration as to weight. If it turns out the goods have to be dumped, it still shows up as a net gain in City Harvest records. Food picked up through the City Harvest system directly by other operations would also be registered in City Harvest sums. These were considered so "lucrative" that internally they were referred to as "goldens."

Many of the pickups were not from restaurants or bakeries at all but were more commonly the leftovers of Wall Street office luncheons or cafeterias. Often, it cost more to pick these up than the food was worth, both because the amounts were limited and because the driver might have to wait hours to access the food. As might be expected, many of these Wall Streeters have also made cash donations to City Harvest.

Then there's the problem of feeding operations to which City Harvest will deliver nothing. One open-air kitchen run by homeless people shacked up in a contemporary Hooverville on the Lower East Side was rejected by Palit as not clean enough. City Harvest staff were so appalled that they took a collection and bought twenty-five pounds of rice to give. "Health issues" would be the excuse for turning down less formal operations. Coming from the people who claim prevention of starvation is the "health issue" they are addressing, the excuse is flimsy at best. Then again, encouraging real community-based, grass-roots self-help has never been the aim of the discard market.

Just because City Harvest looks a little shaky isn't reason to condemn the entire "prepared and perishable food program" (PPFP) network. Nevertheless, where there's one, there's two. The self-chosen terminology of the network says it all.

The Real Benefits

It is not surprising that APCO Associates, the consulting group of one of the country's top tax shelter law firms, Arnold & Porter, guide fledgling prepared and perishable food programs along. Steve Farr, an APCO consultant, says, "They are really growing"; achieving a separate identity from food bankers et al.

The PPFPs are funded by a broad mix of public and private sources, events, and individuals, depending on the locality. United Parcel Service (UPS) Foundation is the leading contender for the preeminent benefactor award of the PPFPs. On occasion, when other means were not available or reasonable, City Harvest used UPS services to deliver packages outside Manhattan, for which they paid the going rate. The usual tax benefits for donations go to UPS; plus, the more of these programs there are nationwide, the more likely it is that they will purchase UPS services.

An impressive, three-inch-thick, plastic-jacketed technical assistance manual entitled "Fighting Hunger with Prepared and Perishable Food" was underwritten by the UPS Foundation. It provides a wealth of information in the event you want to start one of these babies. No doubt the "hungry" appreciate the extras that went along with the production of this loose-leaf wonder. As for environmental concerns, it would be hard to exaggerate the amount of wasted material in it—large type, lots of bullets, heavy pages, most printed on only one side, plastic tabs galore.

In addition to advice on getting money and dealing with the media, there is an entire section devoted to "understanding liability." Among its altruistic treasures is a reprint of an article entitled "Leftovers: The Question of Liability." The subtitle reads, "Food donors are [italics in text] protected under the law." The text assures, "In all the years since the first [good samaritan] law passed, 'not a single case has been reported of an injured party filing suit against a good-faith donor.' " It does not say there have been no injured parties. In the corresponding appendix are letters from various PPFPs to demonstrate mail solicitation decorum. From the [Washington] DC Central Kitchen, Inc., a brief paragraph covers DC's version of the do-good law, claiming it "provides immunity from both criminal and civil liability to a donor of food when that food inadvertently, or even negligently [emphasis added], harms the recipient of the food."

I'd like to think it is needless to write, but just in case, the manual also offers a hefty section on tax deductions.

In some cases the PPFPs carry some food, even some exceptional food to food kitchens and pantries. Leftover breads from local bakeries are popular, for instance. These could be handled by the existing banking network, and to some greater or lesser degree already are. But all the expenses and deductions and plain old money spent make no sense when they feed only a fraction of poor people (very few poor children) a fraction of the time, putting them at risk while washing all other parties' hands of any.

With the possible exception of hardened street people and shut-ins (who have their own food programs), most poor people, even adult men, do not need these programs to survive. The real beneficiaries of the prepared and perishable food programs once again are those who get paid by them, get tax deductions, or just get their charitable rocks off without understanding the consequences to those they (don't) serve. In 1991 a feature item on network TV declared the DC Central Kitchen a major success, providing 175,000 meals annually. The approximate number of people below the poverty line in Washington, D.C., at the time was 100,000. Add those who get no benefits and/or are homeless—those who, for one reason or another, don't appear in government stats. Even with the food banking system stash, is that one and three-quarters meals per poor person each year or ten to twenty meals per poor adult male? Either way you look at it, the claims and kudos are absurd.

It's Expensive Keeping People Poor

The vast panoply of discard food distributors seems innocent enough, perhaps even worthy. Until you get up close. They do not make a dent in the need. At the same time, the relentless advocacy for increased funding has had very concrete, negative effects on virtually all poor people. The TSAR campaign has had profound consequences.

Sooner or later money flowed from every level of government (in most areas), from foundations dizzy on the movement, from wealthy individuals lured by glitzy affairs, celebrity participation, and minimal information. The discard market proponents were birthing little empires (and new bureaucracies) in the guise of "feeding" poor children, women, homeless men.

Advocates busily whittled away at the restrictions in all the programs. The ratio of program money to operation/administration began regressing—even with the federal dough. For salaries, for refrigerators, for stoves, for trucks and vans, for warehouses, for . . . The money was essential to maintaining the ventures, not the food. When volunteers got tired of volunteering, they could just walk away. Paid staff became essential. Without salaries, some distribution sites would not have come into being in the first place; most would have failed to keep regular, scheduled hours so people could line up. Year after year, program heaped upon program, the funding for this once "free food" market expanded nationwide. Because year after year, good people went bonkers to help the poor by giving themselves money.

In the 1970s poor people helped one another, as they continue to do. And they did it with far fewer resources and far greater success. In a kind of round-robin, neighbors borrowed from one another when the check and food stamps ran out. (Their benefits came on different days.) Each year, though, it has become harder and harder to get by.

Welfare departments and even the food stamp program ultimately had a system for giving emergency assistance out, but it was a capricious system, one that could have benefited from heightened consciousness. Had it been the target of the kind of robust, relentless advocacy that produced the discard market, there's no doubt each family, each individual, would have been better off than they are today. As bad as welfare is, if you make it through the labyrinth, you leverage much more than just a half meal or two, or a night's lodging. It, at least, recognizes that people are whole beings with more needs than this alternative could produce even if it were perfect.

Poor people were becoming more poor with every congressional or legislative session that put money in the FEMA pot or any of thirteen food programs run by the U.S. Department of Agriculture alone, not to mention those tugged out of Health and Human Services, the General Services Administration, or any other federal, state, or local agency for similar purposes. At no time did the obvious question of the increasing povertization of the people "served" get any serious consideration. Advocates who bulldozed the cheese didn't even put the key into the ignition regarding income standards.

We do not need to build a better food bank or fix the rotten mess in any way. Most people alive eat. Since most poor people are not being helped by this industry, it's obvious that in one way or another they are accessing food. Must they continue to do so with less and less money? Do we need to increase government spending? Not really. Truth is, billions are pissed away in soup kitchens and the like. Shut them down.

At political rallies in the thirties, people carried placards reading, "End the Breadline: Vote Roosevelt." When I was growing up, the breadlines and soup kitchens elicited neither fond memories from those old enough to remember them nor civic pride. They were cause for national shame—not evidence of our humanity. Not now.

How did this happen again? Was it a conspiracy? I doubt it. It was one of those historic moments when too many inappropriate interests converged, producing an effect sometimes referred to as the mobilization of bias. Whether it started in the boardrooms of private foundations, where primarily wealthy men make philanthropic decisions; or the charity balls, where wealthy women jockey for status by raising money and throwing great tax-deductible parties; or in government, where short-sighted officials attempted to bring expenditures down; or at corporate conferences, where the garbage problem seemed to intersect nicely with social responsibility; or with real estate interests that caused the evictions and burn-outs of so many poor people; or at the hands of the mob of social welfare professionals holding on to the last vestiges of the Great Society; or in the newsrooms of journalists who listened to these others and reported it so uncritically hardly matters.

Chapter 6

The Creation and Marketing
of Homeless People

Until the lions have their historians
Tales of hunting will always glorify the hunter. —African proverb

Under the rubric of helping homeless people, little empires were built, expanded, and strengthened, careers were boosted, and media stars created overnight. The twin of the discard market was born. Here too the problem has been obfuscated, yet it's relatively simple: there is too little habitable housing for all who need it at rents poor people can pay. The solution is equally obvious: more low-rent housing must be obtained. In the nexus between the problem and solution is money; therein lies the rub. Characteristic of most problems generated by poverty, the burning question is not a shortage of dollars but their allocation. The constant is politics.

Few people who actually have the money (*$1,000 weekly* and more)[1] that is now spent to shelter just one family in New York and other places across the country would find it impossible to live adequately in a home. How to spend the money, however, is not left up to

162

them. Instead, that decision is made by politicians and administrators, modified by the myriad advocates whose stars rise and fall with the disposition of each wave of policy on the ever-growing legions of homeless individuals and families. Instead of taking on the issue of the inadequacy of people's income or producing additional low-rent housing, shelter development became yet another growth industry.

Arguably, recognition of the plight of the growing numbers of homeless people began in states like New York, but it was hardly limited to New York's largest city. In Westchester County, the expenditures on homeless families doubled virtually every year through the 1980s. Advocates in Nassau, another "affluent" county, argued during the same period that it held the largest per capita percentage of homeless people in the state. Across the state, claims were made of a significant and growing problem.

Nor was it solely a New York phenomenon. Though estimates vary (ranging from a low of 350,000 to a high of 3 or 4 million), there has been general consensus that homelessness constitutes a national problem if not a crisis. Whatever the actual number nationwide, the condition is serious and the prognosis grim.

In Los Angeles, which until the mid-1980s had a virtual *non*policy on homelessness, a field was finally set aside for an encampment of homeless people. By July of 1987, approximately 600 people had moved in. Work farms not unlike those of the 1920s were even reintroduced in California. In Massachusetts, shelters much like New York's sprouted first in Boston, then spread like a wicked case of psoriasis across the state. Seattle reportedly approved a million-dollar tax levy to produce low-income housing, especially apartments for homeless people. At about the same time, Denver voters rejected a "right to shelter" initiative. No state or city, however, came close to the breadth of the predicament or the level of expenditures that "both" New Yorks spent on emergency "shelters."

Despite these, shantytowns were built all over the city by homeless people who refused to enter the shelter system. The forced "sweeps" of these people by the Dinkins administration have only exacerbated the problem, as people pushed out of one place go on to another. And, although it has become ever more obvious that the most significant need of homeless people is more housing, in the fall of 1991, Mayor Dinkins proposed another twenty-four shelters to be built all over the city. The uproar has been loud, if not heard. Though a "progressive" coalition put him into office, his policies toward homeless people have made his predecessor, Ed Koch, look like a saint.

Homeless people continue to attempt to insert their own vision into rapidly evolving homeless policies. For one, they want the shelters closed down. For most of the decade there wasn't any significant outpouring of support for their views from "homeless advocates"—particularly because the *advocates* typically *ran* the shelters. Social welfare types wanted to *help* homeless people, not house them. In some cities the organizing of homeless people has continued more successfully, but those with the real power largely ignored the people and muted the response. Those who represented themselves as spokespeople *for* "the homeless," and the media who reported on *them,* bear no small share of the culpability. So it was almost inevitable that resources intended for poor people without homes were squandered on everyone and everything but.

The Shelter Revolution Takes Off

It could be argued that the shelter revolution took off when, in 1980, Robert Hayes declared his intent to sue for the right of homeless men on the streets to "shelter."[2] To those who didn't really understand the stakes, it all sounded decent and humane. Hayes appeared selfless and determined, his intent, laudable. He was those things, but he was coming into the politics of poverty with no apparent background in it. Until this crusade, he had been working at a Wall Street law firm. It was something like a dentist deciding that if he could pull teeth he could amputate legs. Of course, poverty politics is about the only "profession" that automatically confers its imprimatur on practitioners who have no education or experience in the field.

Maybe it was because, even in 1980, upscale urban dwellers were disturbed by having to contend with homeless people flanking their pathways and doorways. Whatever. Overnight, Hayes was yanked in, showered with funds, and made into a celebrity, a virtual Nobel laureate in a field he knew almost nothing about. Instead of taking the time to understand the perspective of those who would live with the results, he invaded, unwittingly followed by whole battalions of paid mercenaries who would propel one of the most colossal social errors of our time. The National Coalition for the Homeless, of which Bob Hayes was both executive director and cochair, became the primary lens through which the nation learned to think about the issue, because of its nearly complete hegemony with the press. Actual homeless people tried to influence the coalition's policies, but usually they were expelled from the meetings of the board of directors, which was dominated by shelter providers and developers.

When Hayes finally began to quell his own rhetoric concerning "shelters"—about seven years later by his own admission—and started to emphasize housing, it was too late. The process of institutionalizing shelters and committing large amounts of public funds for them well into the future was epidemic.

'The shelter industry became strong enough in short order to squeeze dollars out of even the federal government at a time when few initiatives were funded in the name of "the poor." One result was the McKinney Act—the single worst piece of "housing" legislation in the nation's history. It started out bad, funding the discard market and shelters generally. It evolved into a holy terror, with ever new and dramatic variations on how to provide more and more services—offering counseling for personal problems and drug treatment, redefining the very idea of shelters to "transitional housing," and in the process undermining tenancy rights and mental health services, and obviously postponing any production of actual housing. The only beneficial aspect of the act was the provision of some funds for defense against evictions.

Historical Contours and Contradictions

Homelessness was not new in 1980, whatever anybody thought. Nor was shelter development. However, years ago, they were not called shelters. They were called poorhouses. The historical debate is rooted in the virtually inevitable conflict between poor people and those who make their living off them. The classic social welfare battle in the late nineteenth and early twentieth centuries was over "outdoor relief" versus poorhouses for those people and families unable to eke out a subsistence living. Outdoor relief was usually cash assistance, predating our current social security and public assistance systems. Receipt of outdoor relief meant that people could live in their own homes; in other words, *outdoors from a poorhouse*.[3]

Advocates of outdoor relief were convinced that environmental (and not genetic) factors caused poverty. They believed the most humane and rational solution to poverty was direct income transfers. Certainly income assistance has always been the solution of choice of poor people, especially mothers whose children might be taken away if they were forced into a poorhouse.

Those opposed to outdoor relief believed the problem was intrinsic to the breeding of the lower classes—especially those descended from southern and eastern Europeans. These were the people who ultimately swelled the rolls of the early poorhouses. An entire science of "eugenics" was formulated to explain mendicancy and determine the most effective means of altering the breeding habits of the poor. Throughout this struggle, a range of poorhouses were developed—those with few "services," work farms, those purposely designed to separate families, those with multiple services intended to correct the defects that were thought to have caused the poverty in the first place. A lot of thinking had gone into the "service strategy." No one, then or now, had stopped to consider whether the so-called deficiencies of these populations were particularly different from those of more "successful" people.

There were also the fiscal arguments that swung some pols. Poorhouse proponents, like shelter proponents today, originally predicted reduced government costs, but these failed to materialize even as poorhouses proliferated over several decades. As social experiments escalated in form and scope, it became increasingly obvious that, at least from the financial perspective, the poorhouses were a disaster. Then and now, many service workers were living off the concepts embedded in poorhouse philosophy. Social work generally was trying to become a respected profession. The health care industry was also horning its way in, taking responsibility for the "mentally ill" by the creation of monstrous institutions to hold them and encouraging mass sterilization for still others. Both sets of do-gooders needed somebody to "fix."

Unions of employed and unemployed people struggled for dignity in opposition to the social welfare professionals who were just getting a foothold in the United States. Politicians switched sides as befitted the situation. Poorhouse inhabitants were not generally consulted. It was dirty, nasty politics from start to finish. In the struggle for Social Security Roy Lubove described it as "one of the most bitter conflicts in the history of U.S. philanthropy."

The case for income security in the United States had been gaining ground for some time (witness the Social Security Act of 1935) when Hitler came into his own, in some measure sealing the fate of the poorhouses. German "scientific" experiments on Jews had taken the theory of genetic inferiority to its horrible conclusion—if they are not quite perfect or human like we are, it's okay to experiment on them for the betterment of *real* people. If their inferiority were the consequence of genes, then nothing could "bring them up to Aryan code" and genocide would have become acceptable. The Nazis' methods and reasons were different from those of the social welfare "reformers." Nonetheless, the world was appalled. No one could be sure where "scientific" social work could and would go. For the time being, the poorhouses were dead.

Some public housing was built, but never enough, and it was never intended to house the truly poor. It was for the "working" poor and other acceptable lowish-income people (in today's liberal parlance: low- to moderate-income people). Housing continued to be a major problem for those with insufficient means.

Periodically, the issue of homelessness would come to the fore—usually because of attention from journalists with short memories or little experience. In 1947, for instance, the return of large numbers of veterans to New York City and the beginning of the baby boom created a greater than usual shortage of low-rent housing. The settlement house founders and other reformers adopted neighborhood preservation concepts—improving code enforcement, planning, and rent control. New housing construction for the returning veterans was stimulated by federally subsidized mortgage loans and the restructuring of the nation's tax system. Still, the numbers of people in need always exceeded the supply. Families who could not find housing were placed in welfare hotels even then. To divert the media scandal, the city's first shelter for welfare families was built. When it turned out that the shelter cost more than the hotels had, the welfare department returned to using hotels.

Between that time and the next major homeless/hotel scandal—in 1970, when the homeless *family* population had grown much bigger—almost nothing was done to address the low-rent housing shortage. To the extent that additional housing was built, more often than not "urban removal" was the consequence—poor families were displaced. Much was done *to* poor people, but little was done to *benefit* them. (The "one-third of the nation [who were] ill-housed" in 1937, according to Franklin Roosevelt, were in fact never housed at all.)

The rash of vituperative press stories in 1970 about families in hotels—especially decent hotels—prompted action. In response, Mayor John Lindsay bumped heads with top Housing Authority officials to increase the number of welfare (homeless) families allowed into the thousands of public housing units that became available each year. By allowing additional welfare families into these units, the authority temporarily ameliorated the crisis, and the hotel population dropped precipitously. The National Welfare Rights Organization (NWRO), with its significant presence in New York City at the time, influenced several agendas—including this one.

By the midseventies, when NWRO had generally dissipated and DWAC came along, "homelessness" had lost the attention of all but those intimately involved—either because they were homeless or because they worked with those who were. Certainly all of us at DWAC were aware of the problem. Sometimes it was one of us. Many women who joined the Redistribute America Movement, in fact, lived in the welfare hotels and other makeshift accommodations for victims of burn-outs, eviction and rental policies, and other family disasters. It was these women—statistics with a face—who knew the degree to which welfare itself was a factor in creating their homelessness.

The Welfare System as a Cause of Homelessness

Tim Casey, then at Community Action for Legal Services in the unforgiving job of citywide government benefits coordinator, produced a comprehensive study of churning for DWAC.[4] It showed that tens of thousands of people—individuals and families—were cut off the welfare rolls every month by administrative fiat, only to appear back on weeks or months later. In the interim, some became homeless, as evictions for nonpayment of rent would often result. (Technically, evictions could have been prevented, but the housing court had no effective way to deal with events occurring at the Human Resources Administration (HRA). As a practical matter, the policies of the two governmental sectors collided, with poor families caught in the middle. If you didn't have a lawyer and/or a judge who understood the confluence of events—and only a few did—you were out of luck.)

Being churned cut families off everything—welfare, food stamps, medicaid. Everything they relied on for day-to-day sustenance, however little it was, disappeared into thin air. The practice made no sense unless it reduced government expenditures. Given the administrative burden it imposed on an already inefficient bureaucracy, even this was debatable. The theory of fiscal advantage was disputed by HRA, which itself had coined the term *churning* to describe the phenomenon. In spite of the obvious crippling effect it had on families still in need, some officials promoted churning because it was thought to deter people from getting back on the rolls (too much hassle), as if all the people cut had alternative means of support readily available. Alternative means, if they existed at all, would probably have meant crime of some sort—prostitution, drugs, stealing. The data certainly didn't support that either. Any way you looked at it, churning was hardly rational social policy.

As Tim's initial study showed, churning intensified rapidly from 1975 to 1981. By 1981 case "reopenings" actually exceeded *new* case openings in the city. "Reopenings" were cases of those who had been churned. More often than not, reestablishing eligibility was as hard as getting on the rolls in the first place, even if you could prove *the welfare* was in error. You started at square one, as if you'd never existed before. Not many years later, Tim produced another study showing the same patterns throughout the United States.

Churning put people into what came to be called a prehomeless syndrome.[5] It was by no means the only cause of homelessness and foodlessness, but it was certainly one of them. One HRA worker closely connected to the intake of emergency shelter families told me in confidence, "Three out of five families coming into the shelter system would not be there except for some failure on the part of the welfare system to provide legal entitlements to those in need."

In 1984, while I was working at the state Department of Social Services, New York State produced a study of this phenomenon, using essentially the same data and concluding the same things about the magnitude and risks of excessive case closings in New York.[6] I could not get the policy hotshots to swallow the canary whole, but they were surprised to find the data matched and did begin to complain to the city.

The argument against churning became so widely acknowledged that on March 10, 1987, Mayor Koch issued a press release conceding that numerous such "case closings" posed a threat of homelessness. It was his argument that recipients lost benefits because they "fail to comply with recertification and other administrative requirements." (He didn't mention that the most common reason for "failure to comply" was a consequence of letters demanding information that never made it into the recipients' hands. If there was a "failure to comply," one might ascribe it to the post office but not to the person who never received the letter.)[7]

I was cut off the rolls that way once—at a time when I was counseling as many as one hundred families and individuals a week on the requirements for establishing and maintaining eligibility. When I received the cutoff notice, I made a mad dash to the welfare center to explain that I had been cut off in error. The letter I was holding in my hand said I was cut off for not returning a previous letter asking me to check off whether or not I still needed welfare. I told them I never received the prior letter. Certainly, doing the work I was doing would have guaranteed my immediate attention. You could hardly have been more informed about the consequences of ignoring such a request than I was. I was known by most of the workers at the center, so they couldn't have doubted my eligibility. I informed them of the error but was advised that it didn't matter—even though my case was still in the computer, I would have to reapply as though I had never been on welfare at all, a process that took weeks.

These were the dangerous weeks or months that sent people over the edge. Koch's press release said cases that "fell through the cracks" would be given special care. He claimed to be establishing a new "case alert program," which would be activated to aid only those clients cut off at least *two* times in the same twelve-month period! Once wasn't enough. He did not say anything would be done to reduce case closings—like making certain *before* the fact that the people cut off were not eligible. (It was widely known and often even announced to the press over the years that just one recertification letter would automatically knock many thousands of people off the rolls.) In any event, it would not be too "off the mark" to say that the government—first the state through DSS, then the city—reacted (however feebly) to the charges we had been making since 1980, before most of the "homeless advocates" even knew what was going on.

Subtracting Fuel, Adding Fire

With one hand the welfare was throwing you out of your apartment; with the other, the public housing authority was slamming a door in your face. During the early 1980s, Mayor Koch expressed his interest in increasing the numbers of what he referred to as members of the "working class" in public housing. Of course, like so many others, he did not perceive that welfare recipients are also members of the working class, even if temporarily disjointed from the waged labor market. If more "working-class" people were to be moved into the housing, inevitably fewer welfare recipients would get in, as these two economic groups were the only ones who would technically qualify under the housing income guidelines.

Since welfare recipients were "the poorest of the poor," they were the most likely to become homeless. Reducing either the rate at which they entered public housing or the net number would be at best counterproductive. If those who were displaced from the projects became homeless, the cost of sheltering them would move into the stratosphere. It was just plain stupid. But that's what happened.

Even though I hadn't worked at DWAC for some time, poor women managed to track me down for assistance of various kinds, which led to some interesting discoveries about New York City's public housing. A number of women complained that, when they tried merely to get on the waiting list, they were told it was a waste of time, since public housing wasn't taking any more welfare families. After hearing a number of variations on this theme, in early 1984 I obtained data from the Housing Authority for the years 1980 through 1983 using a Freedom of Information Act request.

It is not surprising that both the number and rate of welfare families as a percentage of all public housing tenants had dipped. There were 20,000 fewer children in public housing in that period alone. Whenever we raised the practical (and historically successful) matter of *reducing* the number of homeless families by *increasing* their tenancy in public housing, the administration would whine that there wasn't enough turnover, the vacancy rate was down, and so forth. Well, the data did show the vacancy rate was down, but, because of the magnitude of New York's public housing, that still meant thousands of available apartments every year. Surely they could have increased the intake of welfare families immediately. Every 100 families in pretty much meant another 100 out of the costly hotels and, later, shelters.

Also, welfare families made up only about one quarter of the total families living in public housing, but they represented well over half the waiting list.[8] It took a deliberate act to reduce the welfare population in light of the numbers as well as the so-called guidelines, which claimed this priority system for the available units: "(a) families in emergency need of housing; (b) families living under severe hardship conditions; and (c) families living under substandard physical, occupancy, or hardship conditions."[9] Somebody was fibbing again.

The data also revealed a few other interesting things. The number of tenants who were overincome for public housing was double the number on welfare, and the gap was growing. (This occurs in part because people usually do not leave public housing without someplace better to go. They could not be evicted just because their incomes went up after they were made eligible.) Whites were disproportionately overrepresented in relation to income guidelines and the general city population, and they tended to stay in public housing longer than all other tenants. Whites and people of color are also segregated, for the most part, with white projects located in predominantly white areas. The homeless population in New York City is about 95 percent black and Hispanic. It wasn't until a new Housing Authority commissioner was appointed toward the end of the Koch administration that the trend of decreasing access to public housing for welfare families began reversing, also deliberately. However, that commissioner, Joseph Shuldiner, was replaced when David Dinkins became mayor. Homelessness and the welfare rolls are again on the rise.

New York City public housing is among the best in the nation, and the demand for it is high. In 1992 the newly appointed chair of the Housing Authority, Sally Hernandez-Pinero, announced that the authority would not be accepting any more homeless families. She maintained that homeless families were violent and contributed to the declining quality of life in the projects. No evidence was offered to prove the point. Certainly violence experienced by people in low-income areas of the nation is cause for alarm, but identifying its source takes more than a hunch. This time Mayor Dinkins wanted more. Within a month the Housing Authority had retreated from its position and agreed to continue accepting homeless families.

As for private housing, then and now, discrimination against welfare families is legal. Female householders with children have always dominated the welfare population. Their disconnection from a man has led to an implicit social policy derived from the widespread bias that the *mothers, not the men who weren't there,* are failures. Only widows with children occasionally surmount that obstacle.

So even when the welfare department offered to pay more in rent than nonwelfare people could pay, landlords consistently refused to allow welfare recipients in. You can't discriminate against potential tenants on the basis of race, religion, or ethnic background, but you can refuse to rent to families on welfare. Attempts by some legislators to change that have never succeeded. Those landlords who do rent to welfare recipients often milk the buildings by overcrowding and eliminating services, until they become literally uninhabitable. Voilà—welfare families dominate the homeless population.

God knows, there were many other causes for homelessness— landlords who burned buildings down to collect the insurance, even "friends" who burned them down because "their" women rejected them, the city's failure to manage the housing stock it has acquired through foreclosures, welfare policies, housing court goofs, gentrification . . . The list is virtually endless. One of the most frequently mentioned causes in New York State is probably one of the least likely—the closing of large mental health facilities, where the mentally ill used to live. Truth of the matter is, this "dumping," as it's often referred to, occurred approximately twenty years ago. Most homeless people today—even adults—are not old enough to have been in these institutions. Nevertheless, had the community residences that were to replace the institutions been built and had the single-room occupancy units not been all but wiped out, even the mentally ill would be able to go home at night.

With Help Like This . . .

In recent years there have been initiatives sponsored by private nonprofits and government to create housing opportunities or preserve existing ones for poor people. From a distance they seemed to be commonsense responses. The problem is, our social welfare system suspended common sense years ago.

The homeless advocacy movement spurted forward, initially targeting the visible homeless population (single adults), which indeed was growing. Less attention was paid to a much more invisible population (homeless families), if for no other reason than that those new "homeless advocates" didn't know they existed. Still, welfare hotels holding homeless families were filling at ever-increasing rates. In other cases, homeless families were doubling and even tripling up in apartments too small for the first family. Some mothers lived with their children in such places as empty elevator shafts or the steam canals under the city, or they rode the subways back and forth very late at night. Unlike single adults, mothers had to hide "homelessness" because it could be grounds for forced removal of the kids to foster care.

Among those trying to address the problem of homelessness were Legal Aid and the Coalition for the Homeless. The homeless attorneys and advocates often missed the point—that what families and other homeless people needed was housing, not a cleaner welfare hotel or another shelter—so the strategies they pursued were almost always contrary to the goal of accessing permanent housing. In 1983, for instance, Legal Aid initiated one of what I called "toilet paper lawsuits." These suits demanded a host of things that were essentially already required of hotels but not enforced—like a mattress for each person, heat in the winter, and items like sheets and toilet paper. Conditions did not improve.

Another suit, brought by the Coalition for the Homeless, was downright silly. It won the right for homeless people to vote. (Hardly any did. With all their other problems, voting would have been about the last thing on their minds.) These attorneys sometimes did help to elevate the issue in the public eye. Of course, that had its minuses, too.

With inappropriate "solutions" at the fingertips of advocates and providers, and dollars rolling into their bank accounts, all manner of foolishness was perpetrated on homeless people, not to mention the U.S. Treasury. For instance, the primary method of funding for the shelters and hotels for families began with a subsidiary program within AFDC called Emergency Assistance to Families (EAF). Stretching the interpretation of the regulations, cities and counties across the United States tapped EAF for daily payments, called per diems, required by the hotel owners and shelter operators.

The resulting numbers were and still are staggering. Reagan administration officials complained endlessly about the growth in expenditures in AFDC. Well, yes and no. Emergency Assistance to Families, as a part of AFDC, seemed rocket propelled, while standard AFDC payments were in free-fall with respect to their purchasing power. For instance, in New York State alone, expenditures through EAF per family more than tripled in 1988 compared with 1981. Nationally, EAF payments per family during that period more than doubled. National *AFDC* payments to families from 1981 to 1988 were up only one third in actual dollars, but in constant dollars welfare benefits had fallen in every state, as the reader will recall.

Plus, by the mid-1980s, many "emergency" payments were (for technical reasons) "hidden" by states in regular AFDC totals. The numerical consequence was that payouts in AFDC appeared larger per family and in total. Conversely, the payouts in "emergency" funds showed up lower than they actually were. Soon "emergency" funds would form the bedrock upon which the shelter industry would be built, for which homeless families were used, and through which taxpayers were royally fleeced.

Even while the advocacy community was laying the groundwork for the growth of the shelter industry, they began calling for an increase in the rent portion of New York's welfare grant. Superficially, this made sense. But it would merely have given slumlords more for the caves they already rented. Absent more and better housing at low rents, which could only have been produced through a rational housing policy, because the market would not or could not produce it, the problem would not abate. Undaunted by logic, Governor Cuomo reacted by raising the rent portion of the grant by an aggregate 51 percent over a four-year period.

Predictably, rents soared as landlords moved swiftly to gobble up the increases. Housing availability and quality did not improve. Higher rents did not diminish the ever-increasing ranks of homeless families. Worse, even though the landlords—not the recipients—got the raises, federal rules caused food stamps to be reduced one dollar for every three dollars in increased rent. Because more dollars passed through recipients' hands on the way to landlords, fewer "dollars" were available for the purchase of food. Some deal! Keeping the nonrent portion of the grant so low that mothers couldn't pay for even the basics always meant they would come to a crossroads where the decision to "heat or eat" had to be made. That thought was never even factored into the equation of those promoting the rent increases.

From the Other Side

While the prosperous Coalition *for* the Homeless was composed primarily of shelter developers and other service providers, the Union *of* the Homeless attempted to establish a base—perhaps a counterforce—to represent their own interests. They tiptoed gingerly around the coalition *for* them and other evolving media stars, like the late Mitch Snyder, seeking to minimize confrontation. The coalition and Snyder sought to produce what they called shelters; the Union of the Homeless called them concentration camps.

The union started in Philadelphia and was attempting to go national. Its early stages in New York were auspicious, but as soon as the primary leaders (the most skilled organizers) moved out to expand elsewhere, it went downhill and fast. This city is too complicated a place to organize a venture like that without very strong leaders at the helm. The obstacles were too great, and the union was an easy target for takeover by groups that would try to distort rather than enhance its agenda. It wasn't long before the New York City Union of the Homeless dissipated.

There were still other groups of homeless people organizing themselves. One group of homeless families in New York hotels found themselves fighting policies that came into place in good measure as a consequence of the lawsuits and political demands made "on their behalf" by Legal Aid et al. The crowning achievement of this group, primarily of mothers, was a stark reminder of how little the advocates understood either the people they represented or the inevitable fallout of apparently benign advocacy. In this instance, Legal Aid attorneys and other advocates had been oozing naive swill about shutting down the welfare hotels.

Indeed, they *were* squalid places to live, but the existing alternatives were generally worse. This was true of both the available low-rent housing and the newly created "shelters." In the late 1980s, the then mayor, Ed Koch, capitulated. He announced that all welfare hotels would be emptied and shut down. All the families would be moved to either shelters or permanent housing. It had been coming for some time, largely because professional advocates and shelter developers had successfully convinced the public and the policymakers that the *hotel* industry should be replaced by the *shelter* industry.

On the final day for them to leave the welfare hotel (the name of which changed from Grenada to Brooklyn Arms), they staged a sit-in—or, more accurately, a sleep-in. For days they retained control of the hotel and their residences. Ultimately, of course, the multiple powers that be simply detonated the resistance, and it was over.

Why did the families try to stay in these wretched places? Clearly they had reason to believe that both the shelters and so-called permanent housing were worse. And, as usual, the bulk of advocates for the homeless were truly out of touch with the people they *thought* they were serving. Most of the alternative shelters that the good guys and the media proclaimed to be so superior to the hotels provided even less space and tended toward arbitrary and authoritarian practices that these women rejected outright. Seems the helping hands had lost their grip.

In one horrible sense it was gratifying to have demonstrated for the rest of the city what a farce had evolved—particularly from the recipients' point of view. It must have come as quite a surprise that poor people had a different way of looking at things. Why wouldn't they? Their vantage point is so radically different. As Michael Katz wrote in the notes to his book on poorhouses, "The history of welfare looks very different when the historian perches on the shoulder of a poor person and looks outward than it does when the story is told from the perspective of governments, agencies, or reformers."[10]

Looking from the Inside Out

In New York State, the not-for-profit shelter construction phase began with the passage of the Homeless Housing Assistance Act and a first-year allocation of $20 million. In 1983, within the state Department of Social Services, the Homeless Housing Assistance Program (HHAP) was established to set priorities, review proposals, allocate funds, and oversee development.

That same year, after Cesar Perales had been appointed commissioner of the DSS, I applied for a job there. It was at least conceivable that government could operate with integrity and a view toward caring even for its poorest people. Perales and I had collaborated when he was head of the regional office of the U.S. Department of Health, Education and Welfare, now Health and Human Services, in combating the onslaught of two-party rent checks when Jimmy Carter was president. I suppose there were signs from the beginning of a serious mismatch, but we both ignored them. Perhaps each of us thought the other would change.

Our initial meeting of consequence was my interview for the job, during which Perales asked me two crucial questions. The first was whether I could be trusted. The second was whether I would make trouble for him. To the first I said that if he was asking could I be trusted to represent the interests of poor people, in particular poor women and children, I absolutely could. But if he meant could I be trusted to lie for him or any policy handed down that would not conform to their interests, the answer was no. I thought that was pretty clear. When he asked me if I would cause him trouble, it would have been foolish to hedge, given my history. I told him that of course I would make trouble. It seemed to me that anyone hiring me as a special assistant would have to be suspicious of any other response. We laughed.

He also asked me a question I could not answer. He wanted to know why one of my references, Ruth Messinger, qualified her recommendation of me so much as effectively to sabotage my getting the job. But my chief advocate for the job was a board member of DWAC whom I considered a trusted friend. She was very close to Perales. How much pressure she applied is anybody's guess. I suppose Perales thought the grown-up paycheck would be the vice I'd get accustomed to, as he must have quite some years ago. Suffice it to say, when all the paperwork and background checks were done, I was offered the job and I took it.

Perales first assigned me to work under Nancy Travers at the newly created HHAP, which needed to be up and running fast, given the political exigencies. I told her I was particularly interested in the issue of families in need of permanent housing. She nodded in agreement and mumbled some affirmative words. It started out looking like we, too, might actually be on the same track.

After all, the legislation defined homelessness as living *either* on the street *or* in a shelter. This was a condition we were supposed to change. It stood to reason that if living in a shelter meant a person was homeless, then the way to change that status had to be to give that person someplace to live over the long haul, someplace to call home. Building more shelters would not satisfy that aim. But the request for proposals for the $20 million to be distributed annually was targeted from the first at social welfare agencies—not housing groups.

Travers had an inside lock on it. Kim Hopper, her husband to be, was cochair of the Coalition for the Homeless. He and many of their friends shared an undivided loyalty to the idea of building shelters. Most shelter advocates had little experience in poverty issues. Plus, any bureaucrat who wants to get ahead must find a way to continue to be needed. If housing were built and the funds to build more depleted, what role would there be for HHAP? None. But the very nature of shelters require ongoing monitoring and regulation. So, whether consciously or not, the tendency of bureaucrats and bureaucracies to sustain themselves naturally swayed toward the shelter movement.

Politics, of course, played its own role. There were several job openings for people working in housing, since the $20 million plus was supposed to get distributed annually (and indefinitely). Even my closest friend, Tom Sanzillo (whom I later married), decided to apply for a job. He had been organizing tenants for some years with considerable success and had acquired a good deal of knowledge in the field. He also expected we would be producing or rehabilitating permanent housing, *not* shelters.

Even before we began formal work on the housing issues, Nancy Travers's oversight of the FEMA food funds fiasco, which I described in Chapter 5, unsettled me. We were wrapping it up as the new people came on to work at HHAP. Instead of attempting to optimize the benefit to poor people who were the legislated target of the funds, Travers had almost completely dealt from a political deck. She would *say* she cared, but nothing in her deeds hinted at it. Clearly she had bosses over her, but it was equally clear that she wasn't putting up any serious resistance.

The Homeless Housing Assistance Program itself was an unusual beast in that it was set up to do development work that under normal circumstances would have been done in the state's chief housing agency, the Division of Housing and Community Renewal (DHCR). Instead, for reasons practical and political, it was placed within DSS. That meant that technically Perales had the final word. In fact, in the early years he was little more than a front. Bill Eimicke, Governor Cuomo's chief housing adviser, called the shots, presumably with directions from *his* boss.

Eventually Eimicke became the "housing czar" for Cuomo. He wasn't particularly talented or well schooled in housing development, but he had supported Cuomo over Koch in the run for governor. Perhaps most important, Eimicke was working for Koch at the time. Eimicke had tossed a coin in a volatile market, and for taking that risk his stock shot sky high. (He was booted out of the Cuomo administration some years later.) He and Nancy Travers had worked together in the New York City Department of Housing Preservation and Development. She went with him when he left.

Eimicke was one of several slick but not very competent people in high positions in the administration. He had a flair for *un*subtlety that reached its apex when he called the senior DHCR staff together shortly after he took on the additional post of commissioner. According to one staff member present, he said that "merit in decision making" was not important. What was important was how policy decisions played in the press—how good the governor *looked,* not what actually happened.

Another dull tool of particular significance to the shelter development program was David Emil, a budding mandarin whose wealthy father had supported Cuomo "early and often." Emil, with delusions of adequacy, became general counsel to the Department of Social Services. He may have had a law degree, but he didn't seem to know squat about the subject matter on which he would be making countless crucial decisions. He made any number of what appeared to be foolish errors in developing fundamental policies that would have impact for years to come by supporting the unwarranted expansion of the shelter system. He may have put the screws to homeless people with his highly suspect legal decisions, but apparently he served his boss(es) well.

As the months went by, it became eminently clear that poor people in general were not going to be the primary objects of this money. These were tight times as far as new government funds for poor people were concerned. Federal bucks had gone the way of the dodo bird. And *big* "food" distribution dollars were not really flowing yet either. So this grab bag was high stakes, with many prospective customers.

Well-connected slackers didn't have to worry, though, since "merit" in the awarding of contracts is generally a rhetorical posture, not a substantive agenda in government politics. While we were finishing up the FEMA mess, for example, one employee told of a prior application for funds for a battered women's shelter that was so inferior she could find no basis for approving it. She was surprised by just how much pressure was brought to bear. The man in charge of this DSS fund at the time told her quite literally that if she didn't change her evaluation and recommend the project, she would be out of a job. This contract was meant to go to a program with no track record whatsoever in services for battered women. Its leverage was its close connection with William Del Toro. His "programs" were notorious, but Assemblymember Angelo Del Toro is his brother. Quite simply, DSS was and is a patronage trough. If a program slated to get funds happened to be good, that was fine, but it was not *essential* by any means.

Travers did work hard. She put together a staff where none had been, put out a request for proposals, and had us reading HHAP funding proposals in a matter of weeks. We read them by the bushel. In themselves, they were enlightening.

First off, only one of the nonprofits that submitted proposals for the first round of funding intended to build or rehabilitate *permanent* housing for homeless families. Almost no organization wanted to accept truly mentally ill homeless people, in any facility, either. There was a strong bias for sheltering seniors, especially women. The only demographic surprise was a substantial number of proposals for sheltering single men. In those that contemplated taking in single mothers, and their children of course, there were a number of by now familiar "extras": forced counseling and other required services premised on the idea that these women (a) were inferior and (b) could be "cured" by the social work industry through behavior modification techniques, not unlike the poorhouse breeding strategy of old.

Some of the women might have needed and wanted services of some kind, just as middle- and upper-class women do from time to time. I know of none of the latter who invite their therapists to move in with them, though. I know of none who are not free to reject the services of professionals they consider incompetent. Whatever the situation, the homeless families had one common and distinct *need*—housing. That's not what they got.

In fact, instant eviction for those who resisted was a basic premise in most of the initial proposals. That became glaringly evident when Nancy Travers and I attended a meeting of ambitious shelter developers called by and held at the Community Service Society (as per a DSS contract to provide technical assistance on shelters). An attorney from Lawyers for the Public Interest (another nonprofit) had been called in to report on the legal status of people residing in shelters. In particular, she had been charged to find out whether they could be evicted at will, without notice. She began by explaining that normally a request for information on how to evict poor people was not the sort of work her organization did, but because it was coming from this group of social welfare types, she took on the job. No doubt she was completely in the dark as to where this would all lead. She couldn't even see their tongues hanging out as she began.

They were disappointed to hear that even homeless people were entitled to a modicum of due process. That's why later on these shelter providers and developers came up with the concept of "self-help evictions." When new tenants moved in, they were required to sign a paper saying if they broke any of a number of rules, they would *evict themselves*. The good guys wanted to circumvent due process issues and thought this would do the trick.

Sure, there were some tough situations that erupted in shelters, but there were already other remedies available. For instance, if a tenant appeared out of control and a threat to either her- or himself or the other tenants, medical professionals could be called in to take the tenant to Bellevue or another city hospital if necessary. For that matter, the HHAP funds could have been requested specifically for homeless mentally ill people, with safeguards built in to the day-to-day operations.

Instead of self-help, the self-evictions predictably became the tool to enforce arbitrary abuses of power over desperate people. And, of course, they were used in very different ways against women than against men. Let's face it, just by virtue of having children with her, a mother would be more vulnerable to all kinds of unreasonable demands. Some women told of being rounded up at 3:00 A.M. to see if men were in their rooms. (There is no real legal reason why they couldn't be.) Others were evicted for minor infractions—such as feeding their kids in their rooms. In the barracks-style shelters, others told of lights kept on twenty-four hours a day to make sure they didn't hit their kids. Sounds a little like torture, no? Still others were threatened with the removal of their kids to foster care if they didn't follow some capricious and often demeaning order of staff people. Families were supposed to receive certain items, like enough mattresses for all the kids, but they were afraid to complain.

Self-eviction policies also allow cover for many hidden agendas. Catholic Charities, for instance, runs a shelter ostensibly for pregnant women. A woman who finds herself waiting in an emergency-assistance unit with her two-year-old child may not think it's such a great idea to continue her pregnancy. But if she is suddenly offered a place at this shelter—a sure way out of sleeping in an office with dozens of other families waiting to be placed—she just might take it, in spite of the caveat: she must agree to carry the pregnancy to term or face certain eviction. If she changes her mind and has an abortion a week after entering this shelter, she and her two-year-old are dumped from the facility. Her right to choose is abrogated, and issues of church and state are muddied no end. In this and other ways, the social welfare establishment blackmails women into accepting their ideas of what it means to be human.

In one shelter, a media campaign in the late eighties led to measuring all the kids for new winter coats at Christmas. Each time another journalist showed up, some kids would be measured again. Then the big day came when a truckload of brand-new coats was to be delivered. It made great television. But as soon as the media were gone, the coats all disappeared. It wasn't enough that these kids were hurting just by being in this place, but their hopes were built up and dashed, consciously, at Christmastide. None received a coat—new or old. Who would dare complain? After all, the mothers had signed that piece of paper when they walked in the door.

A toys program did deliver. All age-inappropriate toys. Books for toddlers were received by adolescents. Three-year-olds received games meant for much older children; nobody got what she or he wanted. Nobody was asked. Somehow I think a mother could have managed that task with considerably more success. Practically speaking, the kids came away empty-handed again. In the end, you and I paid for the mistakes. Every gift was tax deductible, and the organization delivering it was operating on tax-deductible money—some of it maybe even direct government expenditures.

The point is, right from the beginning, HHAP and DSS policymakers had the definitive say in what could and could not go on in the shelters, particularly because they held the purse strings. The policies that evolved were dreamed up, legitimized, and carried out by very specific people—not some invisible hand. Whether these were invidious at the conceptual stage or merely the consequence of an abundance of ignorance is of little distinction to those who have to live with them. And no matter how obvious the potential for abuse embedded in a proposal, if friends of Travers or political influentials refused to budge, potential became practice. Practice became policy.

The active players with substantial clout in addition to the DSS officials and Eimicke were largely either friends of Travers—several of whom were conveniently placed on the Governor's Task Force on the

Homeless—or random social welfare professionals with a stake in a given policy and enough power to move the agenda—like representatives of the Catholic Church, the Sal[i]vation Army, and other power blocs. That came to include the governor's son Andrew. They were for most intents and purposes free to decide policy from the start. *They were not stuck with outdated, practically ingrained, politically entrenched regulations unsuited to the moment.*

The Development of Family Shelters

There were a few people who recognized the lucrative potential of "not-for-profit" organizations sheltering families right from the beginning. It caught on. The very idea was praised by the press, who actually believed the public relations people at DSS citing the litany of so-called advantages of shelters over hotels, especially the "cost containment" features. These PR people would refer to specified Title 18 dollar amounts that could be given out to maintain these shelters.[11] They implied that these were *maximum* amounts, as if some regulation were taking place, whereas in fact the figures had long since ceased to mean much of anything. The costs of funding every form of shelter were so staggering, no one at the city or state level wanted the public to know. Just as hotels would negotiate set rates on an individual basis, so would the family shelter providers. In most cases these were far higher than any hotel rates. The sham was accomplished bit by bit—not always in apparently benign ways. The endgame was a doozy.

In their role as shelter developers, not a few advocates worked ceaselessly to decimate housing codes in their quest for the most lucrative shelters. Plumbing, electricity, and other construction codes were sometimes waived to make the physical structures cheaper. Space requirements were all but abolished in order to cram as many bodies into as small a space as possible. It was all done quietly, behind the scenes.

Publicly, advocates stuck to their stance of wiping out the evil welfare hotels, whose business they wished to take over—you know, to help the poor. They would claim the shelters were necessary because people were in need of immediate help. Except it took just as long, if not longer, to build shelters as it would have to build permanent housing.

Logic was not one of the long suits of the shelter development advocates. Except, that is, the logic of getting and sustaining money for themselves and the institutions they represented—even subconsciously. Once built, the stake in sustaining the shelters would be rock solid.

Among the first to fiddle with potential regulations was Jack Doyle, who headed the American Red Cross's shelter development team. Doyle and others shared a homesteading cooperative with Nancy Travers and Kim Hopper. All these four were either on the Governor's Task Force on the Homeless or allowed to participate in its meetings.[12]

It was my misfortune to be the first reviewer of the Red Cross proposal. There were a number of fishy things about it. For instance, the Red Cross claimed they were prepared to "commit" $100,000 to the project. (They were seeking the rest of the development cost from HHAP.) As explained in an August 31, 1983, letter addressed to Travers by their controller [sic], they had plenty of bucks to do it with. Beyond their current revenue as reported in the proposal of nearly $13,500,000, the American Red Cross received "additional revenue in excess of $2,000,000, mostly from earnings on reserve funds of over $11,000,000." Even though the organization was rolling in dough, they weren't actually intending to *give* this money to the project: they were *lending* it to the project. And for their trouble, they would charge the state 12 percent interest per annum. The words *lending* and *interest* never appeared in the documents, as that wouldn't have been quite kosher. As they put it, they "would not borrow to raise the $100,000 commitment" but would use their own money, which they figured if they invested would yield them about 12 percent a year. Forgoing this interest they termed, in proper nonprofitese, an "opportunity cost." When the shelter was up and running, they would factor the 12 percent opportunity cost into what they charged the state for letting in homeless families. So much for the not-for-not-for-profit. Remember, these were taxpayers' dollars in the first place—one way or another—that Red Cross was generously planning to charge one more time to taxpayers!

The financial shenanigans were not the worst of it. The proposal's objective was to take a twenty-seven-unit single-room occupancy previously intended for single individuals and turn it into shelter for eighty-four people in families without expanding the space one inch. They claimed (it was never verified) that for purposes of occupancy of a facility of this kind, more small children than older ones could be packed in legally. The rumor going around among several of the potential shelter providers was that for occupancy purposes—space requirements—babies under two years old didn't count at all, and children aged two to twelve only counted half. But for purposes of getting paid a daily fee by the welfare department, each person after the first was assigned an equal value. If this were the case, they could really pack 'em in and enhance their revenue streams for operating costs. This was one of the reasons that the projects seeking to shelter families generally would not allow entrance at all to those with children thirteen years or over. To the extent that there were "ancient" New York City codes with varying age limits and space, they had been created to prevent overcrowding. These shelter advocates wanted just the opposite.

In defense of the not-for-profit policy to overcrowd, Travers personally wrote, "The proposed room size of 150 square feet is almost double the NYC code requirement of 80 square feet per person." Well, not quite. Since these rooms were intended for families of three and four and not single individuals, they fell short of even being legal by those standards, no matter how few one-year-olds were put in. After that, I started a joke that swiftly made the rounds of the office. Q: How many poor people can you pack on the head of a pin? A: As many as you can get DSS to fund you for.

As for Doyle, I thought he should be ashamed of himself. He had a baby of his own at the time. I wondered—out loud—how he thought a toddler could learn how to walk or a ten-year-old do his homework in the midst of such overcrowding. The simple fact is, one thing the welfare hotels generally had was plenty more space than this plan intended to provide. (Likewise, a proposal I read from Henry Street Settlement sold the overcrowding line—its rooms were eighty-one square feet. A couple of us walked out the space on the floor of DSS, each of us barely able to imagine the good guy who dreamed it up.)

Travers was not happy about my unrelenting opposition, in particular over space. She gave the proposal to another staff person she thought would cave and give it a positive review. She didn't. It took still a third to get an actual recommendation on paper. Even then the tone was negative. He, too, objected to the space limitations including a final "The community center is *small,* where are the children going to play!" The early announcements to the media of programs to be funded by Governor Cuomo included the Red Cross proposal. They were to be given $380,000 in HHAP funds. But it wasn't over till it was over. To get from funding recommendations to contracts takes time.

I knew that regulations governing family shelters were being drafted up in Albany by staff from another department. I made calls to find out who was involved and started asking questions. When they understood what was going on, I began to get essentially anonymous calls from them, leaking developments as they were occurring. The draft regulations proposed sixty square feet per person *to be applied to babies as well as all other children and adults in the household.* I then sent a memo to my supervisor, Liz Searles, who clearly felt pretty much the same as most of the rest of us on staff regarding this. (She had two little ones of her own.) I outlined the projected family shelter regs and compared them with the regs already governing young adult shelters. I added that "if and when these regulations are 'activated' several of our present [family shelter] proposals would clearly be out of compliance were they to be funded."

This should have been cause for alarm. It was. Instead of requiring it to have more space or fewer people, Travers sped to the rescue of the all but doomed Red Cross project. She got a copy of the draft regulations and, with her own hot little hands, slashed some of the best provisions in them—including those specifications regarding space. According to one Albany worker, she argued that homeless people in New York City were accustomed to living in tight quarters. She won. To date, the family shelters are the only form of licensed residence in the state with no dictated minimum square footage at all, eclipsing even jail cells.

The Red Cross proposal still needed one thing—community board approval. A couple of well-placed calls to friends in the mostly black Bedford-Stuyvesant neighborhood and the Red Cross project was killed—by black community leaders. Still, not long after, Red Cross moved on to bug New York City government for the dough. Sure enough, they got it.

From Bad to Worse

The Koch administration itself was insisting on being handed a bundle for various housing projects. In spite of numerous staff protests on several proposals, there appeared to be some political obstacle that we could not overcome. One of the largest grants HHAP ever made was for the city to complete a project expanding the Amboy Street Houses. Several RAM members had lived at Amboy (it was a street name but was used by tenants there interchangeably as the name for the houses). None of them had anything but harsh words for the project. It was originally used for burned-out families. It was run by Colony South Brooklyn, an agency with more political ties than good reputation. But none of us on staff was able to prove anything that would have prevented them from getting control over still more poor people's lives and an *awful* lot of government money. That they were known to have a negative image among those they "served" was not in the least germane to whether they would get a contract.

Since that time, the mystery organization has come under even closer scrutiny by the Brooklyn District Attorney's Office. In the fall of 1991, Bill Banks, who was "in charge of checkbooks at . . . Colony South," was put on trial.[13] The original indictment allegedly included charges for political check writing, but, for reasons unknown, the charges that actually went to trial were only those involving checks and credit card expenditures at places like Saks Fifth Avenue and Tiffany's. Banks was acquitted.

I was getting blue as these homeless dollars were falling out of the sky onto places of ill repute. So I went to see Cesar Perales, where the biggest shock came—until they dumped me from my job, that is. I was choking up with actual tears as I described to him what was going on at HHAP, with particular emphasis on the Red Cross and the family shelter regulations, thinking if he knew he would simply put a stop to it. He asked if I wanted to be transferred to other work with another supervisor. I did, but that wasn't the point, I explained. Didn't he see what was happening? He turned to me and said, "Theresa, I don't know. I don't want to know. Don't you understand? *I can't afford to know.*" It was like a boomerang returning smack into the socket of your eye. He didn't know but he did know. He wasn't calling the shots, but he wasn't fighting them either. It was just the way the game was played.

Whenever people—Travers, Perales, whoever—wanted to get out from under a bad decision, they always said, There's nothing I can do about it, it's coming from upstairs. That meant the governor's chambers. It could have meant the governor himself. Sometimes it meant Bill Eimicke. Sometimes *upstairs* meant Andrew Cuomo, both before and after he left his government job.

A number of other HHAP staff and I (no longer working directly with them) continued to meet in secret in the hope of reaching some resolution of outstanding concerns respecting the quasi, if not legally, corrupt funding decisions at HHAP. There was a lot of talk but no imminent solution. Meantime, ever more funding decisions and policy directives were accumulating. Mostly bad. In order to ward off one particularly obnoxious proposal from Bill Del Toro and his crew, several HHAP staff wrote a five-page memo, giving it a boot that would be hard to overcome. The very existence of such a direct document would give them pause. It did. Nancy Travers wrote an obligatory response, defending the project. It would be approved because somebody among them had a political or personal stake in it. There was only so much that we could do from the inside.

Not long after, articles about HHAP appeared in *The Village Voice*. They were not flattering to either the American Red Cross proposal or the plan to boost some loot to another of Bill Del Toro's projects. Bill's brother, Angelo, was head of the Social Services Committee of the assembly at the time. The late Paul Du Brul, a former *Voice* writer, was then employed by DSS and reported directly to Perales. According to Paul, *Voice* writer Wayne Barrett spoke to him about the upcoming article and the issues involved, even though it wasn't the kind of thing Paul would have known anything about. Apparently Wayne dropped names, assuming Du Brul would be discrete. Before I knew it, Du Brul was talking to Perales, and I was out of a job. The appearance of the news items was presumed to have been the consequence of my handiwork. Whistle-blowers aren't treated with any kind of respect. My husband was also harassed to leave, but the protections covering his job as one of many direct HHAP staff and other maneuvers saved him.

Upon being given notice, I went over to yell at Perales, who had reached an all-time low in my book. He didn't realize I was standing outside his door as he was talking to a new senior staff person about Angelo Del Toro and the now defunct HHAP grant to his brother, Bill. (Too much publicity made it untenable, so it was dropped. In 1991, Bill Del Toro and another of his government-funded schemes were under investigation.)[14] Perales was explaining how Angelo should have been able simply to *expect* that any such request by him for funds coming out of DSS would automatically be honored, irrespective of issues of merit. So this one was Cesar's baby. He was in it up to his eyeballs, too! He felt so secure about the conversation that he had it with his office door open. Only he didn't expect Bigfoot to be hanging just outside his peripheral vision. When I walked in, he fumbled for some words to the effect that I'd probably misunderstood what he had been talking about. However, I hadn't even said I heard anything. When the door was shut, I tore into him. Like I said at the outset. I was the one who should have understood from the beginning. Shoot, virtually everyone else at DSS did. There were quid pro quos all over the place.

I just couldn't seem to shake the sense that this was poor people's money they were blowing away. I still can't. Whether it goes directly into someone's pocket or simply advances someone's career doesn't matter if it ends up hurting the people it is supposed to help—negligently or by design.

Andrew Cuomo Walks on Water for Poor Families

As I see it, no single person did more harm or received more accolades for his work in the development of shelters for homeless families than Andrew Cuomo. Of the governor, the infamous questions should have been asked: What did he know? and When did he know it?

When Governor Mario Cuomo first took office, his son Andrew took a government job next to Pop, charging the taxpayers only one dollar a year for his services. During the time he worked in Albany, he was without question the most influential, one of the youngest, and, obviously, the figure closest to the governor. For reasons known probably only to him and his father, Andrew took a shine to the problem of homeless people, especially homeless families in New York. It may very well have been in part quite a charitable impulse. It certainly did not stem from a personal background in housing or welfare issues—the combination most essential for dealing with the problem. It is generally conceded by those close to the source that the ideas he espoused and made into his cause were by no means of his own design.

For that matter, the governor himself had a limited understanding of the realities. At one of the few meetings I attended at which the governor was present, various legislators said they wanted to call a halt to further development of temporary shelters. They also wanted to restrict the state's housing development for homeless families to permanent housing. The governor insisted that the state wasn't building any "temporary" housing. The legislators were taken aback, each of them with some direct knowledge of one or more of the shelters. But they didn't quite know how to pick up the ball after he fumbled it. At the end of the meeting, Assemblymember Nettie Mayersohn gestured to me to come where she was waiting to speak to the governor privately about it. She indicated that I should say something to set the record straight, so I did, telling him that temporary shelters were indeed being built all around the state. He looked at us and in earnest said he had seen some of them and could assure us "they were really quite solid and would last a long time." What did he think we were talking about—tents? If nothing else, that story entertained any number of people as it was told and retold.

If Dad was that far off base, it's not exactly a surprise that Andrew, with virtually no background in the field, could and did become a spokesperson for the issue. In due time he was moving big bucks, too. He had political will, public and private access, and, it was believed, the capacity to put almost anyone he wanted out of (or into) government and other powerful jobs. He is known, like his father, for his ruthlessness.

Andrew apparently could not shake his "calling" even after he left his job with government and went into private law practice. Our Ollie North of homeless policy, Andrew apparently ran an "off-the-shelf government," telling various policymakers what he wanted done and when to do it. Lawyers, commissioners, and other high-level staff jumped to his beat to put together a system of shelters for his own nonprofit organization, HELP. They were costly, cramped, ugly, and foolish public expenditures from construction to operation.

Andrew thought of the units as apartments because many had the semblance of separate sleeping and living quarters, complete with mini-kitchens. Albany HELP's floor plans show "studio" apartments (that is, consisting of only one room, including kitchenette, plus bath) of 271 square feet, counting the 50-square-foot bathroom. A three-room unit in Albany HELP is only 357 square feet, not counting bathroom. (The units can be modified by locking or unlocking various doors to increase for larger families and shrink for smaller.) In Jacob Riis's *How the Other Half Lives,* written over one hundred years ago, there is a remarkably similar floor plan for poor people's housing. Its smallest apartment—two rooms, not counting bathroom—is 274 square feet. Its three-room apartments, not counting bathrooms, are minimally 436 square feet. New York City journalists (most of whom knew little about the industry) by and large touted the HELPs as revolutionary in both design and quality. Andrew was even invited to present his model in various other parts of the country! If Riis could see us now . . .

Andrew brought the Red Cross in to run the first one, in Brooklyn, amidst great public fanfare. His toy apartments were touted as more humane and cheaper than the welfare hotels. In fact, to those with eyes and perhaps ears, and a knowledge of the strict rules that governed them along with the generous payments to them, they were neither. Grown women were treated like children who hadn't the slightest idea what was good for them or their kids. HELP was the pinnacle of a tyranny of kindness.

As one woman stalled in the system because of the tragedy called HELP 1, put it in a *New York Newsday* article, February 3, 1992: "I lived in one house on one block for 40 years before we were foreclosed on and forced to move. . . . I've worked, raised kids. I don't need living classes, I just need a damn apartment." She had two choices before entering HELP 1, where she is automatically infantilized by the rules and rituals common to the place. She could go there and potentially qualify for an early referral to a permanent apartment (quite an incentive) or she could opt for a welfare hotel, where her family could stay for years before being referred out to a private apartment. The whole thing is rigged to ensure that families will *choose* particular shelters. P.S. HELP 1 enjoys the distinction of having the highest number of self-help evictions of all the shelters in the entire city.[15] (They aren't called self-help anymore, though.)

How HELP Works

The mechanisms utilized to produce the HELPs could as easily have been put to the development of permanent, decent, affordable housing for the poorest people—those most likely to become homeless. No one dared tell Andrew that he was inappropriately twisting arms of government employees to make his shelters happen. People did what they were told—at the welfare departments and housing departments of the city and state and at the Housing Finance Agency (HFA), which issued bonds to capitalize them.

To the press Andrew asserted the work was donated or done "at cost" by the private sector, making the HELPs sound cheap, if not free. Journalists took him at his word. Certainly, using government staff time was not "free." Actually, little of the development, construction, or operational work was done for free in the normal sense of the word. Among other questionable expenses during a six-month period in 1988 were professional consultants at $36,216 and promotion and advertising at $19,050.[16] This latter expense certainly wasn't required to get homeless people to come into the program; they are automatically "blackmailed" into it by HRA. A mock-up model of HELP 1 was also made (part of promotion and advertising?) for just over $19,000. I'm sure they could have found an art or architecture school class to do it for less. But then, what was it needed for anyway? Contributions of $35,402 were made by HELP 1 in that six months to HELP Homeless Service Corporation, one of many subsidiaries set up to produce, operate, and promote HELPs.

As of the last IRS reports available to me, there were seven intertwined HELP corporations—several with multimillion-dollar budgets. There is one for each location where a project is built, one central not-for-profit (HELP Homeless Service Corp.), and one for-profit (HELP Homeless Housing Corp.). Andrew Cuomo is on all HELP governing boards, Jeffrey Sachs is on most, and John Kennedy is on some. Very few others are on any. Public documents indicate that there are several more operative HELP shelters currently (winter 1993), so presumably there are more corporations.

Andrew's own income from HELP would be indirectly derived, from payments made to his organization via welfare recipients' benefits. Each of the HELP housing projects pays a cut ("a legal kickback?") of the per diems to the corporation known as HELP Homeless Service, which pays Andrew. (If all this *help* stuff is getting confusing, don't worry, it's probably intended to be.) HELP HSC, too, shovels out money for public relations and advertising. The one fund-raising event noted in 1988 reports grossed $883,392. It cost $358,133. Hopefully, a good time was had by all, since the taxpayers ultimately footed the bill.

The individual charges per family far exceeded those scheduled to be paid on a per diem basis to welfare hotels, and even to most other nonprofit shelters operating in the city. The recipients did not get any choice about whether to turn the payments over, no matter how absurd they seemed (as compared with those for any, including luxury, housing in the city). Among the services purchased and provided/required, only day care is nearly universally desired. The others, which are not *exactly* mandatory, cover the gamut—all there at the homestead. There's the expected, like psychiatric counseling; the useful, like family health care; plus everything from nutrition and parental leadership guidance to high school equivalency classes, even, and this is one of Andrew's favorites, Little League. Maybe some of these are actually useful, but there's certainly no reason they have to be provided on site and exclusively to tenants of Andrew's buildings.

The per square foot construction costs were astronomical, in spite of the many quality and safety corners that were cut (and housing codes that were ignored) to produce these units. Although HELP 1 has been occupied for barely two years, chipping paint speckles the place, even where people who live there could never reach (on external beams, for instance). All the expenditures, including pay for numerous staff who worked on every phase of the projects, were either wholly paid for by

New York taxpayers or shared by taxpayers around the country through tax shelters for "donors" and AFDC payments, which are split among federal, state, and local government.[17]

On top of all this, the way Andrew structured the deal, HELP would reap rewards for a long time to come. He went for public dollars in a big way, convincing HFA to float the bonds that would assure the capital necessary for his projects. Private investors would purchase the bonds. The revenue derived from the sale was then passed along to HELPs, at an interest rate of seven eighths of a percent, to be paid back over a ten-year period out of welfare monies—our tax dollars and the recipients' checks, that is. If HELP were to default anywhere along the way, New York taxpayers still have to pick up the tab on the bonds.

HELP did the deal. A private developer took on the physical development work "at cost." Construction firms were hired to build. After the buildings were up and ready to run, HELP subcontracted the operation and management of the buildings and services to agencies like the American Red Cross for the next ten years (barring early termination for unforeseen circumstances). At the end of ten years, HELP has no further contractual obligation. Not coincidentally, the depreciation schedule for the payoff of debt service would be completed in ten years also. In other words, after the taxpayers were soaked for ten years through inflated AFDC payments to the HELP/Red Cross (or other operational organization) project, the building, free and clear of debt, need not be operated as a shelter any longer. In fact, Andrew maintained that if the shelters were not "needed" for families in the future, they could be turned into housing for senior citizens (because the apartments are so small). HELP would not be required to continue using them for the purpose or the people for whom they were built in the first place. Not bad. During that ten years, HELP would have minuscule functional connection to the operation. It was merely the deal doer, negotiating things like the daily rate paid to the shelter per family with the appropriate state and local government departments. It was not, and is not, a service provider. Notwithstanding, HELP managed to squeeze some (possibly legal) annual payments from each of its toy apartment complexes through the negotiated per diem rates.

Andrew's muscle propelled the negotiations—with HFA, the banks, the communities, and with the welfare departments who would have to pay the per diems over the next ten years. In some communities, like Mount Vernon, HELP was opposed because it was producing shelters rather than housing. Of course, community opposition was no sweat.

Usually, the strongest objections were over the money. In the early stages, localities were led to believe these projects were a bargain. (Even now, most of the press thinks these abominations are cheap.) When they got closer to the finish line, it would become all too apparent that the costs would exceed anything the local governments were already paying out to hotels, motels, or even other shelters—notwithstanding HELP's incorporation papers, which state their purpose as providing "safe, and sanitary temporary habitable space for homeless families . . . as a cost effective alternative to welfare hotels."[18]

Even though per diems paid to the Red Cross exceeded the official standards for payments to hotels, within the first year of operation, the Red Cross demanded and received *retroactive* increases to make up for a claimed operating deficit. A January 23, 1990, letter from DSS was sent to New York City's welfare department raising the daily rate per family to $114.30 backward to December 21, 1987. It's amazing how creative government employees could be with AFDC monies when they wanted to.

Fighting with Andrew was presumed to be hazardous to one's future, so a number of extraordinary measures were taken to assist him along the way. Top-level staff in various government departments handled business for Andrew's HELPs that under normal circumstances would not have been a part of their jobs. Some of these actions are described in detail, others hinted at in a memo from Nancy Travers to Andrew Cuomo dated October 28, 1988. The memo is written "to set the record straight." It does. In the course of discussing the "record," Travers gives us a glimpse of an off-the-shelf government operation at work for Andrew Cuomo and his HELP organization.

States with large homeless populations were concerned that federal reimbursement for most hotel/shelter payments to families was in jeopardy because of the Department of Health and Human Services's reinterpretation of a long-standing payment principle and its desire to end the federal share. These issues were of particular concern to Andrew because his ten-year commitments for the HELP projects relied on specific state-federal agreements. They were also of concern to state and local governments with high rates of long-term homelessness among families. If the federal share of family shelter costs were eliminated, state and local costs would soar. But Andrew Cuomo apparently wanted more than a basic cease-fire between the feds and the states on the matter. If Travers is to be believed, he wanted specific commitments tacked on to the final legislative package for his/HELP's advantage.

In the memo, Travers explains DSS's reluctance to tie specific HELP-related amendments to what was called the Stanton moratorium (which would checkmate the federal government's plan to discontinue paying its share of the family shelter burden). She writes, "The language that *David Emil* drafted for you was something neither the Department nor myself was aware of. As I understand it, *it was delivered on plain bond and was never part of the Department's legislative agenda in Washington* [emphasis added]." Travers's memo, too, was written on plain bond. In other words, these written transactions were not sanctioned job-related activities, but they surely would affect how government business was getting done. She goes on to imply that had she known of the language to advance Andrew's interests, she would have lent her support, irrespective of the potential for negatively affecting legislation of major importance:

> the Department [DSS] does have fairly strict protocol about lines of communication—particularly with Washington and the Gov's office. Lowly program folk [i.e., her] are not supposed to involve themselves with such serious and esoteric goings on. But it certainly can be arranged in the future and we would be more than happy to track any legislation of interest to you and can assure you that it won't fall between the cracks—nor will there be mixed signals regarding support.

She proceeds. Apparently at the highest level of DSS, tying together the HELP and Stanton moratorium amendments as an "all or nothing package" was perceived to have "serious fiscal implications for the state . . . and its entire system of shelter payments to everyone on AFDC." Legitimately so. But, according to Travers, that did not stop Michael

Dowling, previous head of Income Maintenance at DSS, now chief aide to Governor Cuomo on social welfare issues, whom she describes as intervening with DSS personnel and Senator Moynihan and his staff on Andrew's behalf. The memo is clearly intended to tell Andrew how faithful a servant Travers has been to him and to explain away any potential misreading he may have had of her role in these events.

Her next topic is setting the per diem for HELP in Albany. She places blame for a snag in the negotiations on a reluctant Albany County welfare official, even naming her. As the state's top shelter regulator, whose responsibilities included rate-setting arrangements, Travers could have been expected to keep such potentially damaging discussions off paper. Certainly the extraordinary measures she took to assist HELP had an appearance of impropriety if not worse. She probably would have been more discreet, but, according to the memo, Andrew hadn't been returning her calls. She says she would have been more helpful in the negotiations if she had known sooner that there was a problem. (Albany's welfare department may have wanted to keep costs down. Sooner or later it would have had to cave. The mayor of Albany, one of the first to support Governor Cuomo in the primary, had been repaid, frequently. At some point, the mayor would have to ante up again.)

The tour de force begins, "Finally, I'd like to request some closure on the second floor job [in other words, working with the governor more directly.] It's clear that there is some problem or combination of problems—either with the BCI [Bureau of Criminal Investigations], continuing resistance on the part of other second floor players, *a loss of your confidence* [emphasis added], or a combination of all three." She adds, parenthetically, "If it's a BCI problem, I would at least like to know just which murder I forgot to report."

What does the head of a nongovernment agency (Andrew) have to do with government job decisions? How could the state's chief shelter regulator possibly treat the project of a man who's holding her future in his hands with objectivity? Likewise, Emil, who couldn't manage to make an adjustment in the state plan to produce permanent housing, even at the request of several of the state's legislators from both houses, did, according to Travers, come up with language for HELP, as part of a very crucial "package deal" from Congress. How could the general counsel of the state Department of Social Services put the whole AFDC population, the state of New York, and other states at risk of losing everything for one project?

Lackluster David Emil, who selflessly sat through endless meetings to help HELP along, who intervened in matters normally dealt with by lower-level staff (like negotiating the HELP 1 budget with Jack Doyle of Red Cross),[19] shortly became the head of Battery Park City, a multi-billion-dollar public authority dedicated to building housing and undertaking other development activities for affluent New Yorkers. Travers did not end up with the "second floor" job; she did soon leave DSS for a higher-level appointment at the state's Division of Housing and Community Renewal.

As for Cesar Perales, Mayor Dinkins made him social welfare czar of New York City. The job is preposterous in that he is given some authority over several major city agencies, including the Human Resources Administration and the Health and Hospitals Corporation. If no single person has ever been able to make a dent in the problems of one of these superagencies, to imagine an individual "making a difference" over more than one is simply lunatic. Then again, Cesar was not known for his innovations, aggressive style, or significant accomplishments. He was known for following orders.

Stalking the Alternative: Permanent Housing

In 1987, during part of the extended Feast of Saint Andrew, patron saint of the downtrodden, I snagged a fellowship accompanied by a placement with the Joint Legislative Women's Caucus of New York State. I took on a project to explore solutions to the problem of homeless families. (Insofar as homeless families are 90 percent female headed, it was an appropriate issue for the caucus.) From the outset I maintained that families who were homeless needed a permanent place to live, irrespective of any other problems they might have. Assemblymember Helene Weinstein (chair of the caucus) initially seemed pleased that I was interested in working on housing issues, notwithstanding my focus on homeless families, and permanent housing as opposed to shelters.

She directed me to meet with Assemblymember Nettie Mayersohn, chair of the Women's Housing Committee. Mayersohn's housing interests were not particularly with homelessness, but she became intrigued by the information I provided her regarding the excessive expenditures shelters required and why permanent housing for homeless families was superior to and cost less than hotels or shelters. At the time, most people still believed shelters were cost saving. I outlined for her the extent of purchases of service at the expense of a possible housing alternative. We agreed to call a meeting of other members of the working group.

At the initial meeting, a variety of issues and potential legislative actions to alleviate the housing crisis for homeless families were raised. The last suggestion I made briefly outlined a solution that would significantly enhance the production and long-term sustenance of permanent housing I was currently exploring. "The plan" as it came to be referred to colloquially, generated exceptional enthusiasm among many legislators as we introduced it more broadly.

In short order the working group began to grow, and a succession of meetings resulted in a planned hearing on the subject. I continued to do research and met with various legislative staff. As we progressed, more legislators outside the caucus agreed to cosponsor the hearings. Among them, Assembly Housing Committee Chair Pete Graniss expressed considerable interest, lending a much needed boost to the more cautious members of the group.

Events unfolded rapidly. Things were going almost too well, it seemed. I waited for the inevitable bomb to drop. Nothing that involved big bucks could be this easy. I went about my business and traipsed through a series of meetings in which I explained, ad infinitum, various aspects of the problem of homeless families and attendant actions that could be taken to mend the situation.

The working group proceeded with unusual intensity on this—meeting for two and three hours each week, sometimes at the expense of other things the legislators were doing. In time, the anticipated bomb began to descend. First, some of the handful of items I had been working on started to smoke. For instance, one concern was the City Housing Authority's covert practice of reducing their welfare population, thereby exacerbating already disastrous market conditions for these families. This was also happening in some communities outside the city. Mayersohn, on the heels of objections by Helene Weinstein, forcefully objected to pursuing the issue.

Though it was never overtly articulated in racial terms, those opposed to even checking into it maintained that their reelection by a largely middle-class constituency would be threatened if it were perceived that they were working to expand the concentration of welfare families in their neighborhoods. Once the reelection concerns were raised, everyone backed off, as if it were a common courtesy independent of issues.

Assemblymember Barbara Clark and Senator Velmanette Montgomery—both black women with strong grass-roots ties—emerged as the most supportive right from the start. Senator Olga Mendez, who joined the group after it was off the ground, also began promoting aggressive action, though she leaned toward restricting the group's drive to a single item—the plan. Mendez's strategy appeared to be geared to avoiding conflicts that would arise if multiple problems were taken on, thereby making consensus harder to achieve. Finally, two main areas of inquiry were settled on for the hearing—the plan to promote permanent housing development and the administrative accountability of the welfare department. Beneath the surface, discontent was brewing. After Mendez joined, another member came on board, as if to balance the committee and keep Weinstein's invisible hand stirring the pot.

I continued my research, preparing paperwork geared to the hearing. Some of my best sources were people within DSS and HRA with whom I had maintained friendly relations. They led me to others who could zero in on very discrete and sometimes esoteric details necessary to proving the validity of the plan. In other cases I would be sent documents and papers that would have been difficult for me to obtain on my own. I was also directed to crucial reports and other public documents I could request but wouldn't even know about without help. Some advocacy groups and individuals who hadn't capitulated to the current shelter development trend also provided support.

In order to "professionalize" the plan, it was agreed that I would consult with the Pratt Institute in Brooklyn to get computerized printouts to support my assumptions. I explained the basic factors essential to the plan, and Dean Zias of Pratt worked with me, plugging the numbers into various housing configurations to determine the projects' viability over time. I explained the results and showed the initial computer runs to the Women's Housing Committee. The cautious were relieved and the hopeful ecstatic. Malcontents were silent.

The plan in fact was almost obvious but had not been put together in quite the same form by anyone previously. Actually, all the elements were in place in one or another currently functioning project. However, because of the Byzantine nature of welfare law and practice, and the vested interests threatened by the plan's potential, obfuscation was easy to create, keeping people with less knowledge in a quandary. Both some staff and legislators kept finding ways of blocking the plan's release. In some respects, the opposition was a mystery. In others, less so.

One veteran legislative employee theorized that some other legislative staff, especially those on the social services committees, were responding to a perceived turf threat. She said it would be likely that people whose specialization was similar to mine would be concerned that an outsider, particularly a "fellow," would have as extensive—or worse, more extensive—background than they. Since they were *paid* to examine the same issues and make recommendations, they would resist "foreign" ideas that could call their competence into question.

If this were so, it would be one more example of people who make a living off tax dollars getting in the way of progress. That was standard operating procedure at DSS, so why shouldn't it be here? These staff certainly played a role in stalling approval of the hearing, stepping on every possible detail required to implement the event. For instance, under normal circumstances, if a legislator wanted a hearing date (to secure a room, staff, and so on), only a day or so was necessary to set it. Not this one. In spite of having more sponsoring legislative bodies, it took weeks and a good deal of haggling by me and some of the legislative women to get a date, and even that kept changing.

As days and weeks went by, it became apparent that the resistance was also coming from at least some members of the women's caucus. The working group would meet and agree on a course of action, only to have it changed by one of Weinstein's directives to me (as chair, she could dictate what I did). It was turning into a full-fledged battle among the women, splitting those in the caucus who were participating at all almost straight down ethnic and racial lines. Not surprising, most of the black and Latina women remained supportive, worked hard, and even took some abuse in the process.

Without their perseverance under considerable pressure, the hearing never would have taken place. One by one, most of the others succumbed to the unscrupulous leadership of Helene Weinstein. Still, so much controversy was stirred up that in the end the hearing was cosponsored by six legislative bodies. The odd bottom line was, everyone was sick of the proliferation of shelters and believed there had to be a way of stemming that tide without getting Reagan's explicit permission. Sentiment among the legislators who had to face their constituencies every time another shelter went up in their neighborhoods was more than favorable to permanent housing.

At the worst point, Weinstein served me with a veritable gag order. She told me not to speak to the senators, particularly Montgomery and Mendez, or Assemblymember Clark anymore. If they called me, I was to refer them to her and not answer any of their questions. I was in the untenable position of clamming up on the most supportive women or ignoring a direct order. I found myself running from meeting to meeting, spending most evenings and weekends on the phone at home, trying to set up the hearing that almost wasn't. The pressure was excruciating.

In the process, I learned a few things about Weinstein. She was the legislative point person for increasing soup kitchen and pantry funds and sometimes shelter funds through the Task Force on Food, Farm and Nutrition, which she also chaired. She was heavily supported by, and highly supportive of, the social welfare people who stood to lose by the very essence of the plan. How far up the political chain opposition went, I cannot say. Had it not been for the aggressive and active support of Clark and Montgomery especially, in spite of the obstacles, the hearing never would have taken place. That's certain. The symbolic power of the plan was its contradiction of the poverty politics that pitted poor people against their "keepers." I hoped the hearing would hasten the end of what I perceived to be a condensed rerun of the historic battle over outdoor relief and the poorhouses. In spite of its success, that hasn't come to pass. Yet.

The Plan's Essence

The plan was really quite simple. It had always been politics that stood in the way. Shelters and hotels receive enormous daily payments from the welfare department throughout the life of their contracts. The costs are astronomical in the short and long run. (During the information gathering for the hearing, Nancy Travers admitted that DSS and HRA were paying as much as $150 per day per unit to a shelter whose parent organization's board chair was Robert Hayes. These payments would be made even if no family occupied the unit, because employees had to be paid on a regular basis, and so on.) Most of these expenditures actually have nothing to do with the operating and maintenance of the buildings. As much as 90 percent can be for nonshelter-related items, especially service workers and fees accruing to any bank that may have put up a piece of the financing.[20]

Check it out: if 100 units of temporary housing of this sort were paid $150 per day, the total cost per year would be $5,475,000. If only 10 percent of that is for housing-related expenses, the remainder—$4,927,500—is being spent on something *other than housing*—generally, services of one kind or another. The $4.9 million could be recaptured for the production of additional units of housing instead of wasted on often unnecessary, unwanted, and duplicative services.

Over a fifteen-year period, more than $82 million (assuming *zero* inflation, hardly likely) would be spent to shelter only 100 families at any given time. This is nearly $74 million more than would have been necessary simply to house 100 families, whose service needs could easily have been met through other, already existing neighborhood centers designed—and government funded—for that purpose. Multiply these numbers by just 1,000 (there are over 10,000 families in New York's shelter system alone at this time), and you quickly run into the tens of billions of dollars. Try ten thousand . . . As long as the primary mode for dealing with a housing and income shortage is temporary housing of any kind, these expenditures will continue to rise, exponentially.

I proposed a variation on the theme already in practice but utilized mostly for temporary housing at the time. In brief, this plan would have utilized government and private monies available to pay for the initial construction of as many actual apartments for needy families as possible. For the first year or two of operation, these would officially be emergency residences. As such, they would be paid negotiated per diems in the same manner as the hotels and shelters. At the end of the "emergency" period, the family would have the right to stay, receiving a standard rental lease for permanent housing at rent levels affordable to the poorest people—essentially welfare rent maximums in New York City.

Instead of paying for services up the wazoo, the purpose of the per diems would be to build a capital reserve. Clearly, the reserve would be so high that it could sustain the operating and maintenance of the initial construction for the life of the units *and* produce additional housing for more poor and homeless families. The same principles could be applied to this housing, creating yet another pool for additional units as well as maintaining the building at very low rents indefinitely. There were some technical hurdles to be dealt with, but these were all quite surmountable. And the money poured down the sinkhole of modern-day poorhouses would be saved.

Mathematically, legally, and rationally, it worked. It certainly beat paying banks for debt service over and over again. There were many possible sources for the initial capital—not the least of which were HHAP and DHCR. Only political will held the plan back. It would have been a savings to taxpayers and the treasury, and an incalculable benefit to the human beings who would otherwise continue to be shifted from one shelter to the next. Only someone with a stake in shelter development would have any real reason to oppose it.

The Hearing, at Last

Up on a stage, a surprising number of legislators appeared to question the witnesses. At times the dais set up for the occasion could not accommodate all those who wanted in. I sat behind the chair, able to hand notes as necessary to whoever was speaking. The most telling testimony would be that of Nancy Travers and others from the Department of Social Services. Without overtly rejecting it, Travers swirled around the plan like a dog chasing her tail. To every question posed regarding it, she gave a bureaucratese answer—distorting issues she felt legislators would not have the background to challenge. It wasn't just personal either. Something was driving her that made no practical sense. The mechanisms the plan utilized were already in place. Quite simply, the state could decide to do it.

As luck would have it, Travers's partner from DSS for most of the grilling was Jack Hickey, whom I had known for many years and who in fact had been helpful on many occasions. He was also one of the few people at DSS who had a real grip on the technical details of AFDC. I had gone over the theoretical underpinnings of the plan with him previously. He agreed with me, but, until he testified, I wouldn't know what was going to happen.

During his testimony, much to my relief, he confirmed that in principle the details raised in opposition to the plan were mere technicalities that could be overcome. He confirmed that most of the variables in question already existed in one form or another in a number of current and on-line future projects to house homeless families.

Pete Graniss, chair of the Assembly Housing Committee, continued to pursue the issues with Travers quite effectively. Finally, he said to both, "I would like to see the reasons it can work, rather than the reasons it can't."[21] Travers responded, "Certainly." So did Hickey.

David Emil had not been present during most of the Travers-Hickey testimony. Clearly, he was needed, since Travers had not managed to put the plan to rest. So when the head of HRA, William Grinker, took his turn, Emil hung around. Grinker had really not read the plan and apparently had no idea of the prevailing political distress at DSS; so he foolishly said things in his opening statement like "The key to preventing homelessness, I believe, lies in the development of permanent housing" and "I just want to say up front, my belief, that the problem of homelessness is really a basic problem: part of a larger problem in this country of poverty; and that we're not going to solve the problem of homelessness until we really grapple nationally with that issue." He also said that the number of homeless families in the city had risen over 500 percent in nine years. His statistics were gritty: 40 percent of all families coming into the system are classified as pregnant or mothers with newborns; their average length of stay is 13.4 months.

When he completed his opening statement, the questioning began. Initially, Grinker said there was nothing legally prohibiting use of the money in the way the plan suggested. Emil was on his heels: "I'm the general counsel to the Department of Social Services—" Graniss cut him off. But Emil did manage to slip in the possibility of legal implications that had not been discussed.

Quite some time later, Ron Schiffman of the Pratt Institute for Community Development raised a concern regarding lawyers that would be echoed in the coming days by others. "I think lawyers have usually been paid to be creative. I think the difference is that lawyers who I work with when we're doing a development project . . . find a way of solving the problem. Lawyers who work for public entities find that unless they cover somebody's rear-end, they're in trouble." He went out of his way to avoid pointing a finger, but he probably didn't know how correct in the specific he was.

Later Steve Banks, a Legal Aid lawyer heavily involved in the McCain case for safe and habitable *emergency* housing, reinforced the need to stop building more shelters and turn public policy toward the production of permanent housing. He put to rest a number of issues that had been raised—mostly by Travers and Emil—to oppose the conversion plan. He made it clear that in various ways the city and state already utilized the mechanisms that were in the plan, but for different purposes, much as Hickey and, inadvertently, Grinker had said. Banks's bottom line was this: "Logically, there is no reason why it [the money] cannot be used [to expand the production of permanent housing for welfare families]." We may have had our strategic differences, but Banks was legitimately concerned about the flood of shelters, and by this time he knew a breakthrough was essential.

At the end of the hearing, Travers made a rare gesture. She returned to the hearing room and walked up to congratulate me. Odd.

The day after the hearing, Pete Graniss called a meeting with David Emil. He pressured Emil to work out the sticking points. Emil was his usual pouting self, with a touch of nervousness showing through the patrician veneer. After all, there were a serious number of legislators present, each staring straight at him. I was also present, to ensure he didn't get away with obfuscation this time.

Emil knew quite well that all the principles in the plan were already operational somewhere. Unable to dismiss it on any actual legal grounds, he finally claimed that the reason it couldn't be done was that it wasn't in the "state plan" that had already been submitted to the federal government. So, unless and until the state plan were amended, it was a moot issue. Graniss pressed him to do it, if that was the only real problem. Emil claimed that it was hard work and took a lot of time. He failed to mention that he had been working directly with Andrew Cuomo on the sticky issues to produce the HELP abominations.

Emil never did amend the state plan to accommodate Graniss and the rest of us. He did, however (if Travers's memo is to be believed), intervene on behalf of HELP in Washington before leaving DSS.

Two days after the hearing, the Assembly Democratic Conference voted to allocate $370 million for housing development—a portion of which was intended for homeless families and individuals. Weeks later, the senate came to a similar agreement, with details worked out the next session. Graniss had been suggesting that some of these funds be used as initial capital for the plan, presuming Emil et al. did their homework. That didn't happen.

Some Permanent Housing Built

Contrary to the trends at the time, a few buildings were rehabilitated or built as permanent residences for homeless adults and families. The first not-for-profit permanent family housing developed in New York City with HHAP money was the result of the Cooper Square Committee (a community group) and my husband's dogged persistence in the face of every conceivable bureaucratic obstacle. After the first one, it did get easier, as long as the permanent housing advocates on staff (as the staff matured, so did the goals) stayed out of the political gestures HHAP continued to make. (The city itself utilized some millions of HHAP money on so-called permanent housing. One such project was called the 145th Street Cluster. Even after more than a million dollars was sunk into it, the housing remained a disaster. One day I received a call from a woman living in one of these units. She needed help because the bathtub from the upstairs apartment had fallen through the ceiling into her apartment! Staff at HHAP involved had an impossible time staying on top of the entire project, as more and more funding for it went some-where—probably not into the buildings for the most part, though das-tardly deeds were never proven, nor actually pursued for that matter.)

Finally, two years ago, my husband, Tom, put the essence of the housing plan discussed at the legislative hearing into operation in Orange County. He found a willing partner in Shirley Cook, the conservative welfare commissioner there, who could see the cost savings and simplicity in the idea. With the eager assistance of two local minority-run nonprofits, RECAP and PODER, they pulled it off. Curiously, Nancy Travers was still the head of HHAP. She did not try to stop it. It is still, as of this writing, the only permanent housing for homeless families produced this way. If something could be done to produce life-size *permanent* apartments, HELP wouldn't look so hot anymore.

Human Misery: The Cost of (Perhaps) Good Intentions

The fact is that power relations changed when Governor Mario Cuomo took office in 1983. His rhetoric of compassion and the election delivered a mandate to address the homeless population. He brought a number of people into state government to do the job. A Task Force on the Homeless was established that included Doyle, Hopper, and Hayes, among others, as advocate advisers to carve out the homeless program. These people were not pawns, but along with Travers, Emil, and Andrew Cuomo they were the vanguard of the South Africanization of New York, however "sensitive" they appeared. The actual and provable fact is that they all enhanced their careers through the development of shelters, purported to "speak for the homeless," misrepresented the interests of homeless people repeatedly for their own gain, and did so with impunity—occasionally out of ignorance. Given the imprimatur of the governor and the press, armed with a barrelful of options and ultimately hundreds of millions of dollars from multiple sources, they chose shelter development over housing development. A barrage of policy decisions followed that made matters even worse.

Often it is not in the rhetoric, grand schemes, and legislation that the poor get screwed. It is in the details worked out behind closed doors.

Those who argued for the services—like the National Association of Social Workers, the Red Cross, Nancy Travers, and Andrew Cuomo—seemed to have forgotten the deep rootedness of these families' problems. For one, poverty itself and dealing with a welfare system designed to humiliate and degrade people did become internalized. No social service would change these fundamentals. The domestic imperialism tied in to our social policies has the same effects that colonization anywhere does. We just don't choose to call it that.

Being poor does not by definition mean being sick. Being poor does mean needing help. At a minimum that means income and housing. You can't buy a loaf of bread with a social worker. After all, most social workers are not the merciful equivalent of rocket scientists, and Mother Teresa is neither the model nor the norm for the profession. Social work, like most other professions, accommodates a fair share of incompetents, the unethical, the greedy, and "control freaks" (as we used to say in the not so long ago sixties). More than anything else, shelter development became another way to expand their share of the pie. And no one would hold them accountable if they failed to "fix" or "cure" the families.

Chapter 7

Charities and Fraud

Our well-wishing can be unlimited, since in it we need to do nothing. But doing good is harder. —Immanuel Kant

I just got home from the hospital after six days. In that time there have been three deaths and two others wounded by guns. I look at my kids and think, I know I have to live. Nobody would take care of them the way I do. Nobody would take my place.
—A welfare mother and friend, in Brooklyn

Charities come and go, some lasting only long enough to promote the promoters, others enduring a century or more. Sooner or later they involve money, often vast sums of it, and multiple agendas. Some may have been started with truly beneficent intentions, but even these finally give way to a pragmatism that shifts focus away from "helping the poor" and toward sustaining the institution. These dual objectives come increasingly to be at odds; the motivations behind them begin to diversify and encompass a host of additional interests.

For instance, in the past decade the issue of homelessness has swirled like a tornado, picking up random pieces of debris and hurling them every which way. There were those who were genuinely motivated by the desire to help homeless people find a place to live. At the same time, there were those whose primary desire was to cleanse the streets of human misery so they wouldn't have to confront it as they entered or left mansions and luxury condos. There were those who wanted to cart every homeless person off to therapy, like broken furniture needing repair. (Soon every city would be full of carpenters.) There were civil libertarians, who understood the dangers of shaving the rights of home-less persons to be in public places or to beg on city streets. (Helping homeless people in this case also helps everyone, by upholding the constitutional rights of all of us.) And more.

A contrary movement to prohibit public begging was kicked off by some charities and New York's then mayor, Edward Koch. They argued that poor street people were annoying. Giving money was not only a waste, and an encouragement to others, but actually *harmful* to the beggars. They urged those with cash to spare to donate to a *worthy* cause—a charity—instead. The fact that the charities not only begged on the streets but followed people right into their homes to ask for money via the mail, television, newspapers, phone, or fax didn't seem to be so bothersome. Nor did most people care that the dollars they contributed this way might very well do nothing more than help pay for the next mailing or advertisement.

The competition for money and jobs generated by the very exis-tence of poor and homeless people began to dictate social policy. While poor people have gotten poorer in the past twenty years, *social work in many forms has become a growth industry.* The social welfare establishment has prospered beyond anyone's wildest dreams, even through the Rea-gan administration. A Bureau of Labor statistics survey of fifty job catego-ries in New York City from 1977 to 1987, for instance, showed that social services to families increased by 422 percent! This occurred while the dollar value of the maximum welfare payment for a family of three—and the minimum wage—had fallen by 50 percent, far below the poverty line. The social welfare establishment has become so big that it wields significant power in the development of social policy and the election of politicians. It was all but inevitable that it would substitute its own mottled interests for those of the people it claimed to serve.

Nowhere is this more glaring than at the top. Like other industries, large social welfare corporations play a mediating role with government at some times and supply it with employees at others. The less than "objective" consequences are obvious. If some real estate magnate takes a high-level government position, it is not surprising when conditions for

213

real estate development become more favorable. The same sort of thing happens in the world of social welfare. The unseasoned might expect the conditions of poor people themselves to elevate when these professionals take government jobs, but that is rarely true. What is more likely to happen is that conditions for the kinds of institutions these professionals come from improve—conditions for *their* future employment, with respect to both pay and power.

The contradictions are endemic in both the grand foundations like Ford who give away money and the huge and influential social service agencies who get that money along with megacontracts from government. Many of the agencies also have millions of dollars in endowments. Often the names of their directors (founding and current) read like the social register. These board members wield considerable power over social policy at the local and national levels, either purposefully (those who attend meetings, chair committees, hire executive directors, and so on) or by default (those whose major contribution is cash, a name, and a consenting silence). They can be, and often are, as ruthless as board members of any for-profit corporation. If poor people get hurt in the process, that's too bad. It's also too bad that the U.S. Treasury is being looted at their expense. No one is looking, hardly anyone seems to care, almost anything goes as long as the magic words *for the poor* precede the action.

Hands Across America: Electroshock Charity

In addition to the advent of shelters and soup kitchens, the 1980s produced its share of charitable flash floods. In the first TV megatron of its kind, USA for Africa permeated the airwaves with a singable song and a music video that aired worldwide. It didn't do much for starving Africans. It did generate a lot of publicity for its stars and promoters. So much so that Hands Across America (Hands) was hatched to help some of our own. The much publicized event that generated the money was a brilliant stroke. Citizens of the United States joined hands at the same time on the same day to create a human chain stretching from one end of the continent to the other. President and Mrs. Reagan, Donald Duck and Mickey Mouse, and countless others joined the line. The hands didn't stretch far enough, what with the desert and all, but hey.

Hands employed over 450 people full-time and dozens of others during its peak. Fancy digs housed the central operation. Coast-to-coast flights and expensive hotels pampered the organizers. It took some $16 million to raise barely $15 million. The men in control had done it again. The rest of us got snookered.

Hands designated varying amounts to go to each state. They proclaimed that the spending decisions would be made by the people in that state, from across the political, ethnic, racial, class, and cultural spectrum. Even poor people would be encouraged to participate. Democracy would triumph. In a pig's eye.

The Deal in New York State

Some states were all but finished making their decisions for spending the money before New York was even beginning the process. That wasn't because New Yorkers are reluctant to deal with money. The slow start was due to political calculations by the men in charge in La La land. Grass-roots politics in New York has a long and complicated history. They thought they could avert potential trouble by putting us on a hot deadline. The warp speed imposed from Los Angeles also jettisoned any truly democratic process. But, then again, no state had a "truly democratic" process. That was part of the shell game from the start.

The structure of Hands began with a wobbling rubber stamp board of central glitzies—Michael Jackson, Harry Belafonte, and so on. Marty Rogol, a leftover sixties slickster, headed the staff and manipulated the board. There was also a national advisory board composed mostly of the from-hunger crowd, like Ron Pollock, former director of the Food Research and Action Center, and Bob Greenstein, food stamp honcho under Jimmy Carter. Among the few others on this national advisory board was Diane Morales, working for then Manhattan Borough President David Dinkins. Each state set up a separate apparatus to oversee distribution of their allocation, subject to approval from Rogol (who claimed the board had the real decision-making power, when he wasn't putting it down, that is). New York's allocation was just under $900,000.

In the fall of 1986, I took the job of pulling together and staffing the New York State Committee for Hands Across America on the condition that the group would have significant representation of poor people, not just tokens for the show. Except for heads of coalitions (i.e., Russell Sykes) or other blocs (i.e., Kathy Goldman) and the big charities (United Way et al.)—who were excluded as per Rogol's instructions—our committee was supposed to reflect the broad racial, ethnic, class, and cultural diversity of the state.

The only way to get significant participation of poor people, given the late date and the absence of an extant statewide organization, would have been to put out public service announcements on radio and TV and in newspapers. Rogol bristled at the very idea. The compromise we wrestled was to keep the New York Committee small so as to ensure that the few active poor people who could be brought in on short notice would be heard among the glut of service providers who would otherwise dominate the process.

In 1987 I would reach forty—the age at which the ancient Greeks believed one became an adult. By this time I should have known from the start when a solid sham was in the works. But I still wanted to believe.

It wasn't long before we were inundated by manipulators from New Jersey to Los Angeles functioning at the behest of Marty Rogol, who was most anxious to steer New York. The various interlopers were profoundly interested in soup kitchens and food pantries. They thought highly of inserting "case management" into the serving game. Ann Herman, a former welfare mother (left without a stitch by her husband after five children) and now a paid employee at two full-time jobs, put her two cents in quickly. She said people were sick of the red tape already thriving in those places like algae on a stagnant pond. Herman knew that case management (in social work vogue) was just a euphemism for snooping into women's private business. Just what was needed—another social worker—before a bag of almost food was handed out!

Our first meeting seemed to be getting nowhere, between the attempts by an LA-controlled enforcer from New Jersey to scuttle New Yorkers' democratic discussion and the general difficulty of getting any group of strangers to come to some sort of working conclusions. Finally, John Mohawk (a professor of Indian law) breached the impasse. He spoke about transferring power to people who are powerless. Picking up from him, Robin Morgan, feminist author and activist, formulated the magic motion that was unanimously adopted by the group: "We are committed to the politics of justice as opposed to the politics of charity. More specifically, we support advocacy, education, and empowerment as the means to achieve it." Henceforth we would have these principles to guide future decision making. From LA, Rogol et al. reacted as if we were speaking in tongues.

Robin Morgan was railroaded (supportively) into becoming the committee chair. Over the many months we worked on this project, virtually all votes were unanimous. On occasion, one or at most two people opposed a motion. Trouble was, at the beginning of almost every meeting we found ourselves rehashing decisions that had been concluded the meeting before. It became apparent that until some members of the home team got their marching orders from outside, they never knew what to oppose or support, so they would raise settled issues *after* they had voted for them. It kept happening.

It wasn't as if we had no service representatives on our committee. In fact, half the group, including some of those from poverty backgrounds, were service providers of one sort or another, with the largest single plurality being the food people. Three out of seven of New York's food bank heads were on the committee. (Two of them were put on the committee by LA.) Each belonged to one or more of the foodie coalitions and had overlapping boards. They complained that the committee had "too many antipoverty" people on it, as if the issue of hunger were somehow distinct from poverty. It was absurd and persistent.

We sent out mailings to hundreds of groups for their insights. Of course, since no outreach was done or allowed, poor people themselves (except for the handful on our committee) didn't get these mailings. One priceless and revealing response came from Helen Palit from City Harvest. She wrote, "Allocate funds to anti-hunger groups . . . that gave staff and/or board level participation in the Hands Across America event. Such groups, including ours . . . [have] a right to expect that the expenditure of time and money has direct benefit to its program." Did every participant in the United States expect to get something in return? What was the point, anyway? The other food groups would have agreed with everything she wrote except City Harvest's right to anything versus theirs.

Knowing the New York committee would have to distribute some funds to the service organizations, the first and only approved decision we made targeted $150,000 to those direct service and advocacy groups that had something, however flimsy, of "a track record of adhering to the principles of justice." That was concession dough. As for the remainder of our recommendations, we might as well have been on the moon. Rogol claimed to be in full support of everything we were trying to do but expressed his distress at what he considered to be its radical nature—not that he wasn't radical himself. Unhuh—radical chic with grease.

Rogol sent another emissary to dissuade New York from continuing with a plan that would have had far more impact on the lives of poor families than anything the discard market proposed. Unfortunately, as the board member in question listened to the concerted voices defending New York's proposal, he found himself unable to reject it. In fact, he said it was the most creative he knew of from any state, and he would personally guarantee that it got a full hearing with the board—the glitzy one. For reasons now unfathomable, we believed he could deliver on his promise.

Marty Rogol must have imploded. He had sent a messenger who forgot the message. He had tried what effectively amounted to bribery (without calling it that, of course), by suggesting that we could all walk out of this with a good chunk of change for our own organizations, as most state committees did. That didn't work. He went out of his way to demonstrate his connection to David Dinkins, a maneuver whose motivation at the time made no sense to us. No amount of bullying was working.

All the contradictory messages and convoluted maneuvering spun the timetable out of control. Rogol started burrowing from within. We were well past the January 31 deadline. Tom Ferraro, head of a food bank in the Rochester area who voted with everyone else on most motions, suddenly resigned. Not long after, on March 11, John Chicerio, head of a food bank in Nassau, sent Robin Morgan a five-page single-spaced treatise questioning every substantive aspect of the draft of the New York State proposal. He had been at every meeting; he had participated in almost every facet of drafting it except for the typing, for heaven's sake.

On March 16 a slow-burn, detailed letter went back to John from Robin, explaining the many ways his concerns had been accommodated since day one. She pointed out that at the last full meeting he'd voted with everyone else on a solidarity motion to proceed as previously agreed to after long hours of discussion, compromise, and resolution. At the end of that meeting, she had deliberately said, "It would be refreshing if we did not receive any disconcerting missives on issues that should have been taken up before adjourning." Her letter ended with a P.S.:

> I was just about to deliver this completed letter for posting, when I just now learned that, in fact, . . . *you wrote your March 11 letter specifically at the request of Marty Rogol in L.A.* . . . Speaking as Chair of the Committee, I must say that the Committee's patience is (understandably) wearing thin. Speaking for myself as an individual—having volunteered valuable time, reputation, and expertise to this endeavor—my own patience is fast approaching brittle.

Irrespective of Rogol's clear distaste for our work, we had come up with a proposal that would have produced funding for poor people's own political agendas for years to come and would actually put some of it directly into their pockets. We had a backup proposal also, in the event that he didn't like the idea of long-term gains for poor people. We knew the money couldn't do every poor person any good under almost any circumstances, so we decided to let it do some poor people some real good by giving away thousands of $100 sums per child. A lottery system would be set up in seven project sites around the state.

To most of us, it beat paying salaries to soup kitchen workers. It beat buying refrigerators for the kitchens or a night at the local welfare hotel. From the beginning we had effectively made a decision "to do no harm." Going down the path Rogol was trying to shove us onto would mean helping pave the way for the institutionalization of the emergency industry and promoting the social welfare establishment. That, we believed, *would* cause serious harm.

We had reached a stalemate when Rogol revealed the true underpinnings of Hands. In the wake of another presidential defeat, (Reagan versus Mondale), disgruntled Democratic party operatives decided to raise money in this bravura style for two reasons. First, the whole episode would embarrass the White House by calling the world's attention to poverty in the United States. (Suddenly, the appearance of the Reagans in the line made sense.) Second, by allowing targeted elected officials like Dinkins to distribute the patronage, so to speak, Hands would be strengthening their future candidacies. Clearly, there was nothing wrong with our proposal; it simply didn't do what it was supposed to do—strengthen the organizational base for these politicians in future elections. Giving the money to poor people, or even making it accessible primarily to promote advocacy of the kind that really represented their interests, wouldn't have the sort of implicit quid pro quo Hands was looking for in its grantees. Rogol also said Hands intended to use some of the dough to set up a "voter education" operation in Washington for the next national election. We had been had.

Diane Morales told us she had talked it out in her office, letting her boss know she planned to resign from the Hands committees (New York State's and the national advisory board). Oh no she wouldn't, they said. The implicit message she got: Resign from the committee, resign from the job! Even she had not known what was going on until the process was almost over.

On May 1, 1987, most of us held a press conference. We told Hands to "go with our plan or disband us." (I had been relieved of the responsibility of taking a paycheck for my work by then.) Robin began the press conference: "The Hands Across America guidelines say that donated funds should go to fight poverty, hunger, and homelessness. Our proposal took that mission seriously. But the Hands Across America bureaucracy would prefer we fund New York City's institutionalized poverty pimps." We promptly became the Hands Across America Committee in Exile.

Hands Across America Postscript

The "unofficial list" of new Hands' committee participants for New York State, listed the address as c/o Manhattan Borough President's Office. David Jones, general director of the Community Service Society (CSS), one of the oldest and best-endowed social welfare agencies in the country, hosted the new committee and became its chair. For the most part, the rest of the committee members were connected in some way or another to the established charities, community action agencies, foundations, and myriad food distributors and shelter operators now salting the state. I guess by "broad diversity of people" Hands meant social welfare types. This committee did not concern itself with a proportional or significant representation of actual poor people. (Other states really hadn't either. That was part of the hype, not the general practice.) Nor did it feel any compunction about giving funds to itself.

Finally, among organizations the replacement committee listed as receiving funds on December 29, 1987—nearly a full year later than the inviolable January deadline we'd started out with—were the discard market elite. The Nutrition Consortium, the Community Food Resource Center, the Hunger Action Network of New York, and so on were all funded, along with dozens of service-oriented groups around the state. There's every reason to believe that very little of the money went to purchase food or housing for poor people. And none went into poor people's pockets. I know that makes a world of difference to the "hungry and homeless."

Dinkins obviously got what he wanted; virtually every social welfare institution in the city participated legally and not so legally to get him elected mayor. That's what giving away contracts and funding is all about. This was just one of those opportunities *not to help the poor* but to further small-*p* political ends. Without the political motive, Hands Across America was merely pathetic. With it, it was diabolical.

Poor people got stiffed. The people who put hard-earned dollars and many hours into Hands got fleeced. Consumers who purchased "Brands Across America," the corporate companion to Hands, were also ripped off if they thought their purchases would result in benefits passed on to poor people. One way or another, you can be sure the "donations" were factored into the prices of the products and the tax deductions with the IRS. If any single event or effort were responsible for the growth in corporate "giving" (dumping) that we all now pay the price for, it had to be this one.

The Old Guard

The electroshock charities were nothing compared with the old-timers. The latter had stable long-term money to work with, much more of it over time, powerful and wealthy people on their boards, and decades of deceptive practices to emulate. They had also played a role in the evolution of social policy for generations. These "experts" were the good guys, the ones government looked to for advice on social issues, the ones government contracted out public services to, the ones who most distinctly pulled the ears of welfare commissioners and their ilk. As a group, they could wield enough power to slice a commissioner right out of his job. Soon I would get a look at them from the inside, too.

In 1989, I wrote an article for *The Village Voice* that gave me a glimpse of the dynamics of some of the oldest, wealthiest, and most powerful charities in the world. It started with *The New York Times* Neediest Cases Fund, which passed on money solicited by *The Times* to eight charities—mostly of the old guard.

Beginning around Thanksgiving and ending in February, *The New York Times* annually prodded readers with Dickensian stories designed to loosen purse strings round the world for its Neediest Cases Fund. Poignant tales of desperately poor people appeared side by side with touching accounts of donors like "the children in many classrooms who . . . scrape together pennies to help less fortunate youngsters." A daily tally of the take appeared along with the repeated assertions that none of the money went to administration or fund-raising. *The Times* reported that the money was turned over to "eight social service agencies to be distributed to the people in greatest need."

According to *Times* lore, the fund was started back in 1911 on Christmas Day, when Adolph S. Ochs, publisher of *The Times,* was approached on the street by a beggar. After deciding the guy looked "respectable," Ochs gave *him* (not some charity) the few dollars required for a night's lodging. Perhaps to his surprise, Ochs found that giving money directly to a poor person made him feel good. The next year, *The Times* started the tradition of reporting the 100 neediest cases that has since been parlayed into a multimillion-dollar collection service for eight of the city's most entrenched and—except for one—rich social welfare establishments.

When asked their impressions of the Neediest Cases Fund, most people said that "none of the money goes to administration," echoing *The Times*'s own refrain. They believed that it provided money for clothes, food, rent, or even toys for poor people. The fund was presumed to supply tangible goods to distressed New Yorkers—in much the way that Ochs originally did, albeit now through the agencies, which were to act out the charitable impulse for *The Times*.

In 1989, Samuel and Helen Pfiefer of the Bronx, both octogenarians, donated $50 in memory of "our dear son Sidney, who died after a very tragic accident many years ago." Like many other givers, they wanted to target their gift and requested the $50 be used "to make a 10 year old boy happy." Mrs. Pfiefer said that one of the main reasons they decided to give to this fund was that "no money is taken out for administration." They wanted all their money to go directly to a poor child.

It is possible that a ten-year-old received this donation by accident, but certainly not by design. Truth is, much of *The Times* Neediest Cases' money simply doesn't get to the poor, either directly or indirectly. And neither *The New York Times* nor the eight recipient agencies scarfing up the booty could prove otherwise.

In 1989, the eight agencies received over $4 million from this fund. The eight are the Children's Aid Society; Community Service Society; United Jewish Appeal/Federation of Jewish Philanthropies; Catholic Charities, New York; Catholic Charities, Brooklyn; Federation of Protestant Welfare Agencies; Brooklyn Bureau of Community Service; and Staten Island Family Services. (Since my article appeared, this last, the smallest of the lot, has been dropped by *The Times*.) Most of the agencies used the money for general operating expenses—salaries, et cetera. But when I called *The Times* for information about the fund, a spokesperson said, "One hundred percent of the money is received by the people in need; there is no overhead; none of the money goes to pay employees [at *The Times* or the eight recipient agencies]." She said the agencies pay their employees out of other funds, not the Neediest Cases Fund.

Fred Hechinger, then president of The New York Times Company Foundation and the New York Times Neediest Cases Fund, is a gracious, grandfatherly man. He described the fund as "a charity that uses the good services of *The Times* to persuade people to contribute either money or bequests to be distributed to needy people through eight social service agencies which have been serving that purpose for [years]." I read him several quotes from *Times* articles that said almost exactly the same thing and asked him how he thought readers would interpret them. He said, "It means just what it says. . . . I'm puzzled [by the question]; it's not confusing."

It apparently was true that neither Hechinger nor his staff nor any reporters covering the fund were paid from the solicited money. In like manner, the agencies were expected to provide staff from other pockets of money. *The Times* was "not paying for staff—that staff would be there anyway." In fact, the agencies were chosen in part because they already did social service work, had substantial resources, and wouldn't need to hire additional staff to distribute the money. Hechinger maintained that though the money didn't pay for staff, it "extended" what staff could do. For instance, a client being helped through the welfare system receives money to pay back rent, thereby staving off eviction while getting assistance in making it through the welfare bureaucracy. The social worker's normal service—advocacy—is "extended" by the *Times'* cash assistance.

Some published case histories of the neediest, though, only described a service supplied by one of the agencies. There was no mention of cash assistance or any other tangible item given out. Yet the constant refrain that the money "goes to the needy" and not to administration of the fund was never far from the reader's perception. "To me," Hechinger said, "the most important aspect both as a reporter . . . and . . . more recently in the foundation business . . . is everything we collect goes to support the needy. I think that is one of the attractions [to donors]."

Hechinger was also particularly proud that *The Times*'s annual campaign set a precedent, with many newspapers following suit. Indeed, *The Tablet,* a Catholic journal in Brooklyn, has been collecting funds annually for their "Bright Christmas" program. The editor, Ed Wilkinson, said they collect about $30,000 each year, and "every penny goes directly to poor people" in the parishes. The parishes distribute it directly to needy families and individuals in the community.

One parish priest who received and distributed *Tablet* funds said that any amount was very helpful for families in crisis and that he could use much more, especially for rent arrears and food emergencies. However, to his knowledge, none of the several hundred thousand dollars given to Brooklyn Catholic Charities by *The Times*'s Neediest Cases Fund were available to his or any other parish. "It doesn't trickle down," he said. Apparently, Robert Mundy of Brooklyn Catholic Charities agrees. He estimated that only $40,000 to $60,000 of their $300,000 plus grant was distributed to the "needy."

When asked what reports the agencies were required to file with *The Times* to account for the millions, Hechinger said there were no actual requirements. The agencies "stay in touch." Periodically (every few years as records show), Hechinger sent out a "reminder" to the agencies. They then sent letters back thanking *The Times* for the grants with the magic words somewhere in the text that none of the money was used "to cover overhead or administration." Hechinger maintained there were no other written contracts between the agencies and the fund. In other words, *The Times* distributed $4 million—often collected in quarters and single-dollar bills—on a handshake! If any government bureaucrat even considered doing that with public dollars, *The Times* and most other newspapers in town would kick down the doors for answers.

The Agencies

The smallest of the eight agencies reaping *The Times* windfall (at least until after this article appeared) was Staten Island Family Services (SIFS), which claimed to do family counseling. Executive Director Harvy Rosensfit admitted outright to using the Neediest Cases Fund for general operations, saying it paid for building costs, phones, salaries, and other expenses.

According to the directory in the building, SIFS takes up three floors. On the first of these, a receptionist sits with several empty desks behind her. At no time during the half hour a researcher waited in vain to be seen did any client enter or leave the room. Nor did the phone ring even once. There *are* poor people in Staten Island; they compose 8 percent of the borough's population.

In a phone interview days later, Rosensfit said the Neediest Cases Fund was SIFS's biggest single source of revenue. The second largest came from fees paid by clients to the agency, which charged between $30 and $50 per counseling session. Medicaid was not accepted. Clearly, poor people simply could never pay the fees. Pressed as to whether any clients were served for free, he finally implied that there were some. Unable—or unwilling—to be more precise, he put the yearly number at "less than ten."

The King Midas of the eight recipients is the Children's Aid Society (CAS). Government alone paid out $11,690,731 in fees to them in 1988. The Children's Aid Society's Charities Bureau report looks like a who's who in philanthropy. That year nearly $6 million more came in than was spent. The year before, revenue exceeded expenditures by almost $10 million. This, of course, dwarfs the less than $500,000 this nonprofit gets from the Neediest Cases Fund. Philip Coltoff, executive director of CAS, is paid an annual salary plus fringe benefits (not counting the hidden perks available to these execs) exceeding $150,000. He said the revenue windfalls are in part the capital gains from property and stock sales. Hechinger said he has "no way of knowing" whether the *Times*'s money is sitting in a vault. Or, for that matter, whether fund receipts aren't being used as "gambling" capital (the Children's Aid Society turns over $300 million annually in a whirlwind of stock transactions.) Coltoff claimed the reserves were a hedge against years when the stock market maneuvers produce losses; CAS has an endowment of over $77 million. He said about one third of the Neediest Cases Fund money goes to direct relief. The truth is, since there was no Neediest Cases program per se at CAS, Coltoff had no way to be sure what happened to the money. Some of these agencies are so big they could bury oil tankers in their budgets without being noticed.

It wasn't always this way, according to Monsignor John Ahern, who was responsible for *The Times* Neediest Cases Fund at New York Catholic Charities during the 1960s, when extensive reporting requirements were standard. Ahern and other Catholic Charities' staff spent considerable time not only distributing and reporting on the funds but debating the propriety of various expenditures, including whether or not the money could or should be used to pay for social workers and other agency personnel. They concluded, for instance, that paying a home care aide could be done only if the aide was *not* one of their own employees. In this sense, the payment would be like giving the person or family rent money for the landlord or food money for a grocery store; it would purchase a needed commodity. The agreed-upon standard was one of direct payments to meet specific needs of poor people. Ahern said, "We were not being virtuous, that's how it was represented [by *The Times*]."

In more recent years, government funding to cover payments to the aides became widely available, and staff at these agencies knew how to leverage it. Only in the rarest circumstances would there be an occasion to pay them from any other fund. So, agencies claiming they spend *Times*'s money to cover home care aides might be "double dipping," spending on administration of the service or just plain bamboozling *The Times* and its donors.

Monsignor James Murray has headed New York Catholic Charities since 1973. According to him, not much has changed since Ahern's days. He claimed the agency spent more than $1 million on direct relief for the year ending August 31, 1989. Murray said none of the *Times* funds paid salaries, "because that's our perception of how the money might best be used. It goes back to the 100 Neediest Cases [precursor to the Neediest Cases Fund]. We just carry on the tradition. You're always going to have situations where people need a little financial help beyond what the government or social service agencies provide by themselves." The money was used to pay doctors' bills, pay rent, or buy groceries for poor people. Murray said no verbal or written communication had been supplied by *The Times* outlining any policy changes regarding the use of their funds since he took over at Catholic Charities.

Murray stuck to his claim that at New York Catholic Charities the fund was distributed directly to the poor, but Kevin Sullivan, head of Social Development, did not. For instance, the "schedule of direct relief" Murray supplied to me indicates that 3,574 immigrants were given a total of $225,500 to "subsidize fees." Sullivan and others confirmed that these were not court fees but in fact charges to immigrants who were required to *pay* Catholic Charities for their services. He also said the vast majority of nearly 500 immigration clients each month were poor, but very few receive the service for free. According to him, the *Times* fund actually underwrites staff and overhead.

Few institutions inspire more fear and dread in government bureaucrats than Catholic Charities, which attends many a meeting with outstretched hands. For them, social service is business. Occasionally they float some venture capital on "emerging needs," but generally only for a short period until the government steps in to foot the continuing bill. As with nearly all the large human service agencies, most of what they take credit for is done with government payment.

Leonard Becker, assistant executive director of the Brooklyn Bureau of Community Services, reversed himself on the organization's use of the *Times* funds over the course of two conversations and twenty minutes. First he insisted that 100 percent of the money was distributed in a concrete manner: for food, clothing, rent, et cetera. He said the bureau even supplements it from outside sources. Asked if any was spent on salaries, he said, "Of course not, we have a fiduciary responsibility to *The New York Times* to spend the money the way our contract with them demands. We have been recipients of this fund from the very beginning. It's always been for direct goods for the poor, and we have always done it that way. We do provide services, and services are provided by people [to distribute food, clothing, and so on], but we make up the shortfall [in salaries] out of other funds. That's the whole idea behind the original fund when it was started by Ochs."

Later, while I was on a call to yet another of the Big Eight, I was interrupted by a harried Becker, who must have spoken to someone. (By that time lots of someones must have spoken to one another.) Becker wanted to amend his previous statements: "I'm sorry, I'm afraid I misinformed you. Some of the money does go to salaries." A new party line must have been in formation.

The Brooklyn Bureau of Community Services is puny compared with the United Jewish Appeal/Federation of Jewish Philanthropies, which has $312 million in assets. In most years it ranks first or second in *Times* fund market share. *The Times*'s fund head, Fred Hechinger, maintained that the allocation formula was based on relative numbers of poor people served by a given agency. But is it? In New York City the poor are not primarily white. Yet not one photo of a black or brown person appeared in the Jewish Federation's glossy forty-four-page 1989 annual report, designed as a public relations and fund-raising tool. The text indicates this massive agency serves primarily Jews, without much regard to poverty status. The only explicit mention of "nonwhites" is in the president's message affirming opposition to apartheid in South Africa. Nor do any of those pictured from contemporary photos appear poverty stricken. "Needy," said one staffer, "doesn't necessarily mean being poor." The only cash distribution program mentioned in the annual report is one that assists poor families to "meet extra expenses for Passover." Certainly it is reasonable for any people to preserve their culture and heritage. However, promoting their heritage is hardly the same as serving poor people regardless of race or ethnicity.

One member affiliate highlighted (and one of the few that deals with poverty) in the annual Jewish Federation report is the Metropolitan New York Coordinating Council on Jewish Poverty. During my employment at New York State's Department of Social Services in the mid-1980s, the council submitted a grant proposal for homeless housing funds. They proposed to shelter Jews traveling from such locations as Florida to New York for religious holidays, who they argued would be technically homeless at the time. Significant pressure had to be applied to get them to understand that if they were going to take state money to shelter homeless people, they couldn't exclude the majority of homeless people from their facilities simply because they were not Jewish, not to mention the absurdity in their definition of "homeless."

Repeated attempts to interview the Jewish Federation's executive director were unsuccessful. An employee sent one unattached sheet purporting to list *Times* Neediest Cases Fund disbursements to five "needy" organizations, including two not within *The Times*'s stated boundaries—the five boroughs. Almost $250,000 went to Long Island and Westchester. The Jewish Federation made no claim that any of the *Times*'s money was distributed directly to poor people. Even though *The Times* was about to launch its 1990 campaign, the federation still had over $100,000 in *Times* funds waiting to be allocated to the needy. How hard can it be to give that money away?

It's definitely easier to find out how to give to the fund than it is to find out how and where to get from it. As Brooklyn Catholic Charities' Bob Mundy described it, that's because the *Times* articles are written "in terms of the donor, not the clients." In fact, the articles never do tell anyone how to access the funds. For the most part, in fact, the agencies that receive the funds from *The Times* have had no identified or identifiable program corresponding to their allocation, at least not in recent years. Persons in need can go to these agencies for help, but more likely than not they will be told the agency has no fund to help them in a direct way. Even community organizations have virtually no way to tap into the funds to get help for individuals they work with. Certainly DWAC attempted in the late 1970s to get assistance from the Community Service Society (CSS) for some welfare recipients or applicants who needed tiding over till their welfare checks came through. All came back empty-handed.

More recently, a small community group that was helped by a CSS social worker, Black Veterans for Social Justice (BVSJ), ran into a quick cutoff. One of the group's functions is to help homeless vets get jobs and get out of shelters. According to staffer Dusty Fox, CSS did help twelve of their members in 1989 with small individual grants between welfare checks or before employment income came through. Shortly, however, CSS said they couldn't keep distributing cash assistance this way. (They had spent a total of $2,133 on fifteen requests from BVSJ, mostly for carfare and food. Twice money was used to prevent eviction.) The CSS cut of the *Times* fund in 1989 was just under $1 million.

The last request from the group that year was for James Dawkins, a homeless vet living in a shelter. Although he had begun working on voter registration, Dawkins hadn't yet been paid when he learned that his mother, who had cancer, was dying in Maryland. The black veterans' group came up with partial travel money and went to CSS for the rest. They were turned down. Days later, Dawkins finally was paid and with his group's contributions went to Maryland. His mother died while he was en route. The CSS intake sheet showed a zero in the grant column next to the name James Dawkins. Dusty Fox said CSS acted like *The Times* Neediest Cases Fund is a "big secret." That certainly had been my experience, ten years and two CSS executive directors earlier.

Community Service Society gets more money from the *Times* fund than most of the other groups. The 1988 campaign netted them nearly a million dollars out of the just over $4 million pot. But, CSS serves relatively few needy people directly. In fact, over the years, a number of former CSS employees have maintained that on occasion CSS (in the past) would use composites for *The Times*'s sob stories that lure in the bucks. In other words, they were *theoretical poor people*.

Then again, with all their money, CSS made few claims regarding direct service to poor people. A CSS spokesperson at the time (1989) conceded that not much of the Neediest Cases Fund went directly to the needy. She said it paid for salaries for staff, most of whom have no interaction with poor people—at least not through their jobs.

Keeping Up with Jones

Community Service Society's current executive director, David Jones, has a long and questionable history when it comes to distributing money—whether from the city treasury or from public donors. In 1989 a *60 Minutes* segment on whistle-blower and youth organizer Gerard Poppa tagged the New York City Youth Bureau as a dispenser of funds to "nonexistent programs or no-show jobs." The head of the Youth Bureau (a city agency) during much of the time in question was Jones. His second in command was Steve Krause, who left with Jones to become number two at the Community Service Society.

A contemporaneous audit of the Division for Youth (a State agency) by state comptroller Edward Regan saved its most damning criticism for the Youth Bureau, during (and after) Jones's tenure. It reads, "The lack of fiscal monitoring makes funds more vulnerable to abuse and illegal acts." And, "approximately $53,242 in personal services were paid [by the Youth Bureau to an unnamed provider] when there were no youths in the program." The report also suggests that field staff at the Youth Bureau suspected extensive no-shows in the program.

As of 1990, Jones was compensated $145,000 plus perks for his time at CSS, Krause, $111,000 plus for his "services" to the community, because, at CSS, those who do "good" really do well. In financial statements filed with the Charities Bureau in 1989, CSS listed five other employees reaping cash incomes in excess of $63,000 annually; another sixty-nine employees earned over $30,000. How many *Times* donors think their contributions are defraying salaries like that instead of buying winter coats?

Most of CSS's vast resources are spent on sponsoring and attending meetings, doing research, producing studies, and getting press coverage of the results—most consistently from *The New York Times*. (Mrs. Heiskell, the wife of a prominent *Times* editor, also happened to sit on the CSS board of directors a decade ago.) Some of these reports are competent, and a limited number of the staff at CSS even do decent public policy advocacy work. Whether or not the organization ever does *any-thing* useful for its poor constituency is not the point. Rather, readers and poor people have a right to expect the distribution of their money to mirror the nature of the solicitation proffered by *The Times* each year. Certainly poor people would rather have the cash.

In any case, CSS certainly doesn't need *The Times*'s money for other purposes; it has an endowment of nearly $90 million and an annual budget of over $11 million—most of which comes from investment income. Among the investments of this do-gooder operation (as of their 1989 financial report to the Charities Bureau) are holdings in IBM, which was still doing megabusiness in South Africa. They also had stock in a major tobacco company, part of an industry in which diversification means getting people in third world countries and poor U.S. urban areas hooked on cigarettes because the overall U.S. market is in decline. And CSS had holdings in *The New York Times*.

If there were any lingering doubts as to the political nature of the institution, they should quickly dissipate upon reading the reports to the attorney general's office for fiscal year 1990—the year David Dinkins became mayor of New York City. The Community Service Society established what they called the Institute for Community Empowerment, whose purpose was to "eliminate barriers to voter registration." They spent $770,703 on "voter participation" and claim to have registered 6,100 new voters for the primary and general election. Even if one were to be ridiculously generous and presume that each and every person CSS claims to have registered actually *voted,* that comes to a cost of over $125 per head. Shoot, they should have done it the old-fashioned way and simply given the money to the new "voters"—it would have gone a lot further to ensure that they actually pressed a lever in some voting booth. Cash works for a lot of things.[1]

That same year, aside from the usual monetary gush generated by the endowment, government gave CSS a total of just under $1 million, including $157,155 from the city of New York ($671,422 from the feds, the rest from the state). Frequently throughout the 1980s at least, CSS was so flush they were not able to spend their full budget. This never stopped either *The Times* or the government from handing them more. In more recent times, CSS's money glut led them to give some of their own funds to other organizations. Why would anyone call CSS a non-profit?

Well, that way they don't have to pay taxes on their properties. And, in theory, no one exactly "profits." They're not a "service" provider as most people think of them; you don't catch many poor people at CSS unless somebody's studying them or registering them to vote at one of their outstation posts, i.e., anyplace but at the spiffy Charities Building they own on Park Avenue South.

You have to go back to CSS's original incorporation papers to find out their "mission." The Community Service Society was actually a merger of two older charities. Their philosophical underpinnings reveal a great deal about their "concern for the poor." One thing is certain, it came neither out of real sympathy for the plight of those less fortunate nor out of a simple respect for human life. Their motivating force would more accurately be characterized as disdain. The older of CSS's forebears, the New York Association for Improving the Condition of the Poor (NYAICP), was founded in 1848, when various parties decided that volunteers (women) alone were not doing enough to solve the problem of poor people in the mist. To remedy the situation, men were hired to do some of the work to root out this plague. The professionalization of being human, to become known as social work, was begun.[2] It would elevate the "physical and moral condition of the indigent." The Charity Organization Society (COS) of the city of New York came along in 1882 "to be a center of intercommunication between the various churches and charitable agencies in the city. To foster harmonious co-operation between them, and to *check the evils of the overlapping of relief"* [emphasis added].

As these organizations and others like them grew, there emerged a long, drawn-out battle over outdoor relief. The agencies wanted to continue the practice of taking children away from their mothers simply because they were poor. Poverty was the excuse, more money for their own coffers and, in some cases, cheap labor to boot was the consequence of limiting outdoor relief.

In those days, there wasn't much pretense about it. The Charity Organization Society, along with the Russell Sage Foundation and the Brooklyn Bureau of Charities, led the opposition to mothers' pensions—

the precursor to AFDC that several states ultimately enacted. There were a number of ideological strands evolving to oppose the charities—a reform movement of child welfare experts who believed taking children from their mothers was unhealthy for the individuals and the society; the temperance movement; and still others seeking tenement house reform. Most of the reform movements were inclined to attribute poverty to systemic factors. Because private charities that were solely service-providing oriented already had a lock on the fund-raising, reform movements had barely a chance in hell to mount an effective campaign. Often McCarthyite attacks on reformers led to accommodation, just as they do today.[3]

It didn't always work. Most outstanding were groups of women organized ad hoc to institute mothers' pensions because they realized the injustices placed on poor families. After all, they'd often visited them before more formal arrangements shunted women aside. These women knew the mothers and knew they were not by definition bad. What they were by definition was poor. In 1897, in New York City, an amazing bill to provide mothers an allowance equal to the amount otherwise allowed for institutional care had passed the legislature. The charities were powerful enough to convince the New York City mayor to veto it. An advocacy group of young women led by Sophie Irene Loeb and Hannah Einstein emerged and against overwhelming odds defeated the giant charities in 1915. According to Roy Lubove,

> Their [the charities'] defeat in 1915, by the enactment of the New York State Child Welfare Law, was a watershed in the history of American social welfare. The doctrine that voluntary welfare institutions should serve as the community's chief relief resource was successfully challenged.
> . . . Private social work . . . seemed to view money as the commodity least needed by the poor.

In March of 1939, COS and NYAICP joined forces to continue the work they'd been doing independently—to keep people from double dipping, so to speak—and, as the incorporation papers read, "to repress mendicancy by [securing work for those capable] and by the prosecution of impostors." I always thought there was something less than altruistic and do-good about CSS. The movement to professionalize charity work did not die. It moved along from the mid-nineteenth into the twentieth century, with emphasis on fixing poor decadent, alcoholic, and later presumed promiscuous adults whose behavior had "caused" their poverty.

Whereas the staff and boards of the original organizations were all men, the newly merged CSS, like other agencies of the time, put some women (very wealthy ones or those with very wealthy husbands) on the board to be volunteers—especially for fund-raising. The first CSS board was almost one third women—most notable among them was Mrs. John D. Rockefeller III. Now, Ms. Rockefeller may have been a perfectly decent human being, but one thing is certain: she could not have the slightest notion of the problems poor people faced. Nor did any of the other board members. Nevertheless, these people all had votes on policy matters before their organization—matters pertaining to the treatment of poor people in the agency and therefore in the city itself as well as the ideology governing the view of poor people. Given their economic and social status, they could steer the press and lawmakers with respect to any issue. The staff they hired, especially the executive directors, could also steer them. These were, and for the most part at the top continue to be, men. (Even in those days, mothers and their children dominated the poverty population.)

Through fund-raising parties, government funding that could be wheedled out of politicians eager to please the rich and famous, and bequeathed legacies when one of those rich and famous croaked, CSS built their formidable war chest. Though the board now includes some middle-class people, the organization traditionally makes little or no effort to include politically active poor people on it.

The Federation of Protestant Welfare Agencies: Doing Little, Getting More

Another Neediest Cases Fund recipient, the Federation of Protestant Welfare Agencies (FPWA), had a long and embarrassingly barren history in social welfare circles—even among the big charities. Incorporated in 1922, FPWA was a potential tabula rasa when Tracy Huling became their head of policy, advocacy, and research in 1987. Till then, FPWA was just a hanger-on with the other major charities that broker much of New York's public policy.

Huling asked if I would work for her on poverty and welfare policy. I had read a paper she wrote on teenage pregnancy and was impressed. These were the days when social welfare agencies had elevated that issue in a major public way, and every level of government was dropping a bundle on them to study it, service the population, and keep the myths alive. Among other things, Huling's was the first paper I had read by a social welfare "advocate" that acknowledged that both the number and rate of teenagers having babies had been declining for years. This little-known fact was not difficult to ferret out, but suppressing it *was* useful to keep those babies-having-babies dollars flowing. Unfortunately, all manner of bad policies came hand in hand with the distortion of facts, including those pertaining to welfare recipients in general.

I consented to work as a consultant for Huling and FPWA. We also agreed that our priority would be to work on raising welfare benefits, if the executive director and board bought it. Usually all involved in these organizations will buy it, if for no other reason than they don't expect to be successful. The federation certainly had no reason to believe that their lackadaisical organization would become a driving force behind it. So, with their sanction, we went into labor.

One of my reasons for taking on the work was to see whether and how the power of these institutions could be wielded to advance the interests of poor people. Normally, the charities act more as agents for their own needs, but somewhere in their recesses there is still a moral mandate to serve rather than be served. If that mandate could be tapped, the consequences would be worth the effort. Although FPWA had accomplished nothing of consequence for many years, they did have access to power brokers, the media, a stellar board of directors, a paid lobbyist in the state capital, and the other social service entrepreneurs that regularly played collective footsie with one another as the need arose. Their modest, if not downright laughable reputation in the field might have been a hindrance under certain circumstances, but I was willing to bet that they had a "turn" coming. They did.

In spite of opposition from FPWA's paid lobbyists, Malkin and Ross, who "understood Albany" and urged a less comprehensive agenda, we went forward with a plan to raise the basic welfare grant. Ross recommended that FPWA lobby for more and cheaper milk for poor kids. But Huling had already cleared raising welfare benefits with the executive director, Megan McLaughlin, and she was not persuaded otherwise.

Given Ross's clear resistance to a welfare agenda of this nature, the strategy to effect it was worked out primarily between Huling and me. I agreed to produce a revised version of the *Children on Welfare: Families in Need* fact book that had been so helpful in the welfare rights campaign years earlier to raise benefits. It would include an updated analysis of the shortfall in the basic grant since the so-called standard of need had been established in 1970. The grant analysis would be essential to convince people the increase was needed.

While working on the new publication, I stayed well in the background. Huling attended most of the meetings of the various social welfare types whose imprimatur would be needed to make this agenda take off. Had most of them known from the start that I was feeding her information, unnecessary resistance might have precluded their serious participation. When researchers from the other agencies looked at the same material, they invariably managed to botch something and were pressed to return to the calculator and historical documents they'd over-looked. Within months, most of those who counted were in agreement with a strategy calling for the restoration of the original grant.

Several of the agencies that had been disinclined to go along with the larger coalition (especially Catholic Charities), were swept up by the momentum. Refusing to back the others openly would have been impolitic. It was one thing to fudge the data and muffle the offensive in the face of DWAC's work. It was quite another to tell the Protestant Federation to take a hike.

The statistical conflict DWAC had had with the social welfare establishment through the early eighties was enjoined by one of their own, with none of them the wiser—not even FPWA themselves. (McLaughlin didn't know the history, nor did most of the board.) The board expressed satisfaction with the work's compelling quality. It seemed to bolster McLaughlin's credibility internally as well as the federation's reputation externally. By the time the data were released, most of the quibbling agencies (whose statisticians and researchers had been unable to challenge the facts or compel any other strategy) had already fallen into line with FPWA.

So here's the shocker. For a variety of reasons, in less than one year, raising the welfare grant had become the grist of which New York politics is made—the media were down; politicians were lining up like tin soldiers; the social agencies, the shelter developers, the food distribution types were all on board. When the governor mentioned it in his state of the state message (in spite of his reported distaste for the idea and rising state budget deficits), we only needed the other top legislators to pull it off. The FPWA lobbyists publicly got into the act near the very end, but even then they waffled. We didn't wait on them, though. In 1988 a basic welfare grant increase was officially incorporated in the next year's state budget. All the ifs, ands, and buts had been put to rest.

It was simply astonishing. In spite of the shortcomings (there was no organized recipient contingent seriously involved), this "impossible" thing had come to pass. Without doubt, these social agencies could move agendas other than those that served themselves overtly. (The board and, for a while, the executive director of FPWA were pleased the agency's profile had been elevated in the course of raising benefits.) The power they held over social policy was indisputable. It had taken DWAC three long and hard years to get welfare benefits raised. Compared with moving the identical agenda as a welfare rights organization, this was an awesome piece of cake. Maybe too awesome.

Not far beneath the veneer of charity and the fleeting snowflake's depth of justice, a core of callous disregard abounded at the Federation of Protestant Welfare Agencies. It was something I wondered about with most of these charities that had so much and did so little. Why, year after year, were they given so much money for being so demonstrably inept? Why did people bequeath legacies to them? How could FPWA, for instance, with nearly $10.0 million in savings and an annual budget in the range of $2.5 million, shamelessly claim tax exemption without having to produce much of anything more worthy of note than an annual charity ball?

Parties like those organized by the federation or by wealthy individuals are like exclusive clubs, where all kinds of business is done in a pleasurable setting under cover of benefiting some cause—only these are all *tax deductible*. From the caviar and the extravagant floral bouquets to the dance band, all of it is paid for by us. Every check a donor writes out to the federation or any other charity at such an event is a tax expenditure from the U.S. Treasury.

People might dislike the idea of giving money to beggars on the street on the assumption that without the moderating force of a charity it might be spent on booze or drugs of another kind, but donating to a charity that is not even obligated to report its annual liquor bill to any government or funding agency rarely seems to bother anyone. Black tie affairs held by FPWA at Tavern on the Green didn't come cheap.

But there was more to it than that. There was a blatant disregard, perhaps an absolute certainty that no amount of mismanagement or worse would ever be seriously challenged—it never really had. Not long after Megan McLaughlin took over as executive director, on December 4, 1987, the Long Range Planning Committee of the board made the following points:

- Federation Program: Unfocused; lacks priorities; no identifiable outcomes.
- Members: Undefined relationship with unclear benefits.
- Purposes: Federation purposes not understood by its various constituencies in the community.
- Deficit: Reliance on inadequate budget processes and negative consequences for program (over 20 years).
- Information: Inadequate information; information flows; and systems.
- Public Image: Low and indistinct visibility; programs are not seen as vital to the community.
- Unacceptable Status Quo and Failed Previous Efforts: It is clear that our current situation is unacceptable to everyone.[4]

The board *knew* the federation was, for most intents and purposes, brain dead. (The Department of Policy, Advocacy, and Research campaign to raise welfare benefits was about to put them on the map, if only momentarily.) At a minimum, FPWA had been mismanaged for years. Politics, along with the sizable chunk of change churned out from the endowment year after year and a run-down but stunning landmark building on Park Avenue South, kept them alive. There were also established connections between the newly hired chief executive and then Borough President David Dinkins. (One of Dinkins's first fundraising keynote speeches after becoming mayor was for the federation.)

The facade began to crack in 1988, when the finance director of FPWA, after being on the job for only months, became concerned about what she perceived to be innumerable fiscal improprieties.[5] She attempted to rectify certain slipshod practices, but the harder she tried, the more resistance she encountered from McLaughlin. She had hoped FPWA would be a refreshing and heart-invigorating change of pace from the cutthroat financial world from which she had come. Soon, however, she became concerned that the federation was leading her into a cesspool of mismanagement, or even improper fiscal entanglements. The financial controls at FPWA were characterized as unsound to the point of recklessness. She maintains that in light of this, and because her signature appeared on checks demanded by McLaughlin without supporting documentation, she sought counsel. At least one fiscal agent advised her to stop signing checks. She began confiding in Tracy Huling, who was also concerned because McLaughlin was telling her to make misrepresentations to the board with respect to expenditures.

When attempts to resolve an increasing number and magnitude of discrepancies at the professional staff level were clearly revealed to be hopeless, the two took their concerns to the board chair, James Dumpson. Instead of taking the issues seriously and attempting to rectify the wrongs, Dumpson marshaled those in control of the necessary board committees. They circled their wagons and sought not to remedy the situation but rather to eliminate the women calling the institution into question. A blitzkrieg of paper harassment was followed by the swift dismissal of the finance director and, shortly, the coerced resignation of Huling. Not long after, the comptroller and most other professional policy employees also left. Even a number of board members jumped ship as the deceit and intrigue mounted.

The executive director and some of the board under Dumpson's leadership played political hardball with the accusers despite well-documented appeals. (Dumpson was a former commissioner of the Human Resources Administration. During his watch, HRA had come under fire for "midnight raids" on the homes of welfare mothers by caseworkers hunting for men.) Finally, with little internal recourse, charges were brought to the state attorney general's office. Employees at the charities office began a quest based on voluminous documentation of multiple charges of misuse of charitable dollars, including money from the New York Times Neediest Cases Fund.

The claims were not restricted to the *Times* fund. Funds from FEMA (Federal Emergency Management Agency) and SNAP (State Nutrition Assistance Program) conduited through the federation (via the United Way) for soup kitchens and food pantries lacked adequate accountability both from member agencies to FPWA and from FPWA to the funding sources. Accusations were also made that the federation routinely used restricted endowment income and government and foundation grants for purposes other than those for which they were intended.

Documentation demonstrated that grants made by government officials (Dinkins at the city level and Senator Roy Goodman at the state level) were diverted for general operating purposes and accounted for after the fact. One cover-your-ass memo from the head of General Purchasing Services (a project through which member agencies procure goods under the umbrella of FPWA) detailed the ways the Goodman [pork barrel] contract for $50,000 was only by a long stretch of the imagination used for its intended purposes. Nonetheless, an account of how the grant was spent went back to the state from FPWA indicating otherwise.

The employees' complaint to the attorney general limited the charges to those they actually had paperwork to substantiate, even though they had seen much more in the swamp of federation files. The organization's General Purchasing Services, for one, deserved far more attention than they actually got. As documentation from City Harvest shows, not everything that General Purchasing Services bought was of much use to the member agencies, and a good deal of the total dollar amount in motion seemed to get lost in the shuffle. Other agencies claimed that the reason they used the so-called service was not because of the cut rates advertised by FPWA (they weren't cut) but because they believed they were too small to make these purchases directly from the companies the federation used.

In the beginning, FPWA actually made the purchases for members.

As time went by, the federation shed the procurement work, acting only as an agent linking smaller organizations directly to distributors of various goods. Given this change, there was really no reason the smaller agencies shouldn't have been able to make the purchases on their own, with just a simple referral. In spite of the very limited role played by FPWA, they charged a fee to the members and a cut (in excess of $100,000) of the distributors' profits was sent back to the federation. In spite of the comfortable financing arrangement, for some reason, FPWA was never able to make General Purchasing Services pay for themselves—even with government grants added to the pot. Whether the "fees" returned to FPWA went into the pockets of individuals or the coffers of the federation remains unknown—at least to me.

There was also evidence of questionable use of federation funds for the personal benefit of staff, including excessive payments to certain staff upon their departure. Depending on the cloud under which they left, either a shower of silver rained on them or a cold northern wind just blew them out. Keep in mind, this was a *nonprofit charity*, not a multinational corporation. The prior executive director allegedly left with as much as a year's advance salary. The prior assistant vice president (the finance director with another name) was promised compensation in salary; health, dental, and life insurance benefits; and tuition reimbursement of approximately $30,000 under very dubious circumstances. In part, his handiwork had precipitated the concerns of the new finance director, yet, when she was summarily dismissed, *he* was brought back to FPWA to clean up the shop.

There was more. Some worse—such as endangering the health and well-being of employees because of long-standing fire hazards—some more benign. One board member who resigned shortly after these matters came to light noted that even though he was chair of the Planning Committee for the Annual Meeting and Luncheon, he was never provided with its often requested financial report. That's probably because it was becoming an annual party—costing more and netting less as time went by.

Claims made in *The Times* regarding FPWA would have us believe they performed a vital function in the distribution of Neediest Cases Fund money. Right. In 1988, according to public records filed by FPWA, a full $1,700 was distributed for rent to six families in three boroughs. Another $417 was meted out in singles to beggars who came to the door for handouts in that fiscal year. Of course the total of this direct relief doesn't come close to the hundreds of thousands extracted from the public and doled out to the agency by *The New York Times* each campaign.

The complaint lodged against the federation with the attorney general's office in August 1989 noted the "extraordinary proportion of these funds [Neediest Cases] which go to its [FPWA's] own administrative expenses" and charged, "Revenue received from the *New York Times* Neediest Cases campaign . . . was used historically and during our tenure to fund the Federation's general operations. The funds were not used to help the needy as portrayed by the Federation to the *New York Times,* nor by The New York Times to the public."

You see, FPWA's share of the Neediest Cases Fund was sunk into the general operating account (not a practice exclusive to them). Along with other money in the budget, it can be presumed to have defrayed 1988 costs, such as $27,445 for staff travel or $50,359 for conferences and meetings. They do put out a good lunch at the federation. But poor people are not invited to partake—just professionals. Perhaps the fund helps to pay for messengers at the organization. In 1988 Megan McLaughlin reportedly sent a federation-paid messenger to Tiffany's to pick up a gift for a family member at Christmastime, just as the Neediest Cases were being hawked by *The New York Times.*

Did the largely blue blood board of FPWA know how *The Times*'s money was being used? (Addresses for board members tilt to Park and Fifth avenues and middle to upper East Side streets. Among the luminaries listed on the board then were Harry Helmsley and Mrs. Jonathan Bush, sister-in-law to President Bush.) They should have. A document presented at the board meeting on October 27, 1986, pointed out the federation's "increased reliance on the New York Times Neediest Fund."

If one were to argue that instead of giving cash or other tangible goods FPWA provides services to the poor, one would have difficulty proving it. Other than a shaky scholarship program for disadvantaged youth (for which the federation has separately bequeathed legacies), FPWA neither provides direct services to poor people (except referring people who come in for help to some other place to get it) nor claims to—at least not in recent annual reports. The federation only offers services to other organizations that purport to help the "needy." After their practices were exposed, this thirdhand method of *potentially* helping was passively deemed an acceptable interpretation of the Neediest Cases intent.

Some time after his office began looking into the allegations, Attorney General Robert Abrams announced he was running for the United States Senate. What had seemed like a genuine effort by staff attorneys to get to the bottom of the federation's murky practices appeared to melt like Cheez Whiz in a microwave. Was the need for a Dinkins endorsement a factor? After all, during Dinkins's campaign, Abrams was never more than a photo-op away from the mayoral candidate. Was FPWA board chair Jim Dumpson's appointment by Dinkins to a blue ribbon committee a factor? Or the federation's affluent board? I doubt the answer to those questions will pop out any day soon. I do know that a serious investigation is carried out swiftly, and thoroughly, without giving the potential perps an excessive opportunity to cover up. That's not what happened in this case.

On March 15, 1990, more than a year after the issues in question were brought to his attention, Jim Dumpson wrote a letter on behalf of the federation to "Dear Bob" (Abrams), asking him to intervene. The complainants were never contacted by the AG's office after they brought the charges, though any serious investigation should have resulted in multiple communications, as the complainants were told it would. The disturbance quietly receded, chalked up to "personality conflicts."

The federation retreated to their normal ineffectual standard. Tax dollars or poor people's dollars, depending on how you look at it, continued on the standard course of earlier times. An expensive Washington, DC, consulting firm was brought in to analyze (whitewash?) the situation at FPWA. It was the third such firm brought in since McLaughlin had been hired. The report was kept highly secret. The AG's office never secured a copy—at least they said they didn't. They had agreed to look at certain documents at the federation building without obtaining copies that would then be subject to public scrutiny through the Freedom of Information Act. Why the agreement? If there was nothing damaging in the report, why the secrecy?

The Community Service Society and the Federation of Protestant

Welfare Agencies differ from the others receiving Neediest Cases funds in that they provide so little in actual services—certainly for the dollars—to poor people themselves, or any other individuals for that matter. The "newspaper of record" was probably hoodwinked, but no admissions were ever made. Slowly, *The Times* has revised the spin they put on the fund—most likely because it would be difficult to continue the solicitations in the same old way in light of New York's revised (during the 1980s) charity laws. After all, they do purport to understand the English language.

For one, the law regarding "the solicitation and collection of funds for charitable purposes" specifically prohibits *"a false pretense, representation or promise, transaction or enterprise in connection with any solicitation for charitable purposes."* Furthermore, *"To establish fraud neither intent to defraud nor injury need to be shown"* (emphasis added). Donors and the average person believed the Neediest Cases money was distributed to poor people because that's what *The Times* repeatedly asserted. The very nature of the arrangements between *The Times* and the agencies created a climate in which inefficiency, mismanagement, and waste could easily cross over into fraud, deceit, and worse. Nonprofits are run by people, not saints.

In February 1992, somebody at *The Times* finally got it straight. The column on the Neediest Cases explained, "The newspaper covers all the *campaign's* [emphasis added] overhead so that every dollar collected can be passed on directly to seven charities." No claims regarding the use of the money by the charities for administration were included. Fred Hechinger no longer runs the Neediest Cases Fund either.

Charities and Fees for Service

Catholic Charities, the Brooklyn Bureau of Community Services, the Children's Aid Society, and, in a different way, even the United Jewish Appeal/Federation of Jewish Philanthropies do provide services, if not anything tangible, to a sizable population, poor or otherwise. Like Red Cross and so many so-called charities, most of the "services" they all count among their do-good activities are paid for by contracts with various government entities, usually on a per capita basis. (In other words, for these, there is no need for the Neediest Cases Fund for "services.") Just between nursing homes for the elderly and foster care services, these organizations reap tens of millions of dollars, each and every year, directly out of government treasuries. Forget the issues of church and state, which haunt every contractual arrangement with the biggest of these providers—Catholic Charities and the Jewish Federation. (Even though they take major bucks from government, these charities are not required to file the same kinds of nonprofit reports. They must show certain financial information to secure new money for a project, but there is no centralized government entity to which they must report on the whole shebang. They set up subsidiary entities with the regularity of for-profit multinationals. Their corporate veils are probably even more difficult to pierce since they don't pay taxes either. So no one, outside of their own accountants perhaps, knows the full range of their financial deals with the government.)

There is a bottom line—they are invariably paid more than most of us could imagine for, say, one child in foster care, another growth industry. Depending on the kind of foster care, $30,000, $40,000, $50,000 annually is common. There is no logic to the negotiated payments; there are no economies of scale. It would not be a stretch to argue that they (and other providers) have a financial stake in keeping children in the system—another monstrosity. They reject children the state does not agree to pay for, even if they have room for them.

In many ways the agencies serve the same warehousing functions that children's "asylums" did at the turn of the century. One likely reason for the ultimate success of reformers promoting mothers' pensions was that the government was not yet footing the bill for the voluntary agencies' zeal. So while the agencies were powerful, they were not *as* powerful as they are today. Plus, until the government took over the funding job completely, the child-swiping venture required endless fund-raising activities, eventually becoming burdensome to some agency executives.

When children are "voluntarily" given up to foster care, most often it is because their mothers are too poor to care for them at home or have no home to care for them in. Doesn't it make sense to help these families at home by allowing them to rise out of desperate poverty rather than throwing the kids into institutional barbarism and the mother into hell? One has to ask if poverty is still a legitimate reason to take kids away from mothers. About $3.5 billion is spent nationally on foster care, for an estimated 300,000 children. That comes to about ten times the average per capita (including administrative) costs for a child on welfare.

Another common misconception is that child abuse is confined to the family. Not so. Abuses in foster care are endemic. In just one afternoon of looking at the financial reports for the Brooklyn Bureau of Community Services, for instance, I came across two pending wrongful death suits. People want to believe that the abuses of "orphanages" have all been left in the past. They've merely been swept under the rug. One instance that didn't escape notice was New York's recent highly publicized case with Covenant House's Bruce Ritter, who left after multiple reports of sexual abuse of minors surfaced. He showed up back here later, raising money for poor "families" in India—the Albert Schweitzer of child molesters.

The scandal-ridden United Way also "carefully" distributes billions of dollars annually to organizations that, for the most part, don't need it. (All *The New York Times* Neediest Cases agencies get a cut, for instance.) In 1992, the United Way's national boss, William Aramony (income circa $500,000 annually), was driven out of his job as his extravagant excesses began to percolate in the media. Aramony described himself as a "social worker." Until the story broke, if you had ever read a story about the United Way in *The New York Times,* you would have had to believe the agency was a pillar of respectability and responsibility. Had *The Times* or any other "objective" journalists looked, they would have found not only that the United Way had been squandering funds on amenities for employees for some time but also that they largely restricted their assistance to the establishment, often well-endowed, poverty pimps. Shunning any appearance of a political function, the United Way nevertheless served one—to swing as many donated dollars into the status quo organizations as possible. It hasn't been a secret.

Fortunately, the story of financial indiscretions, at least, caught hold. Within weeks, Susan Edelman, in an investigative series for *The Record* (a Bergen County, New Jersey, paper), revealed that the head of the Tri-State United Way (New York, New Jersey, and Connecticut),

Calvin E. Green, had recently retired from service with a good-bye package totaling nearly $4 million—mostly in cash. New York's United Way head didn't escape scrutiny either. His reported annual take has been nearly $500,000 in bucks and perks, including but not limited to a $4,500 a month apartment in New York City's silk stocking district (even though he was living upstate), a Lincoln Town Car and driver, and many other precious items unwitting donors and taxpayers footed the bill for. (He claims he's giving up the apartment.) The kinds of financial improprieties he engaged in for the most part are of the same nature most charities replicate daily—pissing away poor people's dollars on themselves.

The American Red Cross gets its blood money, in every sense of the word. Their president has a salary in the $200,000 range. Next time you see the Red Cross streak out to a disaster site, ask yourself if they would be there if they didn't expect to be paid. Franklin Thomas, closet reactionary and head of the Ford Foundation, is paid over $400,000 annually for his services. That's more than the salaries of the president and vice president of the United States combined. The Sal[i]vation Army is dishing up soup (for a price) in the United States and selling donated clothing they got for free to desperate people in other countries. AmeriCares hopped the first jet out to set up soup kitchens in what used to be referred to as the Eastern bloc nations. The independent federations of Protestant, Jewish, and Catholic charities. Hands Across America. *The New York Times* Neediest Cases Fund. Second Harvest. HELP . . .

Seriously, help. The list is almost endless. Most of the money is squished up at the top. Following the United Way debacle, *The Chronicle of Philanthropy* did a survey of national charities and found that the plurality of salaries for top executives "fall between $100,000 and $200,000." Compensation among those surveyed ranged from a low of $50,000 to a high of $500,000.[6]

Closing down the top ten human service charities plus the United Ways would directly net more money than the federal share of AFDC. That doesn't even take into account the tax expenditures their combined budgets represent, as every dollar donated to them is discounted by Uncle Sam. Nor are their assets in buildings, stocks and bonds, and other properties counted—or taxed.

The Charity Fraud Stereotype

Most people think of charity fraud as something that occurs when too much money is spent on fund-raising and not enough on doing good or when funds intended for the organization end up directly in some individual's pocket. The people who take the dough are your basic "poverty pimps." True. But those who get the money in salaries and perks and who get control over millions of dollars intended to help poor people and fail to deliver are the same. A poverty pimp making a *salary* in the six-figure range doesn't need to put his hand in the cookie jar. It's attached, like an ancillary appendage. Its presence goes a long way toward keeping social policy framed so as to advance the views of a narrow few—none of whom is poor or usually ever has been.

There are countless ways organizations can hide what they do and do not do. It is easy to make claims about their good deeds so spurious as to be ludicrous. Reports to the IRS are often replete with phony information, as the big poverty pimps do not wish to reveal much about their business. Fund-raising expenses are generally underreported. A little simple mathematics and some knowledge of the organization would tell you, if they claim to spend $25,000 on fund-raising but buy $50,000 worth of ads in *The New York Times* and hold fund-raisers at Tavern on the Green, somebody's lying or can't add. Nonetheless, perfectly reputable accounting firms all over the country apply seals of approval to hokey budgetary information about the agencies every year.

The other common con is the big fudge over how much they spend on "program" versus "administration." They exaggerate the former and bury the latter. Who's to say otherwise? Since they are not being watched and aren't regulated, they can be as slippery as time, will, and political connections permit. Until and unless some district attorney indicts someone in the organization, there will never be a real review. And even in cases where legal action is taken, courts are notoriously reluctant to get involved. If they rub the snake oil in right, the social welfare agencies, their staffs and boards, are virtually immune from prosecution for misrepresentations, mismanagement, malfeasance. As my mother used to say, "One lies and the other swears to it."

Political Penury

A revealing advertisement for a budding opportunist ran in the jobs section of *The New York Times* on Sunday, February 2, 1992. It read (in part):

COLLEGE GRAD ADMIN ASST
FOR POLITICAL FUNDRAISING, (GOV'S/US SENATORS) AND SPE-
CIAL EVENTS. . . . KNOWL OF POLITICS AND NY CHARITIES
HELPFUL. . . .

Why would a political fund-raiser need a knowledge of New York charities, when the two are supposed to be mutually exclusive? (Charities must be nonpartisan and must abide by severely restricted lobbying laws to retain their nonprofit status. They may not endorse political candidates. Officially, that is.)

That same Sunday, *New York Newsday* ran an article on the city's projected budget. In it, Mayor Dinkins suggested that he would *increase* the amount of services contracted out to private firms and nonprofits. In theory, these are services currently provided by municipal workers. The jobs would switch from the public to the private sector. What Dinkins did not say was that the best way to get and maintain a political foothold over time is through pervasive patronage routes, that is, control over the distribution of jobs. The political motivation was not lost on FPWA's Megan McLaughlin, who was also quoted in the article. Rather than emphasize providing higher-quality services or even less expensive ones, her comments focused on the bottom line: "With this contracting out goes jobs and all kinds of other things." She questioned how the administration would divide up what she called *"this bonanza"* (emphasis added).

A dwindling industrial base coupled with a service economy spinning out of control and a new city charter that puts all contracting authority into the hands of New York's mayor shift the balance of economic and therefore political power. As a political tool, the "bonanza" is the moral and practical equivalent of buying an election staff without the personal hassle of raising large amounts of money. The nexus between politicians and the social welfare agencies who pimp for them is at the heart of the matter. It is democracy in reverse.

Next to a government contract to build highways or run a naval base, most individual social service contracts are peanuts. Not all. The second largest individual organizational contract in New York City in 1991 is to Andrew Cuomo's ballistic shelter/service organization, HELP, Bronx, for well over $175 million (for fifteen years).[7] It is the city's largest "non-profit human service contract." The more money any individual controls, the more jobs he controls. The more jobs he controls, the more powerful he becomes. Is it any surprise that when faced with the option of developing permanent housing, with its modest overhead, instead of shelters, which continue to be labor intensive for the life of the project, Andrew chose the latter and the logic that would support them? If he were not the governor's son, would he have been able to negotiate the deals with the Housing Finance Agency, the welfare departments, the private sector, or even Washington? If he were not the governor's son, would he have been able to set the tone of many media presentations about homeless people?

But it is in the aggregate where the real killing takes place. New York City's nonprofit human service sector alone hauls in more money annually than the total federal share of AFDC. *And it continues to grow faster than the pace of inflation.* Currently, nearly half the income of New York's service agencies is acquired from government. Twenty-one percent of the agencies account for 90 percent of the money. In other words, the dollars—and power—are concentrated. Laughably, the single service most frequently provided by the social service sector in New York is referred to as information and referral. That means when needy people go to one charity for help, they are advised to go someplace else to get it. New York's may be the biggest nonprofit boondoggle, but it is by no means alone in its capacity to steer local politics, its deceptive practices, or its wealth—and power—compared with other sectors of the economy.

As for quality control, well, there is none. The attorney general's response to both *The Times* Neediest Cases Fund and the Federation of Protestant Welfare Agencies demonstrated that unless they catch you with your hand directly in the till and the money on your person, it virtually doesn't matter what you do. No one is forced to measure and produce *x* amount of any product or result. No one is watching, nobody cares, and not a soul will ask the people who receive the "services" to evaluate them.

When affluent people decide some service they want for themselves isn't up to snuff, they vote with their feet and their pocketbooks. In that sense, markets work quite well for anyone with the power to participate in them. As long as poor people are prohibited from having a choice—a say in deciding which services they need and which providers are most capable of satisfying them—the competitive element, if there is one, is entirely in the hands of Big Brother. Most of the people in every form of this business know this: *there is no accountability in the social service field.* None demanded, none supplied.

The Poverty Industry

"Not-for-profits" sprout like mung beans in spring water while, single mothers, in spite of being employed outside the home in ever greater numbers, become more frequently and more desperately poor. A rash of emergency responses has turned back the clock on cash assistance: food pantries are today's breadlines, shelters are today's flophouses. Solutions like workfare are simply today's form of indentured servitude.

For varying reasons the charities old and new, food distributors, shelter providers, and the rest are ill suited to care for poor people—especially families with children. They are driven by the logic of self-perpetuation, which almost without fail leads to a relentless pursuit of government contracts and donated dollars. The older the institution, the less scrutinized they become. Their covert function is political—as patronage bases for politicians and to help maintain the status quo at all levels of government. Ultimately, they are accountable to no one, as they are not regulated in most ways that matter. More than half a million charities are now registered with the IRS.[8] (A lot of paper flies around, but it might as well be used for fold-up airplanes for all the good it does.)[9] The simple reality is that most often poor people's interests are not served. They are obscured. Money that could have helped becomes the bludgeon with which poor people are kept down.

According to the American Association of Fund-Raising Counsel, "giving" from all nongovernment sources totaled $122,570,000,000 in 1990. Just over half went to religions (often for charitable purposes in addition to church/temple maintenance). Most of it was raised from middle-class people. Almost all of it from corporate to individual giving was tax deductible. Much, if not most of it is wasted.

Poor mother-only families receive most of their income from AFDC, one of the few shares of the national budget that is actually shrinking over time. The total federal share of Aid to Families with Dependent Children, including Emergency Assistance, is just over $10 billion, with state shares being an additional $7 billion plus. It wouldn't take a grand bite out of the total *donated* money to lift everyone out of poverty if only we wanted to. And that doesn't begin to take into account government spending through contracts with nonprofit organizations to whip poor people into shape.

Shouldn't we be just as angry about a child raised in foster care to the tune of $50,000 annually who ages out without being able to live independently as we were about the $600 hammers procured by the military during the Reagan administration? Shouldn't we, in fact, be angrier? After all, the foster care agencies are running a business whose costly products are not inanimate objects but people.

The social programs run by the charities might appear to be filling the gap between the inadequate levels of income transfers accorded to people on welfare and what is really needed to survive, especially since the gross dollar amount spent on the poverty industry continues to climb. Unfortunately, this money not only fails to fill the gap but is very often destructive. The cacophony of private interests that compete for government contracts, tax advantages, and philanthropic dollars to correct their version of the problem is nothing short of deafening. Good public policy cannot be made in an environment of crafted chaos. Whether it's the old-timer agencies, the fly-by-nights, or the new operations becoming institutionalized, in New York or New Mexico, the disease is finally the same, the germ, infectious. And it is shameful.

The grant giver or donor, public or private, wields power over the receiver, a power that renders "scientific" research, public policy pronouncements, and a wide range of service delivery schemes suspect. Most research is subject to the bias planted by the funder. The difference between the scientists hired by the tobacco company or the maker of breast implants and the social scientists is one of presumption and public perception. We are leery of the guy who tells us it's okay to smoke a "light" cigarette, because we know his company is making a buck off his "test results." The social scientist, by contrast, is presumed to have moral superiority simply because he works in the "nonprofit" sector. He is good because he says he will do good. The sector itself has achieved a chimera of sanctity that puts it above the scrutiny normally accorded government contractors. Politicians and those who get the contracts have taken full advantage.

The really bad news is, the social regression from the mid-1970s to the present has been long and deep. With remarkable creativity, every time the social welfare institutions discover a need of poor people or redefine an already perceived one, they find a way to get money for themselves, knowing there's little they can do about it as long as people remain so very poor. Consider one of the most talked about issues these days: that of low-birth-weight babies. Many do not make it. Study after study has shown that the most common denominator of the mothers of low-birth-weight babies is poverty, irrespective of race. In other words, poor Hispanics, blacks, Indians, whites—all experience much higher rates of low-weight births than do middle- or upper-class women of any race.

Social service advocates agree that the problem of low birth weights is poverty. Yet the solution they propose to reduce the rate of such births is to increase access to health care in advance of these births—especially for uninsured women. They all but ignore the fact that for most of the poorest, those with the highest rates of low-weight births, medical insurance per se is not the barrier; they have medicaid, which covers health care, however feebly. Still, these women give birth to low-weight babies. If the common denominator is poverty, then the solution must deal with it.

Creating more jobs for health care professionals, advocates, and nutritionists will not change the unalterable fact that eating enough food is and always has been essential to birthing normal-weight babies. Food cannot be prescribed by a physician or dispensed by a pharmacist. Telling someone what is nutritional will not access nutritional food. Only being able to purchase it will. But for some mysterious reason, health care advocates generally leave the income/resource distribution issue alone. The convoluted logic boggles the mind.

The social welfare practitioners and policymakers have acquired a stranglehold on public policy and, to a growing extent, the economy, and they aren't about to let go. A lot of decent people were suckered into it. A lot of not so decent people orchestrate it with intent.

The question is, who do you want to put your trust in: an agency replete with champagne fund-raisers, political deal making, and its own bulging belly to fill, or a mother who is directly responsible for feeding, clothing, sheltering, acculturating, and, yes, entertaining her children?

In part the problem DWAC and organizations like it had in contradicting the social welfare professionals was that of biting the hand that feeds you—more literally than most people think. You see, because they're the good guys, any challenges to them can be tossed off as the ravings of a few ingrates. They had the market cornered on brains (or so they thought), and they didn't see any reason to produce a platform on which poor people could stand. At least not in public. The angry conferences and other confrontations were just part of doing business. As long as we could not control the spin going out to the press, or even in the minutes of the meetings, these things might as well never have happened.

Besides, they had us. If stupid people like me broadcast their obvious conflicts of interest, then the real bad guys might take away not only the junk but salaries and perks, too. Then there would be no one left to "advocate" for the poor. That bugaboo was firmly planted in every poor activist's ear from the moment she became a known commodity. Known, that is, to the social welfare community in one of its many forms. Telling the truth about this industry of helpers, about fraud, perhaps legal graft, abuse of power, and all that goes with it would bring the Wrath of God (or the *Republicans,* whichever came first) pounding on the poor. Trouble was, not telling did, too.

It is obvious to anyone with eyes that families and individuals are becoming more poor and that there are more of them, in spite of the billions tumbling into charities' bank accounts. Fortunately, there are still multiple competing interests at all levels of society—including within the charities themselves. A shift in public will can reverse the trend, or at least modify it. Part III will focus on getting out of the mess.

PART III

Toward a Politics of Justice: Guaranteed Income

In the presidential election of 1992, *change* won in a landslide. Between the electorate who voiced their opinion in the voting booth and discouraged citizens who voiced theirs by not voting, there was an overwhelming mandate to redraw the political, social, and economic map of this country. We may be entering a period of "social opportunity" during which a new debate on a range of issues, including poverty, can and should take place. For decades, social policy has been made in the dark. It's time to turn on the lights so we can see the problem for what it is. Solutions will follow.

Mother-only families who were poor increased from approximately 2.5 million in 1979 to 3.5 million in 1989. More than half of all children in single-female households are poor. The poverty rate of children whose mothers have completed some college (including those with degrees) is almost one out of three, nearly the same rate as that of two-parent families in which the father has not even completed high school. (In other words, more education per se is no panacea, certainly not for mothers.)

Almost two thirds of children in either African-American or Latina mother-only families are poor. Slightly less than half of white children of single mothers are poor. Although there has been some increase in the number and rate of male-only households with children, these remain exceptions and generally are not poor relative to the total poverty population. Of all single-parent families, female households constitute 94 percent of those in poverty. The poverty rate for mother-only families is three times that of father-only families.

The majority of poor mother-only families receive some amount of welfare for some period of time. The majority of poor mother-only families also have wage income for some period. Over the last decade, single mothers have increased their rate of paid employment. Still, their poverty rates have gone up. Physically challenged family heads also tend to have much higher poverty rates than other family heads. When they are women, they are twice as likely to be poor as their male counterparts. No matter how the numbers are cut, the problem is poverty, and the gender is largely female.[1]

Poverty gnaws at the body and spirit, both of individuals and of nations. No mother should have to ride the subways or set up house in an elevator shaft or an empty barn in lieu of putting her children to sleep in a warm bed at night. No one's children should die because her only source of heat—her kitchen stove—explodes. No one who has not broken any laws or in any way neglected her children by any standard definition should be forced into counseling as a precondition for obtaining shelter. No one should be presumed to be less than human simply because she is poor—particularly not women raising children under our system of welfare, a feat whose difficulty is not to be underestimated. My own experience was terrible. The experiences of millions of other poor mothers and their children are unspeakable. None of these women or their children should ever be told that she is lazy, needs a job, and refuses to "work." What they need is income. What the country needs is a healthy dose of reality grounding unfettered by the "good intentions" of those who profit by degrading and infantilizing poor mothers.

As we barrel into the twenty-first century, we are holding on tenaciously to nineteenth-century notions of poor people and the policies that should govern them. There are many reasons that people are or become poor. One thing is certain: nobody chooses poverty. As a country we have no excuse. Many other nations distribute resources far more equitably to those in *and* out of the waged labor force than the United States.

Bad as it is, welfare—cash assistance—has been the lifeblood of millions who defy the odds by making a difficult but successful transition into the mainstream. Still, it is inexcusable that the obstacles are so many, the barriers so dense, and the public will so profoundly sterile that only the strongest, the toughest, the smartest, the most talented, the luckiest, the best educated, have any real opportunity to advance. Advancing means leaving poverty or near poverty, not simply getting a poorly paying job. It is indefensible that our backup systems for simple subsistence are meted out most harshly and disproportionately to people of color and female households of all races. All this in what is arguably the wealthiest nation in history.

It is estimated that one out of every three children in the United States will experience welfare for at least some part of his or her youth by the turn of the century. One out of every two in New York City. These children are all our children. They are also the future of the nation.

Impediments to Real Reform

Welfare as we know it cannot be fixed. Tinkering with it for decades has accomplished little of value. Bureaucracies within bureaucracies have bloomed, mutations of a polluted society. Too many contradictory interests compete at the public trough in the name of poor people. Entrenched charities dwarf any efforts at self-determination and actively muzzle the political expression of the people they purport to represent. Poor people of our inner cities, small towns, and rural countryside exist in a sprawling banana republic where fighting factions of outsiders— institutionalized poverty pimps—battle over which issue, which treatment, what cabal will dominate at any given point in time. Those who live in poverty are the means for the charities to acquire "foreign aid" from dozens of sources, including the U.S. government.

A major impediment to dismantling the existing social welfare programs is the extent to which they have degenerated into patronage troughs. The government contracts to "help" are first and foremost political tools to strengthen the base of elected officials at all levels of government. Often it is said that government budgets are balanced on the backs of the poor. Certainly over the last quarter of a century, that has happened. There *has* been an observable redistribution scheme under way—the most disturbing one this country has ever seen—from poor women and children to middle-class social welfare professionals. We need to reverse the process, redirecting resources from the coffers of stagnant social service agencies to the pockets of poor families, to those with no other source of income as well as those who live in waged poverty.

Decades of half truths, mythmaking, and downright lies, usually for political ends, have gone into stirring up confusion regarding welfare, the people who receive it, and what to do about it. We must see the problem of poverty for what it is in order to pursue appropriate remedies.

Perhaps the most powerful deceit has evolved from the complementary myths that (a) poor families suffer from an inordinate degree of "dependency" and (b) job and training programs are a panacea for curing dependency. In part, these ingrained beliefs stem from the failure to recognize the unique circumstances of mothers on welfare, the facts that welfare is a women's issue and that lack of income—not work—is what keeps women and their children poor.

In spite of increasing acknowledgment of the "povertization of women," there has been no effort of any magnitude on either the local or national level to stem the tide. Mostly, when policy "experts" recommend solutions, they miss the boat by failing to discern the distinctly different nature of women's poverty (because of children and labor force segregation) compared with that of men. On the one hand, they don't understand the problem; on the other, they are inherently pitted against the very people they are supposed to be helping as they continue to carve out an ever larger share of the pie for themselves. The combination of self-perpetuating social welfare agencies, which run the gamut from foundations to service providers, and weak, ineffective, or corrupt politicians is, quite literally, lethal.

If the waged market won't or can't adequately absorb everyone who needs money to buy the basics, and the helping hands are more like a punch in the face, what social policy makes sense? Income security—or a social security system that is truly universal, dissociated from phony distinctions that save one family and throw another away. If income is the problem, then income must be in the solution—a kinder, gentler, simpler, more generous system of resource distribution, one that does not stigmatize and further alienate those who receive it. The real need of poor families to live with dignity can only be met by increasing cash assistance to them. Providing a universal system for true income security in this country is possible. Currently it is off our political table. It hasn't always been that way, and it doesn't have to stay that way.

Chapter 8

Opening the Door to Social Opportunity and Income Security

> *Imagine yourself, if you will, as a single parent. That means whatever "first" thing is happening, you and you alone witness it, crow over it, cry about it. This includes the first step, the first tooth, the first, second and third birthdays.*
>
> *It also includes the first cold. I remember my first child's first cold. I called up my younger sister who already had three children. . . . "Yup," said my sister, "that sounds just like a cold." . . . The first cold lasted seven days. That means seven nights too. I can't imagine a lonelier seven nights than those taken up by the first cold of a baby of a single mother.*
>
> *The support that one has to have from one's spouse is all-important in baby care. Anybody can croon a baby to sleep. That is, except the mother who has had no sleep in two days and two nights too.*
> —Ruth Szold Ginzberg,
> *Children and Other Strangers*

Not many years after mothers' pensions or wages were won in different states (in the early twentieth century), a program came into being that would radically alter the lens through which the nation viewed itself. For the first time, the federal government accepted a measure of responsibility for the economy's inability to absorb everyone successfully. Poverty was largely deemed a consequence of multiple environmental factors. Despite much opposition, in 1935 the Social Security Act became law.

President Roosevelt and his Committee on Economic Security hoped it would safeguard "against misfortune which cannot be wholly eliminated in the man-made world of ours."[1]

It had its flaws. From the start it aimed to protect men—and only incidentally their families—from the vagaries of the marketplace. (Mostly white men. Many of the jobs originally left out of the social security package were those employing large numbers of people of color and/or women.) Nonetheless, it was intended to "insure" most citizens in (or related to someone in) certain jobs, but not mothers separated from living husbands. The elderly—men, by more than two to one because of their labor force participation rates then—were designated beneficiaries of old age insurance. It was also this bill that created unemployment compensation systems, particularly intended to cover males temporarily disjointed from the waged labor market. It also provided for the care of "crippled" children. Widows (the *good* single mothers/wives) and their children were to receive survivors' benefits. (Early on, if the father divorced his wife shortly before he died, she was not eligible for "his" social security benefits.)

Children with living but absent fathers were almost left out. Fortunately, enough political pressure was brought to bear to include them in the act in a separate program first called Aid to Dependent Children (ADC). Kids on ADC were presumed to live with their mothers, as in fact almost all did. But *no sum of money was designated for the women;* that was lost in the political struggle. It wasn't until the 1950s that the caretaker parent was added to the beneficiary unit, and ADC was changed to AFDC, or Aid to *Families* with Dependent Children.

The Social Security Act also created the program everybody loves and calls the real thing—social security. Many people believe the elderly receive these benefits because they paid for them as workers in their preretirement years. Not so. Not quite. Not everybody. Right off the bat, people who qualified for social security never "put in" enough to get out the amount they would receive. In recent years this became so obvious that huge increases in social security taxes were imposed on current workers. This was not only ostensibly to secure *their* futures but also to cover the shortfall on the bill for current social security beneficiaries. Social security *is* an income transfer program. In that sense, it is similar to welfare—the financing comes out of current taxes.

It also happens to make good public policy. For one, people who would otherwise have been poor would have caused an even greater drain on community resources than they currently do. In fact, the very existence of these monthly checks through which basic needs are sustained is beneficial to the economy as it spurs production to meet consumer demand. These are not dollars that will be spent on junkets to see the world.

The political strength of social security is ample evidence of its popularity. Those who get it actively resist any attempt to tamper with it. A simple political principle stabilizes it: it is much harder to take benefits away from people than it is to withhold something they do not yet have. When the people currently receiving the benefits plus those who expect to one day, plus those who would have to support their parents without social security constitute the majority of the population, any attempt to take this program away would be political suicide. Although some people get less than others, and for some the dollar amount is insufficient, compared with welfare *and* in general, social security is a great thing. Those who qualify get a check every month, period.

Cradle-to-grave security for everyone was not always perceived as a dirty, unhealthy, unwise, or impossible goal. In fact, some people have it. Let's face it—inheriting grandfather's fortune has nothing to do with inalienable rights. It's just the law and the luck of the draw—with respect to parentage, that is. It *isn't* the consequence of superior moral behavior.

Social policy in the United States has done far better at the grave end of the meter than at the cradle end. In health care, social and technological advances have been focused far more on extending and improving the quality of life for older people than on protecting children from the ravages of disease, accidents, malnutrition, or despair. In fact, most public health care dollars are spent on the elderly (through medicaid and medicare). Although medicaid was originally set up particularly to provide health care to poor children and families, as a practical matter, most medicaid expenditures are spent on people over the age of sixty-five, especially for long-term care. Three times as many medicaid dollars are spent on people over sixty-five as on those under twenty-one. Nevertheless, the political liability is generally charged against welfare families. The more the "undeserving poor" (welfare families) seem to get, the less politically viable future programs perceived to be for them become.

What they end up with is not more targeted dollars but the implication that through these expenditures they are getting more than their social "share."

Politicians who chatter incessantly about the growth in welfare spending *aren't* talking about cash assistance through AFDC unless they're serious dunces. Remember, AFDC is *less than one percent* of the federal budget and has fallen. It is microscopic compared with the tonnage that will be used to bail out the savings and loans. It is also less than one fourth the cost of medicaid. (And that doesn't touch medi*care*, which is exclusively for older populations.) What politicians are really most often talking about when they assert the growth in welfare spending is medicaid, knowing most people will presume that "welfare" used this way will trigger thoughts of slovenly but healthy adults who spend their days watching TV, spend their nights making babies, drive around in Cadillacs, and eat roast beef three nights a week. For the most part, they won't admit it, but sometimes politicians are covertly talking about social security expenditures (also entitlements), which have soared in recent decades.

With the exception of single women over the age of eighty-five who live alone, poverty among the elderly in the United States has declined considerably in recent decades. In 1969, children were less likely than men aged sixty-five to sixty-nine to be poor. Children in larger families had always tended to be poorer, but children in smaller ones (which are increasingly common) had not. With minimum wages, public assistance benefits, and even average wages tumbling in purchasing power, children in many kinds of households are poor and are steadily getting more desperately poor. By 1979, the children of our country were twice as likely as older men to be poor. From 1966 on, the well-being of children relative to the elderly has virtually reversed itself. The single most dramatic and obvious factor increasing the economic well-being of the elderly has been the expansion of social security benefits—cash transfers for retirees. They have increased, they have been progressively adjusted, and they cover more categories of people than ever before. We have achieved the lowest rate of poverty of the elderly in the nation's history. Most cash assistance is spent through old-age insurance—social security—and it now covers the preponderance of older citizens. Whatever its shortcomings, for most of those who get it, social security and government-funded health care are damn good things.

Social Security Versus AFDC: Myopic Double Vision

Although created for poor children, AFDC is the most miserly program of income transfers in the nation. Unlike social security, AFDC is distributed on a case-by-case basis, with enough strings to hang an elephant. It is meanly administered, hard to qualify for, hard to keep; it provides niggardly benefits and is tough to stomach with all its invasive attempts at behavior modification.

Some children get social security benefits even though their parent(s) are not gainfully employed. There are a variety of ways this can happen. For instance, upon the death of a parent—most commonly the father—"survivors" can receive social security. Even if the mother has never spent a day in the waged labor market herself, she and her children are often covered by these relatively generous survivor benefits. The mother is neither expected nor required to get a job in order to receive them. No one worries about her "dependency" on the system.

What is the intrinsic difference between a "survivor" family and one with an alive but absent father who either refuses to or can't support his children? Not much. The needs and rights of women and children are not determined by some just and universal standard but by the nature and sometimes the duration of their prior relationship to a man. Brava.

The federal government sets social security payments. At a minimum (depending on the political climate), benefits are increased annually, indexed to keep pace with inflation. Per capita, average monthly benefits on social security are more than four times those for AFDC recipients.

By contrast, each state sets its own level of cash assistance in the AFDC program. No amount is too little. Subsequent to a Supreme Court ruling in 1970, every state was obligated to specify an "actual standard of need" for recipients but was not required to pay it. (The Court made allowances for a state "to accommodate budgetary realities.") At the time, the Court stated that while this system "leaves the States free to effect downward adjustments in the level of benefits paid, it accomplishes within the framework the goal, however modest, of forcing a State to accept the political consequence of such a cutback and bringing to light the true extent to which actual assistance falls short of the minimum acceptable." Translation: the difference between what the state pays and what people "need" constitutes the basis for future political discourse, which should facilitate increasing welfare benefits over time. Mostly, in their dreams.

Budgetary flimflam, benign neglect by the mediating institutions "representing the poor," and political hardball have all contributed to the plummeting of the purchasing power of AFDC benefits nationwide. Welfare families have nearly always been the Willie Hortons of politics, among both Democrats and Republicans. It only became advantageous to complain about the Horton advertisements when the Dems felt like translating it into an overtly racial issue. The fact is, although most welfare recipients are white, the not so silent majority identify race as a principal factor in the welfare equation. Politicians know this, and use it—with the tacit complicity emanating from many social welfare agents waiting for contracts and other insider perks.

So (unlike social security) AFDC grants have all fallen far below the poverty line. In the late 1960s, just before the slide began, grants were much higher in constant dollars. In some cases (including New York), grants then exceeded the poverty line, however slightly.

Every Mother Is a Working Mother

A widow on social security can receive benefits until she dies, and neither social policy experts nor politicians will lose any sleep if she never had or gets a paying job. In fact, if she has small children, she is often presumed to be a better mother for taking care of her children full-time. If and when she were to get a job, she could earn thousands of dollars without a reduction in social security. When she reaches an income maximum, cash assistance from the government will still only be reduced 50 cents for every dollar she earns. One cultural effect of this form of resource distribution is that it acknowledges the working role of at least *some* mothers in the home.

Another grouping of women who in recent years have seen some change in the perception of their value in the home is divorced women. Some can now receive social security benefits through their deceased or retired husbands' benefits (albeit much less than their husbands get) if they were married at least ten years before the divorce. Additionally, they can receive substantial community property. Women argued for years that the caring work they did for their husbands and children while the former were out getting paid was of economic consequence to the men individually, to the entire family unit, and to the society. By making it possible for their husbands to optimize their labor force participation and by raising their children to grow up "properly" socialized, these women contributed to the economy perhaps without ever stepping foot into the paid labor market. Now, in spite of their marital status, they can be rewarded *tangibly*. (Of course, they *may not be*. Not a few women become "displaced homemakers," left with nothing after a divorce, sometimes becoming homeless.)

The pressure to leave small children and enter the waged labor market falls most heavily on welfare mothers. Even though it is generally conceded that the labor market is *tight,* and good child care *rare,* when it comes to welfare mothers, virtually *everyone* wants them out. (Here's where somebody says that the majority of mothers in the United States work outside the home whether they want to or not, so why shouldn't welfare mothers? But of those mothers who work at paying jobs, most do not work full-time, year-round, and they work only if doing so improves the economic condition of their families.) If the welfare mother makes such a move, outside minimal work-related expenses, for the most part her welfare check is reduced one dollar for every dollar she is paid. In other words, *her* government check is taxed at a 100 percent rate. With a wage job she tends to be as poor as or even poorer than she was on straight welfare. I used to tell largely female audiences, "If you think he's going to walk out on you, shoot him. Then you'll get to be a widow."

The tasks are endless, especially for women with very young children—who are the bulk of women on welfare. The job is tough no matter what, and tougher when you lack basic subsistence resources. It is true that all poor mothers are not great at the job of parenting. But neither are all mothers of any class. Good mothering is not a function of class. It is also the case that not all welfare mothers wish to stay in the home. Having been a welfare mother and having worked over the years with thousands of other welfare mothers, I can say with some confidence that, if there is one generalization about us that remains consistent, it is that as a group we are very much like the rest of society—all different. Many have less education and most a tougher hide, but otherwise we span the gamut as mothers, cooks, thinkers, doers, givers and users, housekeepers and gadabouts.

The spread of waged labor, especially from the mid–nineteenth century on, changed the meaning of the word *work,* with dire consequences for women. Until then, most families' toil was at the very least independent of an employer. So what was called and conceived of as work was the everyday life of creating and producing subsistence, both inside and outside the home. "Women's work" was primarily in and very near the home—nurturing children, obeying husbands, tending to household matters, and maybe feeding chickens or tending a garden for flowers (beauty) and food. Certainly it was work, and critical to the functioning of the family and community. It still is. It is even acknowledged for certain classes of women, but not for poor ones.

In part because it is not waged or usually in any sufficient way rewarded with the primary means of resource distribution in today's culture—money—"women's work" has lost its extrinsic value. (As Robin Morgan puts it, women's "labor is too revered to be demeaned by wages.")[2] The introduction of the wage system may have been problematic for lower-class men, but mothers and women in general lost big time. Women's valuelessness in the home extends to the paid labor market, where, by tradition, they are poorly remunerated. As late as 1989, nearly three fourths of single mothers with children under age six received less than half the median family income in the United States. Forty-seven percent received less than one fourth. White women fare only slightly better than black women, with Hispanic women close behind. Men of all races fare better than women of all races, on average.[3] The woman who exits from welfare (as sooner or later almost all do) may have higher self-esteem than she had before, but she rarely benefits in dollars, sans marriage, that is.

A black woman hired as a nanny for an upper-class white family is a "worker"; as a mother laboring in the shadow of the wage under adverse conditions to raise her own children on welfare, she is considered a parasite on society. Under certain circumstances her work is *socially* sanctioned as when it is performed in exchange for a wage, whether or not it improves the material condition of the family. Unless the poor *waged* mother has a trusted relative or friend who will take care of *her* children, she must entrust her small child to the cheapest alternative and her older child to the mercy of the neighborhood. Her stress quotient soars. If the local junkies take an interest in her son or the bargain baby-sitter turns out to be a child molester, she lives with the consequences and faces the stigma of being blamed for not being at home when the kids needed her. The trap is sprung.

If every mother is a working mother, then every poor mother is a member of the working poor. So why do so many political creatures— left, right, and center—believe that a welfare mother is, by definition, an unproductive human being who is suffering from a nearly terminal disease, dependency, which can be cured only by a *job?* As Daniel Patrick Moynihan put it in 1972,

> If American society recognized home making and child rearing as productive work to be included in the national economic accounts . . . the receipt of welfare might not imply dependency. But we don't. It may be hoped that the women's movement of the present time will change this.

The job and training programs so prevalent today are rarely much more than mechanisms of torture. Let's face it, if they really work, why is participation in most of them restricted to welfare mothers? Why, for instance, aren't widows on social security offered training slots? Surely, if anyone deserves a shot at self-improvement, they do (not to mention the fact that their benefits cost us all more).

If asked, every governor in the country can probably point to a half dozen women who were actually helped by one of these programs. Certainly they are *not* going to point out *any* failures, in spite of the overwhelming evidence that the programs do not produce jobs or employ many women who would not otherwise have become employed outside the home. And the majority of the programs are costly. (We're talking Economics 101 here, not human costs.) If the mothers who do get jobs remain poor or near poor, where's the return on our investment?

The History of Guaranteed Income

Irrespective of how or whether we measure work, there was a proposal on the country's table that could have made all the difference in the world. It was hotly debated, but it never became the law of the land. It is an old idea—guaranteed income. What does that mean? Allan Sheahen put it succinctly in his book, *Guaranteed Income:* "It's a plan based on the principle that everyone has the right to live. It would provide every American with a minimum level of income. Enough for food, shelter and basic necessities. It is a floor below which no income can fall."[4] Thirty years after the Social Security Act, another truly significant package of social reforms was attempted. It would come to include a proposal for guaranteed income.

The foundation for President Johnson's Great Society was laid by the Kennedy administration, which wished to put poverty on notice. Income maintenance was ruled out immediately; it was thought to breed the degenerative social disease—dependency.

President Johnson declared his War on Poverty in part because he felt some political imperative to pick up where Kennedy had left off, but especially because big spending programs aimed at reducing the effects of poverty had been his political turf as far back as Franklin Roosevelt's New Deal *and* the Social Security Act. Also, Johnson grew up poor and came from a generally poor community when he was first elected to Congress. Unquestionably, on the issue of poverty, his roots were deeper than Kennedy's. Some of his advisers recommended an income maintenance strategy—guaranteed income—to him early on, but, like Kennedy, he rejected it. At least at first. It is likely that he did so for political, not ideological, reasons.

Later on Johnson appointed a Commission on Income Maintenance Programs, which continued into the Nixon administration. Barbara Jordan, then a Texas state senator, was one of the few commission members not from the business community. Robert Harris, who headed the staff of the commission, maintains that Johnson knew at the outset that the committee would end up endorsing the "creation of a universal income supplement . . . to all members of the population in need."[5] According to

Harris, Johnson appointed such stalwart capitalists as Ben Heineman, president of Northwest Industries, IBM's Thomas Watson, and the Rand Corporation's Henry Rowen to the commission in order to lend weight from the business community to the intended mandate for increased income security. Alair Townsend, also on the staff to the commission, says that Heineman was appointed chair specifically because he had already expressed a conviction that income security was the only true method for addressing poverty. Harris maintains that because there were so many others on the commission with less background in the issue who needed to be brought up to snuff, the work lasted much longer than was anticipated. Consequently, its conclusions were handed to President Nixon. There was minimal dissent among the commission members. Most of the dissenters simply argued for *more* income as the starting point; others wanted to place greater emphasis on creating quality child care in addition to income supplements to allow more freedom of choice.

If Johnson wanted the commission to make these recommendations, why did he bog down the War on Poverty with all the service and economic development schemes? The decline in the industrial base was already limiting certain jobs, and Democratic reform movements had put a stranglehold on party machines accustomed to wielding power through the jobs *they* controlled. The War on Poverty must have seemed an excellent chance to rebuild the party machine—with particular allegiance to him. So services emerged with regularity, each new "need" defined by the helping industry and by elected officials shagging dollars or votes.

The Great Society programs were the perfect form for distributing patronage on a grand scale—Community Action, VISTA, Model Cities. . . . The service cum economic development strategy was to achieve a marriage of otherwise feuding factions: mayors, poor people (who at first had cause for optimism), civil rights leaders, liberals, and the press—complete with a dowry no one would reject. Were it not for the Vietnam War, Johnson had every reason to believe his reelection was in the bag. His programs were shoring up a deteriorating political machine while providing the rhetorical posture for an end to poverty. No such political advantage derived from expanding simple cash assistance programs.

Among the designers of the War on Poverty were many holdovers from the Kennedy administration, who continued to exert influence. Of these, Richard Boone is said to have been a virtual Greek chorus on the matter of citizen participation in the programs evolving out of the Office of Economic Opportunity (OEO). Those who supported his theory believed that institutional change was necessary but would only be achieved with the "maximum feasible participation" of people living in the communities (that would receive funding from OEO), along with the usual social welfare and political players.

Community Action Agencies (CAAs, also known as CAPs, Community Action Programs) were hatched to do the job. Community people were to have a say in the planning, structure, budget, and ongoing operation of the programs. It was believed that this would alter the power dynamics in a given locality, breaking down the political barriers that kept poor people poor. As it happened, this theory of participation was only barely understood by the people who made the decision. It wasn't even a part of the congressional debate over OEO when enabling legislation and appropriations were enacted. Those who thought they did understand, according to Boone, did so on an intellectual, not an experiential level.

In spite of the mandate, with the exception of a few highly publicized locations, input by poor people was all but nonexistent. In *Betrayal of the Poor,* Stephen Rose wrote that in none of the twenty cities he studied

> were any poor people, any representatives of the neighborhoods, or members of the groups to be served involved. . . . While these groups appeared at a later date on the boards of directors of the local agencies, their participation frequently did not occur until the local agencies had started operating, had hired staff, and had secured both administrative and program budgets.

Sar Levitan concurred,

> Affluent citizens who happened to live in a "target area" could represent the poor. The law could therefore be observed without having a single low-income person on the CAA board. This was exactly the case in the early days of the Atlanta CAA, where the only person who could claim to be a representative of the poor within the

vague criteria of the provision was Martin Luther King, Sr., a minister living in the poverty area.

Those CAAs genuinely committed to citizen participation were either swiftly defunded, taken over by more moderate executives, or never allowed to get out of the planning stages. Participation of poor people on a national scale that would make a difference never really took place; only the appearance occurred, as my own experience in the 1970s confirmed.

The mirage of participation had considerable value to the agencies, though. The impact of the civil rights, women's, and welfare rights movements was felt strongly through the seventies, so it was politically uncouth for advantaged parties to act without input from the disadvantaged. By manipulating the input, the social welfare establishment could appear to address poverty issues with the imprimatur of poor people (most commonly, women on welfare). The resulting aura of equity made it easier to get and maintain government and private foundation grants. The pretense of poor people's participation thus legitimized the social welfare institutions.

In 1962 and 1967, amendments to the Social Security Act were passed; they also impelled the services solution. The first amendment moved to increase the states' revenue share for family services (programs that utilized—and paid for—social workers as opposed to income maintenance going directly to recipients) from 50 to 75 percent. The second allowed states to contract these services out to *nongovernmental agencies* (previously, local welfare departments were the sole service providers using federal dollars).

States that had previously and systematically denied welfare benefits to millions of needy families (especially black families) were now eager to qualify for the windfall revenue sharing. But they had to find people categorically eligible for welfare. Furthermore, states would actually have to pay the families welfare benefits (which were also federally subsidized, but not so liberally in most cases). Not to worry. Because cash assistance levels were set *by* the states, it was (a) possible to find families eligible for welfare (to leverage the federal services dollars) and (b) *set AFDC levels so low that families would stay poor.*

The welfare rolls climbed so fast that the phenomenon was characterized as an "explosion." This legislated windfall to states (combined with the War on Poverty strategy of delivering megabucks to state and local governments for "services" to the poor) set off a spending spree that was peaking just when the purchasing power of AFDC benefits began to decline. The decrease in welfare benefits was coupled with an increase in rhetoric about "dependency" and the necessity for women to "work."

In due time, both President Johnson and President Nixon attempted to insert guaranteed income into U.S. domestic policy. (George McGovern also proposed a form of guaranteed income in his 1972 bid against Nixon for the presidency.) President Nixon introduced Congress and the nation to the Family Assistance Plan (FAP), which could have made a giant leap on the road to guaranteed income.[6] In essence, FAP would have replaced our present welfare system with a guaranteed minimum income. In effect, it would have been similar to extending social security to those currently unprotected from the vagaries of the waged labor market and the realities of child rearing. In order to overcome perceived potential disruption of the labor market, people who had low-wage employment would also receive some cash assistance from the government. The higher the job pay, the lower the government checks would be. Again, it was similar to social security, although its initial levels of support were not as generous, and the "tax-back" began with the first dollar earned. The econometric model employed was referred to as a "negative income tax," the theoretical paradigm usually attributed to conservative economist Milton Friedman.

Support for and opposition to FAP were as complex as for any issue in the nation's history. NWRO wanted a higher income standard set from the beginning and the work requirements canned. All groups were divided on the issue for a host of reasons, not the least of which was work. The president's commission never intended forced-work requirements to be a prerequisite to guaranteed income, but, to make it politically palatable to some of the naysayers, Nixon's people inserted what were considered strong forced-work components. The National Welfare Rights Organization argued that mothering *was* work and mothers should be exempted from work requirements, at least until they stopped being their children's primary caretakers.

Some opponents were apoplectic at the thought that guaranteed income would discourage "work" and virtually destroy the economy. In a sense, they were talking about two different populations. At the time, welfare mothers were generally not expected to "work," and the new provisions would not force them into a program until after their youngest child turned six. Most welfare mothers have a small child in the home, so they would not have been affected. The real and most pervasive fear was that virtually the entire working class would opt out of the labor market if they were not forced to work. And the higher the income level without forced work, the more likely people would be to reject work altogether. So if there wasn't much faith in the welfare population, when it came down to it, there was almost none in the so-called working class either. (In my view the working class and the welfare population are really the same, entering and exiting one status or the other as fate and personal circumstances change.)

People unfamiliar with the history of income maintenance are often surprised to learn that a *conservative* economist, Milton Friedman, developed the negative income model and a *Republican* president, Nixon, first proposed a bill to implement it. As a practical and political matter, though, it makes sense. In theory, this plan wiped out much of the entrenched multilayered, self-perpetuating welfare bureaucracy. It would have been simple to administer. It would not have been cheap, but it would have been clean. It also potentially cut into the social service sector, a bastion predominantly cornered by Democrats. And its "work incentives" kept employment desirable by subsidizing low-wage work. According to the French theorist Andre Gorz, "In its right-wing version, the idea of guaranteed income . . . aims to make the growth of unemployment and poverty socially tolerable, for these are considered the inevitable consequences of a free market economy."[7]

On December 13, 1970, President Nixon addressed the decennial White House Conference on Children:

> The great issue concerning family and child welfare in the United States is the issue of family income. For generations social thinkers have argued that there is such a thing as a minimum necessary family income, and that no family should be required to subsist on less. It is a simple idea, but profound in its consequences.
>
> On August 11, 1969, I proposed for the first time in America's

history we establish a floor under the income of every American family with children.

We called it the Family Assistance Plan. It has in turn been called the most important piece of social legislation in our nation's history.

You know the story of this legislation. In April it passed the House of Representatives by a margin of almost two to one. Then it became mired down in the Senate.

It is still stuck, but it is not lost. There is still an opportunity for the 91st Congress to change the world of American children by enacting Family Assistance. . . .

The welfare system has become a consuming, monstrous, inhuman outrage against the community, against the family, against the individual—and most of all against the very children whom it was supposed to help.

We have taken long strides toward ending racial segregation, but welfare segregation can be almost as insidious.

Think what it can mean to a sensitive child. To take only one example—the free lunch program. . . . The welfare children [are] herded into an auditorium for their free lunch, while the others bring their lunches and eat in the classroom. We have got to find ways of ending this sort of separation. . . . The point is the stigmatizing by separation of the welfare children, *as* welfare children.

He went on to describe his own experiences of poverty "back in the Depression" at some length. Then he returned to say,

Today's welfare child is not so fortunate.

His family may have enough to get by on. They may even have more, in a material sense, than many of us did in those Depression years. But no matter how much pride and courage his parents have, he knows they are poor—and he can feel that soul-stifling, patronizing attitude that follows the dole.

Perhaps he watches while a case-worker—himself trapped in a system that wastes, on policing, talents that could be used for helping—while this case-worker is forced by the system to poke around in the child's apartment, checking on how the money is spent or whether his mother might be hiding his father in the closet. This sort of indignity is hard enough on the mother—enough of a blow to her pride and self-respect—but think what it must mean to a sensitive child.

We have a chance now to give that child a chance—a chance to grow up without having his schoolmates throw in his face the fact that he is on welfare, and without making him feel that he is therefore something less than other children.

Our task is not only to lift people out of poverty, but from the standpoint of the child to erase the stigma of welfare and illegitimacy and apartness—to restore pride and dignity and self-respect.

I do not contend that our Family Assistance Plan is perfect. . . . But it is a good program, and a program immensely better than what we have now. . . . For the Senate to adjourn without enacting this measure would be a tragedy of missed opportunity for America.[8]

They did and it was.

The Family Assistance Plan was flawed—it certainly didn't provide enough money to lift families out of poverty, for instance. Social security didn't do that in the beginning either. But the longer FAP held out, the worse it got, as lobbyists from every conceivable corner found fault with it or tried to make it advance their own agendas. Given the strength and diversity of the opposition, FAP was doomed. It seems clear today, however, that FAP in its original form could have changed everything about the politics of poverty and set a universal standard minimum income, irrespective of employment status.

While Nixon has hardly been remembered as a "liberal tax-and-spend" kind of guy, for reasons that only he could tell us, failing to pass FAP remains one of his greatest disappointments. So he says. But there is also a political basis that he could not have missed. At some point, if people have sufficient income to live decently, they have less need for the social service agencies. Republicans have occasionally dented the political allegiance most of these have for the Democratic party, but they have never achieved a significant shift. When the Republicans control the patronage, studies may produce more conservative "results" and "conclusions," but even with a Republican president, most of the minutiae of social service patronage are controlled by Congress, which has been dominated by Democrats for decades. (Republicans have had more success in controlling military patronage. They are not *above* it.) So, whether Nixon wanted to end poverty or whether he wanted to shrink the size of the active opposition isn't clear. It was probably some of both, not unlike Johnson's probable impetus for the Great Society.

Important principles died with the bill. Unfortunately, though we didn't get the good parts of FAP, we do have its worst aspects—forced work and spurious training programs—embedded in our current welfare system, as well as all the mess we had before plus some.

The Rebirth of an Industry

After Nixon abandoned FAP, the professionalization of being human took off again, bloating under government contracts. For every poverty problem, a self-perpetuating profession proposed to ameliorate the situation without altering the poverty itself. In *The Politics of a Guaranteed Income,* published in 1973, Daniel Patrick Moynihan noted the "astonishing consistency" with which middle-class professionals "improved" the condition of lower-class groups by devising schemes that would first improve their *own* condition. Neither simple efficiency nor social justice was to get in the way for some time to come.

Like the nineteenth-century opponents of outdoor relief, today's stars of social welfare keep the "service" engine stoked by ascribing every manner of failure to the families. Laziness. Cheating. Dependency. Drugs. Ignorance. The families lack the resources to defend themselves, though the "helping" institutions always have government and/or foundation funds to lobby (ostensibly in the families' behalf) for *more* funding to fix these deficient humans. This time around, the service sector is more powerful than ever, buttressed by a litany of social "scientific" material produced to prove hypotheses that keep its proverbial pockets bulging with the bounty of good intentions.

Coined by Ken Auletta, the term *underclass* deserves special attention because its implications have spawned more questionable social policy in recent years than almost any other social "discovery." And it helped to deep-six any public discussion of increasing incomes for millions of welfare families.

After a few weeks of watching and studying people in a work and training program, Auletta came to a number of conclusions. The group had been divided into deviant subgroups by the agency running the program, the Manpower Demonstration Research Corporation (MDRC). These were drug addicts, criminals, the psychologically traumatized, and welfare mothers. Why women who remained the caretakers of their children without benefit of a supportive partner were lumped into this study is beyond my comprehension.

Auletta noticed that the mothers were most "successful" in the program. As a result, he took it upon himself to promote workfare for welfare mothers. If he had understood how out of whack their very placement in the grouping was, his "findings" would not have come as much of a surprise. Beyond that, why he looked favorably on the behavior modification strategy (forced work) without considering the host of issues like child care that emanated from it is baffling. Why didn't he question the wisdom of removing mothers from direct caretaking irrespective of their skills, desires, or family needs, if his theory of this deviant "underclass" grouped together in given neighborhoods were indeed accurate? Why leave children without parental supervision in a dangerous neighborhood just so their mother can "work" and stay poor?

Auletta's book helped consolidate the chorus of policymakers around the need for welfare mothers to get out of the house, be trained, and "work." He had observed a very small universe for only a few weeks: "A group of twenty-six trainees . . . became the narrative spine for [the] book." Auletta nevertheless generalized his observations, and few serious academicians challenged the soundness of extracting so much from so little.

Ever since, innumerable political scientists, journalists, and, to some extent, even the general population have used Auletta's term, bemoaned the genesis and woes of the "underclass," ignored the offensive notion embodied in the very word, and made recommendations on what to do about it—often without so much as stepping foot into the neighborhoods involved. A barrage of like-minded literature helped to reaffirm ever-increasing workfare demands by politicians and bureaucrats. It culminated in another welfare reform bill in 1988, which resulted in all kinds of behavior modification strategies, including sexual practices (eugenics) but didn't bother with the issues of helping mothers and their families out of poverty.

In the conservative welfare-bashing bible, *Losing Ground,* Charles Murray places much of the blame on the Great Society. Murray, it seems, mixed the "welfare state" with "welfare." Be that as it may, he believes that the growth in domestic spending attributable to Lyndon Johnson's Great Society has had the unfortunate result of encouraging "dependency." Calling AFDC the "bête noire" of social welfare, he argues that recipients opted out of the job market in favor of easy and plentiful dollars doled out from the Great Society years through 1980.

As I have pointed out, it may be true that government spending on social services and programs for nonpoor people (i.e., medicare) expanded, but for most of the period with which Murray is preoccupied (post-1960s to 1980), cash income in real dollars contracted for *poor families on AFDC.* The welfare *state, not* individual grants to poor people, had expanded wildly. To hold water, Murray's theory would have required the opposite, as he hypothesizes poor people's behaviors directly attributable to the ease of access and increased value of public assistance benefits. Murray is another of those brief social welfare stars whose background was really not there and who later retreated to (perhaps) safer ground—the Apollo space program.

Nevertheless, Murray's choice of culprits—the Great Society—was at least partly correct. It initially emphasized a service strategy to the near exclusion of income security—with the long-term effect of *eroding* the income security of millions, tens of thousands of whom ended up homeless. The conceptual framework that fostered this deterioration held well into the 1990s, long after the nation surrendered in the War on Poverty.

William Julius Wilson, a black sociologist, moved the debate in a different direction in a book called *The Truly Disadvantaged: The Inner City, the Underclass, and Public Policy.* He focused on black male poverty as a consequence of decreasing job opportunities in recent decades. His data are impressive and compelling in many respects. The figures show a dramatic increase in unemployment of black men from the 1960s to 1980. He argues that the rise in single-parent families among blacks correlates with the rise in male unemployment. (He rejects the notion that welfare has caused the breakup of black families.) One of his central conclusions is that if black *male* employment increased, the poverty of female families would decline. Previously "unmarriageable" [unemployed] men would be marriageable. Families would get together or stay together as they had in the past.

It is true that marriage is the single factor most likely to deliver a poor white mother-only family from the clutches of poverty. What is troubling is Wilson's suggestion that the solution to the problem of poverty of women and children rests first on eliminating the poverty of men. Also, a certain set of basic realities are smoothed over a little too facilely. First, half of all married couples in the United States do not stay together. And most absent fathers do not pay child support with any frequency or to any degree sufficient to live on.

Second, teenagers who have babies (upon whom Wilson dwells) have always been more prone to poverty than older mothers in our society. The real difference in the behavior of teenagers who have babies today—black and white—is more attributable to the fact that *their* mothers know that shotgun marriages don't work. They never really did. Forcing a male to marry will not force him to be responsible, even if he has a job. Marrying him almost always creates an additional set of problems for the overwhelmed young mother—he comes with dirty socks and a lot of machismo.

The rate and number of teenagers having babies have been declining for decades. Still, the ages at which most teens do have babies are essentially what they were twenty or thirty years ago—the older the teen, the more likely she is to sustain a pregnancy rather than abort it.

Few statistical analyses have stirred up more hysteria in our time than those regarding teenagers and babies. The consequent public policy bigotry makes these young women easy prey in the behavior modification sweepstakes lavishing ever more social workers with jobs—especially since teenage mothers tend to stay on the welfare rolls longer than older mothers.

More damage was done by the spin liberals David Ellwood and Mary Jo Banes put on the stats. Looking at the same data other social scientists had in front of them, the results of a multiyear Panel Study on Income Dynamics (PSID), they concluded that whereas the majority of welfare recipients were off the rolls quite rapidly, those who stayed on the rolls longest took up much more of the resources. That is true. If five women stay on welfare for one year each, each *individually* takes up fewer resources than one woman who stays on for five years. They went on to put the fear of God into policymakers with the conclusion that long-term recipients take up more than half the resources of AFDC. The scramble to hustle them off the rolls was stronger than ever.

Long-term welfare receipt is generally considered to be eight years or more. (Two thirds of all recipients are off the rolls in three years or less.) But eight years is certainly not an uncommon period for young widows on social security, and that doesn't get up anybody's dander. Remember, social security is income maintenance, too. Oddly, Banes and Ellwood have not done any analysis of the cost of so many long-term social security recipients on survivors' benefits—the data aren't in any of the literature I've read. Yet, using their fearsome logic, the cost of each individual on social security is probably many more times that of the long-term welfare recipient. There are over 1,783,750 children on social security survivors' benefits (as compared with 8,000,000 on AFDC). The former can qualify in utero (as can an AFDC child) and stay on social security *no questions asked* to age eighteen or nineteen. The checks just keep on coming. The mothers (widows) who care for them can stay that long, too. I have never heard of a person eligible for social security "leaving the rolls" for any reason other than death. The total of social security survivors' payments (to someone other than the "covered worker") in 1989 was over $48 billion. That was six times the potential annual cost of AFDC for "long-term recipients," if Banes and Ellwood are to be taken seriously.

Maybe the real problem isn't long-term receipt of income maintenance as much as it is the low level of payments, which keeps young welfare families so poor. Or maybe the constant refrain from today's culture that says, "You're bad, you're bad, you're bad," to one group (those on AFDC) but not the other (those getting survivors' benefits) has something to do with keeping poor people down. Banes and Ellwood did not take that up.

They did notice an increase in "out-of-wedlock" births among long-term recipients, including teenagers who had babies. Whether two or three decades ago these young mothers would have been married *before* coming onto welfare is irrelevant in budget terms. The point is, teenaged mothers would have been on welfare anyway, because young fathers behave in essentially the same ways whether or not they marry. They walk away from the union and rarely take responsibility for the children. The factors that count with respect to length of stay on welfare—like the age of the mother, the number of children she has to raise, her educational attainment, the health of her and the children—have all remained pretty much the same. Then and now the "creation of a single-parent family" is the single most frequent precipitator of welfare receipt—young, married first, or not.

The greatest rate of increase among women having babies out of wedlock has occurred among white, older, middle- and upper-class women. It is a basic fact of our current culture. Nonetheless, the out-of-wedlock issue permeates public policy decisions. And it is the women on welfare who are pushed to change. The clamor to do something about "illegitimacy" has been awesome. The real furor has been over welfare, not marriage. The misogynistic result has been yet more pressure to fix all AFDC mothers, *not unwed fathers*.

To the extent the teenagers do have babies, the decision is not infrequently the result of intense pressure by young men. Young men who do not take care of these babies, and for the most part do not intend to, often get several girls pregnant and then brag about it. The boy's pressure on the girl to keep the baby usually lasts until shortly after it's born. After that, the girl is a mother and the boy is nowhere to be found. Forced sterilizations of young welfare mothers were common in the seventies and eighties. Now some states are attempting to force welfare mothers to use Norplant, and others are refusing to pay any benefits for some babies born to welfare mothers. But I have never heard of a social policymaker even hint at rendering boys who behave in this manner infertile (by vasectomy or any other means). Why?

Job Training for What?

Another academician whose writing massaged the political process for the workfare movement is Lawrence Meade. He contends that welfare is a one-sided equation. Welfare families get something for nothing, therein breaking the implicit social contract between the individual and society. Meade will not concede that the "social contract" was broken from the start, as welfare families are denied any real participation in the political process or other benefits of our society and the labor of mothers is so denigrated as to *seem* nonexistent. During one televised debate, he argued that the social contract does not require that mothers get jobs paying enough to overcome poverty. It merely requires that the mothers "work" if they get welfare. Between this social contract rhetoric, which caught on handily, the repulsion against longer-term recipients, the "illegitimacy question," and concern for or about the "underclass," welfare "reform" was all but inevitable.

In the great welfare reform debates of the late 1980s, social welfare professionals fell all over each other running after more funding through the jobs, training, and child care provisions of the so-called welfare reform bill, ironically presided over by Daniel Patrick Moynihan (usually credited as the architect of FAP). Forgotten were the words of the President's Commission on Income Maintenance two decades earlier: "Services cannot be a substitute for adequate incomes; they cannot pay rent or buy food for a poor family." (The few surviving organizations of welfare mothers put guaranteed income at the top of their lists, but they are rarely listened to. After all, they have no money.)

What stalled the "reform" act for months was the issue of how much money to allocate for running the job/training programs, and a turf war over whether they would be run by welfare departments or contracted out to private charities. (Everybody knew getting women to work didn't mean getting them out of poverty, so there wasn't any time wasted worrying about their financial condition.) In New York, Russell Sykes, then at State Communities Aid Association, even circulated a paper on how the agencies who got the contracts would have to bite the bullet and participate in cutting off the rolls women who didn't "comply"—the ultimate burden of doing "good" in the nineties.

One of the other things most everybody in the field knew but wouldn't say was that the work programs don't really work, so to speak, for many reasons. One is that in a contracting labor market there simply aren't jobs for the millions of women who would be forced into them. Not to mention, these programs cost more than straight income maintenance does. And everything has pretty much been tried before without success. The Manpower Demonstration Research Corporation had extravagant grants (mostly from the Ford Foundation) to study various state programs. Those who read carefully (that is, the data sans MDRC spins) find that the studies generally demonstrate a waste of tax dollars and most people's time. That wasn't the conclusion workfare pushers who floated the funds wanted, so summary statements of megavolume papers fibbed a little—sounding more positive about the outcomes.

Most of what the millions of dollars spent on multiple studies showed was already known from programs that had existed for years. About a decade ago, at a welfare rights workshop in Texas, a woman from Kentucky on what was then called the Work Incentive Program (WIN) gave a vivid description of her interview with a WIN worker. I wrote some of it down, as close to verbatim as I could:

> She asks me what I made on my last job. She asks me what I'd like to make. Well, I'd like to make nothing less than one thousand dollars an hour—who she think she's kidding? She wastes my time with a whole list of bull doo while she's just trying to stretch [the interview] to lunch. She asks me what I think I can do well and I say I can do her job. At least I wouldn't waste time. . . . She says I don't care how fast you can type, all we have are dish washing jobs. So what'd she waste my time with all that bull doo for?

Two decades ago, the Milwaukee County Welfare Rights Organization had a book published. Chapter 3 is called "Poverty Pimps." Early on it reads, "So who *really* benefits from the poverty program? The people who run it. . . . Since the birth of the Office of Economic Opportunity . . . in 1964, hundreds of corporations have found that they can get richer off poverty itself." The failure of most of the job programs targeting welfare recipients had been known for years. Not the least of the informed were the welfare mothers themselves. There was really nothing new under this sun. So what was going on?

There can be little doubt that at least from the mid-1970s into the 1990s, "welfare" reemerged in social policy debates as a largely negative force in our culture and economy, having staggering implications for both societal and individual development. This sentiment achieved a rare consensus, embraced for varying reasons by most of the left, right, and center. They were so uniformly focused on the question of "work," independent of income, that it became difficult to distinguish the ideologies underpinning the assorted proposals to fix the system. Oddly, many of the policy experts redoubling their efforts for forced work at any wage for welfare mothers were concurrently crying the blues about the loss of high-paying industrial jobs, suffered primarily by men. (Watch a rerun of any of a number of speeches delivered by Bill Clinton during the presidential campaign.)

For many reasons, the tendency to exaggerate the "successes" has dominated public discourse.[9] A 7 percent, or 1 percent, or 10 percent "success rate" is common. In other words, the proven failure rate of the programs is 90 percent or more. That hasn't stopped politicians and the social welfare industry from clamoring for ever more funds from Congress. As Texas politician Jim Hightower says, "Job training for what?" He argues that there are millions of people in the country who are already trained, highly educated, and skilled who can't get jobs because the jobs aren't there.

At some point, even Congress will have to do a reality check—if for no other reason than because the cost of the programs far exceeds their benefits. The red herring that "welfare-to-work" has become should sink of its own weight. When it does, there could and should be a reopening of debate on income security, independent of one's relationship to waged work—i.e., guaranteed income. We have to stop and ask how we can condemn millions of people to lives of desperate poverty when we have been unable to offer any real way out.

A majority of U.S. families are teetering on the brink of poverty. They may not be permanently or presently poor, but any of a number of possible calamities—job loss, death of a provider, illness—could push them over the edge. In his book *Equality* William Ryan postulates, "Included in this vulnerable majority, who have an even chance of spending some portion of their lives in economic distress, are perhaps three out of four Americans." Many millions of people who only a few years ago felt secure in their jobs have recently experienced the reality of downward mobility. For some, new jobs will come at lower wages. For others, the condition of poverty will become permanent.

Even if and when the unemployed return to paid work, their pockets often remain virtually empty. Two major trends in employment patterns in the United States are altering the direction of our economy. The most profound is the increase in service sector jobs, public and private. The greatest growth in that sector has occurred at the bottom of the wage scale, with some growth in the middle, and a somewhat larger growth at the top.

In production industries, technological advances, especially via computers, are creating the second major trend—the elimination of jobs. Most blue-collar job losses can be attributed to successful growth strategies adopted by other countries in conjunction with a reorganization of industries in this country based on high-technology models. As a result, far fewer paid jobs have been created than eliminated.

The robotization of the workplace outside the home divides the labor process so that the work of those at the bottom becomes increasingly deskilled—that is, largely rote. This tendency also diminishes middle-level positions and disintegrates the "ladder of opportunity" that remains the myth of entry-level employment. It is a trend that doesn't appear to be letting up. In the early eighties, estimates in *Fortune* magazine, for instance, predicted the further decimation of production jobs by one third to one half by the end of that decade. By 1990, concurred economist Robert Theobald, "the installation of 10 to 20 thousand robots . . . will create up to 5000 new jobs for robot technicians, but the robots will replace 50,000 auto workers." Close, but no cigar. Ford Motor Company *alone* announced that it would lay off 75,000 workers in 1992. The auto industry in this country is in free-fall. Also in 1992, for the first time in its history, IBM, which had long touted its job security, announced the layoffs of 25,000 workers. The list is long and growing. Not only have the "trades" lost jobs, but many upper-middle-class jobs have gone and are going down the tubes, too.

The growing service sector, which has traditionally been dominated by women and men of color, is also becoming rife with technological displacement. By 1994 AT&T will complete its phaseout of a third of its remaining operators (many had already been phased out with the introduction of long-distance dialing). Recordings will do the talking from now on. Cutting out many operators also cuts out managers—an anticipated 200 to 400 of their jobs are gone, too. Anyone with a bank cash card has had the opportunity to experience the almost eerie quality of midnight banking with no other human being in sight. The flood of catalogs clogging every mailbox speaks volumes on the lot of salespeople in stores. It won't be long before we push buttons at McDonald's and burgers pop out. Estimates of the loss of even high-paying finance jobs on Wall Street exclusively as a result of technological advances reach well into the 20 percent range, in spite of a relatively robust stock market. According to one recent congressional report, 9.2 million workers lost their jobs over the five years from 1985 to 1989 "due to plant closings or relocation, elimination of a position or shift, or slack-work."[10] The nation's productivity boom is taking place independent of opportunities for better standards of living or even the maintenance of their present standard for many people.

If the "strongest" workers in the labor force (white men) continue losing relatively better paying jobs (i.e., steel production, automobile manufacturing, middle management, even finance) and continue a downward spiral into lower-wage work, it is not too difficult to guess who will get pushed out altogether. Women and men of color, for whom the ladder of opportunity was rarely more than a footstool in the past, can expect even less in the future, if nothing is done.

The Triple Revolution

On March 22, 1964, the Ad Hoc Committee on the Triple Revolution sent President Johnson a most prescient and now obscure memorandum analyzing the future of the United States along three major lines of inquiry: (1) the cybernation revolution, (2) the weaponry revolution, and (3) the human rights revolution. The document was signed by a number of notables of the time, most of whom are still active in some way in our collective political life. Among them were W. H. Ferry, Todd Gitlin, Michael Harrington, Tom Hayden, Irving Howe, Dwight Macdonald, A. J. Muste, Gunnar Myrdal, Linus Pauling, Bayard Rustin, Carl Stover, and Robert Theobald, the man most responsible for evolving the twin theories of the cybernation revolution and its inevitably required response: guaranteed income.

Only a couple of women were on this committee, Alice Mary Hilton and Dr. Frances W. Herring. The only reference to women is in the last paragraph. Ironically, in just a few short years, the movement that would have the most profound and enduring effect on a national and worldwide level would be the women's movement. For all intents and purposes, to this committee, as to so many others, women were invisible.

As far as it goes, the document and its underlying premises are nonetheless applicable and even more readily understandable today than when they were written. The greatest attention was paid to the cybernation revolution. I'll take that up last. Vis-à-vis the weaponry revolution, they were right on the money. They argued that because world destruction would be the inevitable consequence of using any of a number of developed and developing weapons, war as a means of resolving international conflicts would begin to disappear. (Little did they know that the Vietnam War was just heating up.) They were not naive; they understood that eliminating war would be a slow and "frustrating process." The big bomb theory postulated a decreased need for vast military assets—especially in the form of people power. Jobs and concomitant expenditures created by the military complex would diminish. Defense spending would become a smaller portion of the gross national products of the United States and other countries. They didn't use the term *new world order,* but that's what they were talking about.

Their "human rights revolution" predicted a universal demand for full human rights. It was clear to them that justice as evidenced by a fair share of economic and social rights in this country for blacks would not be met:

> The Negro is trying to enter a social community and a tradition of work-and-income which are in the process of vanishing even for the hitherto privileged white worker. . . .
>
> The U.S. operates on the thesis . . . that every person will be able to obtain a job if he wishes to do so and that this job will provide him with resources adequate to live and maintain a family decently. . . . Job-holding is the general mechanism through which economic resources are distributed. Those without [jobs can function] as only "minimum consumers." As a result, the goods and services which are needed by these crippled consumers and which they would buy if they could, are not produced. This in turn deprives other workers of jobs, thus reducing their incomes and consumption.

In the opinion of the committee, a just outcome in the human rights revolution depended on the outcomes of the other two revolutions and the responsible development of social policy in reaction to all three. Keep in mind that these were peak cold war years; the Berlin Wall was up and the USSR bound tightly. The fax generation wasn't begun. Nor had VCRs, cable TV, PCs like the one I'm working on, or many other time-saving or entertainment devices become commonplace.

The fastest and certainly up there with the most profound change in human history is the cybernetic revolution: the interaction of human behavior and the virtually cosmic changes being wrought by complex electronic computers. The agricultural revolution took thousands of years; the industrial revolution, hundreds. Cybernation is moving at warp speed. Unfortunately, many of the politically active signatories of the Triple Revolution memo went on to promote "full employment" even though they believed jobs would continue to evanesce. The social, economic, and political burden placed on those effectively banished from the waged labor market has been one of the cruelest ever provoked by self-proclaimed progressives. While some men were kicked out of jobs— losing income, homes, and self-respect with few prospects of regaining any of it—poor mothers were being splayed like so much manure into the disappearing field of dreams.

Here's the triple revolution memo on cybernation:

> In the developing cybernated system, potentially unlimited output can be achieved by systems of machines which will require little co-operation from human beings.
>
> . . . The continuance of the income-through-jobs link to consume—now acts as the main brake on the almost unlimited capacity of a cybernated productive system.
>
> . . . An adequate distribution of the potential abundance of goods and services will be achieved only when it is understood that the major economic problem is not how to increase production but how to distribute the abundance that is the great potential of cybernation.
>
> . . . Wealth produced by machines rather than men [sic] is still wealth. *We urge, therefore, that society, through its appropriate legal and governmental institutions, undertake an unqualified commitment to provide*

every individual and every family with an adequate income as a matter of
right. [emphasis added]

Societies throughout history relied on slave labor to produce much
of their wealth. The ancient Greeks, whose concept of the polis and an
active participatory citizenry is part of our strongest (historically acknowledged) heritage, felt that toil had limited intrinsic value to individual well-being. In fact, they considered it an impediment to the
important things in life. For democracy, for art, for philosophy, for the
proper nurturance of future generations, labor was avoided. Our Protestant "work ethic" colors our perspective. But in an age when computers
and robots are displacing people at ever-increasing speed, it is time to
reevaluate our system of resource distribution, the values we assign to
differing activities in the society, like child rearing (one of the few jobs
no one has begun to figure out how to replace by machine), and what
a just society can do about it.

The triple revolution memo predated the findings of the President's
Commission on Income Maintenance and the Family Assistance Plan.
Each of these was moving firmly in the direction of increased income
supports for varying reasons. The time had not yet come.

Recent History

In his 1970 race for a senate seat, George Bush urged voters to support
President Nixon's Family Assistance Plan. His Democratic opponent
(Lloyd Bentsen) made FAP an issue in the race, claiming it would put all
Texans on welfare. Bush lost. Robert Kennedy opposed guaranteed
income. Eugene McCarthy and George McGovern embraced it; both
used it in their ill-fated presidential campaigns. Support and opposition
to it crossed all standard political lines. Dozens of proposals for increasing
income security and even eliminating the welfare system as we know it
were debated. They included family allowances, negative income taxes
(the less income you have, the more the government pays your family),
and universal guaranteed income, irrespective of family composition.
The Family Assistance Plan was only one among them. It wasn't a
hallucination, and it wasn't so long ago.

Barely a few years after FAP's defeat, the very mention of income redistribution choked the most liberal of politicos. Certainly the so-called advocates for the poor kept their mouths shut from the late seventies well into the nineties. They didn't want to jeopardize their government and private foundation support by a whisper with the power of a nuke. We can hope that that fallout is about to dissipate.

Still, it surfaced in snippets here and there. During George Bush's 1988 presidential campaign, he proposed a child care tax credit that had all the markings of a back-door approach to family allowances, albeit for a limited number of children at a low level of payment. It was the one platform piece unanimously adopted by the Republican platform delegates, without so much as a dissenting word. It would have supplied income not only to those low-income mothers working outside the home but also to those *in* the home. Whether it would have applied to welfare families is debatable. Domestic agendas being his weak suit, shortly after the election, Bush gave up on it.

Many day-care groups opposed it—they wanted all of whatever money was going to be passed around for child care to go to themselves. They saw that the package wasn't big enough (it wasn't) and families could choose not to spend it on them. There were some more astute observers who understood the hidden meaning in the Republican proposal, so it wasn't long before some Democrats were calling for it, too. Then the shouting match broke out. Led by Marian Wright Edelman of the Children's Defense Fund, those with the "true" child-care package strongly supported a service package, with its emphasis on paying for child-care services. Some of the Democratic congressional leaders, such as Representative Tom Downey, were beginning to move toward the "choice" ethic on the child-*rearing* question and funding for it. The clash was bitter and drowned out the possibility of compromise. It also muted any serious liberal reconsideration of how the welfare state should progress into the twenty-first century. Once again the service sector would opt for nothing for poor women over not enough for themselves.

In 1991 Senator Jay Rockefeller's Commission on Children officially reopened the dialogue, recommending a children's (family) allowance as key to reducing the poverty of U.S. children.[11] Edelman was on the commission and supported its recommendations. Now that she and other Washington advocates are beginning to come on board, maybe the time is approaching when debate shifts to what form income redistribution should take, not whether it should be done. Bob Greenstein, who fronted the opposition to it for Marty Rogol at Hands Across America in the late 1980s, is now also publicly supportive of a family allowance.

In the middle of the 1992 presidential election, George Bush was again toying with income assistance, this time proposing a several-hundred-dollar-per-person one-time giveaway, ostensibly to spur the economy. Irrespective of the political reasons for that claim or whether the level of proposed expenditures was high enough to have the desired effect, the notion that it would benefit the economy is important for future discourse. For that matter, Bill Clinton's proposal to invest some billions of dollars to jump-start the economy has the same economic rudiment except that, instead of giving to everyone, he will confine the giveaway to contracts of one sort or another—not unlike the Great Society programs of the 1960s. Clinton's is a top-down approach. Each has its positive and negative arguments. Both put treasury money out to be spent for the same desired effect.

Chapter 9

Ending Poverty as We Know It

To have freedom, one requires a little money. —Winston Churchill

The United States is one of few industrialized nations in the world that does not have a family allowance. It shows. A multitude of cross-national studies have been done in recent years to compare the income security of various demographic cohorts. Most of the countries in the studies tend to be the standard "Western" nations. Nearly all the countries studied other than the United States have a system of cash transfers that includes what are variously called children's, or family, allowances. The allowances by themselves are generally not enough to keep families out of poverty, but, in combination with other tax and transfer benefits, they appear to make a significant difference in child—and therefore family—poverty rates. With respect to children in poverty, the United States bottoms out in comparison with most other nations in the studies.

Family allowances subsidize families with children irrespective of labor force participation and family structure. Regular payments are made (usually on a monthly basis) for every child. The principle is simple. Children are the future of any people, and they cost money to raise and thrive. Children are presumed to be of benefit to the whole society and therefore to be its responsibility. (The same principle is the foundation of our system of public education.) In Sweden the concept extends well beyond children. They call it social solidarity. If the individual thrives, the society will.

Every country with them has its own political history behind the development of family allowances. What they have in common is that none was able to guarantee job income sufficient for all families. The allowance is one way of attempting to mitigate against that failure. To those who claim a family allowance will ruin the economy, ask the Germans, the Dutch, the Swedes. . . . Some might whine about high taxes, but they receive far more than the average U.S. citizen in social benefits: cash transfers *and* universal health care, *and,* in some cases, a standard of living higher than our own.

To those who claim single motherhood in itself is the cause of poverty, ask these countries where the rates of single mothers and out-of-wedlock childbearing are comparable to or *higher than* ours. The usual assumptions and excuses just don't hold water under any reasonable scrutiny. The real difference in the much lower poverty rates of many of these nations is the amount of transfer income, the redistributive policies, available to the people.

Even in the 1980s era of virtually worldwide social retrenchment, and in the more recent economic decline, no country eliminated family allowances. Quite the opposite. Portugal, for instance, to begin bringing its social system up to the higher standards of most of the other nations in the European Economic Community, actually expanded income assistance for children and families considerably.

Family allowances have not totally eliminated poverty, however. Even in many of the most generous European countries, race plays a role in poverty statistics. Immigrants from poorer, browner nations generally do not qualify for the full range of benefits accorded to whites. There can be no doubt that one of the major reasons the United States has failed to make a dent in child poverty rates is the perception that blacks and other people of color dominate the poverty statistics. This isn't true, but even if it were, racism is a barbaric excuse for imposing such suffering on so many families.

Functionally, family allowances are similar to our social security system, though alone they are not as generous. A check is sent—usually to the mother—based on the number of children and a variety of other factors depending on the country. (Social insurance in most other countries covers a far wider range of individuals than our social security does. Its combination with family allowances has considerable impact on the poverty rates of families.) Since most nations have family allowances, it wouldn't be too difficult to figure out the appropriate administrative apparatus for the United States. There are many to choose from.

A family allowance here could have the reverse effect that our current dependent exemptions for income tax have. When figuring income taxes, the more income you have, the more dollar value accrues per dependent claimed. If you are too poor to have taxable income, the dependent exemption is worthless. Families with taxable income in the 15 percent bracket net just over $300 per person in reduced taxes. (The less tax owed, the more money for the family, the less for the treasury.) If the family is making significantly more—say $200,000—each dependent claimed is worth over $650. Given the financial problems so many families are having, it makes little sense to render more cash assistance or fiscal relief to upper- than to lower-class families. That *is* the effect of dependent exemptions. (We also do it with housing subsidies, through mortgage deductions, low-interest loans, some construction and rent subsidy programs; health care expenditures, through deductions or exemptions; and in other areas. The "free" ride for poor families is nothing compared with the other free rides out there.)

Instead of an exemption, a family allowance could be accomplished by establishing a refundable dependent tax credit—say $1,500 per child or member of the household—irrespective of a family's relationship to the waged labor market. Those who do not have taxable income would get $1,500 per child or household member. Those with taxable income up to a specified amount would reduce their taxes by up to $1,500 for each counted individual. (The credit could extend into higher brackets at a lower level until it zeroes out.) A dependent credit would be *progressive* in that the lower the taxable family income, the more value the credit would have and vice versa. There is no reason it would have to be limited to families with children—the same system could be applied to everyone. It could help to support those who take care of elderly parents in their homes, for instance. The broader the coverage, the more it acts like a universal form of guaranteed income; the higher the payment, the more other programs it can begin to eliminate.

Family allowances may be the most politically viable form of increased income transfers on our horizon. They are important in part because they implicitly acknowledge the unpaid labor of women by both increasing family income while they remain at home and helping subsidize the costs of replacement labor (child care) when they have paying jobs. (Clearly, fathers who do the bulk of nurturing and household work would be accorded the same benefits. If only more did!) A family allowance could be a beginning. It need not be a stopping point.

The Mechanics of Guaranteed Income

A more equitable solution would be to establish a universal guaranteed adequate income. It would eliminate welfare (and a host of other programs) as we know it and could, depending on funding levels and eligibility standards, pretty much eliminate poverty. A guaranteed income would establish a bottom line of income security—a real "safety net"—below which no one could fall. It would include everyone who, for whatever reason, is poorly, inadequately, or not at all connected to the waged labor market. Conceptually, all this means is extending the principle of social security to everyone.

Sound impossible? Not at all. A number of quite sound models have been developed by various economists and social scientists. The hurdle isn't money—it's politics. Whether it is the mean spirited, who would deprive all poor people because a few might slouch, or the poverty industry, which fears for itself and motivates so much of our public policy, or the politicians who bristle over the dole while they hand out do-nothing pork barrel contracts to special interests (theirs), the problem boils down to the same thing. Politics.

The Family Assistance Plan utilized Milton Friedman's "negative income tax" model. It would work like this: the government would guarantee some dollar figure for everyone in the country. For argument's sake, let's say it would be $14,000 for a three-person family (similar to the average payment to a three-person social security survivor family)—a mother and two children. If the family had no income that year, they would receive $14,000 from the government—a full negative income tax. Using a 50 percent tax rate on the guarantee, if the family had wage income of $7,000 the next year, the government's share would be reduced by $3,500 to $10,500, so that family would have a total of $17,500 in income for the year—the guaranteed $14,000 plus half the earnings over the guarantee. (There has been considerable debate over the tax-back rate to give people an incentive to "work" without costing too much. I have used 50 percent because that's the rate on earnings above a certain amount that social security uses. The difference between this negative income tax and the way social security works is that in this model wages are taxed from the first dollar earned. The more the family receives in wage income, the less they get in negative income tax. Based on this principle, a waged worker, i.e., a broom factory worker, would always get more than a nonwaged worker, i.e., a mother.)

Here's what the model would look like for a three-person family:[1] After $28,000, the family would begin paying income taxes. There is no reason the payments would have to be given in one lump sum. Payments could be made on a monthly basis, like social security. For that matter, the program could and probably should be run by the Social Security Administration. Superficially, the cost of guaranteed adequate income

If Your Annual Income from a Paying Job Is	Then Your Annual Income from the Government Is	So Your Total Annual Income Is
$0	$14,000	$14,000
5,000	11,500	16,500
10,000	9,000	19,000
15,000	6,500	21,500
20,000	4,000	24,000
25,000	1,500	26,500
28,000	0	28,000

could be hundreds of billions of dollars annually. However, it would replace dozens of current programs that may not do what we want them to do—alleviate or eliminate poverty. For instance, AFDC would be eliminated, so would food stamps and SSI (Supplemental Security Income to needy "aged and disabled" people), the current earned income tax credit would be subsumed, virtually all the "feeding" programs and the tax expenditures related to the donation boondoggle could go, and so on. The higher the guarantee is set, the more programs would be eliminated. The more programs eliminated, the more redundant bureaucracies that flow from each would go, including some of those dependent on the contracting-out process. The more programs that are replaced with a guaranteed income, the lower the cost. It is even likely that at some point social security itself would be subsumed.

According to Allan Sheahen, author of *Guaranteed Income,* it would actually be "self-liquidating, meaning it would cost nothing. As people's incomes increased, most of the money would be spent on consumer goods. That would stimulate the economy, creating new jobs, new taxpayers, and new income for the government to replace what was given out." In other words, the multiplier effect would have impact as well as the cashing out of inefficient, corrupt, or redundant programs.

The negative income tax is only one form of guaranteed income. George McGovern's 1972 proposal, for instance, was to give *every* needy American $1,000 annually. Social security itself is another, albeit for a limited population. One way to address the income problem of single mothers (or fathers) and their children would be simply to expand eligibility for social security to include all single-parent families, however they are created. In other words, rather than predicate the receipt for "survivors" on the death of a parent, extend it to cover all single-parent households. Again, this would acknowledge the role of caretaker parents and reward their labor. Unlike negative income tax, there is no presumption about work outside the home, no projection that a paying job is de facto superior. The government could continue child support enforcement measures through the IRS to compensate for some of the outlays. Extending social security in this way would surely be more just than our current arbitrary system. It would not, however, extend to poor single individuals and unrelated adult-only households unless special provisions were made to universalize it.

A Family Trust Fund

The most persistent shell game is played over the issue of cost. That is only a problem when it comes to certain items. Perhaps the Gulf War lasted only a few weeks and the cleanup only a year (at least for the U.S. military), but nobody asked the question How much? when a billion dollars a day literally went up in smoke. If the money we will spend on bailing out the savings and loans were deposited into a family trust fund today, in five years the question wouldn't be whether we could pay for such a program but how generous the level of payment should be. In the 1970s, *all* the projections of the future costs of an ongoing program of cash assistance to families were less than the current aggregate expenditures on "human services" agencies we now take for granted. If only 1 or 2 percent of currently accumulating FICA (Federal Contributions Insurance Act or social security contributions) taxes were designated for families' income *irrespective* of their prior relationship to a man and similarly deposited in an interest-bearing account, a family trust fund to universalize income security would soon be a viable reality.

We could also choose to return some inherited wealth to the nation. On the surface, inheritance taxes are high, but in reality there are so many loopholes regularly exploited by the very wealthy that only a pittance of liquid assets—and virtually none of the real property, the wealth—goes to the treasury. The country's natural resources have been turned over to a handful of people, most of whom did no work to get them. Nevertheless, I have yet to hear a social scientist assert the "social contract" issue with respect to this truly dependent group. The list of potential sources to endow a family trust fund is staggering. Those few who benefit so profoundly from the status quo that creates so much despair can and will find other ways of satisfying their greed. In any case, if the rest of the country is relatively healthy in every sense of the word, who cares if these others prosper once again? Clearly, whether it's the "peace dividend" or any other of a host of sources, including a vast reduction in charities' coffers—money, or lack thereof—is not the issue.

Martin Anderson, an adviser to both President Nixon and President Reagan, once told me that the problem with the Democrats was they were so hounded by their own rhetoric that they *couldn't* spend big money anymore. He said Republicans, by contrast, were associated with the opposite rhetoric and never really had to take the money question into account. He cited Reagan's military expenditures and mounting budget deficit as evidence that spending was never really a problem if those who could effect the change wanted it enough. That's clearly an oversimplification, but the fact is, whenever the political will is marshaled, money comes out of a hat in Washington.

Guaranteed Income Experiments

During that period of U.S. history when guaranteed income was seriously discussed, four long-term experiments were done to see what would happen if income were guaranteed. Two groups of low-income people were followed in each experiment. One was given guaranteed income with no strings attached. The other was given nothing they would not have gotten outside the current system. The behavior of both was followed over the next decade. Much has been written about the results, naturally, informed by the political bias of the writers. There are some facts, some surprising, others not.

One major concern of those involved in examining the outcomes was whether income guarantees would stop people from "working." The answer to that question is mixed. Mothers in two-parent families with the guaranteed income reduced their total wage work from 17 to 31 percent (depending on the experiment) over the group with no special treatment. In one of the experiments, single mothers reduced their total wage work by about 12.0 as compared with 22.7 percent for married mothers. In another, single mothers reduced their wage work by only 2 percent. In any case, the reduction was not very high at all and may represent a choice made by some women to be full-time caretakers when they had the financial opportunity. It is arguable that this behavior is socially desirable or, at a minimum, neutral.

Fathers, in two-parent families for the most part, reduced their work hours by much less than mothers: from 1 percent to 7 percent, depending on the experiment. The project director of the Seattle-Denver experiment, Robert Spiegelman, argued,

There are many ways to cut work hours. Over a period of time, you can cut by taking longer to look for a job. By taking more leave without pay. By turning down overtime when offered. We find the most common way is on job turnover. People just take longer to get re-employed . . . by stretching out the periods in which you don't work, you cut your income somewhat, and substitute some leisure and some income maintenance. That's the kind of trade-off that all people make. You don't work as many hours as you physically could.[2]

Whatever the reasons, the decrease in work time of fathers was virtually negligible and not necessarily problematic. For decades, reduction of work hours has been a primary mechanism for increasing leisure as well as spreading jobs to more people. Since the experiments had no way of measuring the effects of increased consumption brought to the communities involved (because of increased disposable income), it is impossible to say whether total wage work was reduced at all. It is quite likely that any reductions in "work" by some resulted in increased hours put in by others as more money was spent in the communities, increasing either employment opportunities or work time for current employees. In all likelihood, *productivity* either increased or stayed the same. Increased "dependency" was not a factor.

The consequence most alarming to some was an increase in the dissolution of marriages by those with income guarantees in one of the four experiments. But this could actually be a positive outcome—allowing people in unhappy marriages to leave. Women in battering relationships, for instance, may have left husbands they might otherwise have felt forced to stay with. Income was based on the number of people in the family, not marital status. People in happy marriages do not have reason to leave when they have a stable income. Increased income does increase freedom. To reject guaranteed income as a means to enforce marital vows would be to argue that families ought to be kept poor. That would be cruel and ludicrous. And the opposite argument has been made for years—that poverty and/or welfare increase the tendency for family breakup. I would reject either argument. Families break up for many reasons. Happy families, husbands and wives who love each other in nonviolent relationships, do not.

The Fifth Estate

The social welfare field continues to grow at breakneck speed, whether it's social workers per se, income maintenance clerks, administrators, hotshot executives, whatever. In a reasonable world with income guarantees, there would be some automatic shrinkage of this sector. Those macroanalytic political scientists who get bent out of shape at the very thought of any diminution of the social service sector are simply off base. It doesn't matter a whit how big the sector is if the consequence of its growth is the increased misery of those it is supposed to serve. That said, there are a number of points to be made regarding those who continue service work, what their roles should be and what a guaranteed income could mean to them also.

People sometimes jump to the conclusion that I am arguing that no poor people want or need social services and all social workers are bad. Not so. I am concerned, however, about who makes the decision to access services, how they get paid for, how to eliminate fraud and abuse, and how to depoliticize the service system.

It is unlikely that any income guarantees in the foreseeable future would be generous enough to allow those with no other means of income support simply to purchase the services they need as they see fit. At the same time, as the welfare state is currently structured, to the extent that there is massive funding of services, it is often for assistance people do not need or will not accept because of the inadequacy of the providers.

As in the case with most economic development schemes, the problem arises from the top-down nature of the funding structures. Usually, services that are made available to people who cannot afford to pay as they go are funded by contract with the government, or through tax expenditures resulting from tax-deducted donations—often with a shove by one or another advocacy group lobbying for its own.

The only sensible way to structure public services is to put them on some kind of market mechanism. There are many ways this could be accomplished. For instance, poor families could be given vouchers worth up to $3,000 to "spend" on services they wished to have. Let's also say that if they do not use the whole allotment annually, half the difference stays in the treasury, the other half goes to the family. (For families with extraordinary difficulties, a special request process could be in place to exceed the limit on a case-by-case basis.) The potential of a financial return for limiting use of the services to essentials would be one way of controlling costs and ensuring that the service hawks who fail to deliver on their promises lose their patrons.

Over time we could eliminate much of the contracting-out system, reducing the guaranteed incomes of countless institutions currently on the government tit. It wouldn't be all that long before unwanted, unused, and unsatisfactory service programs melted away. If people could choose which services they wish to patronize, those most attractive to them would flourish. It wouldn't take long before appropriate services shifted from where organizations wish them to be (often where poor people are not) to where people who go to them want them to be: within some comfortable distance of home. This cannot happen when politicians and public policymakers decide which services or goods to pay for and whom they will pay. Politics and people being what they are, patronage, nepotism, and greed will outweigh merit and the spirit of democracy the way the current system dishes out service contracts. Capitalism works—for those who have access to the means of consumption. Billions of dollars could be saved. There's *more* funding for the Family Trust Fund. And a lot of families could be spared the intolerable injustice of forced counseling by incompetents and all the rest of the foolishness.

If people had enough money to buy real food, the last place you'd find most of them would be at the soup kitchens and food pantries. Not only these, but literally dozens of superfluous competing bureaucracies could be wiped out. The taxes that are forfeited in the not-for-profit discard market scam, replete with champagne and caviar charged off for benevolent balls, would go a long way toward really helping people in need while eliminating waste and corruption in the current system.

Those entities that no longer really depend on foundations or direct government funds for most of their income because they function largely on endowments—like the Community Service Society and the Federation of Protestant Welfare Agencies—have no excuse. They should be required to *prove* that one hundred or so years after they were comfortably established, they are doing work of true value that is worth the price we pay in forfeited national wealth and desired by the people they ostensibly work for: poor ones. It's not enough for them to *say* so. Their much abused political clout would go down the drain right along with the repeated mismanagement and other nonsense we all end up paying for. Dissolve them, sell off their assets, and turn the charitable millions over to the Family Trust Fund.

Close down the latter-day flophouses (shelters, "transitional housing," and so on), with the exception of a very few for true emergencies, such as fires. Homelessness on the scale we now pay for is not an emergency—it's a downright crime benefiting politically connected social welfare racketeers and other nincompoops. If I were a district attorney, I'd be looking at these charities with an eye toward a RICO (racketeer-influenced and corrupt organization) suit. Talk about bid rigging, kickbacks, venal manipulation of the political system, nepotism, and the lot! Convert the savings into money spent on housing, and in ten years the crisis could be over, billions of dollars could be recouped, and we'd all sleep better at night.

A Feminist Issue

If there can be said to be any political home for poor women inside a larger movement, the candidate is the women's movement. Some believe that civil rights movements are more accurately "the place" for welfare and other poverty issues. Whereas it is true that poverty disproportionately affects people of color, it is also the case that AFDC and low-wage work fall vastly disproportionately on women—including white women. And, historically, the civil rights movements have not targeted economic rights, certainly not for the poorest people.

Clearly, a critical factor in the social equation affecting poor women is that "women's work" generally is not assigned any value in the gross national product, even though it has very substantial consequences for any country's economy. Unless we assign inputs to the welfare mother, she can only be seen and treated as extracting outputs from everyone else. (On average she is back in the waged labor force within three years. Then her labor is counted, even if the stigma of prior welfare receipt never quite leaves.) In a brilliant economic analysis of worldwide under-valuing of women's labor, Marilyn Waring's book, *If Women Counted,* reads,

> The public policy implications of imputing women's work into the national accounts are vast. First, per capita GDP (GNP in the US) would change markedly. A more reliable indicator of the well-being of the community would be available, because all caring services, subsistence production, and that vast range of life-enhancing work would be visible and counted. And priorities would change. . . . Unpaid workers could make a realistic claim on the public purse as opposed to being condemned to "welfare."

It isn't enough to "acknowledge" women's work in the abstract. It must be counted. If poor women's labor were counted, these women would have to rank right up there with workaholics. That work includes the usual child-rearing responsibilities plus keeping children from freezing to death because there is no heat, keeping them clothed because there is no money left in a welfare budget after rent is paid, hauling the laundry for blocks because there is no washing machine, thinking constantly about how to raise them, worrying about their future. In a blistering summer heat wave, the job is like working in a twenty-four-hour-a-day, seven-day-a-week sweatshop.

The failure to count unwaged labor in the gross national product has had very concrete consequences for women in or out of the market-place. The valuelessness depresses women's wage potential at almost every level of the income spectrum. Until the women's movement takes this on with the same fervor accorded ERA and other issues, no amount of federal legislation will alter the basic economic equations. We must extend the call for choice from the reproductive sphere to the productive sphere. A true struggle joined in this way would finally bridge the apparent cultural gap that exists between those women who work at home raising children and those who derive their income from waged labor as well as across class and race lines.

Consider some of the following plans being put into effect (or already under way) in some states to blame and punish women for having children. Several states have or are about to implement "learnfare." The idea is that children who don't go to school who are on welfare are cut out of the family's budget. If the problem continues, the mother is cut. (In some cases the mother is the student.) Since skipping school is not a problem exclusive to AFDC families, what's to stop the state from cutting earned income tax credits from other poor families with similar problems?

States are also trying to force Norplant on AFDC women or decrease payments to women who have more than one or two children. (This is not really to save money—the vast majority of welfare mothers have only one or two children. It is an expression of moral hysteria intended to mollify an ignorant, misogynist, and racist political constituency.) Some states are attempting to force unmarried women with children to get married with a plan called "wedfare" or "bridefare." Most politicians supporting these measures claim they are not intended to increase abortion rates among poor women. They maintain that the idea is to convince women to redistribute their "extra" kids by putting them up for adoption. If women are convinced to do anything of the kind, they would be most likely to put the kids into foster care until they can afford to get them out. The swelling of foster care institutions may seem like a fine idea to those who make their living off them, but is it? How different are they from the children's asylums of the nineteenth century? How different is this from the mass shipping of children from the inner cities to rural towns and villages thousands of miles from home, as was done in the early part of this century?

When welfare mothers attempted to resist getting social security numbers for our infants, nobody paid much attention. Today almost any child must have a social security number. Make no mistake: Big Brother is watching. It is time to hear the alarm as well as the cries of distress of our poor sisters. When the rights of women on welfare are abridged, it is only a matter of time before the rights of others are eroded in similar ways. When the bulk of poor women were denied access to abortion by the elimination of federal funding, it wasn't long before all women were facing the potential loss of choice, as evolving Supreme Court decisions have made plain. It is time to wake up.

The Benefits of Guaranteed Income

Removing the pressures of poverty from family life would have incalculable effects well into the future. Poor people would cease to seem like an economic or spiritual drain on the nation. Lifting the shroud of humiliation from the backs of poor people would release a creative energy otherwise camouflaged. (Studies show that the single most important factor in educating a child is self-esteem. How can a welfare child ashamed of his mother, and perhaps father, feel anything but degraded?) There are savings in future health care costs for a host of ills, not the least of which is low birth weight. We would save in prisons as crime would cease to be the only way out of poverty for so many. Reduced crime also means more peace of mind for all of us.

The list of poverty-related ills is so vast, it is almost impossible to imagine all the benefits eliminating it would generate. Guaranteed income would alleviate personal suffering of tens of millions and at the same time improve the quality of life for all.

The skeptical should try to solve this riddle: Take a neighborhood, anywhere—like Scarsdale or Bel Air. A "good" neighborhood. Impose the following conditions on the residents:

1. Freeze all their assets; take all their cars away.
2. Tell one half the neighborhood that they will have their incomes reduced by half. (These are the lucky ones.)
3. Tell the other half they will occasionally, randomly, and arbitrarily receive half their incomes. The rest of the time they will receive nothing. (Churned off the rolls, so to speak.)
4. Besiege the families with red tape. Find and use every opportunity to tell the parents, especially the mothers, that they are inferior human beings. Actually, more like subhuman (underclass?). Make sure the kids hear. At least once monthly have a politician of some stature make them the target of everyone else's woes.
5. Change the rules several times a year. Keep the rule changes complex and quasi-secret, so they can't "comply."

6. Reduce police and firefighting services. Take away quality child-care centers for parents who still have jobs outside the home.

7. Close some schools, fire some teachers; among those still willing to teach there, reduce salaries. Don't bother about learning standards, just move the kids through and out.

8. Create cockamamie make-work jobs and training programs for the mothers that do not help them out. Make sure they work hard and worry a lot about how their children are doing without them.

9. Create a massive labyrinth through which *only* the "best and brightest" can occasionally escape.

10. Send in researchers; study the people, make them feel like animals in a zoo. Wonder why they don't like you. Assume it's an inbred form of hostility that can only be addressed by giving you public dollars. Make sure they know about this.

11. Now and then spend great sums of money on small countries, minor wars, to bail out the savings and loans (in which they have nothing), whatever you can think of. Tell them there's no way you can help them. Say it's the budget deficit thing and, besides, get a job.

What will happen?

How long will it take for housing prices to drop? Stores to close? Banks to move out? How long before speculating turns into gambling? How long before an alcoholic becomes a drunk? How long before a "casual" suburban drug user becomes a drug seller and a desperate junkie needing a fix whether or not he can pay for it? How long before theft, looting, and random violence become a way of life for many? How long before what few stores remain raise their prices sky high to make up from the many others for the actions of the few? How many more guns will be sold? What kind? How long before men who can escape without their families leave them behind? How long before a "nervous breakdown" becomes a full-fledged mental collapse? How long does it take a whole neighborhood to disintegrate? *Any* neighborhood.

The conditions above are essentially those that have been imposed on the poorest neighborhoods all over the country. Try the reverse: Take a neighborhood, anywhere—South Central LA, Watts, East New York—a "bad" neighborhood. Reverse the dynamics:

1. Rehabilitate dilapidated housing where it makes sense; build new housing where reason dictates.
2. Restore welfare benefits to their previous levels, or, better yet, give people without paying jobs the same benefit of the doubt accorded to people on social security *and* the same benefit levels. Restore the value of the minimum wage. Better yet, institute a guaranteed income.
3. Make certain the checks or other means of payment come in regularly and safely for everyone.
4. Reduce red tape to an absolute minimum. Guarantee productive choice as much as reproductive choice, so that women can enter and leave the wage market as *they* determine. Use every means available to lift the self-esteem of parents, especially mothers. Make sure the kids hear it.
5. Put back police and firefighting services. Set up quality child-care services like those produced overnight during World War II, when women's labor outside the home was *needed*, respected, and rewarded.
6. Improve the schools. Make it cool to attend school. Make it fun. Insist that kids who can't read, can't graduate.
7. Encourage the best and brightest to stay or others to come by creating a livable environment with opportunity for advancement.

How long before small businesses pop up because the aggregate income in the community has at least doubled and people can buy basic items like food and clothing again? How long before entrepreneurs start hiring other people? How long before these events spur additional economic growth, not only within this community but outside it as more consumption requires more production of all kinds? How long before children, formerly ashamed of their parents and background, start to be proud and wish to excel? How long before mothers whose self-esteem has soared begin to see options in their lives—and take them? How long before men who can see a productive future return? How long before the underground economy comes aboveground and the most destructive elements begin to wither away, as they are no longer the only possibilities for upward mobility?

Looks tough? Well, politically speaking it is. Practically speaking, it ain't half what it's cracked up to be.

Consider the income element. Any neighborhood that has had nearly half its legal income wiped out will be in trouble, quick. Clearly some mechanism must be put into place to restore the diminished aggregate income in poor communities. Since most of these communities have high proportions of single mothers taking care of their children, merely attempting to establish a job base would not suffice. Improving the economic condition of these areas would have to include increased cash assistance in some form.

Usually forgotten in discussions of economic security is the *positive effect it would have on the economy*. The initial outlay need not be excessive if a fund from which it will come is built up first. Over time, guaranteed income would generate jobs like no other spending program could—as necessary goods and services are produced and sold in the local markets where most people would spend it. Because aggregate consumption begets aggregate production, guaranteed income would even make some wealthy people wealthier, and create new wealth. The multiplier effect throughout the economy would be felt in short order. The new jobs would have an organic, market link to communities, unlike so many "economic development" schemes that foolishly plop money into bumbling top-down enterprises with little or no commonsense relationship to the community.

Guaranteed income could also eliminate price supports and subsidies of all kinds—not just in social welfare but in every field propped up by them. Take dairy products. Every bottle of milk that you (or welfare mothers) buy has a hidden tax in it that, in effect, guarantees an adequate income to the dairy farmer. Once again, we're paying for the income security of a politically determined group. The dairy lobby is powerful.

Guaranteeing income to everyone, irrespective of lobbying capacity, would eliminate the stigma of "welfare." It could also begin to peel away the political cover that provides support to one group at the expense of another sub rosa. A more equitable system of income distribution would be a democratizing process. Industry would change, yes. It could also boom. It is the opposite of trickle-down theory. Call it the sprout-up theory. Call it the vision thing, if you want.

Redistribution is something that this country does, that many other countries do and few reject.[3] It usually works to the economic benefit of both the giver and the givee. For some reason, as a nation we upset

314

ourselves only when we think about giving to our own poor people. Giving to older, even wealthier citizens in the form of social security, or to dairy farmers in price supports, is no sweat. Do we stop giving to foreign nations or U.S. seniors or young widows with small children "for their own good"? Do we really even question it? Not on your life.

Guaranteed income may seem like an exclusively redistributive strategy, but it is also an economic growth strategy predicated on democratic values. Let's face it, one of the reasons the United States introduced the Marshall Plan to rebuild parts of Europe and its counterpart in Japan was to create markets for U.S. goods, services, and technology. For a long time it worked—for all the countries involved. In any event, a socially responsible culture does not cause economic disaster.

When the Berlin Wall came down, one of the first things the West German government did was to give deutsche marks to East Germans, who flooded into West Germany to buy things. To the casual observer, this may have seemed like a magnanimous gesture of unusual proportions. To others it was a brilliant political moment, with virtually all the money quickly flooding right back into West Germany's economy.

One thing is certain—pointing the finger at poor women is neither the answer to the riddle nor the resolution of the problem. If the mean spirit that has prevailed in this country at least since the early seventies regarding poor people ever passes, the relatively simple objective of guaranteeing adequate income can be realized. The fact is that the entire nation would benefit. The true peace dividend is within our grasp. We need only insist upon it with our collective political will. Cynics can chide me for being naive, but they cannot challenge the eminent reasonableness of a strategy to trust poor people just like we trust social security recipients and those who report to the IRS. The honor system.

Real Change?

During the election campaign of 1992, Bill Clinton demonstrated some rhetorical concern about the issues of welfare and resource distribution, but whether he understands the issues remains to be seen. He boasted of Arkansas's work programs, but no one ever took a close look. (Politicians can say just about anything about "welfare-to-work" programs and be taken seriously without proof because their purpose is to get people off the welfare rolls.) Unless you happen to be one of the unfortunate women caught in their net, these Arkansas programs are little more than a joke. The only significant study done on them to date was published in the mid-1980s by the Manpower Demonstration Research Corporation, which followed two groups of "randomly selected" welfare recipients and applicants over a fifteen-month period. One carefully chosen group was forced to take the job training services. The other received no services (just their welfare checks).

What happened? Fewer than one fifth of participants in either group obtained jobs outside the home. But those who did get jobs ended up with less money than they'd had when on welfare. Both groups started out poor, and both got poorer. That's not because Arkansas's welfare grant of $204 monthly for a three-person family is high enough to make paid employment prohibitive either. Notwithstanding, after nine months, MDRC rendered a favorable, if premature, decision on the program, projecting a potential $41 to $224 per participant benefit to society over a five-year period. (No kidding.) Paradoxically, fifteen months into the study, participants who received *no* services or training were taking home, on average, more wage income than those who were "helped." To soften the blow, MDRC dances around the issues raised, but the bottom line is, neither the study they did on Arkansas programs (in two counties) nor those on programs in other states demonstrate any clear advantage to the families pushed into outside work. In some states, they were able to claim a (questionable) few-hundred-dollar benefit to the recipients per year as opposed to the benefit to "society" (which they derived by subtracting the losses in income of the recipient from the reduced expenditures of the state). In fact, the results are clear to anyone who cares to examine them closely: paid employment outside the home for welfare mothers has little to recommend it. And, unless Clinton isn't paying attention, he must know it. The work and training programs are little more than today's form of indentured servitude.

Still, Clinton claims his intent to cut welfare families off after two years if they are not in a private sector or public service job. One has to hope there is more to this than the rhetoric, or the consequences to poor women, who appeared to be virtual whipping posts during his electoral campaign, could be disastrous. (One has to hope that Hillary Rodham

Clinton stands up for the women on this one.) His *Putting People First* reads,

> *Empower people* with the education, training, and childcare they need
> for up to two years, so they can break the cycle of dependency.
> . . . After two years *require those who can work to go to work,* either in
> the private sector or in community service; provide placement assist-
> ance to help everyone find a job, and give the people who can't find
> one a dignified and meaningful community service job.

What jobs? Well, there has been talk of "enterprise zones" as an essential ingredient in producing jobs in poor areas. The principle of bringing jobs and income into the inner cities is laudable; the problem is in the method. Enterprise zones may make good sound-bite economics, but do they make sound policy?

In theory they are tools for economic development. They are created in geographic "zones" and have special privileges that mitigate or eliminate impediments to development. Among these are zoning ordinances, property condemnation laws to allow combining small lots into one large lot, labor laws, building codes, other land use restrictions required by community or planning boards, environmental rules related to industrial pollution of all kinds, and, most of all, tax breaks galore. The idea is to make an area attractive to industry that otherwise might not be. What enterprise zones were not originally designed to do was to access capital, although Clinton recommends a nationwide network of com- munity development banks, which could address this shortcoming. Start- up capital will be needed for some services and small businesses of all kinds pertinent to helping a neighborhood to thrive, but it need not be restricted to enterprise zones.

The idea is not inherently bad, but in practice there have been many problems, including that enterprise zones have created relatively few jobs for the people in the communities they were intended to serve. Indeed, relaxing local labor standards assumes the existence of a large unem- ployed population. Second, the jobs that are created are usually intended for men or are low-wage women's work, virtually ensuring poverty wages to welfare families. Third, the real profits remain concentrated in the hands of a few (whoever gets to control the wealth and the few who make the decisions as to whom the benefit will accrue). In practice, either the best jobs go to people who don't live and spend in the neighborhood or, before you know it, the people who once lived there poorly are displaced to live somewhere else, poorly. Fourth, the products resulting from the enterprise zones rarely have any value to the people in the communities, so they are shipped out. With them go the profits they are intended to produce. The problems of enterprise zones are the same as those inherent in most top-down schemes, with some added features, like seriously gutted labor standards. In a sense, they put labor law in reverse.

Let's face it, as we attempt or are forced by prevailing political and production conditions to extricate ourselves from a military-industrial economic base, we must have an alternative that produces jobs some people need, doing things that people in the community want and will willingly pay for if they have the resources. *That* produces tax revenue, which would move back into the local, state, and federal government. This is no small task, but it is essential if we are to move toward a people-driven market instead of a Pentagon-driven one. It is anticipated that direct defense-related employment will decline from about 6.0 million jobs in 1991 to fewer than 3.5 million in less than a decade.[4] I am not an economist, but added to the jobs that will be replaced by other means, this seems a bit ominous. Actually, one of our problems is that there is no prominent economist with the creativity of a Marx or Keynes today who envisions a way to deal with future resource distribution effectively. Dora Merris, editor of *Flexible Automation,* wrote to *The New York Times* in 1985,

> Economics from Adam Smith on has focused on ways to ration scarce resources. The economic problems of the 1990's and after will have to focus on ways to distribute abundance. . . . It will no longer suffice to base distribution of wealth on wages paid for the creation of that wealth.
>
> We face a frightening psychological prospect: making a very fundamental transformation in the way we think about work, wages, and human activity. My vote for Keynes's intellectual successor will go to the economist who can help us develop a framework for dealing constructively with these changes.[5]

Most economists are still operating on an industrial model, even though that has long since been outdated. We need a visionary to step forward.

Whereas some new jobs would be created in a guaranteed income economy, it is essential to acknowledge that it is highly unlikely that there will ever be enough decent jobs for everyone. There never have been. That's why, even if you can't swallow the notion that women raising children are working, you must accept the concept that resource distribution has to take place independent of job creation per se. A major function of a civilized society is to achieve an equitable mechanism to distribute resources to all members. In a money-based economy, guaranteed adequate income is a prerequisite to any fair distribution. Some will ask, Why not simply guarantee a decent job to everyone? Setting the question of mothering work aside, if it could have been done, it would have been.

Curiously, guaranteed income will probably only come about if and when at least some of the hack social welfare agencies hop on the bandwagon. In other words, they will, as they occasionally have, represent the interests of poor people when the bandwagon becomes so swollen they look bad by not being on it. Some organizations will also join the fray because individuals in them truly do want to see change, and they will work from within to promote an agenda of income security.

Robert Kennedy had a habit of paraphrasing Dante when he wanted to inspire people to action. He would say that in Dante's *Inferno* the last rung in hell was reserved for those who sat on the sidelines and did nothing. In fact, they are on *no* rung in hell but whirl hopelessly at its gates. Dante wrote that "Hell will not receive them since the wicked might feel some glory over them." It was Dante's contention that these souls—the opportunists—were neither positive nor negative forces in life, looking out only for themselves. John Ciardi's introduction to Canto III of the *Inferno* explains, "They took no sides, therefore they are given no place. As they pursued the ever-shifting illusion of their own advantage, changing their courses with every changing wind, so they pursue eternally an elusive, ever-shifting banner."

Many, if not most of those who toil in the helping professions haven't the slightest idea of the politics that envelop and employ them

319

at the expense, directly and indirectly, of those they seek to help. However, many *do know* what they are doing and why, how they achieve prestige, fill their pockets, advance their power. If these will not move on their own, it is up to the rest of us to move them. Sitting on the sidelines is not enough.

Two caveats need to be taken into account. First, there really are no monoliths. No institution or political force ever really has ideological hegemony. No group is all bad or all good. There are dominant and subordinate players, complete with the interweaving of personal standards of integrity, public images, and professional competence. And there are structural dynamics over which no one person has full control. So, as the welfare mother complaining at a conference once said, "If the shoe don't fit, don't wear it." If you feel you have come under attack in this book, you may not have. Or you may have. In the end, it is in part the responsibility of those who have crafted the mess to search their consciences and help get us out of it. It is not likely that a $100,000-plus-a-year executive at one of the do-nothing charities will find it difficult getting a job elsewhere in the marketplace anyway.

The second caveat is to guard against despair. Despite what may seem to be the overwhelming angst of this book, it is intended to generate some optimism. And some activism. In the shifting terrain of economic insecurity lie the seeds of social opportunity. It is possible to join the interests of a wide variety of people around the issues of income/resources in a way that includes poor people not as an afterthought but as an integral constituency to achieving social parity and economic security. Compassion has no party. Whatever the political motivation, raw, unabating poverty in our midst is shameful. When the opportunity for serious change arises again, let's hope the people with the power to do something about it don't botch the job. A good deal of debate necessarily precedes political action of the monumental kind. I hope that I might be contributing in a small way to the sum of experience that finally evolves into significant change. I hope the same for you.

NOTES

Introduction

1. Some working-class constituents also obtained jobs in the early stages, usually on the lower rungs of the agencies. Over time, and as they became more educated, some would move up the ladder.

2. Social welfare professionals are not always social workers per se. The industry is so large that it accommodates a wide range of jobs—executives, researchers, comptrollers, and so on. However, in this book, I use the terms *social workers* and *social welfare professionals* interchangeably, in particular because it was the professionalization of social work that gave rise to the rest.

Part I: The Welfare: Inside Out
Chapter 1: The Mothers' Shift

1. Some names have been changed.

2. In January 1990 there was a slight but almost negligible increase in aggregate benefits in New York. There has been no increase since. (Figures for welfare benefits, family demographics, and social and economic trends in this book come from a variety of sources. Most are drawn from either a New York City Human Resources Administration Publication, *Dependency,* or federal government publications from the Department of Health and Human Services *Social Security Bulletins;* Department of Commerce *Current Population Reports, Series P-60, 1991 Green Book,* and a variety of publications by the General Accounting Office and the Bureau of Labor Statistics.

3. When a welfare mother takes a paying job, she is generally eligible for payments for certain essentials like day care without which she would otherwise be unable to work outside the home. The welfare department doesn't *supply* these items, but to some extent it was and is obliged to pay for them. Although the specific rules governing these benefits have changed since my time, there are still benefits for which she is theoretically eligible. The 1988 Welfare Reform Act improved some of the benefits but left states free to pay less for child care than actual market rates. The tendency is to pay less than the rates required for *quality* child care. Families are also eligible now for medicaid benefits for a year after they leave the welfare rolls.

4. Theresa Funiciello, *The Number One Killer of Our Children: Poverty.* (New York: Federation of Protestant Welfare Agencies, 1988), p. 2.

Chapter 2: The Brutality of the Bureaucracy

1. This is a slight oversimplification. Some states have a higher "standard of need" than "payment standard." The bottom line was that you had to have ten dollars less than the payment standard to qualify, even though you could apply with a higher gross income. The resource limit varied from state to state, with zero being the lowest. The disparity between welfare benefits in low-paying states like Mississippi and high-paying states like New York has diminished somewhat, because the value of welfare benefits in high-paying states has fallen more precipitously than it has in low-paying states and the value of food stamps is higher in low-paying states, which helps to offset the difference. There are dozens of requirements besides income built in to the system both to qualify for welfare and to stay on it, even if your income needs remain constant.

2. One study produced by Mary Ellen Boyd's organization, Nontraditional Employment for Women (NEW), and the state's League of Women Voters soon showed that for every entry-level job advertised in newspapers across the state, there were an average of nineteen applicants, and often experience required on the most menial of them.

3. The irony of CETA was that as it sought to employ more disadvantaged workers, it became proportionately less viable politically. Dick Wagner at the Department of Labor, who kept extensive data (at least well into the eighties) on the Public Employment Program, which evolved into CETA, maintained that the death knell was sounded when the thrust changed from countercyclical (jobs for laid-off Lockheed types) to counterstructural (jobs

for disadvantaged workers). Out of the program after thirty days, the former retained a 70 percent placement rate in unsubsidized jobs, while the latter managed only a 30 percent rate.

Several studies also showed that many of the so-called disadvantaged workers were in fact temporarily laid-off municipal workers who had been placed in their old jobs using CETA funds. Of the 30 percent who retained employment then, only a fraction were actually from the truly disadvantaged population. Wagner maintained that few of these workers had acquired transferable skills during their CETA employment. Politicians made mincemeat out of CETA costs versus results. According to Wagner, CETA's main function became injecting money into the economy and keeping people busy. There was not political support for this even in the Carter administration. (Interview, 1984.)

4. Most of the press did not cover this first case of welfare center brutality that we officially encountered, except the *Guardian* and the Brooklyn Catholic paper, *The Tablet,* on June 21 and August 24, 1978, respectively. As the cases and cruelty increased, many more press accounts were filed. On occasion, we were even brought into cases by newspapers such as *The Staten Island Black Press,* which in a story headlined "White Cop Beats Black Woman; Woman Arrested for Assault" identified DWAC as the place to go for help with similar complaints.

5. Name changed.

Chapter 3: Challenging the Myths

1. *1991 Green Book.*

2. Timothy Casey and Mary Mannix, *Quality Control and the "Churning Crisis"* (New York: Center on Social Welfare Policy and Law, 1986).

3. The data for this section are drawn from several U.S. and New York City government documents, the most recent and comprehensive of which is the *1991 Green Book* published by the U.S. House of Representatives, Committee on Ways and Means. Information has also been taken from *Social Security Bulletins,* the U.S. Department of Health and Human Services, *Dependency* by the New York City Human Resources Administration, and Funiciello, *The Number One Killer of Our Children.*

4. Most other states do not separate checks the way New York does. Because of the historic use of separate components, and the likelihood that landlords would respond by raising rents, it would make little sense for New York to switch now.

5. Tim's story was even more interesting than that. When Tim was very young, his father became disabled and ceased to live with the family. His mother went on welfare. Tim is quick to describe the humiliations and poverty of welfare. After a few years, his father died, and the same family became recipients of social security. Everything changed for Tim—especially his self-esteem. Now he's an attorney practicing welfare law.

6. When President Reagan came into office, these rules were abolished, so families could once again be forced onto two-party checks and direct vendor payments.

7. Milwaukee County Welfare Rights Organization, *Welfare Mothers Speak Out* (New York: Norton, 1972), p. 31.

8. There is no comprehensive national data on the work programs, but it is generally conceded that they do not employ significantly more people than would have been employed without them and that the women involved remain poor. One 1985 report on "welfare grant diversions" (one of many job programs) done by Manpower Demonstration Research Corporation on six states showed the following:

> *Arizona:* became operational June 1982; by the end of 1984, "Arizona had enrolled 163 participants and placed them in positions. . . . However, half of the participants had terminated employment . . . within 6 months."
>
> *Florida:* first-year goal: 800 participants; "20 participants had been placed in OJT [on-the-job] positions."
>
> *Maine:* Goal: 600; placements: 63.
>
> *New Jersey:* Goal: 500; placements: 56.
>
> *Texas:* Goal: 890; participants (not placements): 18.
>
> *Vermont:* Goal: 200; placements: 15.

Income for each of these programs was far below the poverty level after job-related expenses. Virtually all the studies of these kinds of programs show the same or worse.

9. Human Resources Administration, *Dependency* (New York, 1991).

10. U.S. Department of Commerce, Bureau of the Census, *Money Income of Households, Families and Persons in the United States, 1990* (August 1991).

11. William Julius Wilson, *The Truly Disadvantaged: The Inner City, the Underclass, and Public Policy* (Chicago: University of Chicago Press, 1987).

12. Roy Lubove, *The Struggle for Social Security, 1900–1935* (Cambridge, MA: Harvard University Press, 1968), and Michael B. Katz, *In the Shadow of the Poorhouse* (New York: Basic, 1986).

Chapter 4: Upping the Stakes

1. The Bureau of Labor Statistics Lower Living Standard for a four-person family in 1967 was $6,021. If occupational expenses, social security payments, personal taxes, and rent were subtracted from the total, the result would have been $4,237 annually—still in 1967 dollars. (Recipients didn't have work-related expenses, and rent would be met through a separate grant.) An upward adjustment was made to meet prices for 1969 by using the consumer price index and then reduced in various ways to end up with a preadded allowance budget for welfare recipients of $2,720 annually. This figure was implemented in 1970 for a four-person family on welfare in New York State. In 1971 it was cut yet another 10 percent. In 1973 the cut was restored. It was finally increased in 1974 to reflect *1972* prices of goods and services that had been deemed essential by the state legislature *in 1969*. That's where New York's basic allowance remained until 1981.

2. She even formally accused us of discriminating against whites at one point.

3. The basic grant did not actually increase for technical reasons, but the equivalent of 15 percent ($38.70) was added to the monthly allowance of $258.00. Combined, the new monthly preadded allowance (before rent) was therefore $296.70. By the time the grant would take effect, inflation would be over 200 percent. To have kept pace with inflation, the grant would have had to more than double in 1981, to something in excess of $516.00 per month.

4. *Leadership development* was the commonly used phrase to describe an organization's efforts to train new leaders as they were brought in.

Part II: Filling the Gap: A Charitable Deduction

1. Service contracts are arrangements made between government and charities wherein government agrees to pay private (usually nonprofit) agencies in exchange for services provided to the public. Often, but not always, these contracts are negotiated on a per person, per family, or per diem (day) rate. The contracts range from thousands to hundreds of millions of dollars— much like contracts for military procurements from the defense industry. Tax expenditures are the means by which government provides indirect payments to individuals and corporations through an extensive array of tax deductions, exclusions, and credits related to social policy objectives. Every dollar the treasury does not take in is a dollar someone else's tax burden must make up for.

2. Carter proposed technical changes in the administration of AFDC, like "retrospective budgeting" and "monthly reporting," which would have adversely affected recipients' incomes but which died when his welfare reform bill failed to pass. He also increased "quality control" measures, which were intended to prevent recipients from getting overpayments or payments they weren't supposed to get. Since there was no concurrent incentive to prevent underpayments or nonpayments to eligible people, local welfare departments went loco cutting people off the rolls in spite of continued eligibility. The Carter administration also fiddled with food stamps, which resulted in cuts. Reagan got these and more cuts through the budget process without independent and hard-to-pass major legislation.

Chapter 5: City Silos and the Pop-Tart Connection

1. Jan Poppendieck, *Breadlines Knee-Deep in Wheat* (New Brunswick: Rutgers University Press, 1986).

2. Stephen G. Greene, "Product Donations Confuse Charity Ledgers, Tempt Some to Cook the Books," *The Chronicle of Philanthropy*, vol. 4, no. 4 (January 1, 1992), p. 29.

3. Stephen G. Greene, "Product Donations Confuse Charity Ledgers, Tempt Some to Cook the Books," *The Chronicle of Philanthropy*, vol. 5, no. 4 (December 1, 1992), p. 28.

4. *Case Study: Kroger Company*, Second Harvest promotional literature received 1991.

5. U.S. Department of the Treasury, Internal Revenue Service, *Statistics of Income Bulletin*, vol. 10, no. 4 (Spring 1991), p. 118.

6. Second Harvest portfolio of promotional literature received 1991. Grocery Manufacturers of America data from undated item *The Food Industry Speaks*.

7. *Food Assistance*, General Accounting Office Report to Congressional Requesters, May 1991, pp. 1 and 2.

Chapter 6: The Creation and Marketing of Homeless People

1. Data released to the Legislative Women's Caucus in 1987 showed a shelter charging $150 daily per family of four. HELP 1, the first of Andrew Cuomo's shelters, came in "cheap" at just about $800 weekly for 1989. Barracks-type "Tier 1" facilities run by the city and nonprofits are seas of

cots in massive rooms and have been estimated to cost between $58,000 and $70,000 per annum. In 1987, the state's published (official) rate was $54 per four-person family, but most providers were negotiating per diems individually and sub rosa for higher rates.

2. *Callahan et al.* v. *Carey et al.* Index No. 42582179, Supreme Court of the State of New York.

3. The ideas on this history of the poorhouses and shelters are more fully developed and well documented in Roy Lubove, *Struggle for Social Security;* Roy Lubove, *The Professional Altruist: The Emergence of Social Work as a Career, 1880–1935* (Massachusetts: 1965), and Katz, *In the Shadow of the Poorhouse.* Diane Gordon, "A Hotel Is Not a Home," in *City Limits: Barriers to Change in Urban Government* (New York: Charterhouse, 1973). Some primary resource material, such as incorporation papers of early charities, was also used.

4. Casey and Mannix, *Quality Control and the "Churning Crisis."*

5. Transcript of New York State public hearing, "Homeless Families: Causes and Solutions," testimony of Dr. Anna Lou Dehavenon, June 23, 1987.

6. *Administrative Closings of New York City Public Assistance Cases* (New York State Department of Social Services, April 1984).

7. Casey and Mannix, *Quality Control and the "Churning Crisis"; Administrative Closings of New York City Public Assistance Cases;* "The Talk of the Town," *The New Yorker,* June 6, 1983; Bella English, " 'Errors' Lopped 25% off Welfare," New York *Daily News,* May 18, 1984; Anna Lou Dehavenon, *New York City's "Churning" Crisis and the Tyranny of Indifference,* April 15, 1986; Evelyn Brodkin and Michael Lipsky, "Quality Control in AFDC as an Administrative Strategy," in *Social Service Review* (University of Chicago, 1983); Downtown Welfare Advocate Center, by experience. From the midseventies well on into the eighties, pressure to decrease welfare rolls vastly increased the incidence of "administrative errors," resulting in drastic actions against millions of poor people.

8. New York City Public Housing Authority, "Conventional Public Housing Applications; Eligible Applicants—Waiting List," Quarter ending June 1983.

9. New York City Housing Authority, Memo from Bernard Moses, Director of Management, to District Chief Managers and Project Managers, November 17, 1980.

10. Katz, *In the Shadow of the Poorhouse,* p. 293.

11. Title 18 is the official rules and regulations of the Department of Social Services.

12. Travers and company had it both ways. They worked at lucrative jobs *helping the poor* and helped themselves to some of the benefits. Travers, in particular, had worked first for the city under Bill Eimicke, who was in charge of the very program under which this co-op was established. Her income was substantial and her rent cheap, allowing her to cash in on a form of gentrification for years. In the meantime, poor families who desperately needed the apartments taken up by her and her friends went without. Travers and Hopper were ultimately married and bought a house of their own, selling out their share of the co-op at a reportedly low price.

13. Jim Dwyer, "Public Charity, Private Theft," *New York Newsday*, October 23, 1991, p. 2; and subsequent phone conversation with Dwyer.

14. Michael Powell, "Suspended Charity Got State Aid: Housing Group Led by Del Toro Given $600,000," *New York Newsday*, October 22, 1991.

15. Council of the City of New York, Committee on Housing and Buildings and Committee on General Welfare, Report on Tier Two Shelters (October 21, 1992), p. 25.

16. HELP 1, Statement of Support, Revenue, and Expense, six months ended June 30, 1988.

17. These percentages vary from state to state. In New York, the 50 percent state share is subdivided equally between state and local government. Of course, New York was only one of many states where nonprofit shelter development was taking off. Almost all these costs, too, were borne by taxpayers and continue to be.

18. Andrew Cuomo did produce a small amount of permanent housing in more recent times also.

19. Memo to William Eimicke from David Emil re: HELP 1—Red Cross Proposals, January 27, 1987.

20. The maximum rental payment in a "regular" welfare grant in New York City for a four-person family is $312 per month. It is possible for this sum to cover normal operating and maintenance costs of a full-size apartment unit in a building in good condition (which, if it were new, it should be), as long as there are no unnecessary services, including no debt service to a bank. If a shelter is getting as much as $150 per day for the same family, its monthly income for one unit is over $4,000. Since $312 is less than 10 percent of the shelter payment in this case, *more* than 90 percent of the

shelter unit cost is spent on items other than housing per se—social workers of every ilk and debt service.

21. These and subsequent quotations regarding the hearing are all in the transcript of the hearing "Homeless Families: Causes and Solutions."

Chapter 7: Charities and Fraud

1. In 1992, in spite of the impending presidential election, CSS decided to cut back on this project. For some reason, without a clearly political connection to the big-time candidates, voter registration and education became less important to CSS.

2. Some of this history is drawn from primary sources. Most of the rest is based on Katz, *In the Shadow of the Poorhouse,* and Lubove, *Struggle for Social Security.*

3. Lubove, *Struggle for Social Security.*

4. The Federation of Protestant Welfare Agencies, internal board of directors document.

5. Information drawn from documents provided via a Freedom of Information Act request to the New York State attorney general and several interviews, on and off the record, with eyewitnesses.

6. Stephen G. Greene, "How Much Should Charities Pay?" *The Chronicle of Philanthropy,* vol. 4, no. 11, (March 24, 1992), p. 32.

7. Elizabeth Holtzman, *Statistical Summary Supplement to the Comptroller's Comprehensive Annual Contracts Report for Fiscal Year Ended June 1991* (New York City Comptroller), p. 60.

8. *The Chronicle of Philanthropy,* vol. 5, no. 1 (October 20, 1992), p. 3. As per new report from the IRS.

9. Grant Williams, "Charities Must Prepare to Confront Scrutiny of Their Affairs, Leaders Say," *The Chronicle of Philanthropy,* vol. 5, no. 2 (November 3, 1992), p. 8. In the wake of the United Way scandal, "Some officials said they were concerned that many non-profits were moving too slowly to stamp out mismanagement and violations of ethical and legal standards." The chronicle quotes Elizabeth Dole, president of the American Red Cross, at the annual meeting of Independent Sector (a coalition of grant makers and charities): "For years charities have been largely 'free of public scrutiny, free to pursue our purposes, our own sense of what the public should want, and free to spend their money according to our own rules, standards, and priorities.'"

Part III: Toward a Politics of Justice: Guaranteed Income

1. *1991 Green Book, Overview of Entitlement Programs*, Washington, D.C., May 1991; Report to the chairman, U.S. House of Representatives, Committee on Ways and Means, *Poverty Trends, 1980–1988: Changes in Family Composition and Income Sources Among the Poor* (General Accounting Office, September 1992).

Chapter 8: Opening the Door to Social Opportunity and Income Security

1. *Green Book*, p. 105.

2. Robin Morgan, *Anatomy of Freedom* (New York: Anchor Press, 1982), p. 7

3. *Current Population Survey Trends in Relative Income: 1964–1989*, U.S. Department of Commerce, Economics and Statistics Administration, Bureau of the Census, pp. 51–53.

4. Allan Sheahen, *Guaranteed Income: The Right to Economic Security* (Los Angeles: Gain, 1983), p. 17.

5. *Poverty Amid Plenty*, p. 57.

6. The history here is drawn from Daniel Patrick Moynihan, *The Politics of a Guaranteed Income: The Nixon Administration and the Family Assistance Plan* (New York: Random House, 1973), and several other books, articles, and interviews with people active in the process at the time.

7. Andre Gorz, "(S)he Who Doesn't Work Shall Eat All the Same: Tomorrow's Economy—and Proposals from the Left," originally in *Lettre Internationale*, Spring 1986.

8. Moynihan, *Politics of a Guaranteed Income*.

9. Successes in these programs are defined as job *placements* and reductions (even short-term) in welfare expenditures *not* increased income or family well-being or even the duration of a job. One study in New York showed that the Human Resources Administration was claiming placements of individuals into one-day temporary jobs over and over to increase the appearance of success. One individual placed that way was counted as over 300 successes.

10. Office of Technology Assessment, *After the Cold War*, p. 9.

11. *Children's allowance* and *family allowance* are used interchangeably here. However, as one poor mother pointed out in the Hands Across America

discussion, children do not exist independent of others, usually, minimally, a mother. *Family* encompasses many forms and at the same time acknowledges the importance of durable relationships. The term *family* also allows for social policy to include those who care for the elderly in their homes.

Chapter 9: Ending Poverty as We Know It

1. This is Allan Sheahen's model with a 50 percent tax rate and a $14,000 per family of three guarantee.

2. Sheahen, *Guaranteed Income*, p. 175.

3. Current U.S. "foreign aid" also ends up in the hands of U.S. peddlers, who contrive any number of ways to sell their know-how to the countries in question—even when their ideas make no sense (Graham Hancock, *Lords of Poverty* [New York: Atlantic Monthly, 1989]). To boot, aid is often handed to the wrong people. For instance, in many countries the U.S. has "helped," most agricultural work has historically been done by women, yet aid to improve agricultural production has traditionally been given to men, who neither know how to put it to rational use nor care. To the extent that foreign aid does stay within a given country, a good deal is siphoned into the pockets of bureaucrats, who use it like it's a personal gift.

4. Office of Technology Assessment, *After the Cold War*, p. 3.

5. Dora Merris, "What Will We Do When Machines Do All the Work?" *The New York Times*, April 10, 1985.

BIBLIOGRAPHY

Administrative Closings of New York City Public Assistance Cases. New York State Department of Social Services. April 1984.

After the Cold War: Living with Lower Defense Spending. Office of Technology Assessment. February 1992.

Alternatives to the Welfare Hotel: Using Emergency Assistance to Provide Decent Transitional Shelter for Homeless Families. New York: Community Service Society, 1987.

The American Promise. Arthur I. Blaustein, ed. New Brunswick, NJ: Transaction, 1982.

Arkansas: Interim Findings from the WIN Demonstration Programs, Janet C. Quint et al. Manpower Research Demonstration Corporation. November 1984.

Backlash. Susan Faludi. New York: Crown, 1991.

Betrayal of the Poor. Stephen M. Rose.

Between Money and Love. Natalie J. Sokoloff. New York: Praeger, 1980.

Beyond Entitlement. Lawrence Mead. New York: Free Press, 1986.

Beyond Rhetoric. National Commission on Children. Washington, DC: U.S. Government Printing Office, 1991.

Beyond the Myths: The Families Helped by the AFDC Program. New York: Center on Social Welfare Policy and Law, 1985.

Biting the Hand That Feeds Them: Organizing Women on Welfare at the Grass Roots Level. Jacqueline Pope. New York: Praeger, 1989.

Budgeting for Defense Inflation. Congressional Budget Office. January 1986.

Came the Revolution. Daniel Patrick Moynihan. New York: Harcourt Brace Jovanovich, 1989.

333

The Campaign for Healthier Babies: Fighting the Problems of Low Birthweight in New York City. Greater New York March of Dimes, November 1986.

Capitalism and Freedom. Milton Friedman. Chicago: University of Chicago Press, 1962.

Characteristics and Financial Circumstances of AFDC Recipients, FY 1990. U.S. Department of Health and Human Services, Administration for Children and Families, Office of Family Assistance. 1990.

Charity Begins at Home. Teresa Odendahl. New York: Basic, 1990.

Children and Other Strangers. Ruth Szold Ginzberg. New Brunswick, NJ: Transaction, 1992.

Children on Welfare . . . Families in Need. New York: Downtown Welfare Advocate Center, 1979.

The Collapse of Welfare Reform: Political Institutions, Policy and the Poor in Canada and the United States. Christopher Leman. Cambridge, MA: MIT Press, 1980.

Current Population Reports: "Characteristics of the Population Below the Poverty Level," Series P-60, Washington, DC: Government Printing Office, 1982, 1984, 1990; Nos. 133, 152, 174, 175, 176, 177.

Dependency. "Economic and Social Data for New York City, January–June 1985." New York: Human Resources Administration, 1990.

Dynamic Aspects of Poverty and Welfare Use in the United States. Richard Coe, Greg Duncan, and Martha Hill. 1983. Prepared for Conference on Problems of Poverty, Clark University, 1982, 1983.

The Economic and Budget Outlook: Fiscal Years 1987–1991, A Report to the Senate and House Committees on the Budget, Part I. Congressional Budget Office. February 1986.

Economic Justice for: Pastoral Letter on Catholic Social Teaching and the U.S. Economy. National Conference of Catholic Bishops. Washington, DC: U.S. Catholic Conference, 1986.

Economic Status of the Elderly. "Income of Older New Yorkers." New York State Office of Aging, 1986.

Equality. William Ryan. New York: Pantheon, 1981.

Evaluation of the Pre-added Allowance Level. New York: Human Resources Administration, Office of Research and Program Evaluation, 1977.

Family and Nation. Daniel Patrick Moynihan. New York: Harcourt Brace Jovanovich, 1986.

Feeding Children: Federal Child Nutrition Policies in the 1980's. Congressional Budget Office. May 1980.

Fighting Poverty. Sheldon Danziger and Daniel Weinberg. Cambridge, MA: Harvard University Press, 1986.

Final Report of the Project: "Motivation and Economic Mobility of the Poor." Martha Hill et al. University of Michigan, Institute for Social Research, August 1983.

The First Charity. Robert Matthews Johnson. Cabin John, MD: Seven Locks, 1988.

Food Assistance: Readmitting Private Nonprofit Sponsors into the Summer Food Service Program. U.S. General Accounting Office, GAO/RCED-91-82.

Four Essays on Liberty. Isaiah Berlin. London: Oxford University Press, 1969.

The Great Society's Poor Law. Sar Levitan.

Guaranteed Annual Income: The Moral Issues. Philip Wogaman. Nashville: Abingdon, 1968.

A Growing Crisis: Disadvantaged Women and Their Children. U.S. Commission on Civil Rights. May 1983.

Guaranteed Income: The Right to Economic Security. Allan Sheahen. Los Angeles: Gain, 1983.

The Guaranteed Income. Robert Theobald, ed. New York: Doubleday, 1966.

Homelessness in New York State: A Report to the Governor and the Legislature. Cesar A. Perales. New York State Department of Social Services, October 1984.

Hope or Hassle: A Study of New York City's Welfare to Work Initiative for AFDC Recipients. Statewide Youth Advocacy, 1987.

"A Hotel Is Not a Home." Diane Gordon. In *City Limits: Barriers to Change in Urban Government.* New York: Charterhouse, 1973.

How the Other Half Lives. Jacob A. Riis. rpt. New York: Dover, 1971.

Hunger in America: The Growing Epidemic. Physicians Task Force on Hunger in America. Middletown, CT: Wesleyan University Press, 1985.

The Idea of Poverty: England in the Early Industrial Age. Gertrude Himmelfarb. New York: Vintage, 1983.

If Women Counted. Marilyn Waring. New York: Harper & Row, 1988.

The Inferno. Dante Alighieri. Translated by John Ciardi. New York: Mentor, 1982.

Interstate Child Support: Mothers Report Receiving Less Support from Out-of-State Fathers. U.S. Government Accounting Office, GAO/HRD 92-39FS.

In the Shadow of the Poorhouse. Michael B. Katz. New York: Basic, 1986.

Joint Public Hearing of the New York State Legislature on Homeless Families: Causes and Solutions. Albany, NY. June 23, 1987.

A Lesser Life. Sylvia Ann Hewlett. New York: Morrow, 1986.

Living Poorly in America. Leonard Beeghley. New York: Praeger, 1983.

Lords of Poverty. Graham Hancock. New York: Atlantic Monthly, 1989.

Losing Ground. Charles Murray. New York: Basic, 1984.

Maine: Interim Findings from a Grant Diversion-funded Employment Program. Patricia Auspos. Manpower Research Demonstration Corporation, June 1985.

Maryland: Interim Findings from the Maryland Employment Initiatives Programs. Janet Quint et al. Manpower Research Demonstration Corporation, February 1984.

Maximum Feasible Misunderstanding. Daniel Patrick Moynihan. New York: Free Press, 1969.

Men and Marriage. George Gilder. Gretna, LA: Pelican, 1986.

Money Income of Households, Families and Persons in the United States, 1990. U.S. Department of Commerce, Bureau of the Census. August 1991.

Mother-Only Families: Low Earnings Will Keep Many Children in Poverty. U.S. General Accounting Office, GAO/HRD-91-62.

The New Consensus on Family and Welfare: A Community of Self-Reliance. Michael Novak et al. Washington, DC: Marquette University, 1987.

The New York Nonprofit Sector in a Time of Government Retrenchment. Lester Salaman, ed. Washington, DC: Urban Institute Press, 1987.

New York State Catholic Conference Commission on the Elderly Final Report 1986 (Data from *A Profile of Older Americans 1985*). American Association of Retired Persons with U.S. Department of Health and Human Services, Administration of the Aging.

"New York's 'Work-Not-Welfare' Program." Theresa Funiciello, *Dissent,* Fall 1987.

1991 Green Book: Overview of Entitlement Programs. U.S. House of Representatives, Committee on Ways and Means. May 1991.

1933–1983—Never Again: A Report to the National Governors' Association Task Force on the Homeless. Mario Cuomo. New York, July 1983.

The Number One Killer of Our Children: Poverty. Theresa Funiciello. New York: Federation of Protestant Welfare Agencies, 1988.

Old, Alone and Poor: A Plan for Reducing Poverty Among Elderly People Living Alone (Excerpts from Report of the Commonwealth Fund Commission on Elderly People Living Alone). 1987.

Organizing the Movement: The Roots and Growth of ACORN. Gary Delgado. Philadelphia: Temple University Press, 1986.

A Passion for Equality. Nick Kotz. New York: Norton, 1977.

The Political Economy of Welfare Reform in the United States. Martin Anderson. Stanford, CA: Hoover Institution Press, 1978.

The Politics of a Guaranteed Income. Daniel Patrick Moynihan. New York: Random House, 1973.

The Politics of Housework. Ellen Malos, ed. London: Allison and Busby, 1980.

The Politics of Welfare: The New York City Experience. Blanche Bernstein. Cambridge, MA: Abt, 1982.

Poor Kids. Alvin Schorr. New York: Basic, 1966.

Poor Support. David Ellwood. New York: Basic, 1988.

Poverty amid Plenty: The American Paradox. Report of the President's Commission on Income Maintenance Programs. November 1969.

"Poverty and Welfare Dependence Across Generation," 3. Martha S. Hill and Michael Ponza. *Economic Outlook USA,* Summer 1983.

Poverty in New York State: Statewide and National Trends, 1970–1980. New York State Department of Social Services. June 1983.

Poverty in the United States, 1990. U.S. Department of the Commerce, Bureau of the Census. August 1991.

"The Poverty Industry." Theresa Funiciello. *Ms. Magazine,* November–December 1990.

Poverty Trends, 1980–1988: Changes in Family Composition and Income Sources Among the Poor. U.S. General Accounting Office, GAO/PEMD-92-34.

Private Lives/Public Spaces: Homeless Adults on the Streets of New York City, 1982. Ellen Baxter and Kim Hopper. New York: Community Service Society, February 1981.

The Promised Land. Nicholas Lemann. New York: Knopf, 1991.

Putting People First. Bill Clinton and Al Gore. New York: Times, 1992.

Quality Control and the "Churning Crisis." Timothy Casey and Mary Mannix. New York: Center on Social Welfare Policy and Law, 1986.

"Racial Differences in Low Birth Weight." Joel C. Kleinman and Samuel Kessel. *New England Journal of Medicine,* vol. 317, no. 12, pp. 749–53.

"Reason, Passion, and 'The Progress of the Law.'" William J. Brennan, Jr., Benjamin Cardozo Lecture, September 17, 1987.

The Reconstruction of Family Policy. Elaine A. Anderson and Richard C. Hula. New York: Greenwood, 1991.

Reducing Poverty Among Children. Congressional Budget Office. 1985.

Reforming Government. Daniel L. Feldman. New York: Morrow, 1981.

Rent Levels and Housing Conditions in New York City: A Comparison of Public Assistance and Other Poor Tenants. New York Department of Housing Preservation and Development. 1982.

Report on the California Workfare Program. Sacramento: Coalition of California Welfare Rights Organizations. 1985.

Report on Tier Two Shelters. Council of the City of New York, Committee on Housing and Buildings and Committee on General Welfare. October 21, 1992.

A Report on Welfare in New York City. Human Resources Administration, Department of Income Maintenance. November 1977.

Revolution from Within. Gloria Steinem. New York: Little, Brown, 1992.

The Right to Be Lazy. Paul Lafargue. Chicago: Kerr, 1975.

"Rights and Redistribution in the Welfare System." William Simon. *Stanford Law Review,* vol. 38, p. 143.

The Road to Equality. George Bernard Shaw. rpt. Boston: Beacon, 1971.

"(S)He Who Doesn't Work Shall Eat All the Same." Andre Gorz, *Dissent,* Spring 1987.

Social Security Bulletin, Annual Statistical Supplement. U.S. Department of Health and Human Services. 1990 and 1992.

Statistical Summary Supplement to the Comptroller's Comprehensive Annual Contracts Report for Fiscal Year Ended June 1991. Elizabeth Holtzman. New York City Comptroller, June 1991.

The Struggle for Social Security, 1900–1935. Roy Lubove. Cambridge, MA: Harvard University Press, 1968.

The Third Wave. Alvin Toffler. New York: Bantam, 1980.

Toward a Policy for the Amelioration and Prevention of Family Homelessness and Dissolution: New York City's After-Hours Emergency Assistance Units in 1986–87. Anna Lou Dehavenon. New York: East Harlem Interfaith, 1987.

Toward Social and Economic Justice. David Gill and Eva Gill, eds. Cambridge, MA: Schenkman, 1985.

The Triple Revolution. Ad Hoc Committee on the Triple Revolution, Advertising Age. 1964.

The Triple Revolution: Social Problems in Depth. Robert Perrucci and Marc Pilisuk. Boston: Little, Brown, 1968.

The Triumph of Politics. David Stockman. New York: Avon, 1986.

The Truly Disadvantaged: The Inner City, the Underclass, and Public Policy. William Julius Wilson. Chicago: University of Chicago Press, 1987.

The Tyranny of Indifference and the Re-institutionalization of Hunger, Homelessness and Poor Health. Anna Lou DeHavenon. New York: East Harlem Interfaith Welfare Committee, 1986.

Uncontrollable Spending for Social Services. Martha Derthick. Washington, DC: Brookings Institute, 1975.

The Underclass. Ken Auletta. New York: Vintage, 1983.

The Undeserving Poor. Michael Katz. New York: Pantheon, 1989.

Unemployed Parents: Initial Efforts to Expand State Assistance. U.S. General Accounting Office, GAO/PEMD-92-11.

U.S. Children and Their Families: Current Conditions and Recent Trends. 1987.

Virginia: Interim Findings from the Virginia Employment Services Program. Marilyn Price. Manpower Demonstration Research Corporation, May 1985.

The Vulnerable. John Palmer, Timothy Smeedling, and Barbara Boyle Torrey, eds. Washington, DC: Urban Institute Press, 1988.

The Way Home. New York City Commission on the Homeless. February 1992.

Wealth and Poverty. George Gilder. New York: Basic, 1981.

"Welfare in the Cuomo Years: Less Is Less, Sandford Schram and Theresa Funiciello. In *New York State Today,* ed. Peter Colby and John White. SUNY Press, 1988.

"Welfare Mothers Earn Their Way." Theresa Funiciello. *Christianity and Crisis,* 1984.

Welfare Mothers Speak Out. Milwaukee County Welfare Rights Organization. New York: Norton, 1972.

Welfare to Work. U.S. General Accounting Office, GAO/HRD-92-118.

West Virginia: Interim Findings on the Community Work Experience Demonstration. Joseph Ball et al. Manpower Demonstration Research Corporation, November 1984.

Work-related Programs for Welfare Recipients. Congressional Budget Office, 1987.

Years of Poverty, Years of Plenty. Greg Duncan et al. University of Michigan, Institute for Social Research, 1984.